MICROSOFT
Word 97
Complete Concepts and Techniques

MICROSOFT
Word 97
Complete Concepts
and Techniques

Gary B. Shelly
Thomas J. Cashman
Misty E. Vermaat

SHELLY
CASHMAN
SERIES®

COURSE TECHNOLOGY

COURSE TECHNOLOGY
ONE MAIN STREET
CAMBRIDGE MA 02142

an International Thomson Publishing company I(T)P°

CAMBRIDGE ALBANY BONN CINCINNATI LONDON MADRID MELBOURNE

MEXICO CITY NEW YORK PARIS SAN FRANCISCO TOKYO TORONTO WASHINGTON

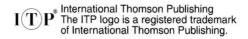
© 1998 Course Technology
One Main Street
Cambridge, Massachusetts 02142

I(T)P® International Thomson Publishing
The ITP logo is a registered trademark
of International Thomson Publishing.

Printed in the United States of America

For more information, contact Course Technology:

Course Technology
One Main Street
Cambridge, Massachusetts 02142, USA

International Thomson Publishing Europe
Berkshire House
168-173 High Holborn
London, WC1V 7AA, United Kingdom

Thomas Nelson Australia
102 Dodds Street
South Melbourne
Victoria 3205 Australia

Nelson Canada
1120 Birchmont Road
Scarborough, Ontario
Canada M1K 5G4

International Thomson Editores
Campos Eliseos 385, Piso 7
Colonia Polanco
11560 Mexico D.F. Mexico

International Thomson Publishing GmbH
Konigswinterer Strasse 418
53227 Bonn, Germany

International Thomson Publishing Asia
Block 211, Henderson Road #08-03
Henderson Industrial Park
Singapore 0315

International Thomson Publishing Japan
Hirakawa-cho Kyowa Building, 3F
2-2-1 Hirakawa-cho, Chiyoda-ku
Tokyo 102, Japan

ISBN 0-7895-1338-2

PHOTO CREDITS: *Project 1, pages W 1.4-5* Pen and ink well, hieroglyphics, deers, hunters, book, mallet, Courtesy of Corel Professional Photos CD-ROM Image usage; Computer, monitor, keyboard, stone background, © Metatools, created by Photospin; Computer with CD-ROM provided by PhotoDisc, Inc. © 1996; *Project 2, pages W 2.2-3* Man with newspaper provided by PhotoDisc, Inc. © 1996; *Project 3, pages W 3.2-3* Globe and street sign, Courtesy of Corel Professional Photos CD-ROM Image usage; *Project 4, pages WD 4.4-5* Map image © 1997 Photodisc, Inc. *Project 5, pages WD 5.2-3,* Boat, Courtesy of Corel Professional Photos CD-ROM Image usage; Thomas Jefferson, provided by North Wind Picture Archives; Hieroglyphics, provided by The British Museum. *Project 6, pages WD 6.2, Women With Wheels* newsletter, Courtesy of The Quarterly Newsletter on Automobiles for Women; Landspeed Louise, Courtesy of Louise A. Noeth; *At-Home Dad* newsletter, Courtesy of Peter Baylies; *page WD 6.3, Newsletter Design* newsletter, Courtesy of The Newsletter Clearinghouse; Cat illustration provided by Rod Thomas; *Catnip* newsletter, Courtesy of Tufts University School of Veterinary Medicine.

4 5 6 7 8 9 10   BC   21098

MICROSOFT
Word 97
Complete Concepts and Techniques

C O N T E N T S

Microsoft Word 97   **WD 1.1**

Preface

The Shelly Cashman Series® offers the finest textbooks in computer education. The Microsoft Office 97 books continue with the innovation, quality, and reliability that you have come to expect from this series. We are proud that both our Office 95 and Office 4.3 books are best-sellers, and we are confident that our Office 97 books will join their predecessors.

With Office 97, Microsoft has raised the stakes by adding a number of new features, especially the power of the Internet. The Shelly Cashman Series team has responded with Office 97 books that present the core application concepts required in any introductory application software course, as well as new features such as the Office 97 Internet tools.

In our Office 97 books, you will find an educationally sound and easy-to-follow pedagogy that combines a step-by-step approach with corresponding screens. Every project and exercise in the books are new and designed to take full advantage of the Office 97 features. The popular Other Ways and More About features have been amended to offer in-depth knowledge of Office 97. The all-new project openers provide a fascinating perspective on the subject covered in the project. The Shelly Cashman Series Office 97 books will make your computer application software class an exciting and dynamic one that your students will remember as one of their better educational experiences.

Objectives of This Textbook

Microsoft Word 97: Complete Concepts and Techniques is intended for a two-unit course that presents Microsoft Word 97. No experience with a computer is assumed, and no mathematics beyond the high school freshman level is required. The objectives of this book are:

- ▶ To teach the fundamentals of Microsoft Word 97
- ▶ To help students demonstrate their proficiency in Microsoft Word 97 and prepare them to pass the Proficient level Microsoft Office User Specialist Exam for Microsoft Word 97
- ▶ To foster an appreciation of word processing as a useful tool in the workplace
- ▶ To give students an in-depth understanding of creating announcements, business letters, resumes, research papers, reports, form letters, and newsletters and how to use OLE
- ▶ To expose students to examples of the computer as a useful tool
- ▶ To develop an exercise-oriented approach that allows students to learn by example
- ▶ To encourage independent study and help those who are working on their own in a distance education environment

Approved by Microsoft as Courseware for the Microsoft Office User Specialist Program — Proficient Level

This book has been approved by Microsoft as courseware for the Microsoft Office User Specialist program. After completing the projects and exercises in this book, the student will be prepared to take the Proficient level Microsoft Office User Specialist Exam for Microsoft Word 97. By passing the certification exam for a Microsoft software program, students demonstrate their proficiency in that program to employers. This exam is offered at participating test centers, participating corporations, and participating employment agencies. For more information about certification, please visit Microsoft's World Wide Web site at http://microsoft.com/office/train_cert/.

The Shelly Cashman Approach

Features of the Shelly Cashman Series Office 97 books include:

▶ Project Orientation: Each project in the book uses the unique Shelly Cashman Series screen-by-screen, step-by-step approach.

▶ Screen-by-Screen, Step-by-Step Instructions: Each of the tasks required to complete a project is identified throughout the development of the project. Then, steps to accomplish the task are specified. The steps are accompanied by screens. Hence, students learn from this book the same as if they were using a computer.

▶ Thoroughly Tested Projects: The computer screens in the Shelly Cashman Series Office 97 books are captured from the author's computer. The screen is captured immediately after the author performs the step specified in the text. Therefore, every screen in the book is correct because it is produced only after performing a step, resulting in unprecedented quality in a computer textbook.

▶ Multiple Ways to Use the Book: This book can be used in a variety of ways, including: (a) Lecture and textbook approach — The instructor lectures on the material in the book. Students read and study the material and then apply the knowledge to an application on the computer; (b) Tutorial approach — Students perform each specified step on a computer. At the end of the project, students have solved the problem and are ready to solve comparable student assignments; (c) Other approaches — Many instructors lecture on the material and then require their students to perform each step in the project, reinforcing the material lectured. Students then complete one or more of the In the Lab exercises at the end of the project; and (d) Reference — Each task in a project is clearly identified. Therefore, the material serves as a complete reference.

▶ Other Ways Boxes for Reference: Microsoft Word 97 provides a wide variety of ways to carry out a given task. The Other Ways boxes included at the end of most of the step-by-step sequences specify the other ways to execute the task completed in the steps. Together, the steps and the Other Ways box make a comprehensive and convenient reference unit; you no longer have to reference tables at the end of a project or at the end of a book.

▶**OtherWays**

1. Click Outside Border button on Tables and Borders toolbar
2. On Format menu click Borders and Shading, click Borders tab, click Box, select desired width, select desired color, click OK button

More *About*
Drop Caps

A drop cap often is used to mark the beginning of an article. An alternative is a stick-up cap, which extends into the left margin, rather than sinking into the first few lines of the text. To insert a stick-up cap, click In Margin in the Drop Cap dialog box.

▶ More About Feature: The More About features in the margins provide background information that complements the topics covered, adding interest and depth to the learning process.

Organization of This Textbook

Microsoft Word 97: Complete Concepts and Techniques provides detailed instruction on how to use Word 97. The material is divided into six projects and two integration features as follows:

Project 1 – Creating and Editing a Word Document   In Project 1, students are introduced to Word terminology and the Word window by preparing an announcement. Topics include starting and quitting Word; entering text; adding bullets to paragraphs while typing; checking spelling while typing; saving a document; selecting characters, lines, and paragraphs; centering, bolding, italicizing, and changing the font and font size of selected text; importing a picture from the Web and then resizing the picture; printing a document; opening a document; correcting errors; and using Word Help.

Project 2 – Using Word's Wizards and Templates to Create a Cover Letter and Resume   In Project 2, students create a resume using Word's Resume Wizard. Topics include personalizing the resume using Word's AutoFormat feature and print preview. Then, students create a cover letter using a Word letter template. Topics include personalizing the cover letter; creating and inserting an AutoText entry; dragging and dropping selected text; aligning text vertically with the TAB key; and checking spelling at once. Finally, students switch from one open Word document to another and then close all open Word documents.

Project 3 – Creating a Research Paper with a Table   In Project 3, students use the MLA style of documentation to create a research paper. Topics include changing margins; adjusting line spacing; using a header to number pages; first-line indenting paragraphs; using Word's AutoCorrect features; creating a Word table, entering data into the table, and formatting the table; adding a footnote; inserting a manual page break; creating a hanging indent; creating a text hyperlink; sorting paragraphs; using the thesaurus; and counting the words in a document.

Integration Feature – Creating Web Pages   In this section, students are introduced to creating Web pages. Topics include saving the resume created in Project 2 as an HTML file; creating a personal Web page using the Web Page Wizard; and personalizing the Web page using hyperlinks.

Project 4 – Creating a Document with a Title Page and Tables   In Project 4, students work with tables in a document. Students learn how to add an outside border with color; add color to characters; download clip art from the Microsoft Clip Gallery Live page on the Web; change a floating picture to an inline picture; insert a section break; insert an existing document into an open document; save a document with a new file name; set and use tabs; create a table using the Draw Table feature; change the alignment of table cell text; change the direction of text in table cells; center a table; customize bullets in a list; and change the starting page number in a section.

Project 5 – Generating Form Letters, Mailing Labels, and Envelopes   In Project 5, students learn how to generate form letters, mailing labels, and envelopes from a main document and a data source. Topics include creating and editing the three main documents and their associated data source; inserting the system date into a document; inserting merge fields into the main document; using an IF field; displaying and printing field codes; merging and printing the documents; selecting data records to merge and print; sorting data records to merge and print; viewing merged data in the main document; and inserting a bar code on the mailing labels and envelopes.

Project 6 – Creating a Professional Newsletter   In Project 6, students learn how to use Word's desktop publishing features to create a newsletter. Topics include adding ruling lines; adding a bullet symbol; formatting a document into multiple columns; creating a dropped capital letter; framing and positioning graphics across columns; inserting a column break; adding a vertical rule between columns; creating a pull-quote; adding color to characters and lines; highlighting text; using the Format Painter button; creating and running a macro to automate a task; changing the color of a graphic; and adding text to a graphic.

Integration Feature – Using WordArt to Add Special Text Effects to a Word Document In this section, students are introduced to WordArt, an application included with Word. Using the newsletter built in Project 6, students create a new headline in WordArt and then embed the new headline into the Word document. The following WordArt special effects are introduced: changing the shape of the text, stretching the text, bolding the text, and adding a shadow to the text.

End-of-Project Student Activities

A notable strength of the Shelly Cashman Series Office 97 books is the extensive student activities at the end of each project. Well-structured student activities can make the difference between students merely participating in a class and students retaining the information they learn. The activities in the Office 97 books include:

▶ **What You Should Know** A listing of the tasks completed within a project together with the pages where the step-by-step, screen-by-screen explanations appear. This section provides a perfect study review for students.

▶ **Test Your Knowledge** Four pencil-and-paper activities designed to determine students' understanding of the material in the project. Included are true/false questions, multiple-choice questions, and two short-answer activities.

▶ **Use Help** Any user of Word 97 must know how to use Help, including the Office Assistant. Therefore, this book contains two Use Help exercises per project. These exercises alone distinguish the Shelly Cashman Series from any other set of Office 97 instructional materials.

▶ **Apply Your Knowledge** This exercise requires students to open and manipulate a file on the Data Disk that accompanies the Office 97 books.

▶ **In the Lab** Three in-depth assignments per project require students to apply the knowledge gained in the project to solve problems on a computer.

▶ **Cases and Places** Seven unique case studies require students to apply their knowledge to real-world situations.

Instructor's Resource Kit

A comprehensive Instructor's Resource Kit (IRK) accompanies this textbook in the form of a CD-ROM. The CD-ROM includes an electronic Instructor's Manual (called ElecMan) and teaching and testing aids. The CD-ROM (ISBN 0-7895-1334-X) is available through your Course Technology representative or by calling one of the following telephone numbers: Colleges and Universities, 1-800-648-7450; High Schools, 1-800-824-5179; and Career Colleges, 1-800-477-3692. The contents of the CD-ROM are listed below.

▶ **ElecMan** (*Electronic Instructor's Manual*) ElecMan is made up of Microsoft Word files. The files include lecture notes, solutions to laboratory assignments, and a large test bank. The files allow you to modify the lecture notes or generate quizzes and exams from the test bank using your own word processor. Where appropriate, solutions to laboratory assignments are embedded as icons in the files. When an icon appears, double-click it; the application will start and the solution will display on the screen. ElecMan includes the following for each project: project objectives; project overview; detailed lesson plans with page number references; teacher notes and activities; answers to the end-of-project exercises; test bank of 110 questions for every project (50 true/false, 25 multiple choice, and 35 fill-in-the-blank) with page number references; and transparency references. The transparencies are available through the Figures on CD-ROM described below.

▶ **Figures on CD-ROM** Illustrations for every screen in the textbook are available. Use this ancillary to create a slide show from the illustrations for lecture or to print transparencies for use in lecture with an overhead projector.

▶ **Course Test Manager** This cutting-edge Windows-based testing software helps instructors design and administer tests and pretests. The full-featured online program permits students to take tests at the computer where their grades are computed immediately. Automatic statistics collection, student guides customized to the student's performance, and printed tests are only a few of the features.

▶ **Lecture Success System** Lecture Success System files are designed for use with the application software package, a personal computer, and a projection device. The files allow you to explain and illustrate the step-by-step, screen-by-screen development of a project in the textbook without entering large amounts of data.

▶ **Instructor's Lab Solutions** Solutions and required files for all the In the Lab assignments at the end of each project are available.

▶ **Lab Tests/Test Outs** Tests that parallel the In the Lab assignments are supplied for the purpose of testing students in the laboratory on the material covered in the project or testing students out of the course.

▶ **Student Files** All the files that are required by students to complete the Apply Your Knowledge and a few of the In the Lab exercises are included.

▶ **Interactive Labs** Eighteen hands-on interactive labs that take students from ten to fifteen minutes each to step through help solidify and reinforce mouse and keyboard usage and computer concepts.

Shelly Cashman Online

Shelly Cashman Online is a World Wide Web service available to instructors and students of computer education. Visit Shelly Cashman Online at www.scseries.com. Shelly Cashman Online is divided into four areas:

- ▶ **Series Information** Information on the Shelly Cashman Series products.

- ▶ **The Community** Opportunities to discuss your course and your ideas with instructors in your field and with the Shelly Cashman Series team.

- ▶ **Teaching Resources** Designed for instructors teaching from and using Shelly Cashman Series textbooks and software. This area includes password-protected instructor materials that can be downloaded, course outlines, teaching tips, and much more.

- ▶ **Student Center** Dedicated to students learning about computers with Shelly Cashman Series textbooks and software. This area includes cool links, data from Data Disks that can be downloaded, and much more.

Acknowledgments

The Shelly Cashman Series would not be the leading computer education series without the contributions of outstanding publishing professionals. First, and foremost, among them is Becky Herrington, director of production and designer. She is the heart and soul of the Shelly Cashman Series, and it is only through her leadership, dedication, and tireless efforts that superior products are made possible. Becky created and produced the award-winning Windows 95 series of books.

Under Becky's direction, the following individuals made significant contributions to these books: Peter Schiller, production manager; Ginny Harvey, series specialist and developmental editor; Ken Russo, Mike Bodnar, Stephanie Nance, Greg Herrington, and Dave Bonnewitz, graphic artists; Jeanne Black, Quark expert; Patti Koosed, editorial assistant; Nancy Lamm, Lyn Markowicz, Cherilyn King, Marilyn Martin, and Steve Marconi, proofreaders; Cristina Haley, indexer; Sarah Evertson of Image Quest, photo researcher; and Peggy Wyman and Jerry Orton, Susan Sebok, and Nancy Lamm, contributing writers.

Special thanks go to Jim Quasney, our dedicated series editor; Lisa Strite, senior product manager; Lora Wade, associate product manager; Scott MacDonald and Tonia Grafakos, editorial assistants; and Sarah McLean, product marketing manager. Special mention must go to Suzanne Biron, Becky Herrington, and Michael Gregson for the outstanding book design; Becky Herrington for the cover design; and Ken Russo for the cover illustrations.

Gary B. Shelly
Thomas J. Cashman
Misty E. Vermaat

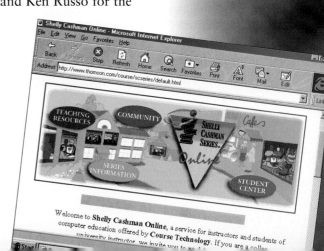

Shelly Cashman Series – Traditionally Bound Textbooks

The Shelly Cashman Series presents the following computer subjects in a variety of traditionally bound textbooks as shown in the table below. For more information, see your Course Technology representative or call one of the following telephone numbers: Colleges and Universities, 1-800-648-7450; High Schools, 1-800-824-5179; and Career Colleges, 1-800-477-3692.

COMPUTERS	
Computers	Discovering Computers: A Link to the Future, World Wide Web Enhanced
	Discovering Computers: A Link to the Future, World Wide Web Enhanced Brief Edition
	Using Computers: A Gateway to Information, World Wide Web Edition
	Using Computers: A Gateway to Information, World Wide Web Brief Edition
	Exploring Computers: A Record of Discovery 2e with CD-ROM
	A Record of Discovery for Exploring Computers 2e
	Study Guide for Discovering Computers: A Link to the Future, World Wide Web Enhanced
	Study Guide for Using Computers: A Gateway to Information, World Wide Web Edition
	Brief Introduction to Computers 2e (32-page)
WINDOWS APPLICATIONS	
Integrated Packages	Microsoft Office 97: Introductory Concepts and Techniques, Brief Edition (6 projects)
	Microsoft Office 97: Introductory Concepts and Techniques, Essentials Edition (10 projects)
	Microsoft Office 97: Introductory Concepts and Techniques (15 projects)
	Microsoft Office 97: Advanced Concepts and Techniques
	Microsoft Office 95: Introductory Concepts and Techniques (15 projects)
	Microsoft Office 95: Advanced Concepts and Techniques
	Microsoft Office 4.3 running under Windows 95: Introductory Concepts and Techniques
	Microsoft Office for Windows 3.1 Introductory Concepts and Techniques Enhanced Edition
	Microsoft Office: Advanced Concepts and Techniques
	Microsoft Works 4* • Microsoft Works 3.0*
Windows	Introduction to Microsoft Windows NT Workstation 4
	Microsoft Windows 95: Introductory Concepts and Techniques (96-page)
	Introduction to Microsoft Windows 95 (224-page)
	Microsoft Windows 95: Complete Concepts and Techniques
	Microsoft Windows 3.1 Introductory Concepts and Techniques
	Microsoft Windows 3.1 Complete Concepts and Techniques
Word Processing	Microsoft Word 97* • Microsoft Word 7* • Microsoft Word 6* • Microsoft Word 2.0
	Corel WordPerfect 8 • Corel WordPerfect 7 • WordPerfect 6.1* • WordPerfect 6* • WordPerfect 5.2
Spreadsheets	Microsoft Excel 97* • Microsoft Excel 7* • Microsoft Excel 5* • Microsoft Excel 4
	Lotus 1-2-3 97* • Lotus 1-2-3 Release 5* • Lotus 1-2-3 Release 4* • Quattro Pro 6
Database Management	Microsoft Access 97* • Microsoft Access 7* • Microsoft Access 2
	Paradox 5 • Paradox 4.5 • Paradox 1.0 • Visual dBASE 5/5.5
Presentation Graphics	Microsoft PowerPoint 97* • Microsoft PowerPoint 7* • Microsoft PowerPoint 4*
DOS APPLICATIONS	
Operating Systems	DOS 6 Introductory Concepts and Techniques
	DOS 6 and Microsoft Windows 3.1 Introductory Concepts and Techniques
Word Processing	WordPerfect 6.1 • WordPerfect 6.0 • WordPerfect 5.1
Spreadsheets	Lotus 1-2-3 Release 4 • Lotus 1-2-3 Release 2.4 • Lotus 1-2-3 Release 2.3
Database Management	dBASE 5 • dBASE IV Version 1.1 • dBASE III PLUS • Paradox 4.5
PROGRAMMING AND NETWORKING	
Programming	Microsoft Visual Basic 5
	Microsoft Visual Basic 4 for Windows 95* (available with Student version software)
	Microsoft Visual Basic 3.0 for Windows*
	QBasic • QBasic: An Introduction to Programming • Microsoft BASIC
	Structured COBOL Programming (Micro Focus COBOL also available)
Networking	Novell NetWare for Users
	Business Data Communications: Introductory Concepts and Techniques
Internet	The Internet: Introductory Concepts and Techniques (UNIX)
	Netscape Navigator 4: An Introduction
	Netscape Navigator 3: An Introduction • Netscape Navigator 2 running under Windows 3.1
	Netscape Navigator: An Introduction (Version 1.1)
	Netscape Composer
	Microsoft Internet Explorer 3: An Introduction
SYSTEMS ANALYSIS	
Systems Analysis	Systems Analysis and Design, Second Edition

*Also available as a Double Diamond Edition, which is a shortened version of the complete book

Shelly Cashman Series – **Custom Edition**® Program

If you do not find a Shelly Cashman Series traditionally bound textbook to fit your needs, the Shelly Cashman Series unique **Custom Edition** program allows you to choose from a number of options and create a textbook perfectly suited to your course. Features of the **Custom Edition** program are:

▶ Textbooks that match the content of your course

▶ Windows- and DOS-based materials for the latest versions of personal computer applications software

▶ Shelly Cashman Series quality, with the same full-color materials and Shelly Cashman Series pedagogy found in the traditionally bound books

▶ Affordable pricing so your students receive the **Custom Edition** at a cost similar to that of traditionally bound books

The table on the right summarizes the available materials.

For more information, see your Course Technology representative or call one of the following telephone numbers: Colleges and Universities, 1-800-648-7450; High Schools, 1-800-824-5179; and Career Colleges, 1-800-477-3692.

For Shelly Cashman Series information, visit Shelly Cashman Online at **www.scseries.com**

COMPUTERS	
Computers	Discovering Computers: A Link to the Future, World Wide Web Enhanced
	Discovering Computers: A Link to the Future, World Wide Web Enhanced Brief Edition
	Using Computers: A Gateway to Information, World Wide Web Edition
	Using Computers: A Gateway to Information, World Wide Web Brief Edition
	A Record of Discovery for Exploring Computers 2e (available with CD-ROM)
	Study Guide for Discovering Computers: A Link to the Future, World Wide Web Enhanced
	Study Guide for Using Computers: A Gateway to Information, World Wide Web Edition
	Introduction to Computers (32-page)

OPERATING SYSTEMS	
Windows	Microsoft Windows 95: Introductory Concepts and Techniques (96-page)
	Introduction to Microsoft Windows NT Workstation 4
	Introduction to Microsoft Windows 95 (224-page)
	Microsoft Windows 95: Complete Concepts and Techniques
	Microsoft Windows 3.1 Introductory Concepts and Techniques
	Microsoft Windows 3.1 Complete Concepts and Techniques
DOS	Introduction to DOS 6 (using DOS prompt)
	Introduction to DOS 5.0 or earlier (using DOS prompt)

WINDOWS APPLICATIONS	
Integrated Packages	Microsoft Works 4*
	Microsoft Works 3.0*
Microsoft Office	Using Microsoft Office 97 (16-page)
	Using Microsoft Office 95 (16-page)
	Microsoft Office 97:Introductory Concepts and Techniques, Brief Edition (396-page)
	Microsoft Office 97: Introductory Concepts and Techniques, Essentials Edition (672-page)
	Object Linking and Embedding (OLE) (32-page)
	Microsoft Outlook 97 • Microsoft Schedule+ 7
	Introduction to Integrating Office 97 Applications (48-page)
	Introduction to Integrating Office 95 Applications (80-page)
Word Processing	Microsoft Word 97* • Microsoft Word 7* • Microsoft Word 6* • Microsoft Word 2.0
	Corel WordPerfect 8 • Corel WordPerfect 7 • WordPerfect 6.1* • WordPerfect 6* • WordPerfect 5.2
Spreadsheets	Microsoft Excel 97* • Microsoft Excel 7* • Microsoft Excel 5* • Microsoft Excel 4
	Lotus 1-2-3 97* • Lotus 1-2-3 Release 5* • Lotus 1-2-3 Release 4* • Quattro Pro 6
Database Management	Microsoft Access 97* • Microsoft Access 7* • Microsoft Access 2*
	Paradox 5 • Paradox 4.5 • Paradox 1.0 • Visual dBASE 5/5.5
Presentation Graphics	Microsoft PowerPoint 97* • Microsoft PowerPoint 7* • Microsoft PowerPoint 4*

DOS APPLICATIONS	
Word Processing	WordPerfect 6.1 • WordPerfect 6.0 • WordPerfect 5.1
Spreadsheets	Lotus 1-2-3 Release 4 • Lotus 1-2-3 Release 2.4 • Lotus 1-2-3 Release 2.3
	Quattro Pro 3.0 • Quattro with 1-2-3 Menus
Database Management	dBASE 5 • dBASE IV Version 1.1 • dBASE III PLUS
	Paradox 4.5 • Paradox 3.5

PROGRAMMING AND NETWORKING	
Programming	Microsoft Visual Basic 5 • Microsoft Visual Basic 4 for Windows 95* (available with Student version software) • Microsoft Visual Basic 3.0 for Windows*
	Microsoft BASIC • QBasic
Networking	Novell NetWare for Users
Internet	The Internet: Introductory Concepts and Techniques (UNIX)
	Netscape Navigator 4: An Introduction
	Netscape Navigator 3: An Introduction
	Netscape Navigator 2 running under Windows 3.1
	Netscape Navigator: An Introduction (Version 1.1)
	Netscape Composer
	Microsoft Internet Explorer 3: An Introduction

*Also available as a mini-module

Microsoft *Word 97*

Microsoft Word 97

Microsoft Word 97

Creating and Editing a Word Document

Objectives:

You will have mastered the material in this project when you can:

▶ Start Word
▶ Describe the Word screen
▶ Change the default font size of all text
▶ Enter text into a document
▶ Spell check as you type
▶ Save a document
▶ Select text
▶ Center a paragraph
▶ Change the font size of selected text
▶ Change the font of selected text
▶ Bold selected text
▶ Underline selected text
▶ Italicize selected text
▶ Import a picture from the Web
▶ Resize a picture
▶ Print a document
▶ Correct errors in a document
▶ Use Microsoft Word Help
▶ Quit Word

Letter Perfect

From Carved Tablets to Computerized Font Libraries

Longfellow speaks of the "footprints on the sands of time" left by great ancestors. Indeed, these recordings of events and accomplishments communicate messages of days long gone. In ancient times, thoughts were shared by making symbols in the sand, drawing on cave walls, and etching hieroglyphics and pictoral carvings on tombs. The Egyptians are credited with creating the first alphabet of symbols and pictures, which in approximately 1000 B.C., was modified when the Phoenicians added consonants and the Romans agreed upon 23 unique uppercase letters. The straight shapes of these Roman letters were created out of necessity, as artists had difficulty chiseling curves in stone.

The Roman alphabet influenced early Latin writing, but scribes developed additional lowercase letters. They handwrote on scrolls made from animal skins or on paper made from organic vegetable material. Their Carolingian script was adopted by the Emperor

Charlemagne as an educational standard during the tenth century. These scrolls evolved into folded manuscript books produced by monks in monasteries and lay people in universities.

Several centuries later, the developing European bourgeoisie longed for multiple copies of documents and reading materials. Thus, when Johann Gutenberg developed the printing press in the fifteenth century, he caused a European upheaval. In 1454, he printed Bibles, which were the first mass-produced books printed with moveable type. To make this type, he painstakingly punched a mirror image of a letter in a soft piece of metal, poured molten metal into this hole, and produced a letter. The letters were arranged in a matrix, inked, and pressed onto paper. By the end of the century, more than 1,000 printers worked in 200 European cities.

During the Industrial Revolution in the 1800s, steam presses cut the printing time by 85 percent. A machine eliminated the need to create punched type by hand. In the 1900s, the need for metal type ceased. Letters were created by the photocomposition process, which projects letters on photosensitive paper. In today's digital age, letters are created by the computer, and an abundance of font styles are available.

Microsoft Word 97 provides a font list that allows you to add variety to and enhance the appearance of your documents. Now, thousands of fonts are available from numerous sources including the Internet and for purchase on CD-ROM.

Each font has a unique name. Some are named after the designer. For example, the Baskerville font was developed by John Baskerville, a teacher turned printer in the seventeenth century. Other fonts named for their designers are Giambattista Bodoni, William Caslon, and Claude Garamond. Times New Roman resembles the letters inscribed on the base of Trajan's Column in the Roman Forum in A.D. 114. As you work through the projects in this book, recall that the letters you type are descendants of the footprints left by our printing forefathers.

Microsoft
Word 97

Creating and Editing a Word Document

*C*ase *P*erspective

Tropical Travel, a local travel agency, specializes in customized vacation packages to locations around the world. One popular package is to Paradise Island. Surrounded by crystal-clear waters and lined with white-sand beaches, Paradise Island offers swimming, surfing, SCUBA diving, snorkeling, sailing, and scenic hiking.

Each month, Tropical Travel prepares a flier announcing exciting vacation packages. The announcement is posted in local retail stores, printed in magazines and newspapers, and mailed to the general public. You have been asked the prepare an announcement for the Paradise Island vacation packages. To add appeal to the announcement, you are asked to include a picture of Paradise Island in the announcement. When you are finished creating the announcement, you print it for distribution.

You surf the Internet for a picture of Paradise Island and locate one at the Web site of www.scsite.com/wd97/pr1.htm. Details for the announcement, such as information about Paradise Island, can be obtained from any travel agent at Tropical Travel.

What Is Microsoft Word?

Microsoft Word is a full-featured word processing program that allows you to create professional looking documents such as announcements, letters, resumes, and reports; and revise them easily. You can use Word's desktop publishing features to create high-quality brochures, advertisements, and newsletters. Word has many features designed to simplify the production of documents. For example, you can instruct Word to create a prewritten document for you, and then you can modify the document to meet your needs. Using its expanded **IntelliSense**™ technology, Word can perform tasks such as correcting text, checking spelling and grammar, and formatting text – *all while you are typing*. Using Word's thesaurus, you can add variety and precision to your writing. With Word, you easily can include tables, graphics, pictures, and live hyperlinks in your documents. From within Word, you can search the Web for documents or create your very own Web pages.

Project One – Paradise Island Announcement

To illustrate the features of Word, this book presents a series of projects that use Word to create documents similar to those you will encounter in the academic and business environments. Project 1 uses Word to produce the announcement shown in Figure 1-1. The announcement informs the public about exciting vacation packages at Paradise Island through the Tropical Travel agency. Below the headline, PARADISE ISLAND, is a picture of the breathtaking scenery at Paradise Island, designed to catch the attention of the reader. The picture is located at the Web page www.scsite.com/wd97/pr1.htm. Below the picture is the body title, Ready For A Vacation?, followed by a brief paragraph about Paradise Island. Next, a bulleted list identifies vacation package details. Finally, the last line of the announcement lists the telephone number of Tropical Travel.

Document Preparation Steps

Document preparation steps give you an overview of how the document in Figure 1-1 will be developed. The following tasks will be completed in this project:

1. Start Word.
2. Change the size of the displayed and printed characters.
3. Enter the document text.
4. Spell check as you type.
5. Add bullets as you type.
6. Save the document on a floppy disk.
7. Format the document text (center, enlarge, bold, underline, and italicize).
8. Insert the picture from a Web page.
9. Resize the picture.
10. Save the document again.
11. Print the document.
12. Quit Word.

headline ►

picture of vacation spot ►

PARADISE ISLAND

body title ►

Ready For A Vacation?

Paradise Island offers glistening, white-sand beaches and swimming in crystal-clear waters. Recreational activities include surfing, SCUBA diving, snorkeling, sailing, and scenic hiking.

bulleted list ►

- Paradise Island vacation packages fit <u>any</u> budget
- Cottages, suites, condos, and inns are available

Call ***Tropical Travel*** at 555-2121

FIGURE 1-1

The following pages contain a detailed explanation of each of these tasks.

Mouse Usage

In this book, the mouse is the primary way to communicate with Word. You can perform six operations with a standard mouse: point, click, right-click, double-click, drag, and right-drag. If you have a **Microsoft IntelliMouse**™, then you also have a wheel between the left and right buttons. This wheel can be used to perform three additional operations: rotate wheel, click wheel, or drag wheel.

Point means you move the mouse across a flat surface until the mouse pointer rests on the item of choice on the screen. As you move the mouse, the mouse pointer moves across the screen in the same direction. **Click** means you press and release the left mouse button. The terminology used in this book to direct you to point to a particular item and then click is, click the particular item. For example, *click the Bold button*, means point to the Bold button and then click.

Right-click means you press and release the right mouse button. As with the left mouse button, you normally will point to an item on the screen prior to right-clicking. In many cases, when you right-click, Word displays a **shortcut menu** that contains the commands most often used for the current activity. Thus, when these projects instruct you to display a shortcut menu, point to the item being discussed and then right-click.

Double-click means you quickly press and release the left mouse button twice without moving the mouse. In most cases, you must point to an item before double-clicking. **Drag** means you point to an item, hold down the left mouse button, move the item to the desired location on the screen, and then release the left mouse button. **Right-drag** means you point to an item, hold down the right mouse button, move the item to the desired location, and then release the right mouse button.

If you have a Microsoft IntelliMouse™, then you can use the **rotate wheel** to view parts of the document that are not visible. The wheel also can serve as a third button. When the wheel is used as a button, it is referred to as the **wheel button**. For example, dragging the wheel button causes Word to scroll in the direction you drag.

The use of the mouse is an important skill when working with Microsoft Word 97.

Starting Word

Follow these steps to start Word, or ask your instructor how to start Word for your system.

More *About* Mouse Usage

Some mouse users bend their wrists frequently while moving the mouse. To help prevent wrist injuries, place the mouse at least six inches from the edge of a workstation. In this location, the wrist is forced to be flat, which causes bending to occur at the elbow when the mouse is moved.

More *About* Microsoft IntelliMouse™

You can use the Microsoft IntelliMouse™ to pan (scroll continuously) through a document or zoom a document. To pan up or down, hold down the wheel button and drag the pointer above or below the origin mark (two triangles separated by a dot). To zoom in or out, hold down the CTRL key while rotating the wheel button forward or back.

To Start Word

1 **Click the Start button on the taskbar and then point to New Office Document.**

The programs in the Start menu display above the Start button (Figure 1-2). The New Office Document command is highlighted on the Start menu.

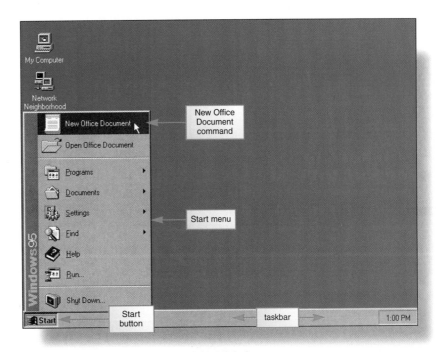

FIGURE 1-2

2 **Click New Office Document. If necessary, click the General tab when the New Office Document dialog box first opens.**

Office displays several icons on the General sheet in the New Office Document dialog box (Figure 1-3). Each icon represents a different type of document you can create in Microsoft Office. In this project, you are to create a new document using Microsoft Word 97.

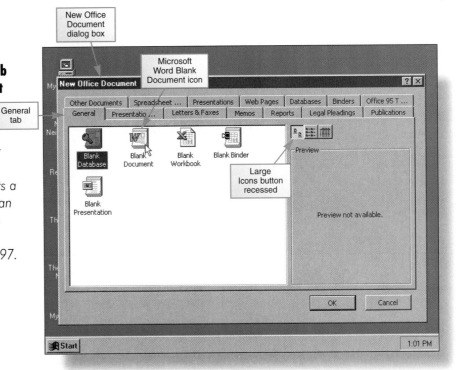

FIGURE 1-3

3 **Double-click the Blank Document icon.**

Office starts Word. While Word is starting, the mouse pointer changes to the shape of an hourglass. After a few moments, an empty document titled Document1 displays on the Word screen (Figure 1-4).

4 **If the Word screen is not maximized, double-click its title bar to maximize it. If the Office Assistant displays, click its Close button.**

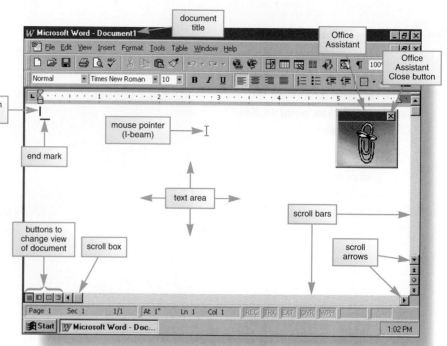

FIGURE 1-4

The Word Screen

The **Word screen** (Figure 1-4) consists of a variety of features to make your work more efficient and the results more professional. If you are following along on a personal computer and your screen differs from Figure 1-4, click View on the menu bar and then click Normal.

Word Document Window

The Word document window contains several elements similar to the document windows in other applications, as well as some elements unique to Word. The main elements of the Word document window are the text area, insertion point, end mark, mouse pointer, and scroll bars (Figure 1-4).

TEXT AREA As you type or insert pictures, your text and graphics display in the **text area**.

INSERTION POINT The **insertion point** is a blinking vertical bar that indicates where text will be inserted as you type. As you type, the insertion point moves to the right and, when you reach the end of a line, it moves downward to the next line. You also insert graphics at the location of the insertion point.

END MARK The **end mark** indicates the end of your document. Each time you begin a new line as you type, the end mark moves downward.

MOUSE POINTER The **mouse pointer** becomes different shapes depending on the task you are performing in Word and the pointer's location on the screen. The mouse pointer in Figure 1-4 has the shape of an I-beam. The mouse pointer displays as an **I-beam** when it is in the text area. Other mouse pointer shapes are described as they appear on the screen during this and subsequent projects.

SCROLL BARS You use the **scroll bars** to display different portions of your document in the document window. At the right edge of the document window is a vertical scroll bar, and at the bottom of the document window is a horizontal scroll bar. On both scroll bars, the **scroll box** indicates your current location in the document. At the left edge of the horizontal scroll bar, Word provides three buttons you use to change the view of your document. These buttons are discussed as they are used in a later project.

Word is preset to use standard 8.5-by-11-inch paper, with 1.25-inch left and right margins and 1-inch top and bottom margins. Only a portion of your document, however, displays on the screen at one time. You view the portion of the document displayed on the screen through the **document window** (Figure 1-5).

More *About*
Scroll Bars

You can use the vertical scroll bar to scroll through multi-page documents. As you drag the scroll box up or down the scroll bar, Word displays a page indicator to the left of the scroll box. The page indicator reflects the current page, if you were to release the mouse at that moment.

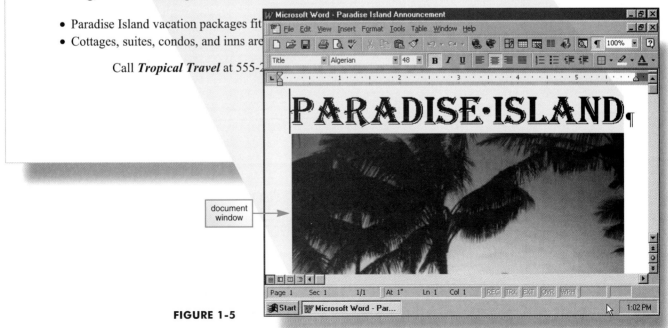

FIGURE 1-5

Menu Bar, Toolbars, Rulers, and Status Bar

The menu bar, toolbars, and horizontal ruler appear at the top of the screen just below the title bar (Figure 1-6). The status bar appears at the bottom of the screen.

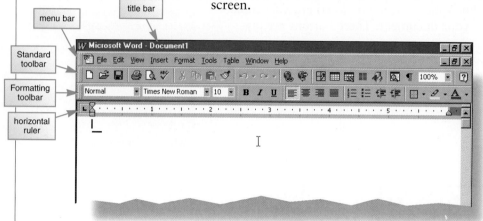

menu bar

title bar

Standard toolbar

Formatting toolbar

horizontal ruler

FIGURE 1-6

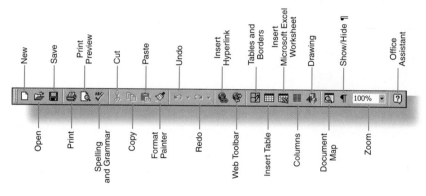

New · Save · Print Preview · Cut · Paste · Undo · Insert Hyperlink · Tables and Borders · Insert Microsoft Excel Worksheet · Drawing · Show/Hide ¶ · Office Assistant

Open · Print · Spelling and Grammar · Copy · Format Painter · Redo · Web Toolbar · Insert Table · Columns · Document Map · Zoom

FIGURE 1-7

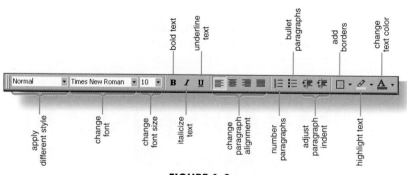

bold text · underline text · bullet paragraphs · add borders · change text color

apply different style · change font · change font size · italicize text · change paragraph alignment · number paragraphs · adjust paragraph indent · highlight text

FIGURE 1-8

MENU BAR The **menu bar** displays the Word menu names. Each menu name contains a list of commands you can use to retrieve, store, print, and format data in your document and perform other tasks. Many of these commands have a picture beside them to help you quickly identify them. For example, the Save command on the File menu has a picture of a floppy disk beside it. To display a menu, such as the File menu, click the menu name on the menu bar.

TOOLBARS The menu bar is actually the first toolbar on the Word screen. Just below the menu bar is the **Standard toolbar**. Immediately below the Standard toolbar is the **Formatting toolbar**.

Toolbars contain buttons, boxes, and menus that allow you to perform tasks more quickly than using the standard menu bar. For example, to print, click the Print button on the Standard toolbar. Each button has a picture on the face that helps you remember its function. Figure 1-7 illustrates the Standard toolbar and identifies its buttons and boxes; Figure 1-8 illustrates the Formatting toolbar. Each button and box is explained in detail as it is used in the projects.

The Standard and Formatting toolbars initially display **docked**, or attached to top edge of the Word window directly below the menu bar. Additional toolbars may display automatically on the Word screen, depending on the task you are performing. These additional toolbars display either stacked below the Formatting toolbar or floating on the Word screen. A floating toolbar is not attached to an edge of the Word window. You can rearrange the order of **docked toolbars** and can move **floating toolbars** anywhere on the Word screen. Later in the book, steps are presented that show you how to float a docked toolbar or dock a floating toolbar.

RULERS Below the Formatting toolbar is the **horizontal ruler** (Figure 1-9). You use the horizontal ruler, sometimes simply called the **ruler**, to set tab stops, indent paragraphs, adjust column widths, and change page margins. An additional ruler, called the **vertical ruler**, displays at the left edge of the window when you are performing certain tasks. The vertical ruler is discussed as it displays on the screen in a later project.

STATUS BAR The **status bar** is located at the bottom of the screen. From left to right, the following information displays about the page shown in Figure 1-9: the page number, the section number, the page visible in the document window followed by the total number of pages in the document, the position of the insertion point in inches from the top of the page, the line number and column number of the insertion point, and several **status indicators**. If the insertion point does not display in the document window, then no measurement displays on the status bar for the position of the insertion point, its line, and its column.

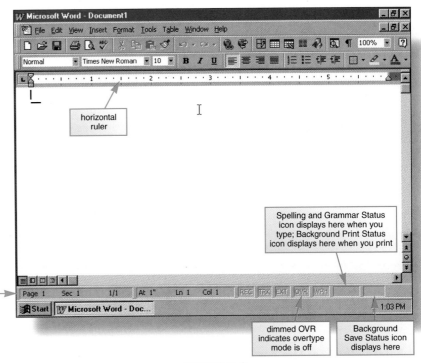

FIGURE 1-9

The right half of the status bar displays several status indicators. Five of these status indicators (REC, TRK, EXT, OVR, and WPH or WPN) appear darkened when on and dimmed when off. For example, the dimmed OVR indicates overtype mode is off. To turn most of these status indicators on or off, double-click the status indicator. These status indicators are discussed as they are used in the projects.

Other status indicators appear as you perform certain tasks. When you begin typing in the text area, a Spelling and Grammar Status icon appears at the right edge of the status bar. When Word is saving your document, a Background Save Status icon appears on the status bar. When you print a document, a Background Print Status icon appears. These status icons will be discussed later in this project.

Depending on how you installed Word and the status of certain keys on your keyboard, your status bar may have different status indicators on or off. For example, the dimmed WPH on the status bar indicates WordPerfect Help is off. If your WordPerfect Help status indicator is darkened, WordPerfect Help is active and you need to deactivate it. When WordPerfect Help is on, the keys you press on the keyboard work according to WordPerfect instead of Word. To deactivate the WordPerfect Help, ask for assistance from your instructor or do the following: Click Tools on the menu bar and then click Options; click the General tab; click Help for WordPerfect users and click Navigation keys for WordPerfect users to clear these check boxes; and then click the OK button in the Options dialog box.

If a task you select requires several seconds (such as saving a document), the status bar displays a message informing you of the progress of the task.

More *About*
Horizontal Ruler

If the horizontal ruler does not display on your screen, click View on the menu bar and then click Ruler. This command is a toggle. That is, to hide the ruler, also click View on the menu bar and then click Ruler.

Changing the Default Font Size

Characters that display on the screen are a specific shape, size, and style. The **font**, or typeface, defines the appearance and shape of the letters, numbers, and special characters. The preset, or default, font is Times New Roman (Figure 1-10 below). The **font size** specifies the size of the characters on the screen. Font size is gauged by a measurement system called **points**. A single point is about 1/72 of one inch in height. Thus, a character with a font size of ten is about 10/72 of one inch in height. The default font size in most versions of Word is 10. If more of the characters in your document require a larger font size, you easily can change the default font size before you type. In Project 1, many of the characters in the announcement are a font size of 20. Follow these steps to increase the font size before you begin entering text.

Steps **To Increase the Default Font Size Before Typing**

1 **Point to the Font Size box arrow on the Formatting toolbar.**

The mouse pointer changes to a left-pointing block arrow when positioned on a toolbar (Figure 1-10). When you point to a toolbar button or box, Word displays a **ScreenTip** *immediately below the button or box. The ScreenTip in this figure is Font Size.*

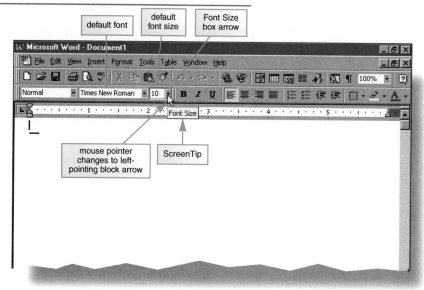

FIGURE 1-10

2 **Click the Font Size box arrow on the Formatting toolbar.**

A list of available font sizes displays in a Font Size list box (Figure 1-11). The font sizes displayed depend on the current font, which is Times New Roman.

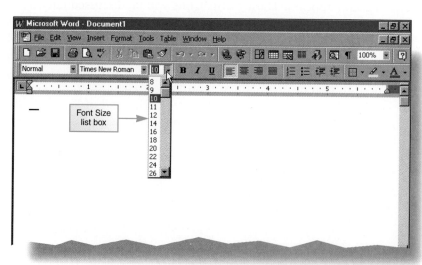

FIGURE 1-11

3 Point to font size 20.

Word highlights font size 20 in the list (Figure 1-12).

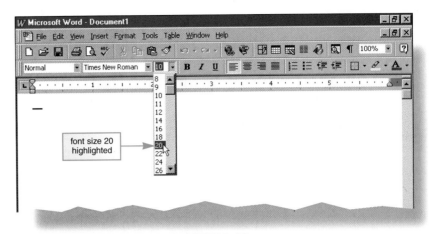

font size 20
highlighted

FIGURE 1-12

4 Click font size 20.

The font size for this document changes to 20 (Figure 1-13). The size of the insertion point increases to reflect the current font size of 20.

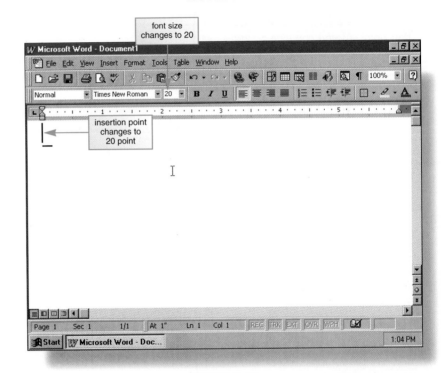

font size changes to 20

insertion point changes to 20 point

FIGURE 1-13

The new font size takes effect immediately in your document. Word uses this font size for the remainder of this announcement.

E ntering Text

To prepare a document in Word, you enter text by typing on the keyboard. In Project 1, the headline (PARADISE ISLAND) is capitalized. The example on the next page explains the steps to enter the headline in all capital letters at the left margin. Later in the project, this headline will be centered across the top of the document, formatted in bold, and enlarged.

Other Ways

1. Right-click paragraph mark above end mark, click Font on shortcut menu, click Font tab, click desired point size in Size list box, click OK button

2. On Format menu click Font, click Font tab, select desired point size in Size list box, click OK button

3. Press CTRL+SHIFT+P, type desired point size, press ENTER

4. Press CTRL+SHIFT+>

Steps To Enter Text

1 **If the CAPS LOCK indicator is not lit on your keyboard, press the CAPS LOCK key. Type PARADISE ISLAND as the headline. If at any time during typing you make an error, press the BACKSPACE key until you have deleted the text in error and then retype the text correctly.**

Word places the P in PARADISE ISLAND at the location of the insertion point. As you continue typing this headline, the insertion point moves to the right (Figure 1-14). The insertion point is currently on line 1 in column 16.

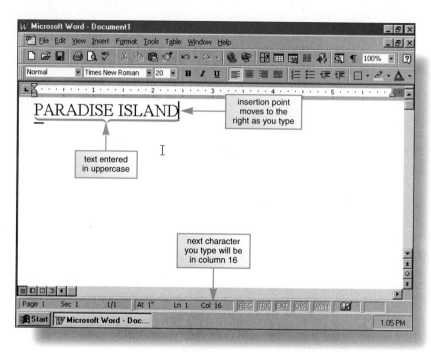

FIGURE 1-14

2 **Press the CAPS LOCK key and then press the ENTER key.**

Word creates a new paragraph by moving the insertion point to the beginning of the next line (Figure 1-15). Whenever you press the ENTER key, Word considers the previous line and the next line to be different paragraphs. Notice the status bar indicates the current position of the insertion point. That is, the insertion point is currently on line 2 column 1.

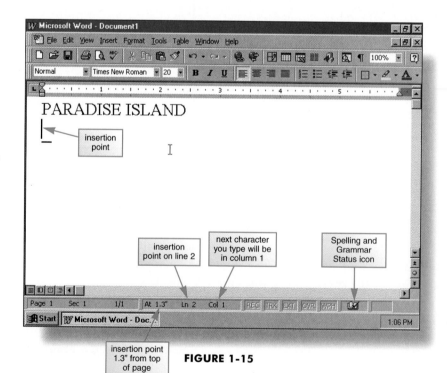

FIGURE 1-15

More *About* Headlines

Because the headline is the first item a reader notices, it should be effective. Headlines of fewer than four words are often typed in all-capital letters.

When you begin entering text into a document, the **Spelling and Grammar Status icon** displays at the right edge of the status bar (Figure 1-15). As you type, the spelling icon shows an animated pencil writing on paper, which indicates Word is checking for possible errors. When you stop typing, the pencil changes to either a red check mark or a red X. In Figure 1-15, the Spelling and Grammar Status icon displays a red check mark. In general, if all of the words you have typed are in Word's dictionary and your grammar is correct, a red check mark appears on the Spelling and Grammar Status icon. If you type a word not in the dictionary (because it is a proper name or misspelled), a red wavy underline appears below the word. If you type text that may be grammatically incorrect, a green wavy underline appears below the text. When Word underlines a possible spelling or grammar error, it also changes the red check mark on the Spelling and Grammar Status icon to a red X. As you enter text into the announcement, your Spelling and Grammar Status icon may show a red X, rather than a red check mark. Later in this project, you check the spelling of these words. At that time, the red X returns to a red check mark.

Entering Blank Lines into a Document

To enter a blank line into a document, press the ENTER key without typing anything on the line. The following example explains how to enter two blank lines below the headline, PARADISE ISLAND.

 Steps To Enter Blank Lines into a Document

① **Press the ENTER key two times.**

Word inserts two blank lines into your document below the headline (Figure 1-16).

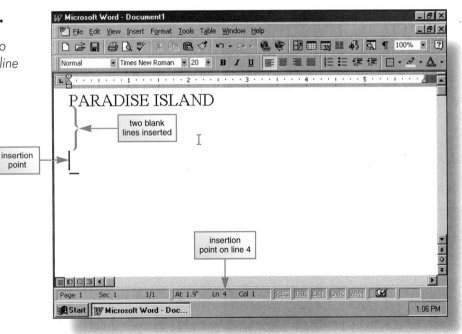

FIGURE 1-16

> **More** *About*
> **Entering Text**
>
> In the days of typewriters, the letter l was used for both the letter l and the number one. Keyboards, however, have both a number one and the letter l. Keyboards also have both a number zero and the letter o. Be careful to press the correct keyboard character when creating a word processing document.

Displaying Nonprinting Characters

To indicate where in the document you press the ENTER key or SPACEBAR, you may find it helpful to display **nonprinting characters**. The paragraph mark (¶) is a nonprinting character that indicates where you pressed the ENTER key. A raised dot (•) shows where you pressed the SPACEBAR. Nonprinting characters display only on the screen. They do not appear in printed documents. Other nonprinting characters are discussed as they display on the screen in subsequent projects. The following steps illustrate how to display nonprinting characters, if they are not already displaying on your screen.

Steps | To Display Nonprinting Characters

1 **Point to the Show/Hide ¶ button on the Standard toolbar.**

Word displays the ScreenTip for the button (Figure 1-17).

FIGURE 1-17

2 **If it is not already recessed, click the Show/Hide ¶ button on the Standard toolbar.**

*Word displays nonprinting characters on the screen, and the Show/Hide ¶ button on the Standard toolbar is **recessed**, or pushed in (Figure 1-18).*

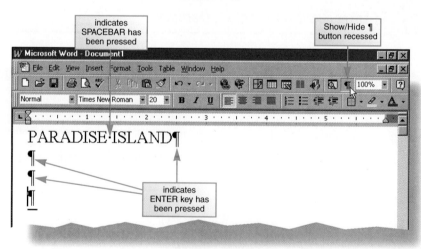

FIGURE 1-18

OtherWays

1. On Tools menu click Options, click View tab, click All, click OK button
2. Press CTRL+SHIFT+*

Notice several changes to your screen display (Figure 1-18). A paragraph mark appears at the end of each line to indicate you pressed the ENTER key. Recall that each time you press the ENTER key, Word creates a new paragraph. Because you changed the font size, the paragraph marks are 20 point. Notice the paragraph mark above the end mark – you cannot delete this paragraph mark. Between each word, a raised dot appears, indicating you pressed the SPACEBAR. Finally, the Show/Hide ¶ button is recessed to indicate it is selected.

If you feel the nonprinting characters clutter your screen, you can hide them by clicking the Show/Hide ¶ button again. It is recommended that you display nonprinting characters; therefore, the screens presented in this book show the nonprinting characters.

Entering More Text

The next step is to enter the body title, Ready For A Vacation?, into the document window as explained in the steps below.

TO ENTER MORE TEXT

Step 1: Type Ready For A Vacation? to enter the body title.

Step 2: Press the ENTER key twice.

The body title displays on line 4 as shown in Figure 1-19.

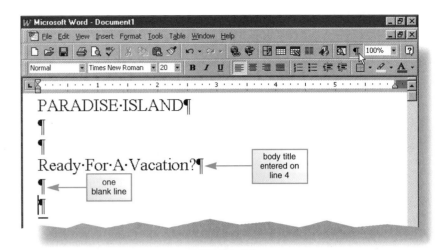

FIGURE 1-19

Using the Wordwrap Feature

Wordwrap allows you to type words in a paragraph continually without pressing the ENTER key at the end of each line. When the insertion point moves beyond the right margin, Word positions it automatically at the beginning of the next line. As you type, if a word extends beyond the right margin, Word also positions the word automatically on the next line with the insertion point. Thus, as you enter text using Word, do not press the ENTER key when the insertion point reaches the right margin. Because Word creates a new paragraph each time you press the ENTER key, press the ENTER key only in these circumstances:

1. To insert blank lines into a document
2. To begin a new paragraph
3. To terminate a short line of text and advance to the next line
4. In response to certain Word commands

Perform the following step to become familiar with the wordwrap feature.

Steps To Wordwrap Text as You Type

1 **Type** Paradise Island offers glistening, white-sand beaches and swimming in crystal-clear waters. **to enter the first sentence in the paragraph below the body title of the announcement.**

Word wraps the word, and, to the beginning of line 7 because it is too long to fit on line 6 (Figure 1-20). Your document may wordwrap on a different word depending on the type of printer you are using.

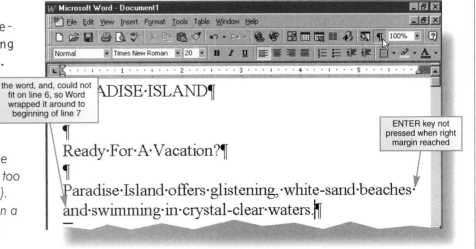

FIGURE 1-20

Checking Spelling Automatically as You Type

As you type text into the document window, Word checks your typing for possible spelling and grammar errors. If a word you type is not in the dictionary, a red wavy underline appears below it. Likewise, if text you type contains possible grammar errors, a green wavy underline appears below the text. In both cases, the Spelling and Grammar Status icon displays a red X, instead of a check mark. Although you can check the entire document for spelling and grammar errors at once, you also can check these errors immediately.

To verify that the spell check as you type feature is enabled, right-click the Spelling and Grammar Status icon on the status bar and then click Options on the shortcut menu. When the Spelling & Grammar dialog box displays, be sure Check spelling as you type is selected and Hide spelling errors in this document is not selected.

When a word is flagged with a red wavy underline, it is not in Word's dictionary. If a word is flagged, it is not necessarily misspelled. For example, many names, abbreviations, and specialized terms are not in the Word's main dictionary. In these cases, you tell Word to ignore the flagged word. As you type, Word also detects duplicate words. For example, if your document contains the phrase, to the the store, Word places a red wavy underline below the second occurrence of the word, the. To display a list of suggested corrections for a flagged word, you right-click it.

In the following example, the word, include, has been misspelled intentionally as incude to illustrate Word's spell check as you type feature. If you are doing this project on a personal computer, your announcement may contain different misspelled words, depending on the accuracy of your typing.

Steps **To Spell Check as You Type**

1 **Press the SPACEBAR once. Type the beginning of the next sentence:** Recreational activities incude **and then press the SPACEBAR.**

Word flags the misspelled word, incude, by placing a red wavy underline below it (Figure 1-21). Notice the Spelling and Grammar Status icon on the status bar now displays a red X, indicating Word has detected a possible spelling or grammar error.

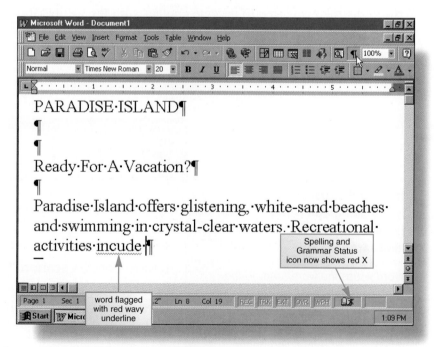

FIGURE 1-21

2 **Position the mouse pointer in the flagged word (incude, in this case).**

The mouse pointer's shape is an I-beam when positioned in a word (Figure 1-22).

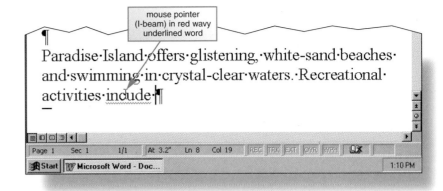

FIGURE 1-22

3 **Right-click the flagged word, incude. When the shortcut menu displays, point to include.**

Word displays a shortcut menu that lists suggested spelling corrections for the flagged word (Figure 1-23).

4 **Click include. Press the END key and then type** surfing, SCUBA diving, snorkeling, sailing, and scenic hiking. **to enter the remainder of the sentence.**

Word replaces the misspelled word with the selected word on the shortcut menu (Figure 1-24 on the next page). The Spelling and Grammar Status icon replaces the red X with a check mark.

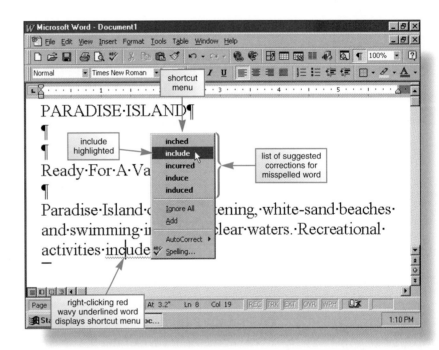

FIGURE 1-23

Other Ways

1. Click flagged word, double-click Spelling and Grammar Status icon, click correct word on shortcut menu

If your word actually is spelled correctly and, for example, is a proper name, you can right-click it and then click Ignore on the shortcut menu. If, when you right-click the misspelled word, your desired correction is not in the list (Figure 1-23), you can click outside the shortcut menu to make the menu disappear and then retype the correct word.

If you feel the wavy underlines clutter your document window, you can hide them temporarily until you are ready to check for spelling errors. To do this, you right-click the Spelling and Grammar Status icon on the status bar and then click Hide Spelling Errors on the shortcut menu.

Entering Documents that Scroll the Document Window

As you type more lines of text than Word can display in the text area, Word **scrolls** the top portion of the document upward off the screen. Although you cannot see the text once it scrolls off the screen, it remains in the document. Recall that the document window allows you to view only a portion of your document at one time (Figure 1-5 on page WD 1.11).

Follow this step to scroll the document window while entering text.

Steps To Enter a Document that Scrolls the Document Window

 1 **Press the ENTER key twice.**

Word scrolls the headline, PARADISE ISLAND, off the top of the screen (Figure 1-24). Your screen may scroll differently depending on the type of monitor you are using.

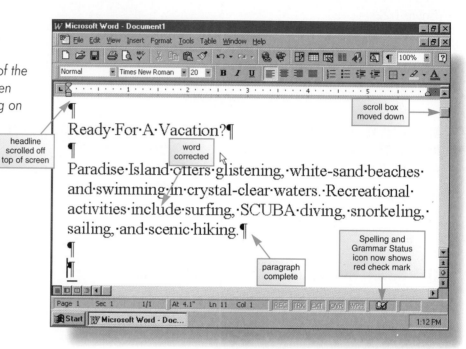

FIGURE 1-24

More *About* **Scrolling**

Computer users frequently switch between the keyboard and the mouse during a word processing session, which places strain on the wrist. To help prevent wrist injury, minimize switching. If your fingers are already on the keyboard, use keyboard keys to scroll; if your hand is already on the mouse, use the mouse to scroll.

When Word scrolls text off the top of the screen, the scroll box on the scroll bar at the right edge of the document window moves downward (Figure 1-24). The **scroll box** indicates the current relative location of the insertion point in the document. You may use either the mouse or the keyboard to move the insertion point to a different location in a document.

With the mouse, you use the scroll bars to bring a different portion of the document into the document window, and then click the mouse to move the insertion point to that location. Table 1-1 explains the techniques for scrolling with the mouse.

TABLE 1-1

SCROLL LOCATION	MOUSE USAGE
Up	Drag the scroll box upward.
Down	Drag the scroll box downward.
Up one screen	Click anywhere above the scroll box.
Down one screen	Click anywhere below the scroll box.
Up one line	Click the scroll arrow at the top of the scroll bar.
Down one line	Click the scroll arrow at the bottom of the scroll bar.

When you use the keyboard, the insertion point moves automatically when you press the appropriate keys. Table 1-2 outlines the various techniques to scroll through a document with the keyboard.

AutoFormat As You Type

The next step is to enter the bulleted list in the announcement. In Word, a **list** is a series of paragraphs. A **bullet** is a small circle positioned at the beginning of a paragraph. Bullets differ from the nonprinting character for the SPACEBAR because bullets print. You can type the list and then place the bullets on the paragraphs at a later time, or you can instruct word to place a bullet character automatically as you type the paragraphs. For example, you can type an asterisk (*) at the beginning of the first paragraph in the list. When you press the ENTER key to add another item to the list, Word automatically changes the asterisk to a bullet character.

This type of automatic change is one of the many **AutoFormat As You Type** features of Word. To be sure this feature is on, click Tools on the menu bar, click AutoCorrect, click the AutoFormat As You Type tab, be sure these two check boxes are selected: Automatic bulleted lists and Format beginning of list item like the one before it, and then click the OK button.

Perform the following steps to add bullets automatically to a list as you type.

TABLE 1-2	
SCROLL LOCATION	*KEY(S) TO PRESS*
Left one character	LEFT ARROW
Right one character	RIGHT ARROW
Left one word	CTRL+LEFT ARROW
Right one word	CTRL+RIGHT ARROW
Up one line	UP ARROW
Down one line	DOWN ARROW
To end of a line	END
To beginning of a line	HOME
Up one paragraph	CTRL+UP ARROW
Down one paragraph	CTRL+DOWN ARROW
Up one screen	PAGE UP
Down one screen	PAGE DOWN
Previous page	CTRL+PAGE UP
Next page	CTRL+PAGE DOWN
To the beginning of a document	CTRL+HOME
To the end of a document	CTRL+END

  **To Bullet a List as You Type**

1 **Type an asterisk (*) and then press the SPACEBAR. Type** Paradise Island vacation packages fit any budget **as the first item in the list.**

The asterisk character must be followed by a SPACEBAR for the AutoFormat As You Type feature to work properly (Figure 1-25).

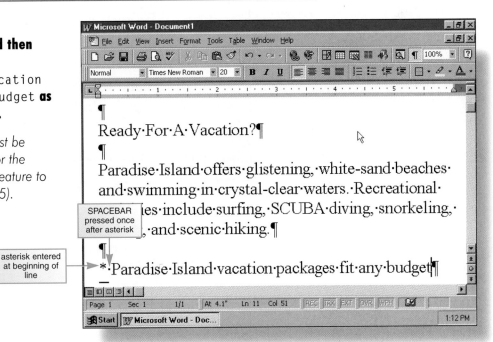

FIGURE 1-25

2 **Press the ENTER key.**

Word converts the asterisk on line 11 to a bullet character and places another bullet character on line 12 (Figure 1-26). Each time you press the ENTER key, Word considers the next line a new paragraph and places a bullet character automatically at the beginning of the line. The Bullets button on the Formatting toolbar is recessed, indicating the current paragraph is bulleted.

asterisk converted to bullet character when ENTER key pressed

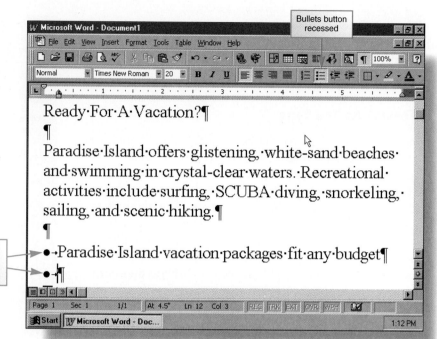

FIGURE 1-26

3 **Type** Cottages, suites, condos, and inns are available **and then press the ENTER key.**

Word places a bullet character on line 13 (Figure 1-27). Because you are finished with the list, you must instruct Word to stop bulleting paragraphs. To stop automatic bulleting, you press the ENTER key again.

bullet character on line below list

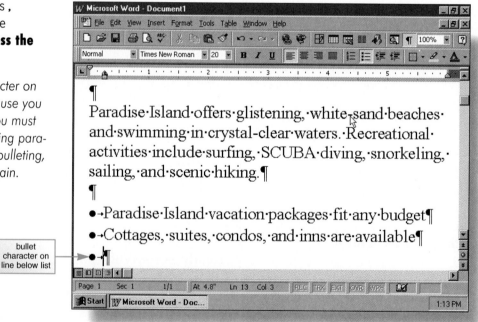

FIGURE 1-27

4 **Press the ENTER key. Type** Call Tropical Travel at 555-2121 **as the last line in the announcement.**

Word removes the lone bullet character after the list because you pressed the ENTER key twice (Figure 1-28). The text of the announcement is completely entered.

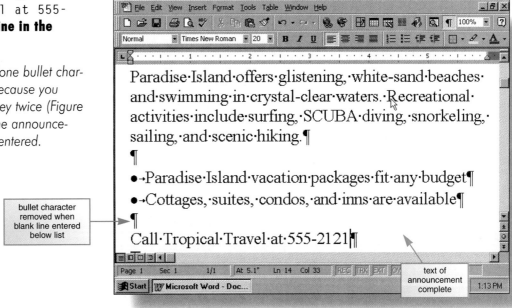

bullet character removed when blank line entered below list

text of announcement complete

FIGURE 1-28

If you know before you type a list that it is to be numbered, you can add numbers as you type, just as you add bullets as you type. To add numbers, type the number one followed by a period and a space (1.) at the beginning of the first item and then type your text. When you press the ENTER key, Word places the number two (2.) at the beginning of the next line automatically. As with automatic bullets, to stop automatic numbering, press the ENTER key twice at the end of the list.

Saving a Document

When you are creating a document in Word, the computer stores it in memory. If the computer is turned off or if you lose electrical power, the document is lost. Hence, it is mandatory to save on disk any document that you will use later. The steps on the next page illustrate how to save a document on a floppy disk inserted in drive A using the Save button on the Standard toolbar.

Other Ways

1. Type list, select list, click Bullets button on Formatting toolbar

2. Type list, select list, right-click selected list, click Bullets and Numbering on shortcut menu, click Bulleted tab, click desired bullet type, click OK button

3. Type list, select list, on Format menu click Bullets and Numbering, click Bulleted tab, click desired bullet type, click OK button

More *About* **Saving**

When you save a document, you should create readable and meaningful filenames. A filename can be up to 255 characters, including spaces. The only invalid characters are backslash (\ ), slash (/), colon (:), asterisk (*), question mark (?), quotation mark ("), less than symbol (<), greater than symbol (>), and vertical bar (|).

Steps To Save a New Document

1 Insert a formatted floppy disk into drive A. Click the Save button on the Standard toolbar.

Word displays the Save As dialog box with the insertion point blinking after the default file name, PARADISE ISLAND, in the File name text box (Figure 1-29). Notice that Word chooses the first line of the document as the default file name. Because the file name is selected initially when the Save As dialog box displays, you can change the file name by immediately typing the new name. If you do not enter a new file name, the document will be saved with the default file name, PARADISE ISLAND.

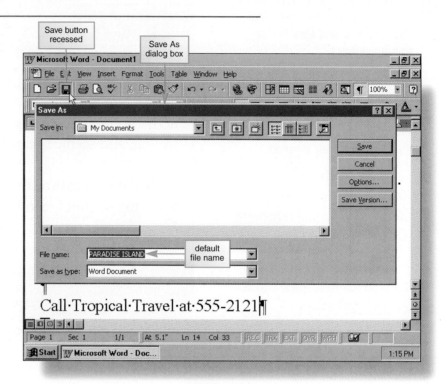

FIGURE 1-29

2 Type the file name Paradise Island Announcement **in the File name text box. Do not press the ENTER key after typing the file name.**

*The file name, Paradise Island Announcement, displays in the File name text box (Figure 1-30). When creating file names, you should be as meaningful as possible. Thus, the first words in this file name (Paradise Island) relate to the nature of this document, and the last word (Announcement) relates to the category of this document. Using this technique, all files relating to Paradise Island, whether a letter, a memo, or an announcement, will be grouped together in a folder. A **folder** is a specific location on a disk. Notice that the current folder is My Documents. To change to a different drive or folder, you must use the Save in box.*

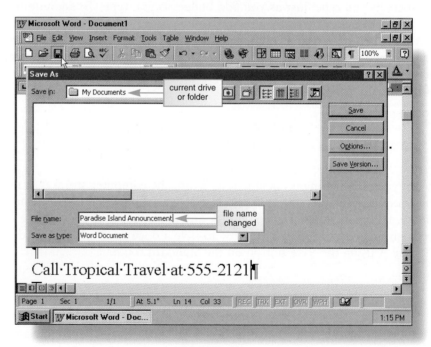

FIGURE 1-30

3 **Click the Save in box arrow and then point to 3½ Floppy (A:).**

A list of the available drives displays with 3½ Floppy (A:) highlighted (Figure 1-31). Your list may differ depending on your system configuration.

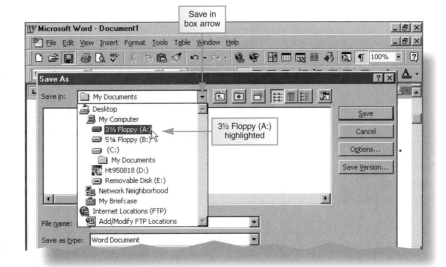

FIGURE 1-31

4 **Click 3½ Floppy (A:) and then point to the Save button in the Save As dialog box.**

The 3½ Floppy (A:) drive becomes the selected drive (Figure 1-32). The names of existing files stored on the floppy disk in drive A display. In Figure 1-32, no files currently are stored on the floppy disk in drive A.

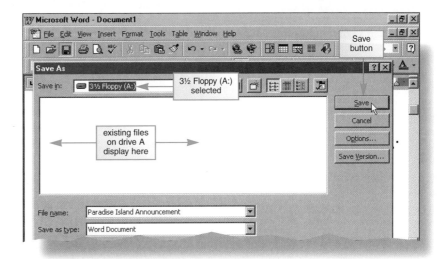

FIGURE 1-32

5 **Click the Save button in the Save As dialog box.**

Word saves the document on the floppy disk in drive A with the file name Paradise Island Announcement (Figure 1-33). Although the announcement is saved on a floppy disk, it also remains in main memory and displays on the screen.

OtherWays

1. On File menu click Save, type file name, select location in Save in box, click Save button in dialog box

2. Press CTRL+S, type file name, select location in Save in box, click Save button in dialog box

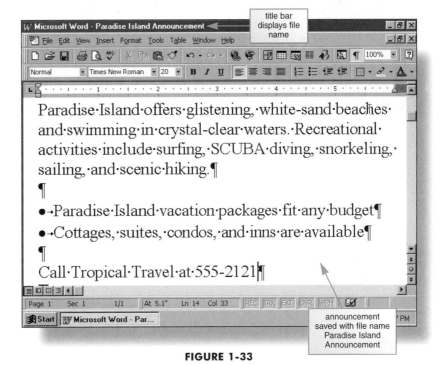

FIGURE 1-33

Formatting Paragraphs and Characters in a Document

The text for Project 1 now is complete. The next step is to format the characters and paragraphs within the announcement. Paragraphs encompass the text up to and including the paragraph mark (¶). **Paragraph formatting** is the process of changing the appearance of a paragraph. For example, you can center or indent a paragraph.

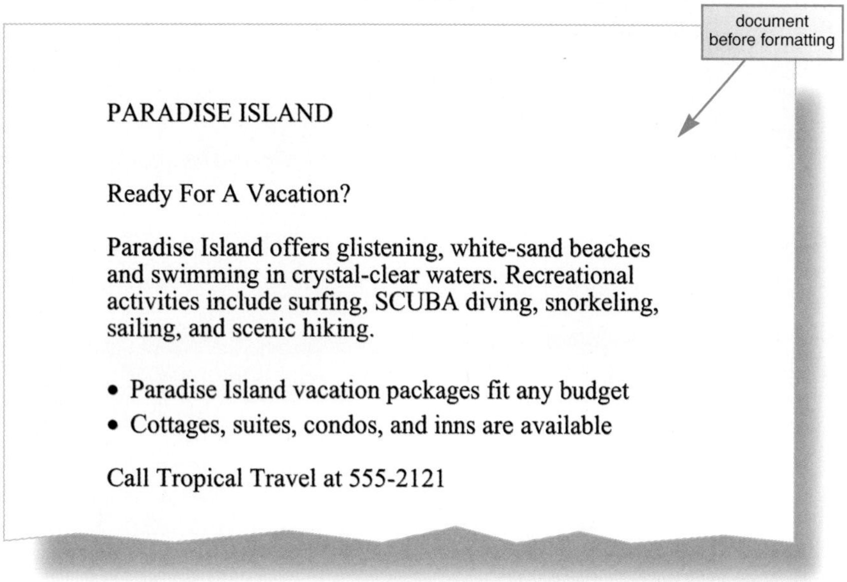

Characters include letters, numbers, punctuation marks, and symbols. **Character formatting** is the process of changing the way characters appear on the screen and in print. You use character formatting to emphasize certain words and improve readability of a document.

With Word, you can format before you type or apply new formats after you type. Earlier, you changed the font size before you typed any text, and then you entered the text. You also used AutoFormat to insert bullets as you typed the list in the announcement. In this section, you format existing text.

Figure 1-34 shows the announcement before formatting the paragraphs and characters in it. Figure 1-35 shows the announcement after formatting it. As you can see from the two figures, a document that is formatted not only is easier to read, but it looks more professional.

In the pages that follow, you will change the unformatted announcement in Figure 1-34 to the formatted announcement in Figure 1-35 using these steps:

1. Center the headline and body title across the page.
2. Enlarge the headline.
3. Change the font of the headline.
4. Bold the headline.
5. Bold and enlarge the body title.
6. Underline a word in the bulleted list.
7. Bold and italicize a series of words in the last line of the announcement.
8. Center the last line of the announcement.

document before formatting

PARADISE ISLAND

Ready For A Vacation?

Paradise Island offers glistening, white-sand beaches and swimming in crystal-clear waters. Recreational activities include surfing, SCUBA diving, snorkeling, sailing, and scenic hiking.

- Paradise Island vacation packages fit any budget
- Cottages, suites, condos, and inns are available

Call Tropical Travel at 555-2121

FIGURE 1-34

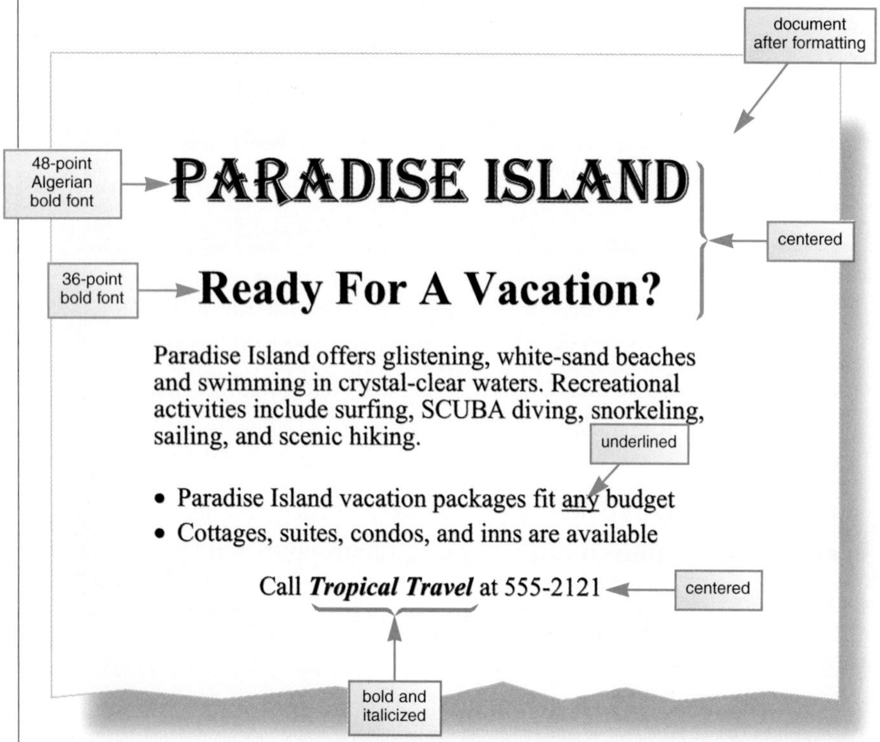

document after formatting

48-point Algerian bold font

PARADISE ISLAND

centered

36-point bold font

Ready For A Vacation?

Paradise Island offers glistening, white-sand beaches and swimming in crystal-clear waters. Recreational activities include surfing, SCUBA diving, snorkeling, sailing, and scenic hiking.

underlined

- Paradise Island vacation packages fit <u>any</u> budget
- Cottages, suites, condos, and inns are available

Call *Tropical Travel* at 555-2121

centered

bold and italicized

FIGURE 1-35

The process required to format the announcement is explained on the following pages. The first formatting step is to center the first two lines of text between the margins. Recall that each line is considered a separate paragraph because each line ends with a paragraph mark.

Selecting and Formatting Paragraphs and Characters

To format a single paragraph, move the insertion point into the paragraph and then format it. To format multiple paragraphs in a document, however, the paragraphs you want to format first must be selected and then they can be formatted. In the same manner, to format characters, you first must select the characters to be formatted and then format your selection. Selected text is highlighted. For example, if your screen normally displays dark letters on a light background, then selected text appears as light letters on a dark background.

Selecting Multiple Paragraphs

The headline (PARADISE ISLAND) and the body title (Ready For A Vacation?) are separated by two paragraph marks. Thus, the headline and the body title are actually four separate paragraphs. Recall that each time you press the ENTER key, Word creates a new paragraph.

To center the headline and body title in Project 1, you must first **select** all four paragraphs as shown in the following steps.

> **More** *About* **Formatting**
>
> Character formatting includes changing the font, font style, font size; adding an underline, color, strikethrough, shadow, outline; embossing; engraving; making a superscript or subscript; and changing the case of the letters. Paragraph formatting includes alignment; indentation; and spacing above, below, or in between lines.

Steps **To Select Multiple Paragraphs**

1 **Press CTRL+HOME to position the insertion point at the top of the document; that is, press and hold the CTRL key, then press the HOME key, and then release both keys. Move the mouse pointer to the left of the first paragraph to be centered (the headline) until the mouse pointer changes to a right-pointing block arrow.**

The mouse pointer changes to a right-pointing block arrow when positioned to the left of a paragraph (Figure 1-36).

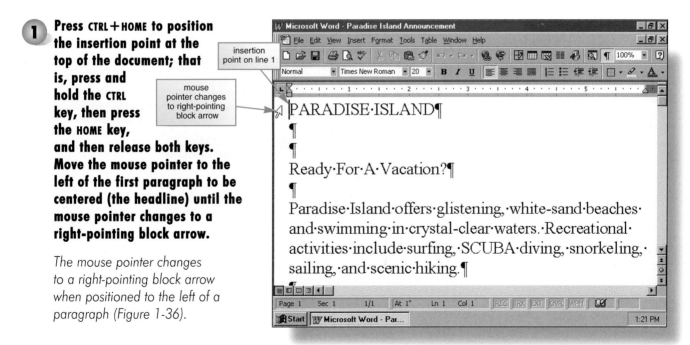

FIGURE 1-36

2 **Drag downward to the last line of the last paragraph to be centered (the body title).**

All of the paragraphs to be centered are selected; that is, light letters on a dark background (Figure 1-37). Recall that dragging is the process of holding down the mouse button while moving the mouse, and finally releasing the mouse button.

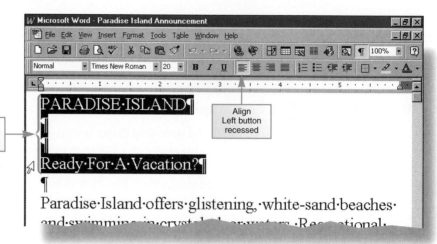

FIGURE 1-37

OtherWays

1. With insertion point at beginning of desired paragraph, press CTRL+SHIFT+DOWN ARROW

Centering Selected Paragraphs

The default alignment for paragraphs is **left-aligned**; that is, flush margins at the left edge, and jagged edges at the right edge. In Figure 1-37, the **Align Left button** is recessed to indicate the selected paragraphs currently are left-aligned. To center selected paragraphs, click the Center button as shown in the following step.

Steps **To Center Selected Paragraphs**

1 **With the paragraphs still selected, click the Center button on the Formatting toolbar.**

Word centers the headline and body title between the left and right margins (Figure 1-38). The Center button on the Formatting toolbar is recessed, which indicates the high-lighted paragraphs are centered.

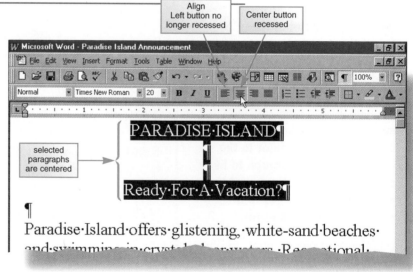

FIGURE 1-38

OtherWays

1. Right-click selected paragraph, click Paragraph on shortcut menu, click Indents and Spacing tab, click Alignment box arrow, click Centered, click OK button

2. On Format menu click Paragraph, click Indents and Spacing tab, click Alignment box arrow, click Centered, click OK button

3. Press CTRL+E

When a selected paragraph(s) is centered, the Center button on the Formatting toolbar is recessed. If, for some reason, you wanted to return the selected paragraphs to left-aligned, you would click the Align Left button on the Formatting toolbar.

The next series of steps selects the headline and formats the characters in it. In the pages that follow, you select the headline, increase the font size of the selected characters to 48, change the font of the selected characters to Algerian, and then bold the selected characters.

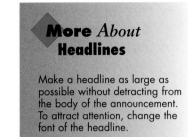

More *About* **Headlines**

Make a headline as large as possible without detracting from the body of the announcement. To attract attention, change the font of the headline.

Selecting a Single Line

To select the headline, the first line of the announcement, perform the following step.

 Steps To Select a Single Line

1 **Move the mouse pointer to the left of the line to be selected (the headline) until it changes to a right-pointing block arrow and then click.**

The entire line to the right of the mouse pointer is selected (Figure 1-39).

headline selected

mouse pointer changes to right-pointing arrow

FIGURE 1-39

Other Ways

1. With insertion point at beginning of desired line, press SHIFT+DOWN ARROW

Changing the Font Size of Selected Text

The next step in formatting the headline is to increase its font size. Recall that the font size specifies the size of the characters on the screen. Earlier in this project, you changed the font size for the entire announcement from 10 to 20. The headline, however, requires a larger font size than the rest of the document. Follow these steps to increase the font size of the headline from 20 to 48 points.

 Steps To Change the Font Size of Selected Text

1 **While the text is selected, click the Font Size box arrow on the Formatting toolbar, and then point to the down arrow on the Font Size scroll bar.**

Word displays a list of the available font sizes (Figure 1-40). Available font sizes vary depending on the font and printer driver.

Font Size box arrow

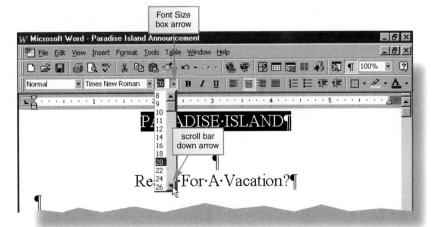

scroll bar down arrow

FIGURE 1-40

2 Click the down arrow on the scroll bar until the font size 48 displays in the list and then point to 48.

Font size 48 is highlighted (Figure 1-41).

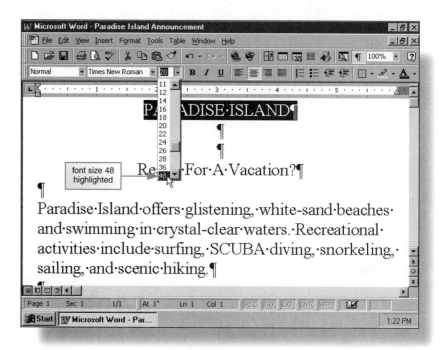

FIGURE 1-41

3 Click font size 48.

Word increases the font size of the headline from 20 to 48 (Figure 1-42). The Font Size box on the Formatting toolbar displays 48, indicating the selected text has a font size of 48.

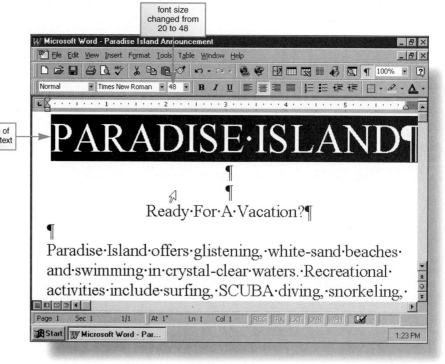

FIGURE 1-42

Changing the Font of Selected Text

Recall that the default font is Times New Roman. Word, however, provides many other fonts to add variety to your documents. Thus, change the font of the headline in the announcement to Algerian as shown in these steps.

Steps To Change the Font of Selected Text

1 **While the text is selected, click the Font box arrow on the Formatting toolbar, scroll through the list until Algerian displays, and then point to Algerian.**

Word displays a list of available fonts (Figure 1-43). Your list of available fonts may be different, depending on the type of printer you are using.

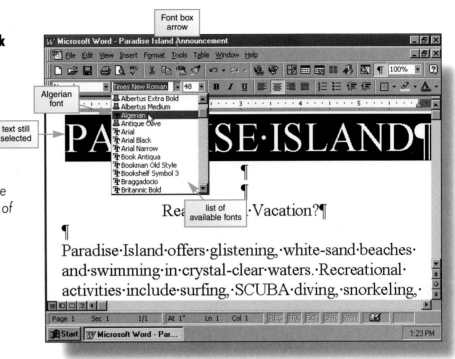

FIGURE 1-43

2 **Click Algerian.**

Word changes the font of the selected text to Algerian (Figure 1-44).

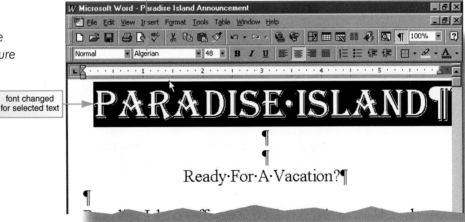

FIGURE 1-44

Bold Selected Text

To further emphasize the headline of the announcement, perform the step on the next page to make it bold.

Other Ways

1. Right-click selected text, click Font on shortcut menu, click Font tab, select desired font in Font list box, click OK button

2. On Format menu click Font, click Font tab, select desired font in Font list box, click OK button

3. Press CTRL+SHIFT+F, press DOWN ARROW key until desired font displays, press ENTER

To Bold Selected Text

① **While the text is selected, click the Bold button on the Formatting toolbar.**

Word formats the headline in bold (Figure 1-45). The Bold button is recessed.

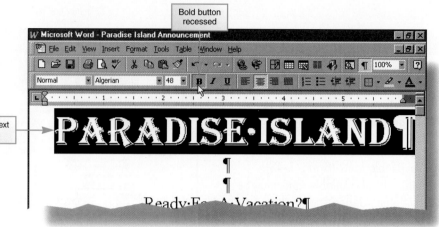

FIGURE 1-45

OtherWays

1. Right-click selected text, click Font on shortcut menu, click Font tab, click Bold in Font style list box, click OK button
2. On Format menu click Font, click Font tab, click Bold in Font style list box, click OK button
3. Press CTRL+B

When the selected text is bold, the Bold button on the Formatting toolbar is recessed. If, for some reason, you wanted to remove the bold format of the selected text, you would click the Bold button a second time.

Continuing to Format Text

The next step is to select the body title (Ready For A Vacation?), increase its font size, and bold it.

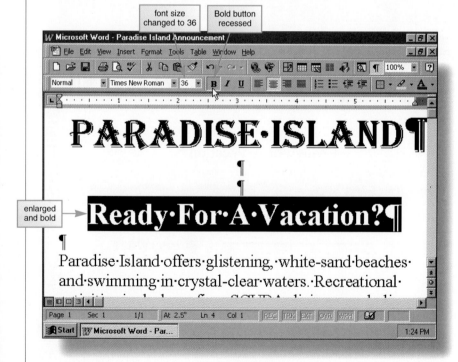

FIGURE 1-46

TO FORMAT A LINE OF TEXT

Step 1: Click to the left of the line to be formatted (the body title).

Step 2: Click the Font Size box arrow on the Formatting toolbar and scroll to the font size 36. Click font size 36.

Step 3: Click the Bold button on the Formatting toolbar.

The body title is enlarged and bold (Figure 1-46).

Scrolling

Continue formatting the document by scrolling down one screen so the bottom portion of the announcement displays in the document window.

Steps To Scroll Through the Document

1 Position the mouse pointer below the scroll box on the vertical scroll bar (Figure 1-47).

2 Click below the scroll box on the vertical scroll bar.

Word scrolls down one screenful in the document (see Figure 1-48 below). Depending on your monitor type, your screen may scroll differently.

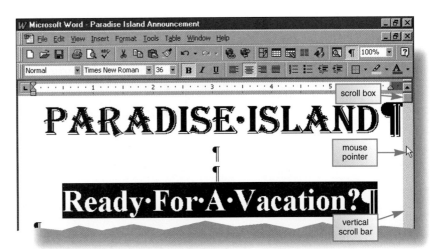

FIGURE 1-47

Other Ways

1. Drag scroll box on vertical scroll bar
2. Click scroll arrows on vertical scroll bar
3. Press PAGE DOWN or PAGE UP
4. See Tables 1-1 and 1-2 on pages WD 1.22 and WD 1.23

Selecting a Single Word

Follow these steps to select the word, any, so it can be underlined.

 Steps To Select a Single Word

1 Position the mouse pointer somewhere in the word to be formatted (any, in this case).

The mouse pointer's shape is an I-beam in a word that has not yet been selected (Figure 1-48).

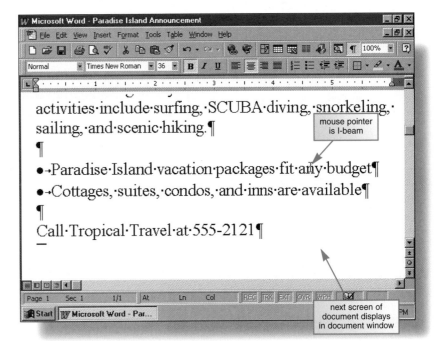

FIGURE 1-48

2 **Double-click the word to be formatted.**

The word, any, is selected (Figure 1-49). Notice that when the mouse pointer is positioned in a selected word, its shape is a left-pointing block arrow.

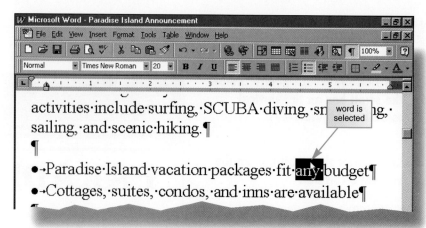

FIGURE 1-49

OtherWays

1. With insertion point at beginning of desired word, press CTRL+SHIFT+RIGHT ARROW

Underlining Selected Text

The next step is to underline the selected word, any.

Steps **To Underline Selected Text**

1 **With the text still selected, click the Underline button on the Formatting toolbar.**

The word, any, is underlined (Figure 1-50). The Underline button is recessed.

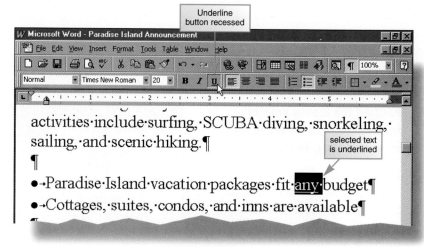

FIGURE 1-50

OtherWays

1. Right-click selected text, click Font on shortcut menu, click Font tab, click Underline box arrow, click Single, click OK button
2. On Format menu click Font, click Font tab, click Underline box arrow, click Single, click OK button
3. Press CTRL+U

When the selected text is underlined, the Underline button on the Formatting toolbar is recessed. If, for some reason, you wanted to remove the underline from the selected text, you would click the Underline button a second time.

Selecting a Group of Words and Formatting Them

The next formatting step is to italicize and bold the phrase, Tropical Travel, in the last line of the announcement. The first set of steps selects the text. Then perform the second set of steps to bold and italicize the selected text.

Steps To Select a Group of Words

① Position the mouse pointer on the first character of the first word to be selected.

The mouse pointer, an I-beam, is at the beginning of the word, Tropical (Figure 1-51).

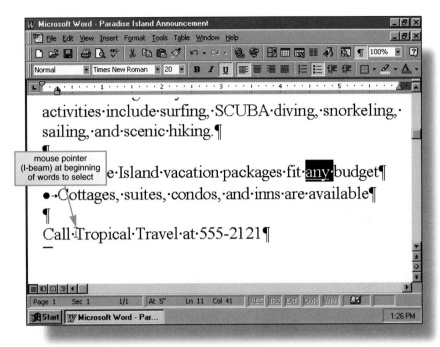

FIGURE 1-51

② Drag the mouse pointer through the last character of the last word to be selected.

The phrase, Tropical Travel, is selected (Figure 1-52).

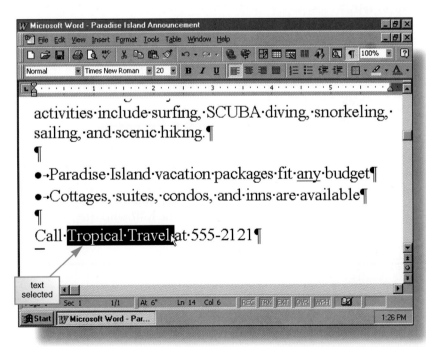

FIGURE 1-52

> *Other***Ways**
>
> 1. With insertion point at beginning of first word in the group, press CTRL+SHIFT+RIGHT ARROW until words are selected

Steps **To Italicize and Bold Selected Text**

1 **With the text still selected, click the Italic button on the Formatting toolbar. Click the Bold button on the Formatting toolbar. Click inside the selected text to remove the highlight.**

Word italicizes and bolds the text and positions the insertion point inside the bold and italicized text (Figure 1-53). When the insertion point is inside the bold and italicized text, the Bold and Italic buttons on the Formatting toolbar are recessed.

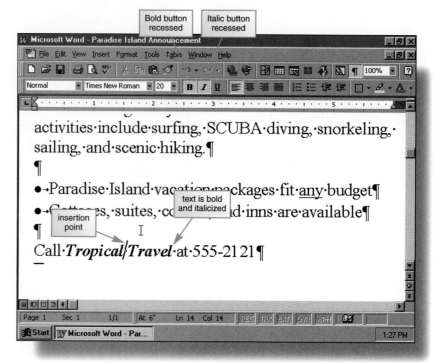

FIGURE 1-53

To remove a highlight, click the mouse. If you click inside the highlight, the Formatting toolbar displays the formatting characteristics of the characters and paragraphs containing the insertion point.

Centering a Paragraph

The last step in formatting Project 1 is to center the last line of the announcement. Recall that paragraph formatting does not require you to select the paragraph. That is, just position the insertion point in the paragraph to be formatted and then format it accordingly.

Perform the following step to center the last line in the announcement.

More *About* **the Formatting Toolbar**

Many of the buttons on the Formatting toolbar are toggles; that is, click them once to format the selected text, and click them again to remove the format from the selected text. For example, clicking the Italic button italicizes selected text; clicking the Italic button again de-italicizes the selected text.

Steps **To Center a Single Paragraph**

1 **Be sure the insertion point is still in the last line of the announcement. Click the Center button on the Formatting toolbar.**

The last line of the announcement is centered (Figure 1-54). Notice that you did not have to select the paragraph before centering; paragraph formatting requires only that the insertion point be somewhere in the paragraph.

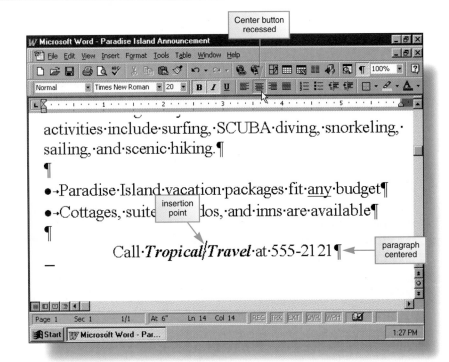

FIGURE 1-54

The formatting for the announcement is now complete. The next step is to import a graphic from the Web and then resize it.

Inserting a Picture from the Web into a Word Document

Graphic files are available from a variety of sources. Word 97 includes a series of predefined graphic files called **clip art** that you can insert into a Word document. These clip art files are located in the Clip Gallery, which contains its own Help system to assist you in locating an image suited to your application. If you have a scanner attached to your system, Word can insert the scanned photograph directly from the scanner; or, you can scan the picture into a file and then insert the scanned file into the Word document at a later time. Instead of scanning your own pictures, you can purchase photographs from a local software retailer, usually on a CD-ROM, or you can locate a picture on the Internet.

Once you have a graphic file, you can then insert, or **import**, it into a Word document. If you locate the picture on the Web, some browsers require you to copy the picture to a file on a local drive and then import the picture from your own disk. Other browsers, such as Microsoft Internet Explorer, allow you to copy the picture to the Clipboard and paste it into your Word document – *without first having to copy the file to a local disk!*

In this project, you locate a picture of Paradise Island at the Web site of www.scsite.com/wd97/pr1.htm that you want to use in the announcement. If you do not have access to the Web, go to the steps on page WD 1.44 to insert the picture from the Data Disk that accompanies this book.

▶ *Other* **Ways**

1. With insertion point in desired paragraph, click Paragraph on shortcut menu, click Indents and Spacing tab, click Alignment box arrow, click Centered, click OK button

2. With insertion point in desired paragraph, on Format menu click Paragraph, click Indents and Spacing tab, click Alignment box arrow, click Centered, click OK button

3. Press CTRL+E

More *About* **Using Graphics**

Emphasize a graphic in an announcement by placing it at the optical center of the page. To determine optical center, divide the page in half horizontally and vertically. The optical center is located one third of the way up the vertical line from the point of intersection of the two lines.

NOTE: The following steps assume you are using Microsoft Internet Explorer as your browser. If you are not using Internet Explorer and your browser does not allow you to copy pictures to the Windows Clipboard, you will need to perform a different set of steps. Your browser's handling of pictures on the Web will be discovered in Step 6 on page WD 1.42. If necessary, you may be directed to follow the steps on page WD 1.44 to save the Paradise Island picture on a disk and then insert the picture into the announcement from the disk.

Steps To Insert a Picture from the Web

1 **Press CTRL+HOME. Position the insertion point where you want the picture to be inserted. Click Insert on the menu bar.**

The insertion point is positioned on the paragraph mark immediately below the headline of the announcement (Figure 1-55). The Insert menu and its list of commands display.

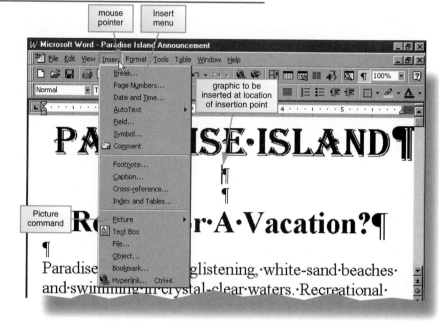

FIGURE 1-55

2 **Point to Picture on the Insert menu and then point to From File on the Picture submenu (Figure 1-56).**

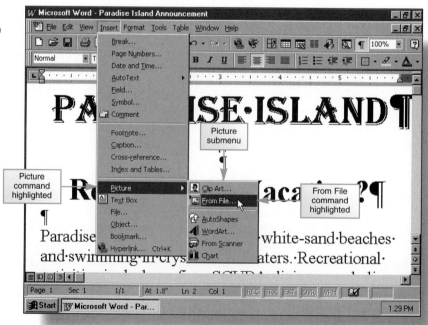

FIGURE 1-56

3 Click From File. When the Insert Picture dialog box displays, point to the Search the Web button.

Word displays the Insert Picture dialog box (Figure 1-57). The current folder is Clipart; graphic files supplied with Word are located in this folder. The Paradise Island picture is located on the Web.

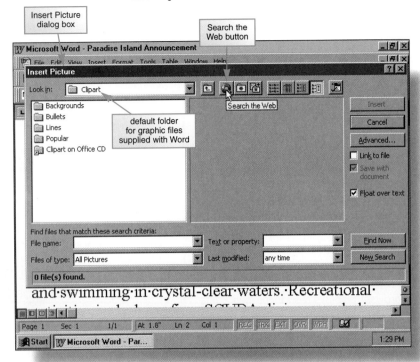

FIGURE 1-57

4 Click the Search the Web button. When the Find it Fast – Microsoft Internet Explorer window displays, click the Address text box to select its contents and then type
`www.scsite.com/wd97/pr1.htm`
in the Address text box.

If you currently are not connected to the Web, Word connects you using your default browser. Word displays the Find it Fast window (Figure 1-58). You can search by words or phrases in the Internet Searches text box; or if you know the exact address of the Web site containing the desired picture, you can enter the address in the Address text box.

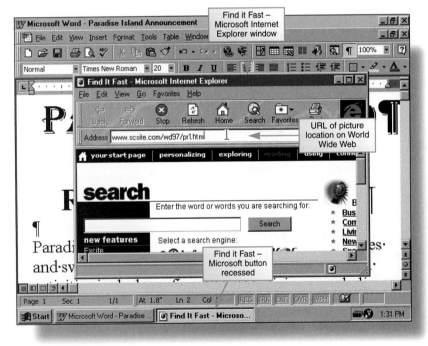

FIGURE 1-58

5 Press the ENTER key. If necessary, maximize the Web page window. Right-click the picture of Paradise Island. Point to Copy on the shortcut menu. (If you do not have a Copy command, go to the steps on page WD 1.44.)

The http://www.scsite.com/ wd97/pr1.htm Web page displays (Figure 1-59). This Web page displays several pictures used in this project. This announcement uses the picture of Paradise Island. Your browser displays a shortcut menu. If you do not have a Copy command on your shortcut menu, your browser requires that you save the picture on a disk and then insert the picture from the disk. Thus, if you do not have a Copy command on your shortcut menu, go to the steps on page WD 1.44 to copy the picture onto a disk and then insert the picture into the announcement from your disk.

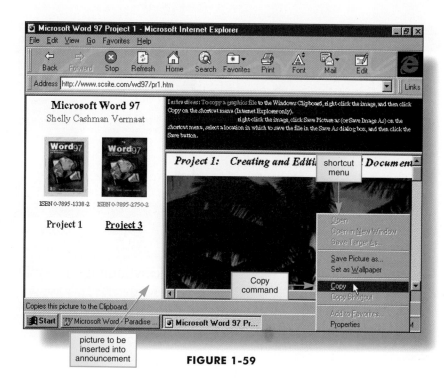

FIGURE 1-59

6 Click Copy on the shortcut menu. Close the browser window. Be sure the insertion point is still on the paragraph mark below the headline in the announcement. Click Edit on the menu bar and then point to Paste Special (Figure 1-60).

*The picture of Paradise Island is copied to the **Clipboard**, which is a temporary Windows storage area. You will paste the picture into the announcement from the Clipboard.*

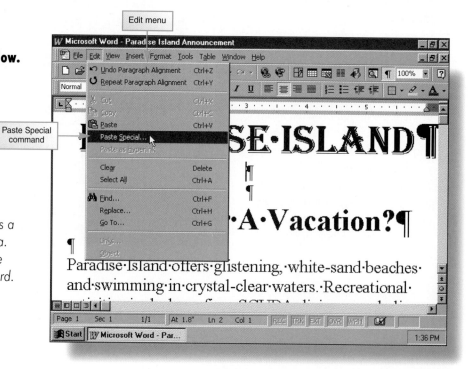

FIGURE 1-60

7 **Click Paste Special. When the Paste Special dialog box displays, click Float over text to clear the check box. Point to the OK button.**

*Word displays the Paste Special dialog box (Figure 1-61). You want to clear the Float over text check box so the picture of Paradise Island is inserted as an inline picture, instead of a floating picture. A **floating picture** is one inserted in a layer over the text; whereas, an **inline picture** is positioned directly in the text at the location of the insertion point. Floating pictures are discussed in a later project.*

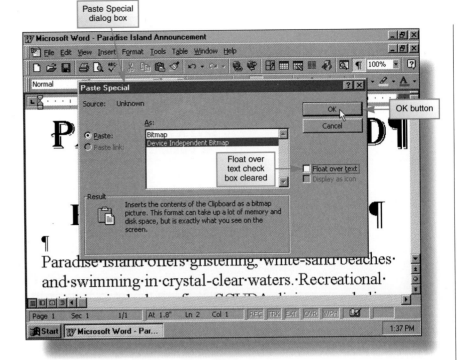

FIGURE 1-61

8 **Click the OK button.**

Word inserts the picture into your document at the location of the insertion point (Figure 1-62).

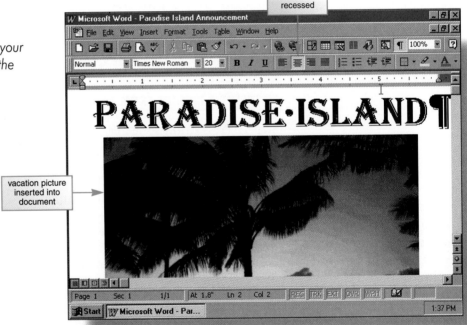

FIGURE 1-62

Because you inserted the picture as an inline picture, it is part of a paragraph. Therefore, you can use any of the paragraph alignment buttons on the Formatting toolbar to reposition the picture. Recall that earlier you formatted that paragraph mark to centered. Thus, the Paradise Island picture is centered across the page.

More *About*
Shortcut Menus

Right-clicking an object opens a shortcut menu (also called a context-sensitive or object menu). Depending on the object, the commands in the shortcut menu vary. A dimmed command in a shortcut menu means the command cannot be used at the current time.

If, when you right-click the Paradise Island picture on the Web, you did not have a Copy command on the shortcut menu, you have to save the picture on a disk and then insert it from the disk. With the shortcut menu on the screen, proceed with these steps.

TO SAVE A PICTURE ON THE WEB ON A DISK AND THEN INSERT IT IN THE DOCUMENT

Step 1: Click Save Image As (or a similar command) on the shortcut menu.
Step 2: Insert a formatted floppy disk into drive A.
Step 3: When the Save As dialog box displays, type a:vacation and then click the Save button. Close your browser.
Step 4: Be sure the insertion point is still positioned on the paragraph mark immediately below the headline. Click Insert on the menu bar, point to Picture, and then click From File.
Step 5: When the Insert Picture dialog box displays, click Float over text to clear the check box.
Step 6: Type a:vacation in the File name text box and then click the Insert button.
Step 7: If Word displays a ruler at the left edge of the screen, click View on the menu bar and then click Normal.

Word inserts the picture into your document at the location of the insertion point as shown in Figure 1-62 on the previous page.

If you do not have access to the Web, follow the steps below to insert the picture from the Data Disk that accompanies this book.

TO INSERT A PICTURE FROM THE DATA DISK THAT ACCOMPANIES THIS BOOK

Step 1: Press CTRL+HOME. Position the insertion point where you want the picture to be inserted (on the paragraph mark immediately below the headline of the announcement).
Step 2: Insert the Data Disk that accompanies this book into drive A.
Step 3: Click Insert on the menu bar, point to Picture, and then click From File.
Step 4: When the Insert Picture dialog box displays, click Float over text to clear the check box.
Step 5: Type a:\Word\vacation in the File name text box and then click the Insert button.
Step 6: Replace the Data Disk with your floppy disk.

Word inserts the picture into your document at the location of the insertion point as shown in Figure 1-62 on the previous page.

The picture in Figure 1-62 is a little too small for this announcement. The next step is to resize the imported graphic.

Resizing an Imported Graphic

Once a graphic has been imported into a document, you can easily change its size. **Resizing** includes both enlarging and reducing the size of a graphic. To resize a graphic, you first must select it. The following steps show how to select and then resize the picture you just imported from the Web.

Steps **To Resize a Graphic**

1 **Click anywhere in the graphic. If your screen does not display the Picture toolbar, right-click the Paradise Island picture and then click Show Picture Toolbar.**

*Word selects the graphic (Figure 1-63). The Picture toolbar floats on the Word screen when a graphic is selected. Selected graphics display surrounded by a **selection rectangle** with small squares, called **sizing handles**, at each corner and middle location of the selection rectangle. To resize the graphic, you drag the sizing handles until the graphic is the desired size. Dragging a corner sizing handle maintains the proportions of the graphic; whereas, dragging a middle sizing handle distorts the proportions of the graphic.*

FIGURE 1-63

2 **Point to the upper-left corner sizing handle.**

The mouse pointer changes to a two-headed arrow when it is on a sizing handle.

3 **Drag the sizing handle outward until the selection rectangle is positioned approximately to the position shown in Figure 1-64.**

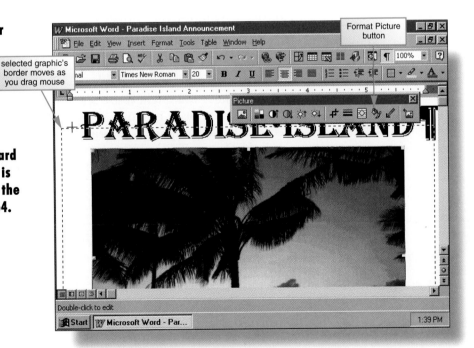

FIGURE 1-64

4 **Release the mouse button. Click outside the graphic, above it or below it in the text, or to the right of it to deselect it.**

Word resizes the graphic (Figure 1-65). The Picture toolbar disappears from the screen when you deselect the graphic.

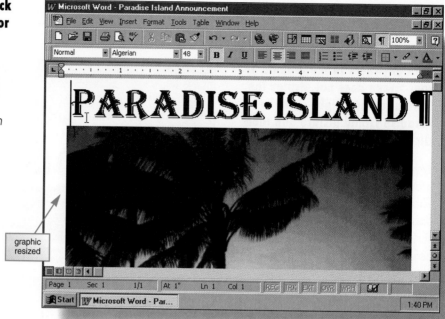

FIGURE 1-65

Instead of resizing a selected graphic with the mouse, you also can use the Format Picture dialog box to resize a graphic by clicking the Format Picture button on the Picture toolbar and then clicking the Size tab. Using the Size sheet, you enter exact width and height measurements. If you have a precise measurement for the graphic, use the Format Picture dialog box; otherwise, drag the sizing handles to resize the graphic.

Restoring a Resized Graphic to Its Original Size

Sometimes you might resize a graphic and realize it is the wrong size. In these cases, you may want to return the graphic to its original size and start over. To return a resized graphic to its original size, click the graphic to select it and then click the Format Picture button on the Picture toolbar to display the Format Picture dialog box. Click the Size tab and then click the Reset button. Finally, click the OK button.

Saving an Existing Document with the Same File Name

The announcement for Project 1 is now complete. To transfer the formatting changes and imported graphic to your floppy disk in drive A, you must save the document again. When you saved the document the first time, you assigned a file name to it (Paradise Island Announcement). Word assigns this same file name automatically to the document each time you subsequently save it if you use the following procedure.

Steps To Save an Existing Document with the Same File Name

1 **Click the Save button on the Standard toolbar.**

Word saves the document on a floppy disk inserted in drive A using the currently assigned file name, Paradise Island Announcement. When the save is finished, the document remains in memory and displays on the screen (Figure 1-66).

FIGURE 1-66

Other Ways

1. On File menu click Save
2. Press CTRL+S

If, for some reason, you want to save an existing document with a different file name, click Save As on the File menu to display the Save As dialog box. Then, fill in the Save As dialog box as discussed in Steps 2 through 5 on pages WD 1.26 and WD 1.27.

Printing a Document

The next step is to print the document you created. A printed version of the document is called a **hard copy** or **printout**. Perform the following steps to print the announcement created in Project 1.

 Steps To Print a Document

1 **Ready the printer according to the printer instructions. Click the Print button on the Standard toolbar.**

The mouse pointer briefly changes to an hourglass shape, and then Word quickly displays a message on the status bar, indicating it is preparing to print the document. A few moments later, the document begins printing on the printer. The right edge of the status bar displays a printer icon while the document is printing (Figure 1-67).

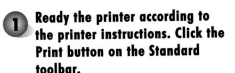

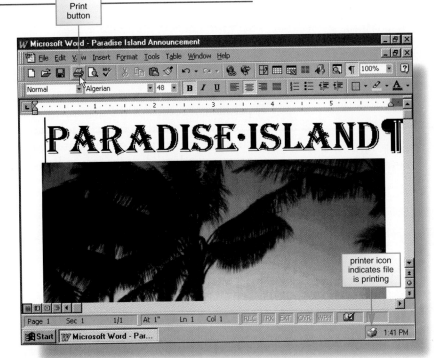

FIGURE 1-67

2 When the printer stops, retrieve the printout (Figure 1-68).

PARADISE ISLAND

Ready For A Vacation?

Paradise Island offers glistening, white-sand beaches and swimming in crystal-clear waters. Recreational activities include surfing, SCUBA diving, snorkeling, sailing, and scenic hiking.

- Paradise Island vacation packages fit <u>any</u> budget
- Cottages, suites, condos, and inns are available

Call *Tropical Travel* at 555-2121

FIGURE 1-68

More *About* **Printing**

To print multiple copies of the same document, click File on the menu bar and then click Print. When the Print dialog box displays, type the desired number of copies in the Number of copies text box in the Copies area and then click the OK button.

When you use the Print button to print a document, Word prints the entire document automatically. You then may distribute the hard copy or keep it as a permanent record of the document.

If you wanted to cancel a job that is printing or waiting to be printed, double-click the printer icon on the status bar (Figure 1-67 on the previous page). In the printer window, click the job to be canceled and then click Cancel Printing on the Document menu.

Quitting Word

After you create, save, and print the announcement, Project 1 is complete. To quit Word and return control to Windows 95, perform the following steps.

Steps To Quit Word

1 **Point to the Close button in the upper-right corner of the title bar (Figure 1-69).**

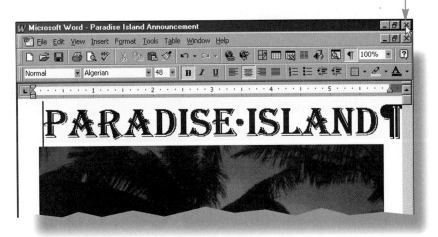

FIGURE 1-69

2 **Click the Close button.**

If you made changes to the document since the last save, Word displays a dialog box asking if you want to save the changes (Figure 1-70). Clicking the Yes button saves changes; clicking the No button ignores the changes; and clicking the Cancel button returns to the document. If you did not make any changes since you saved the document, this dialog box does not display.

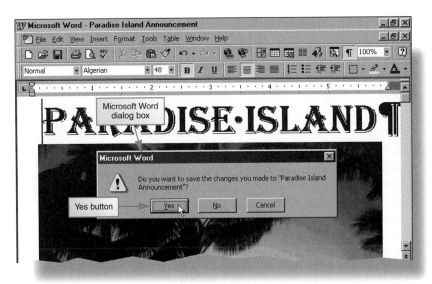

FIGURE 1-70

OtherWays

1. On File menu click Exit
2. Press ALT+F4

Project 1 is now complete. You created and formatted the announcement, inserted a picture from the Web on it, printed it, and saved it as both a Word document and a Web document. You might decide, however, to change the announcement at a later date. To do this, you must start Word and then retrieve your document from the floppy disk in drive A.

Opening a Document

Earlier, you saved the Word document built in Project 1 on floppy disk using the file name Paradise Island Announcement. Once you have created and saved a document, you often will have reason to retrieve it from the disk. For example, you might want to revise the document. The following steps illustrate how to open the file Paradise Island Announcement.

Steps To Open a Document

1 **Click the Start button on the taskbar and then point to Open Office Document (Figure 1-71).**

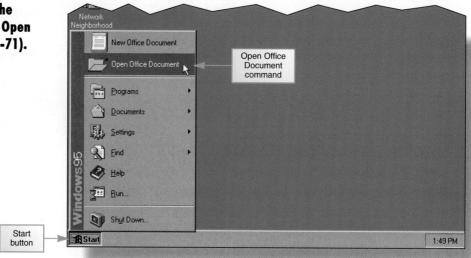

FIGURE 1-71

2 **Click Open Office Document. If necessary, click the Look in box arrow, and then click 3½ Floppy (A:). If it is not already selected, click the file name Paradise Island Announcement. Point to the Open button.**

Office displays the Open Office Document dialog box (Figure 1-72). Office displays the files on the floppy disk in drive A.

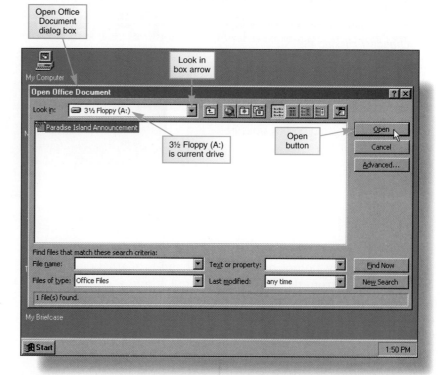

FIGURE 1-72

3 **Click the Open button.**

Office starts Word, and then Word opens the document, Paradise Island Announcement, from the floppy disk in drive A and displays the document on the screen (Figure 1-73).

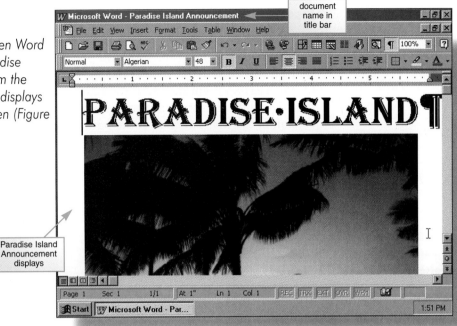

FIGURE 1-73

Correcting Errors

After creating a document, you often will find you must make changes to the document. Changes can be required because the document contains an error or because of new circumstances.

Types of Changes Made to Documents

The types of changes made to documents normally fall into one of the three following categories: additions, deletions, or modifications.

ADDITIONS Additional words, sentences, or paragraphs may be required in the document. Additions occur when you omit text from a document and are required to add it later. For example, you accidentally may forget to put the telephone number in the last line of Project 1.

DELETIONS Sometimes, text in a document is incorrect or is no longer needed. For example, the agency might remove condos from their package deals. In this case, you would delete the word condos from the bulleted list.

MODIFICATIONS If an error is made in a document, you might have to revise the word(s) in the text. For example, SCUBA diving might be offered to only certified divers.

Word provides several methods for correcting errors in a document. For each of the error correction techniques, you first must move the insertion point to the error.

Inserting Text into an Existing Document

If you leave a word or phrase out of a sentence, you can include it in the sentence by positioning the insertion point where you intend to insert the text. Word always inserts the text to the left of the insertion point. The text to the right of the insertion point moves to the right and downward to accommodate the new text. The following steps illustrate inserting the word, beautiful, before the word, crystal, in the first sentence of the paragraph below the body title in Project 1.

Steps To Insert Text into an Existing Document

1 **Scroll through the document and click immediately to the left of the letter c in the word, crystal.**

The insertion point displays immediately to the left of the letter c in crystal (Figure 1-74).

FIGURE 1-74

2 **Type** beautiful, **and then press the SPACEBAR.**

The word, beautiful, is inserted between the words, in and crystal, in the announcement for Project 1 (Figure 1-75). Be sure to include the comma after the word, beautiful, as shown in the figure.

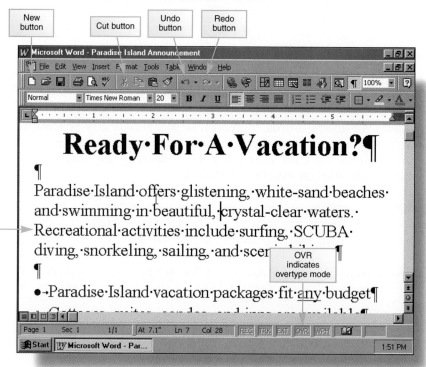

FIGURE 1-75

Notice in Figure 1-75 that the text to the right of the word, crystal, moved to the right and downward to accommodate the insertion of the word, beautiful. That is, the word, Recreational, moved down to line 8.

In Word, the default typing mode is insert mode. In **insert mode**, as you type a character, Word inserts the character and moves all the characters to the right of the typed character one position to the right. In the example just given, you used insert mode to add the word, beautiful. You can change to overtype mode by double-clicking the **OVR status indicator** on the status bar (Figure 1-75). In **overtype mode**, Word replaces characters to the right of the insertion point. Double-clicking the OVR status indicator a second time returns you to insert mode.

Deleting Text from an Existing Document

It is not unusual to type incorrect characters or words in a document. In such a case, to correct the error, you may want to delete certain letters or words.

TO DELETE AN INCORRECT CHARACTER IN A DOCUMENT

Step 1: Click next to the incorrect character.
Step 2: Press the BACKSPACE key to erase to the left of the insertion point; or press the DELETE key to erase to the right of the insertion point.

TO DELETE AN INCORRECT WORD OR PHRASE IN A DOCUMENT

Step 1: Select the word or phrase you want to erase.
Step 2: Right-click the selected word or phrase, and then click Cut on the shortcut menu; or click the Cut button on the Standard toolbar (Figure 1-75); or press the DELETE key.

Undoing Recent Actions

Word provides an **Undo button** on the Standard toolbar that you can use to cancel your recent command(s) or action(s). If you delete some text accidentally, you can bring it back. If you want to cancel your undo, you can use the **Redo button**. Some actions, such as saving or printing a document, cannot be undone or redone.

TO CANCEL YOUR MOST RECENT ACTION

Step 1: Click the Undo button (Figure 1-75) on the Standard toolbar.

TO CANCEL YOUR MOST RECENT UNDO

Step 1: Click the Redo button (Figure 1-75) on the Standard toolbar.

TO CANCEL A SERIES OF PRIOR ACTIONS

Step 1: Click the Undo button arrow to display the undo actions list.
Step 2: Drag through the actions to be undone.

Closing the Entire Document

Sometimes, everything goes wrong. If this happens, you may want to close the document entirely and start over. You also may want to close a document when you are finished with it so you can begin your next document. To close the document, follow these steps.

TO CLOSE THE ENTIRE DOCUMENT AND START OVER

Step 1: Click File on the menu bar and then click Close.
Step 2: If Word displays a dialog box, click the No button to ignore the changes since the last time you saved the document.
Step 3: Click the New button (Figure 1-75 on page WD1.52) on the Standard toolbar.

You also can close the document by clicking the Close button at the right edge of the menu bar.

Microsoft Word Help

At any time while you are working in Word, you can answer your Word questions by using **Help**. Used properly, this form of online assistance can increase your productivity and reduce your frustrations by minimizing the time you spend learning how to use Word. Table 1-3 summarizes the five categories of Word Help available to you.

Table 1-3		
HELP CATEGORY	DESCRIPTION	HOW TO ACTIVATE
Office Assistant	Answers your questions, offers tips, and provides Help for a variety of Word features.	Click the Office Assistant button on the Standard toolbar.
Contents Sheet	Groups Help topics by general categories. Similar to a table of contents in a book.	Click Contents and Index on the Help menu and then click the Contents tab.
Index Sheet	Accesses Help topics by subject. Similar to an index in a book.	Click Contents and Index on the Help menu and then click the Index tab.
Find Sheet	Searches the index for all phrases that include the term in question.	Click Contents and Index on the Help menu and then click the Find tab.
Question Mark button and What's This? command	Used to identify unfamiliar items on the screen.	In a dialog box, click the Question Mark button and then click an item in a dialog box. Click What's This? on the Help menu and then click an item on the screen.

The following sections show examples of the various types of Help described in Table 1-3.

Using the Office Assistant

The **Office Assistant** answers your questions and suggests more efficient ways to complete a task. With the Office Assistant active, for example, you can type a word or phrase in a text box, and the Office Assistant provides immediate Help on the subject. Also, as you create a document, the Office Assistant accumulates tips that suggest more efficient ways to complete a task you performed while creating the document, such as formatting, printing, or saving. This tip feature is part of the **IntelliSense™ technology** that is built into Word.

The following steps show how to use the Office Assistant to obtain information on saving a Word document as a Web page.

 Steps **To Obtain Help Using the Office Assistant**

1 **If the Office Assistant is not on the screen, click the Office Assistant button on the Standard toolbar. If the Office Assistant is on the screen, click it. Type** save Word document as a Web page **in the What would you like to do? text box and then point to the Search button (Figure 1-76).**

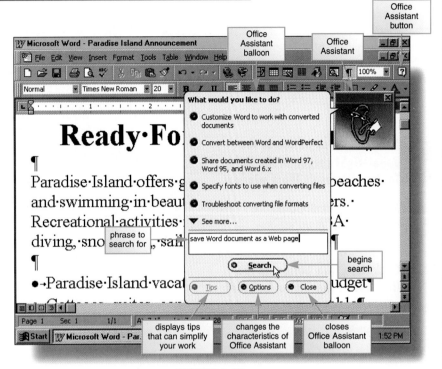

FIGURE 1-76

2 **Click the Search button and then point to the Learn what happens when you save a Word 97 document as a Web page topic.**

The Office Assistant displays a list of topics relating to the phrase, save Word document as a Web page (Figure 1-77).

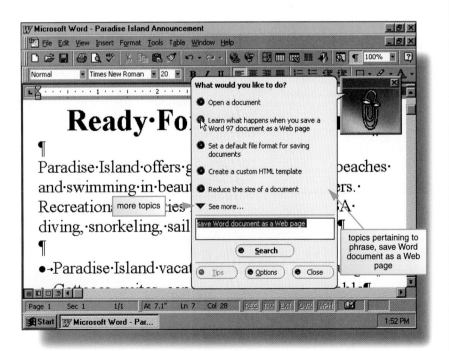

FIGURE 1-77

3 **Click Learn what happens when you save a Word 97 document as a Web page.**

The Office Assistant displays the Help Topics: Microsoft Word window (Figure 1-78). Word Help windows contain a variety of links, which include buttons and green underlined words. When you point to a link, the mouse pointer shape changes to a pointing hand.

4 **Click the Close button in the upper-right corner of the Help Topics: Microsoft Word window.**

The Help window closes and control returns to the Word window.

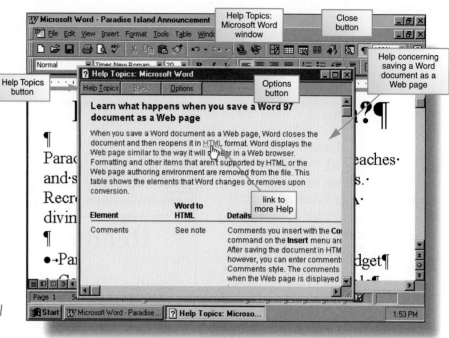

FIGURE 1-78

5 **Click the Close button on the title bar of the Office Assistant window.**

The Office Assistant disappears from the screen.

You can use the Office Assistant to search for Help on any topic concerning Word. Once Help displays, you can read it, print it, or click one of its links to display a related Help topic. To print the Help information, click the Print button if one exists. If the window does not contain a Print button, click the Options button or right-click the window and then click Print Topic. The Help Topics button in the Help window allows you to obtain Help through the Contents, Index, and Find sheets.

DISPLAYING TIPS TO IMPROVE YOUR WORK HABITS If you click the Office Assistant Tips button (Figure 1-76 on the previous page), Word displays tips on how to work more efficiently. Once a tip displays (Figure 1-79), you can move backward or forward through the list of accumulated tips. As you work through creating a document, Word adds tips to the list. If the Office Assistant displays on the screen and it has a new tip for you, a light bulb appears in the Office Assistant window. If the Office Assistant does not display on the screen and it has a new tip for you, the light bulb appears on the Office Assistant button on the Standard toolbar.

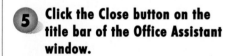

FIGURE 1-79

OFFICE ASSISTANT SHORTCUT MENU When you right-click the Office Assistant window, a shortcut menu displays, which allows you to change the characteristics of the Office Assistant. For example, you can hide the Office Assistant, display tips, change its appearance, select a different icon for the assistant, or view animation of the Office Assistant. These options also are available by clicking the Options button that displays when you click the Office Assistant.

Using the Contents and Index Command to Obtain Help

The Contents and Index command provides access to the Contents, Index, and Find sheets. The **Contents sheet** in the Help Topics: Microsoft Word dialog box offers you assistance when you know the general category of the topic in question, but not the specifics. Use the Contents sheet in the same manner you would use a table of contents at the front of a textbook. The following steps show how to use the Contents sheet to obtain information on getting assistance while you work.

 Steps **To Obtain Help Using the Contents Sheet**

1 **Click Help on the menu bar and then point to Contents and Index (Figure 1-80).**

FIGURE 1-80

2 **Click Contents and Index. If necessary, click the Contents tab. Double-click the Getting Help book. Point to the Ways to get assistance while you work topic.**

*The Help Topics: Microsoft Word dialog box displays (Figure 1-81). This dialog box contains three tabbed sheets: Contents, Index, and Find. In Figure 1-81, the Getting Help topic is preceded by a book icon. A **book icon** means subtopics exist. To display the subtopics associated with a topic, you double-click its book icon. The subtopics are preceded by a **question mark icon**. To display information on a subtopic, you double-click the subtopic. A book icon opens when you double-click it.*

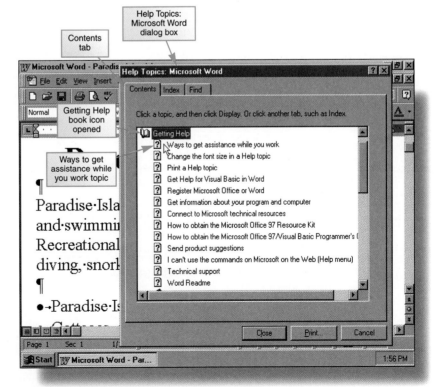

FIGURE 1-81

3 Double-click the Ways to get assistance while you work topic.

Word displays the Microsoft Word window containing tips on Word's Help (Figure 1-82). When you click a link, Word displays additional Help information.

4 Click the Close button in the upper-right corner of the Microsoft Word Help window.

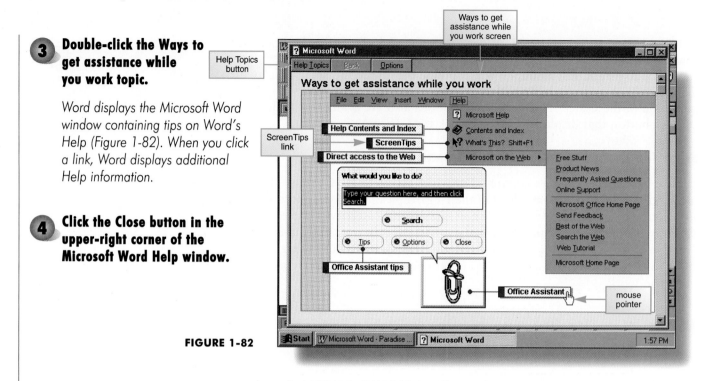

FIGURE 1-82

Instead of closing the Microsoft Word window in Step 3, you could click the Help Topics button in Figure 1-82 to return to the Contents sheet (Figure 1-81 on the previous page).

The Contents sheet in the Help Topics: Microsoft Word dialog box is much like a table of contents in the front of a book. The **Index sheet**, however, is similar to an index in the back of a book. For example, if you wanted help on formatting characters in bold, you would display the Index sheet, type bold (Figure 1-83) and then double-click the bold formatting topic to display Help information on formatting characters in bold. Then, click the Close button.

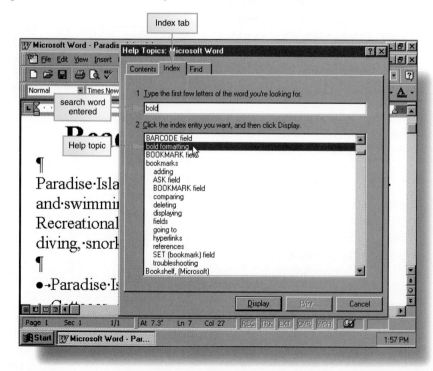

FIGURE 1-83

The **Find sheet** is used to locate a Help topic on a particular word or phrase. For example, if you wanted help on inserting an inline floating picture, you would display the Find sheet, type insert picture (Figure 1-84) and then double-click the Change a floating picture to an inline picture and vice-versa topic. Then, close the Help window.

Obtaining Web Information

To obtain Web-related information, click Help on the menu bar and then point to Microsoft on the Web to display a submenu of Web-related commands. The Help window in Figure 1-82 shows this submenu. If you click any command on the submenu, your system will launch your browser and connect to a corresponding page on the World Wide Web. Use the commands on the Web submenu to obtain up-to-date information on a variety of topics.

Using What's This? or the Question Mark Button

To obtain Help on an item on the Word screen, click Help on the menu bar and then click What's This? To obtain help on an item in a Word dialog box, click the **Question Mark button** that displays in the upper-right corner of a dialog box. Using either technique, the mouse pointer changes to an arrow and a question mark as shown in Figure 1-85. Move the **question mark pointer** to any item on the Word screen or in a dialog box, and then click to display a **ScreenTip**, which offers an explanation of the item on which you clicked. For example, clicking the Print button on the Standard toolbar displays the Help message shown in Figure 1-86.

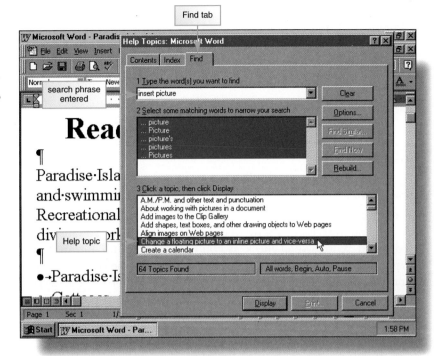

FIGURE 1-84

FIGURE 1-85

FIGURE 1-86

If you click text with the question-mark pointer, Word displays the paragraph and character formatting characteristics of the text on which you click.

Word Help has features that make it powerful and easy to use. The best way to familiarize yourself with Word Help is to use it.

Wizards

Word supplies **wizards** to assist you in creating common types of documents, such as letters, memos, resumes, and newsletters. To use a wizard, click File on the menu bar, click New, and then select the wizard you desire from the appropriate tabbed sheet. The wizard asks you a few basic questions, and then displays a formatted document on the screen for you to customize or fill in blanks. In Project 2, you will use a wizard.

Project Summary

Project 1 introduced you to starting Word and creating a document. Before entering any text in the document, you learned how to change the font size. You also learned how to save and print a document. You used Word's spell check as you type feature and automatically added bullets to paragraphs as you typed them into the document. Once you saved the document, you learned how to format its paragraphs and characters. Then, you imported a graphic file from the Web and resized it. With the technologies presented, you learned to move the insertion point so you could insert, delete, and modify text. Finally, you learned to use Word Help.

What You Should Know

Having completed this project, you now should be able to perform the following tasks:

▶ Bold Selected Text *(WD 1.34)*
▶ Bullet a List as You Type *(WD 1.23)*
▶ Cancel a Series of Prior Actions *(WD 1.53)*
▶ Cancel Your Most Recent Action *(WD 1.53)*
▶ Cancel Your Most Recent Undo *(WD 1.53)*
▶ Center a Single Paragraph *(WD 1.39)*
▶ Center Selected Paragraphs *(WD 1.30)*
▶ Change the Font of Selected Text *(WD 1.33)*
▶ Change the Font Size of Selected Text *(WD 1.31)*
▶ Close the Entire Document and Start Over *(WD 1.54)*
▶ Delete an Incorrect Character in a Document *(WD 1.53)*
▶ Delete an Incorrect Word or Phrase in a Document *(WD 1.53)*
▶ Display Nonprinting Characters *(WD 1.18)*
▶ Enter a Document that Scrolls the Document Window *(WD 1.22)*
▶ Enter Blank Lines into a Document *(WD 1.17)*
▶ Enter More Text *(WD 1.19)*
▶ Enter Text *(WD 1.16)*
▶ Format a Line of Text *(WD 1.34)*
▶ Increase the Default Font Size Before Typing *(WD 1.14)*
▶ Insert a Picture from the Data Disk that Accompanies this Book *(WD 1.44)*

▶ Insert a Picture from the Web *(WD 1.40)*
▶ Insert Text into an Existing Document *(WD 1.52)*
▶ Italicize and Bold Selected Text *(WD 1.38)*
▶ Obtain Help Using the Contents and Index Command *(WD 1.57)*
▶ Obtain Help Using the Office Assistant *(WD 1.55)*
▶ Open a Document *(WD 1.50)*
▶ Print a Document *(WD 1.47)*
▶ Quit Word *(WD 1.49)*
▶ Resize a Graphic *(WD 1.45)*
▶ Save a New Document *(WD 1.26)*
▶ Save a Picture on the Web on a Disk and Insert It in the Document *(WD 1.44)*
▶ Save an Existing Document with the Same File Name *(WD 1.47)*
▶ Scroll Through the Document *(WD 1.35)*
▶ Select a Group of Words *(WD 1.37)*
▶ Select a Single Line *(WD 1.31)*
▶ Select a Single Word *(WD 1.35)*
▶ Select Multiple Paragraphs *(WD 1.29)*
▶ Spell Check as You Type *(WD 1.20)*
▶ Start Word *(WD 1.9)*
▶ Underline Selected Text *(WD 1.36)*
▶ Wordwrap Text as You Type *(WD 1.19)*

 Test Your Knowledge

1 True/False

Instructions: Circle T if the statement is true or F if the statement is false.

T F 1. Microsoft Word 97 is an operating system.
T F 2. The insertion point indicates where text will be inserted as you type.
T F 3. The Standard toolbar initially displays floating on the Word screen.
T F 4. To create a new paragraph, press the ENTER key.
T F 5. Double-click a red wavy underlined word to display a shortcut menu that lists suggested spelling corrections for the flagged word.
T F 6. To save a document with the same file name, click the Open button on the taskbar.
T F 7. Italicizing a word is an example of character formatting.
T F 8. To center selected paragraphs, click the Center button on the Formatting toolbar.
T F 9. A floating picture is one positioned directly in the text at the location of the insertion point.
T F 10. The Office Assistant button is on the Standard toobar.

2 Multiple Choice

Instructions: Circle the correct response.

1. _____ are used to display different portions of your document in the document window.
   a. Status indicators   b. Toolbars   c. Scroll bars   d. Rulers
2. If a word you type is not in Word's dictionary, a _____ wavy underline appears below the word and a red _____ displays on the Spelling and Grammar Status icon.
   a. green, check mark   b. green, X   c. red, check mark   d. red, X
3. To scroll down one entire screenful at a time, _____.
   a. click below the scroll box on the scroll bar   b. click scroll arrow at bottom of the scroll bar
   c. press PAGE DOWN   d. both a and c
4. To place a bullet automatically at the beginning of a paragraph, type a(n) _____ and then press the SPACEBAR.
   a. asterisk (*)   b. plus (+)   c. letter o   d. exclamation point (!)
5. To select a single word, _____ the word.
   a. click   b. right-click   c. double-click   d. drag
6. Selected graphics display _____ handles at the corner and middle locations.
   a. selection   b. sizing   c. picture   d. resizing
7. To erase the character to the right of the insertion point, press the _____ key.
   a. DELETE   b. INSERT   c. BACKSPACE   d. both a and c
8. _____ the OVR status indicator to toggle between overtype and insert mode.
   a. Click   b. Right-click   c. Double-click   d. Drag
9. To close a document and start over, _____.
   a. click Close on File menu   b. click Close button on menu bar
   c. click Close button on Standard toolbar   d. both a and b
10. If Office Assistant has a new tip, a _____ displays in the Office Assistant button or window.
    a. light bulb   b. flashlight   c. paper clip   d. magic wand

Test Your Knowledge

3 Understanding the Word Screen

Instructions: In Figure 1-87, arrows point to major components of the Word screen. Identify the various parts of the screen in the spaces provided.

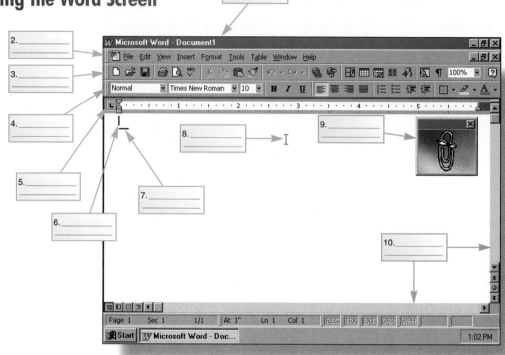

FIGURE 1-87

4 Understanding the Standard and Formatting Toolbars

Instructions: In Figure 1-88, arrows point to several of the buttons and boxes on the Standard and Formatting toolbars. In the spaces provided, briefly explain the purpose of each button and box.

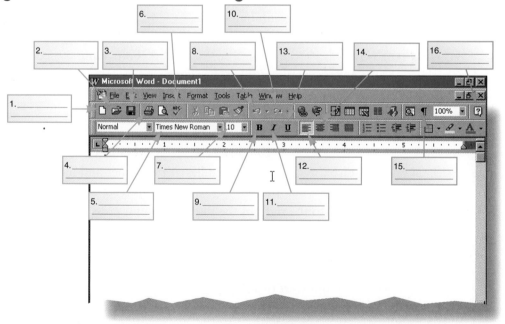

FIGURE 1-88

Use Help

1 Reviewing Project Activities

Instructions: Perform the following tasks using a computer.

1. Start Word.
2. If the Office Assistant is on your screen, click it to display its balloon. If the Office Assistant is not on your screen, click the Office Assistant button on the Standard toolbar.
3. Click Options in the Office Assistant balloon and then click the Gallery tab. Click the Next button repeatedly to view the various assistants. Display Mother Nature. Click the Options tab and then review the different options for the Office Assistant. Close the Office Assistant dialog box. Change the Office Assistant icon back to the original one.
4. Click the Office Assistant to display its balloon. Type select text in the What would you like to do? text box. Click the Search button. Click the Select text and graphics link.
5. Click Select text and graphics by using the mouse. Read the information. Use the shortcut menu or Options button to print the information. Click the Back button. Click Select text and graphics by using shortcut keys. Read and print the information. Click the Close button in the Help window. Close the Office Assistant window.
6. Click Help on the menu bar and then click Contents and Index. Click the Contents tab. Double-click the Key Information book. Double-click the For Customers Using Word for the First Time book. Double-click the What's new in Word 97 topic. Read and print the following help topics: Automating your tasks and getting assistance, Editing and proofing tools, Working with Web tools. Close any open Help window(s).

2 Expanding on the Basics

Instructions: Use Word Help to better understand the topics listed below. Answer the questions on your own paper or hand in the printed Help topic to your instructor.

1. In this project, you checked spelling as you typed. Use the Office Assistant to answer the following questions about checking spelling all at once.
   a. What button do you click to spell check the document all at once?
   b. If you want to do a grammar check with a spelling check, how do you turn on the grammar check feature?
   c. What are the readability scores? How do you turn them on?
2. In this project, you opened a single file from the Open dialog box. Use the Contents tab in the Help Topics: Microsoft Word dialog box to determine how to select multiple files in the Open dialog box.
3. In this project, you imported a Graphics Interchange Format (GIF) file from the Web into the announcement. Use the Index tab in the Help Topics: Microsoft Word dialog box to determine the complete list of graphic file types that may be inserted into a Word document.
4. In this project, you saved a Word document as a Web page. Use the Find tab in the Help Topics: Microsoft Word dialog box to learn how to use the Web wizard to create a Web page.
5. Use the What's This? command on the Help menu to display ScreenTips for five buttons that you are unfamiliar with on the Standard and Formatting toolbars. Print each ScreenTip by right-clicking it, clicking Print Topic on the shortcut menu, and then clicking the OK button.

Apply Your Knowledge

CAUTION: To ensure you have enough disk space to save your files, it is recommended that you create a copy of the Data Disk that accompanies this book. Then, delete folders from the copy of the Data Disk that are not needed for the application you are working on. Do the following: (1) Insert the Data Disk in drive A; (2) start Explorer; (3) right-click the 3½ Floppy (A:) folder in the All Folders side of the window; (4) click Copy Disk; (5) click Start and OK as required; (6) insert a floppy disk when requested; (7) delete all folders on the floppy disk you created except the Word folder; (8) remove the floppy disk from drive A and label it Word Data Disk.

1 Spell Checking a Document

Instructions: Start Word. Open the document, apply-1, from the Word folder on the Data Disk that accompanies this book. As shown in Figure 1-89, the document is an announcement for Computers Made Easy that contains many spelling and grammar errors. You are to right-click each of the errors and then click the desired correction on the shortcut menu. You may need to refer to your Use Help 2 responses to information on how to verify that the grammar checker is enabled.

spelling and grammar errors are circled to help you identify them

Feeling Frustrated?

WE CAN HELP!

Our goal at Computers Made Easy are to take the complexity out of comptuer programs. We offer three three levels of training in each of these application: word processing, electronic mail, spreadsheets, databases, ard presentation graphics. We also offering Internet training!

• Coarses are $99 eacxh for seven contact hours
• Each student is provided with a hands-on textbook

to sign up, call 555-9090

FIGURE 1-89

Perform the following tasks:

1. Position the insertion point at the beginning of the document. Scroll down until you encounter the first error.
2. Right-click the flagged phrase, goal at Computers Made Easy are. Change the incorrect verb in the flagged phrase by clicking the phrase, goal at Computers Made Easy is, on the shortcut menu.
3. Right-click the flagged word, comptuer. Change the incorrect word, comptuer, to computer by clicking computer on the shortcut menu.
4. Right-click the flagged word, three. Click Delete Repeated Word on the shortcut menu to remove the duplicate occurrence of the word, three.
5. Right-click the flagged word, ard. Because the correct word is not on the shortcut menu, click outside the shortcut menu to remove it from the screen. Correct the misspelled word, ard, to the correct word, and, by removing the letter r and replacing it with the letter n.
6. Right-click the flagged phrase, also offering. Change the phrase, also offering, to the correct phrase by clicking the phrase, also offer, on the shortcut menu.
7. Right-click the flagged phrase, these application. Change the word, application, to its plural form by clicking the phrase, these applications, on the shortcut menu.

Apply Your Knowledge

8. Right-click the flagged word, Coarses. Change the incorrect word, Coarses, to Courses by clicking Courses on the shortcut menu.

9. Right-click the incorrect word, eacxh. Change the incorrect word, eacxh, to each by clicking each on the shortcut menu.

10. Right-click the flagged word, to. Capitalize the word, to, by clicking To on the shortcut menu.

11. Click File on the menu bar and then click Save As. Save the document using Corrected apply-1 as the file name.

12. Print the revised document.

In the Lab

1 Creating an Announcement with an Imported Picture from the Web

Problem: You own the cutest golden retriever puppy named Pumpkin. The problem is that you cannot keep Pumpkin because you are moving to a condominium that does not allow pets. You have a picture of Pumpkin in a file called puppy. You decide to prepare an announcement for the sale of Pumpkin. The unformatted announcement is shown in Figure 1-90, and the formatted document is shown in Figure 1-91 on the next page.

> unformatted document
>
> PUPPY FOR SALE!
>
> Pumpkin Needs a Home
>
> Pumpkin is a two-month old, purebred, female golden retriever. A playful puppy with a sweet temperament, Pumpkin is current on all her shots. Owner has a three-generation pedigree.
>
> - Owner is moving and must leave Pumpkin behind
> - Take home this great family companion for $450
>
> Interested? Please call (607) 555-0909

FIGURE 1-90

Instructions:

1. Change the font size from 10 to 20 by clicking the Font Size box arrow and then clicking 20.

2. If necessary, click the Show/Hide ¶ button on the Standard toolbar to display paragraph marks and spaces.

3. Create the unformatted announcement shown in Figure 1-90. Add the bullets to the list as you type by beginning the first item in the list with an asterisk followed by a space.

4. Save the document on a floppy disk with Puppy Announcement as the file name.

5. Select the headline and body title line. Center them.

(continued)

In the Lab

Creating an Announcement with an Imported Picture from the Web *(continued)*

6. Select the headline. Bold it. Change its font size from 20 to 48. Change its font to Comic Sans MS. If the headline wraps to the next line, adjust the font size so it fits on one line.

7. Select the body title line. Increase its font size from 20 to 36. Bold it.

8. Select the words, great family companion, in the bulleted list. Bold them.

9. Select the word, Please, in the last line of the announcement. Italicize it.

10. Click somewhere in the last line of the announcement. Center it.

11. Import the graphic file called Puppy on the paragraph mark below the headline. The picture is located on the Web page www.scsite.com/wd97/pr1.htm and also on the Data Disk that accompanies this book. Enlarge the picture of the puppy about 25%. If the last line of the announcement moves to another page when you resize the picture, make the picture smaller.

12. Check the spelling of the announcement.

13. Save the announcement again with the same file name.

14. Print the announcement (Figure 1-91).

48-point Comic Sans MS bold font →

PUPPY FOR SALE!

36-point bold →

Pumpkin Needs a Home

Pumpkin is a two-month old, purebred, female golden retriever. A playful puppy with a sweet temperament, Pumpkin is current on all her shots. Owner has a three-generation pedigree.

- Owner is moving and must leave Pumpkin behind
- Take home this **great family companion** for $450

Interested? *Please* call (607) 555-0909

FIGURE 1-91

In the Lab

2 Creating an Announcement with Clip Art

Problem: You are the president of The Sports Car Club and you are preparing an announcement inviting new members (Figure 1-92). You decide to use the Sports Car Clip Art from the Clip Gallery supplied with Word.

Instructions:

1. Change the font size from 10 to 20 by clicking the Font Size box arrow and then clicking 20.

2. If it is not already selected, click the Show/Hide ¶ button on the Standard toolbar to display paragraph marks and spaces.

3. Create the announcement shown in Figure 1-92. Enter the document first without the graphic file and unformatted; that is, without any bolding, underlining, italicizing, or centering.

4. Save the document on a floppy disk with Sports Car Club Announcement as the file name.

5. Select the headline and body title line. Center them.

6. Select the headline. Bold it. Change its font size from 20 to 48. Change its font to Arial.

7. Select the body title line. Increase its font size from 20 to 48. Bold it.

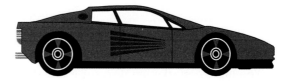

48-point Arial bold font

Zoom into Action!

48-point bold

The Sports Car Club

Do you have a sports car? Do you wish you had a sports car? The Sports Car Club is just for you! At our monthly meetings, members share ideas and learn from knowledgeable guest speakers. Exciting events include an annual **road rally**, **car shows**, **picnics**, **contests**, **fund-raisers**, and a variety of members-only social activities.

- Individual membership dues are $30 per year; family membership dues are $50 per year
- Meetings are the first Saturday of each month from 3:00 p.m. to 6:00 p.m.

Call Dave at 555-4235 for all the details!

FIGURE 1-92

8. Select the word, Zoom, in the headline and italicize it.

9. Select the following words one at a time in the paragraph and bold them: road rally, car shows, picnics, contests, and fund-raisers.

10. Click somewhere in the last line of the announcement. Center it.

11. Import the Sports Car clip art file located in the Transportation category of the Clip Gallery below the headline. That is, click Insert on the menu bar, point to Picture, and then click Clip Art. Scroll through the files, select the sports car, and then click the Insert button.

(continued)

In the Lab

Creating an Announcement with Clip Art *(continued)*

12. Change the clip art from a floating object to an inline object. To do so, click the picture, then click the Format Picture button on the Picture toolbar. Click the Position tab and then clear the Float over text check box. Click the OK button. Click View on the menu bar and then click Normal to return to normal view.
13. Enlarge the graphic if necessary. If the last line of the announcement moves to a second page, then make the graphic smaller.
14. Check the spelling of the announcement. Save the announcement again with the same file name.
15. Print the announcement.

3 Composing an Announcement from a Draft

Problem: You are the marketing director for Water World Park. You want to prepare an announcement of the park and its activities for the public. You have obtained a picture of one of the park's bears to use in the announcement.

Instructions: You are to create the unformatted announcement shown in Figure 1-93. The picture of the bear is located on Web page www.scsite.com/wd97/pr1.htm and also on the Data Disk that accompanies this book. Then, using the techniques presented in this project, format the announcement. Below are some general guidelines:

1. Center the headline and title.
2. Bullet short lists.
3. Use italics, bold, and underlining to emphasize words or phrases.
4. Change font to emphasize text.
5. Increase font size of headline and title.
6. Increase the size of the picture.

unformatted document

Polar Bear Show!

WATER WORLD PARK

Offering fun and entertainment for the whole family, Water World Park is both an amusement park and a water zoo. We have rides for children and adults of all ages. The water zoo has hundreds of aquariums and pools. Our arena has a water show every hour.

Admission is $15 per adult and $8 for children under 10 years
Park is open from 10:00 a.m. to 8:00 p.m. every day between March 1 and October 31

Call 555-0762 for more information

FIGURE 1-93

Cases and Places

The difficulty of these case studies varies: ❭ are the least difficult; ❭❭ are more difficult; and ❭❭❭ are the most difficult.

1 ❭ You have been assigned the task of preparing an announcement for World Wide Communications. The announcement contains a picture to be imported from the Web. Use the following text and picture: headline – Need a Second Phone Line?; picture located on Web site www.scsite.com/wd97/pr1.htm of a girl on the telephone; body title – World Wide Communications; paragraph text – For our current customers, we are offering a special promotion through the month of October. You can have a second telephone line installed into your home without charge. All you pay is $14 per month thereafter for the second telephone line. What a small price to pay for an available telephone line!; first bulleted item – We guarantee installation within four days of your order; second bulleted item – Select a telephone number of your choice; last line – To order, call us at (888) 555-9898. Use the concepts and techniques presented in this project to create and format this announcement.

2 ❭ You have been assigned the task of preparing an announcement for Buckley School of Business. The announcement contains a clip art image from the Clip Gallery. Use the following text and picture: headline – Registration Begins Today!; picture located in Business category of Clip Gallery; body title – Buckley School of Business; paragraph text – Our school offers the finest education in word processing, spreadsheets, databases, presentation graphics, electronic mail, the Internet, computer programming, systems analysis and design, and much more! We have the latest technology and the highest quality instructors, which enables us to provide a job-placement guarantee to all our graduates; first bulleted item – Classes cost $85 per credit hour and parking is $40 per semester; second bulleted item – Fall classes begin Monday, August 31, at 8:00 a.m.; last line – Call 555-8989 to register today. Use the concepts and techniques presented in this project to create and format this announcement.

3 ❭❭ Your Aunt Ruth, a graduate of Green Grove High School, will be celebrating her fortieth high school reunion this year. She has asked you to prepare an announcement that can be sent to each member of the graduating class. The reunion will feature dinner at Broadway Restaurant, live entertainment by The Bakers Band, and a special guest appearance by Joey Williams, a local comedian. The reunion will be held on Saturday, November 14, at 6:00 p.m. Guests will have the opportunity to reminisce about old times, catch up on current projects, and share future plans. Everyone is encouraged to take part in the food and fun. More information can be obtained by calling Mrs. Betty Travis at (576) 555-2223. Use the concepts and techniques presented in this project to create the announcement. Be sure to include at least two bulleted items in a list and insert an appropriate graphic from the Clip Gallery or the Web.

Cases and Places

4 ▶▶ You have just been hired by Nature Valley, a public nature park, as the marketing director. You decide to put together an announcement for the upcoming open house, which has been scheduled for the weekend of September 14 and 15 from 9:00 a.m. to 7:00 p.m. both days. Admission for the open house is $4 per person. Nature Valley offers breathtaking scenery with abundant, lush vegetation and friendly animals. Guests can take nature walks or hikes on trails; swim or boat in crystal-clear lakes; or fish in rippling rivers. More information can be obtained by calling John Gray at 555-9087. Use the concepts and techniques presented in this project to create the announcement. Be sure to include at least two bulleted items in a list and insert an appropriate graphic from the Clip Gallery or the Web.

5 ▶▶▶ Many organizations, such as schools, libraries, grocery stores, child-care centers, and so on, have a place where announcements are posted on a public bulletin board. Often, so many announcements are displayed that some go unnoticed. Find a posted announcement at one of the above mentioned organizations that you think might be overlooked. Copy the text from the announcement. Using this text, together with the techniques presented in this project, create an announcement that would be more likely to catch a reader's eye. Format the announcement effectively and include a bulleted list and suitable graphic from the Clip Gallery or the Web.

6 ▶▶▶ Both small and large companies advertise on the World Wide Web. Some of these advertisements are written as plain text without any formatting or graphics. Surf the Web for an advertisement that you feel lacks luster. Copy the text from the announcement. Using this text, together with the techniques presented in this project, create an announcement that would be more likely to catch a reader's eye. Format the announcement effectively and include a bulleted list and suitable graphic from the Clip Gallery or the Web.

7 ▶▶▶ Many retail stores post announcements throughout the store to promote new or unique products or products on sale. These announcements are designed to encourage consumers to purchase products they were not even considering when they first entered the store. Visit a local electronics store and select an item you believe could have greater sales with increased in-store advertising. Write the text for a promotional announcement and then, using the techniques presented in this project, create an announcement that could be posted around the store to enhance the sales of the item. Format the announcement effectively and include a bulleted list and suitable graphic from the Clip Gallery or the Web.

Microsoft Word 97

Using Word's Wizards and Templates to Create a Cover Letter and Resume

Objectives:

You will have mastered the material in this project when you can:

▶ Create a resume using Word's Resume Wizard
▶ Identify the Word screen in page layout view
▶ Use styles in a document
▶ Replace selected text with new text
▶ Insert a line break
▶ Use AutoFormat As You Type
▶ Select a table
▶ Change the font size of all characters in a table
▶ Use print preview to view and print a document
▶ Explain the components of a business letter
▶ Create a cover letter using Word's letter template
▶ Zoom a document
▶ Create an AutoText entry
▶ Select a paragraph
▶ Format characters using shortcut keys
▶ Insert an AutoText entry
▶ Select a sentence
▶ Drag and drop selected text
▶ Indent the left margin of a paragraph
▶ Use the TAB key to vertically align text
▶ Spell and grammar check a document at once
▶ Switch from one open Word document to another
▶ Close all open Word documents

Resume Writing

Keywords Are the Key to Getting Noticed

Europeans Handwrite

In many European countries, the art of fine penmanship is one of the qualifications to land a job. In France, for example, job seekers handwrite their applications, and some companies spend as much as $30,000 analyzing the handwriting on these forms.

Not so in the United States. With downsizing affecting corporate human resources' staffs, companies have turned to a high-tech method of screening the volume of resumes. This "electronic applicant tracking" system uses an optical scanner to convert a typed page to electronic text, stores the resume in a database, and then uses artificial intelligence to select certain resumes matching the job qualifications. Thus, job applicants today must write a resume that the scanner can read and the computer will choose from the database.

Optical scanners work best when reading a clean, clear, concise document.

The artificial intelligence software screens the resumes, retrieves those matching keywords in up to 20 categories, and then ranks the selected documents according to the number of matching keyword terms, or *hits*. Thus, your goal is to include as many of these words or phrases as possible when describing your talents and qualifications. To do so, use simple, precise nouns instead of verbs. For example, use the phrase, project manager, instead of managed projects. Common keywords are writer, supervisor, production, fluent, analytical ability, assertive, college graduate, communication skills, organizational skills, creative, customer oriented, detail minded, flexible, industrious, innovative, open minded, results oriented, risk-taker, self-starter, supportive, and team player. Jargon is fine, but do not use abbreviations.

As you begin your job search, you may need two versions of your resume: one that is scannable electronically to send to large corporations, and a second, conventional document similar to the one you will create in this project for smaller companies. Both should have similar content. Each resume should be customized to meet the requirements of a specific job advertisement. The ease with which you can create resumes in Microsoft Word 97 makes it a value tool for the job seeker. The Resume Wizard helps you organize your skills, education, and experience in a format that is appropriate for the type of job you are pursuing. The wizard offers several built-in headings that you can place in any order, and you can add your own headings. The wizard also helps you create a cover letter and send the resume and cover letter to a prospective employer by e-mail or fax.

One researcher estimates that nearly 80 percent of resumes today are never seen by humans once they are scanned into the electronic system. Although this method seems impersonal and cold, unlike the European handwritten application style, it is a valuable step to help\you land the job of your dreams.

Get Noticed

Scannable Fonts

Arial

Courier

Times New Roman

Univers

Microsoft
Word 97

Using Word's Wizards and Templates to Create a Cover Letter and Resume

Case Perspective

Caroline Louise Schmidt has recently graduated from North Carolina University with a Bachelor of Arts degree in Technical Writing and an Associate of Science degree in Computer Technology. Because she now is ready to embark on a full-time career, Caroline decides to prepare a resume to send to prospective employers. She wants the resume to look professional while highlighting her education and experience. Once she prepares her resume, Caroline's next step is to prepare a personalized cover letter to send to each prospective employer. As she reads yesterday's edition of the *Charlotte News*, she locates a classified advertisement for a computer textbook proofreading position at International Markson Press, which sounds like a position suited just for her. Caroline immediately begins writing a cover letter to Mr. Samuel Parker at International Markson Press. In her cover letter, she emphasizes her first-hand experience with both computers and proofreading. As she places her cover letter and resume in the mail, Caroline dreams about a career at International Markson Press.

Caroline created her resume using Word's Resume Wizard, which is a tool designed to assist users in preparing a resume. Then, she composed her cover letter using a Word letter template, which produces a properly formatted business letter.

Introduction

At some time in your professional life, you will prepare a resume along with a personalized cover letter to send to a prospective employer(s). In addition to some personal information, a **resume** usually contains the applicant's educational background and job experience. Because employers review many resumes for each vacant position, you should design your resume carefully so it presents you as the best candidate for the job. You should attach a personalized cover letter to each resume you send. A **cover letter** enables you to elaborate on positive points in your resume; it also provides you with an opportunity to show the potential employer your written communication skills. Thus, it is important that your cover letter is well written and follows proper business letter rules.

Because composing letters and resumes from scratch is a difficult process for many people, Word provides **wizards** and **templates** to assist you in these document preparations. A template is like a blueprint; that is, Word prepares the requested document with text and/or formatting common to all documents of this nature. By asking you several basic questions, Word's wizards prepare and format a document for you based on your responses. Once Word creates a document from either a template or a wizard, you then fill in the blanks or replace prewritten words in the documents. Some wizards and templates are installed with Word; others are on Microsoft's Web page for you to download.

Project Two – Cover Letter and Resume

Project 2 uses Word to produce the cover letter shown in Figure 2-1 and resume shown in Figure 2-2 on the next page. Caroline Louise Schmidt, a recent college graduate, is seeking a full-time position as a computer textbook proofreader with a major publishing firm. In addition to her resume, she sends a personalized cover letter to Mr. Samuel Parker at International Markson Press detailing her work experience.

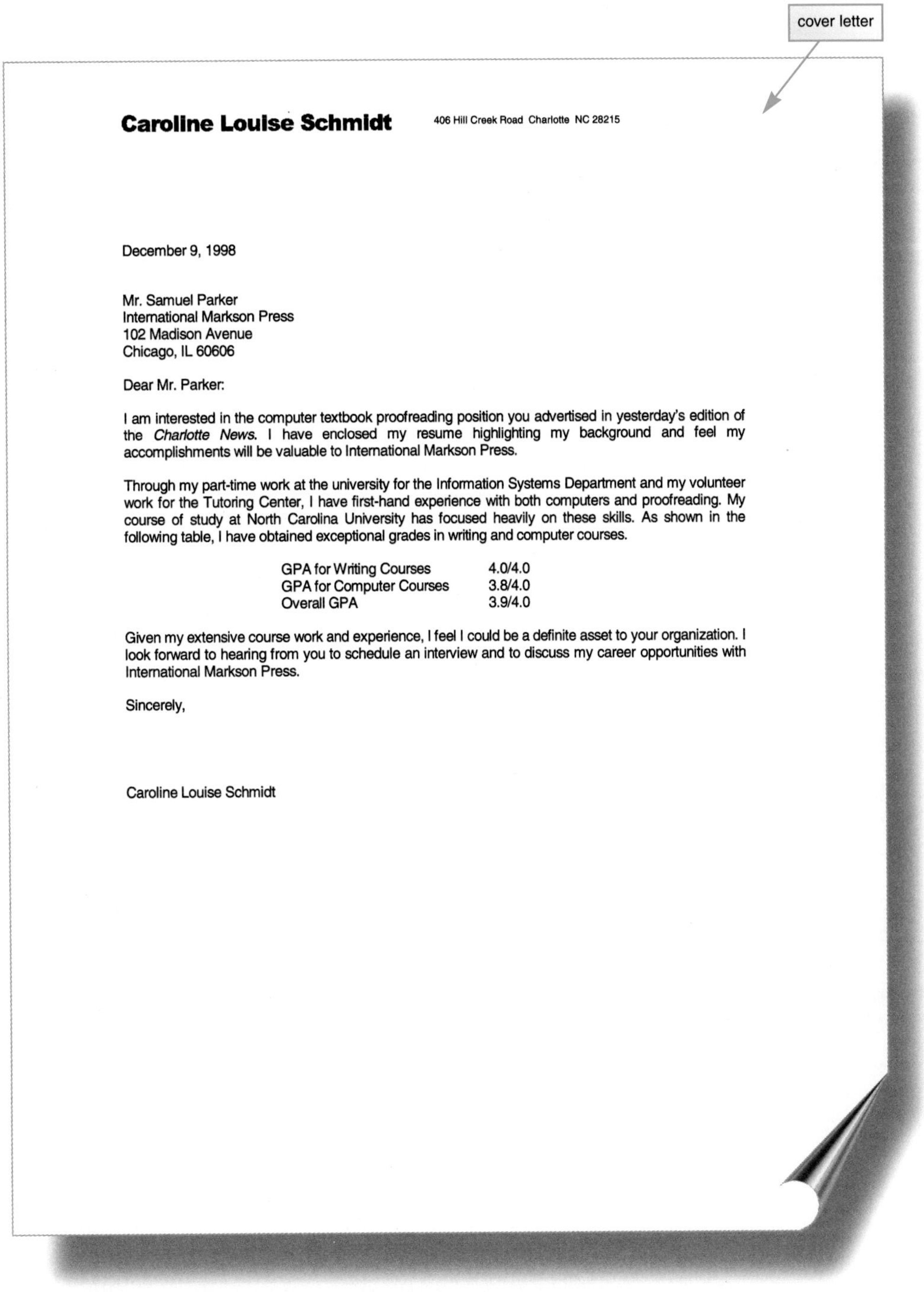

cover letter

Caroline Louise Schmidt   406 Hill Creek Road Charlotte NC 28215

December 9, 1998

Mr. Samuel Parker
International Markson Press
102 Madison Avenue
Chicago, IL 60606

Dear Mr. Parker:

I am interested in the computer textbook proofreading position you advertised in yesterday's edition of the *Charlotte News*. I have enclosed my resume highlighting my background and feel my accomplishments will be valuable to International Markson Press.

Through my part-time work at the university for the Information Systems Department and my volunteer work for the Tutoring Center, I have first-hand experience with both computers and proofreading. My course of study at North Carolina University has focused heavily on these skills. As shown in the following table, I have obtained exceptional grades in writing and computer courses.

GPA for Writing Courses	4.0/4.0
GPA for Computer Courses	3.8/4.0
Overall GPA	3.9/4.0

Given my extensive course work and experience, I feel I could be a definite asset to your organization. I look forward to hearing from you to schedule an interview and to discuss my career opportunities with International Markson Press.

Sincerely,

Caroline Louise Schmidt

FIGURE 2-1

Document Preparation Steps

Document preparation steps give you an overview of how the cover letter and resume in Figures 2-1 and 2-2 will be developed. The following tasks will be completed in this project:

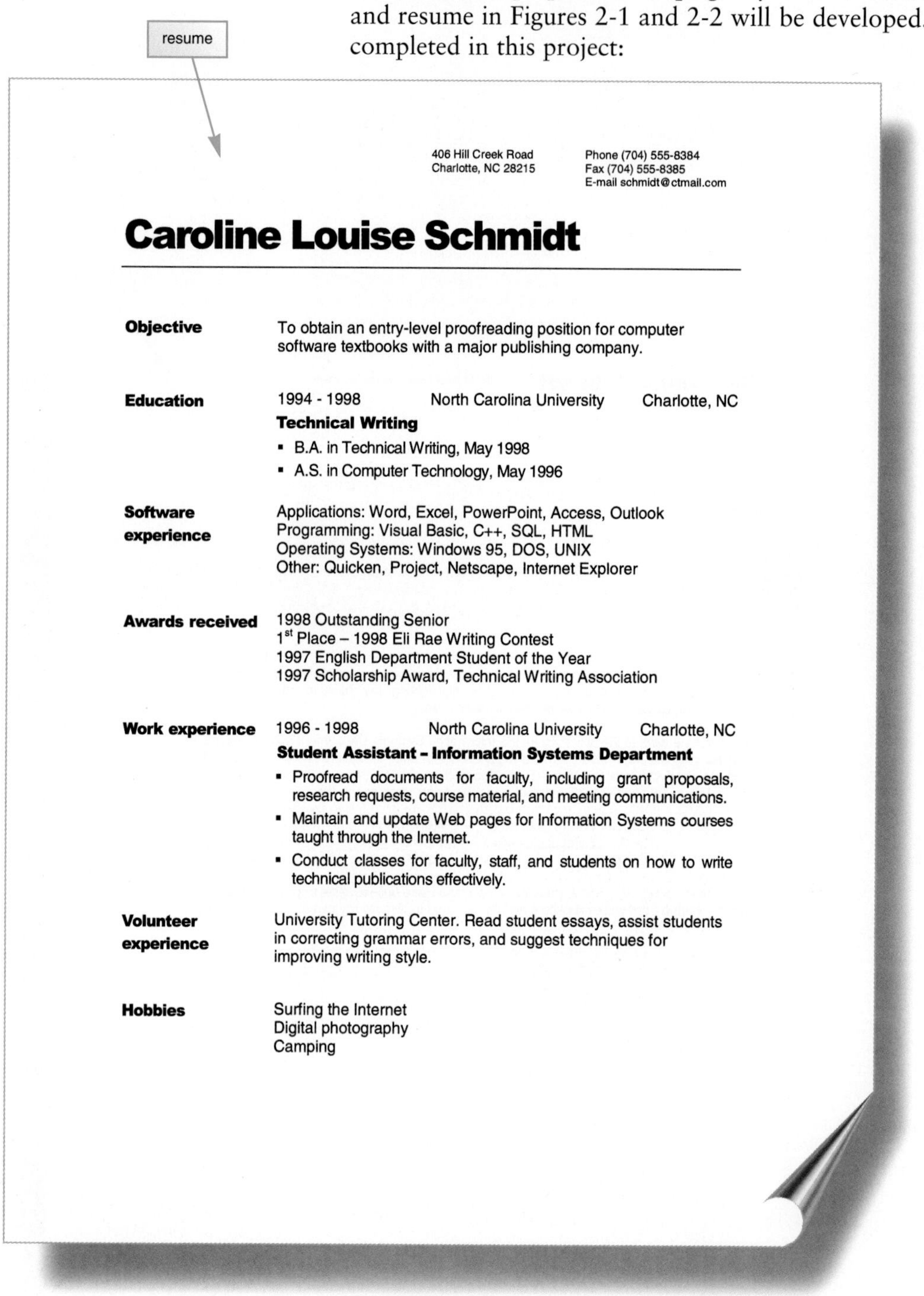

1. Start Word.
2. Use the Resume Wizard to create a resume.
3. Personalize the resume.
4. View and print the resume in print preview.
5. Save the resume.
6. Use a letter template to create a cover letter.
7. Create an Auto-Text entry.
8. Type the cover letter using the AutoText entry.
9. Move a sentence in the cover letter.
10. Spell check the cover letter.
11. Save and print the cover letter.
12. Switch to the resume.
13. Spell check and save the resume.

The following pages contain a detailed explanation of each of these tasks.

resume

406 Hill Creek Road
Charlotte, NC 28215

Phone (704) 555-8384
Fax (704) 555-8385
E-mail schmidt@ctmail.com

Caroline Louise Schmidt

Objective   To obtain an entry-level proofreading position for computer software textbooks with a major publishing company.

Education   1994 - 1998   North Carolina University   Charlotte, NC
Technical Writing
- B.A. in Technical Writing, May 1998
- A.S. in Computer Technology, May 1996

Software experience   Applications: Word, Excel, PowerPoint, Access, Outlook
Programming: Visual Basic, C++, SQL, HTML
Operating Systems: Windows 95, DOS, UNIX
Other: Quicken, Project, Netscape, Internet Explorer

Awards received   1998 Outstanding Senior
1st Place – 1998 Eli Rae Writing Contest
1997 English Department Student of the Year
1997 Scholarship Award, Technical Writing Association

Work experience   1996 - 1998   North Carolina University   Charlotte, NC
Student Assistant – Information Systems Department
- Proofread documents for faculty, including grant proposals, research requests, course material, and meeting communications.
- Maintain and update Web pages for Information Systems courses taught through the Internet.
- Conduct classes for faculty, staff, and students on how to write technical publications effectively.

Volunteer experience   University Tutoring Center. Read student essays, assist students in correcting grammar errors, and suggest techniques for improving writing style.

Hobbies   Surfing the Internet
Digital photography
Camping

FIGURE 2-2

Using Word's Resume Wizard to Create a Resume

You can type a resume from scratch into a blank document window, or you can use a wizard and let Word format the resume with appropriate headings and spacing. Then, you can customize the resulting resume by filling in the blanks or selecting and replacing text. Perform the following steps to create a resume using the **Resume Wizard**.

Steps **To Create a Resume Using Word's Resume Wizard**

1 **Click the Start button on the taskbar and then click New Office Document. If necessary, click the Other Documents tab when the New Office Document dialog box first opens. Click the Resume Wizard icon.**

Office displays several wizard and template icons in the Other Documents sheet in the New Office Document dialog box (Figure 2-3). Icons without the word, wizard, below them are templates. If you click an icon in the Other Documents sheet, a preview of the resulting document displays in the Preview area; thus, the Resume Wizard is selected and a preview of a resume displays in the Preview area.

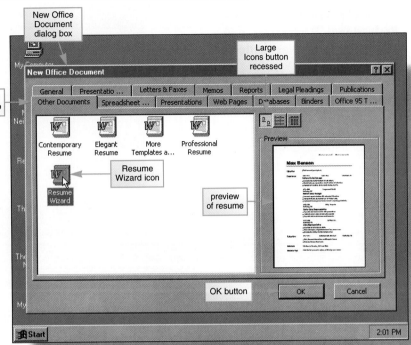

FIGURE 2-3

2 **Click the OK button. When the Resume Wizard dialog box displays, point to the Next button.**

*After a few seconds, Word displays the **Start panel** of the **Resume Wizard dialog box**, informing you the Resume Wizard has started (Figure 2-4). Notice this dialog box has an Office Assistant button you can click to obtain help while using this wizard. Depending on your system, the Word screen may or may not be maximized behind the Resume Wizard dialog box.*

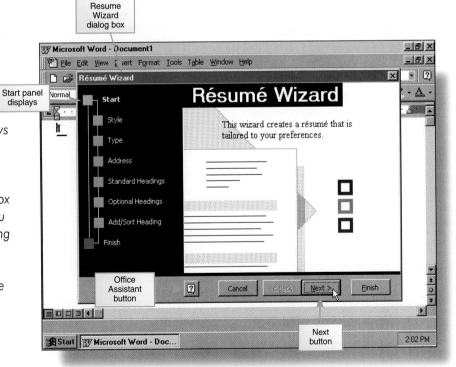

FIGURE 2-4

3 **Click the Next button. When the Style panel displays in the Resume Wizard dialog box, click Professional, if necessary, and then point to the Next button.**

Word displays the Style panel in the Resume Wizard dialog box, requesting the style of your resume (Figure 2-5). Word provides three styles, or families, of wizards and templates: Professional, Contemporary, and Elegant. A preview of each style resume displays below each respective option button in this panel.

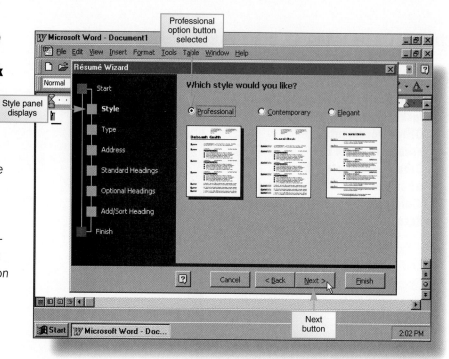

FIGURE 2-5

4 **Click the Next button. When the Type panel displays in the Resume Wizard dialog box, click Entry-level resume, if necessary, and then point to the Next button.**

Word displays the Type panel in the Resume Wizard dialog box, asking for the type of resume that you want to create (Figure 2-6).

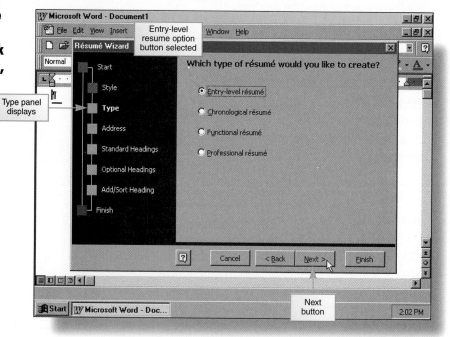

FIGURE 2-6

5 **Click the Next button.**

*Word displays the **Address panel** in the Resume Wizard dialog box, with the current name selected (Figure 2-7). The name displayed and selected in your Name text box will be different, depending on the name of the last person using the Resume Wizard.*

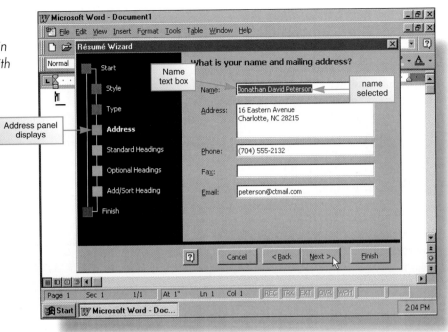

FIGURE 2-7

6 **With the name in the Name text box selected, type** Caroline Louise Schmidt **and then press the TAB key to advance to the Address text box. Type** 406 Hill Creek Road **and then press the ENTER key. Type** Charlotte, NC 28215 **and then press the TAB key to advance to the Phone text box. Type** (704) 555-8384 **and then press the TAB key to advance to the Fax text box. Type** (704) 555-8385 **and then press the TAB key to advance to the Email text box. Type** schmidt@ctmail.com **and then point to the Next button.**

The personal information is entered in the Address panel in the Resume Wizard dialog box (Figure 2-8). Notice that as you typed the name, Caroline Louise Schmidt, it automatically replaced the selected text in the Name text box. When you want to replace text in Word, select the text to be removed and then type the desired text.

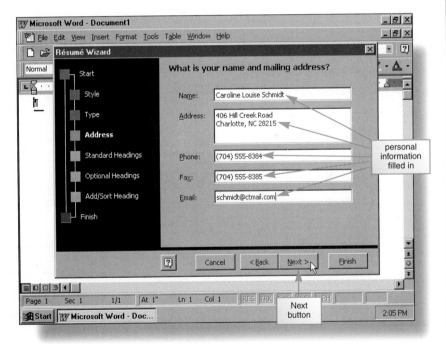

FIGURE 2-8

7 **Click the Next button. When the Standard Headings panel displays in the Resume Wizard dialog box, if necessary, click Interests and activities, Languages, and References to remove the check marks to clear the options. All other check boxes should be selected. Point to the Next button.**

Word displays the Standard Headings panel in the Resume Wizard dialog box, which requests the headings you want on your resume (Figure 2-9). You want all headings, except for these three: Interests and activities, Languages, and References.

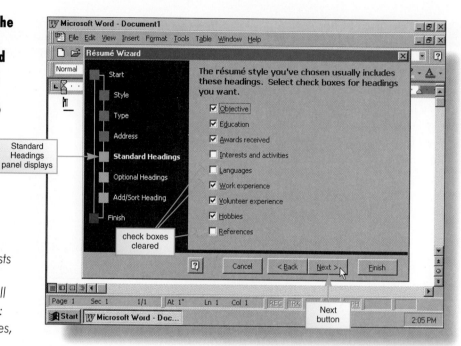

FIGURE 2-9

8 **Click the Next button. Point to the Next button in the Optional Headings panel in the Resume Wizard dialog box.**

Word displays the Optional Headings panel in the Resume Wizard dialog box, which allows you to choose additional headings for your resume (Figure 2-10). All of these check boxes should be cleared because none of these headings is required on your resume.

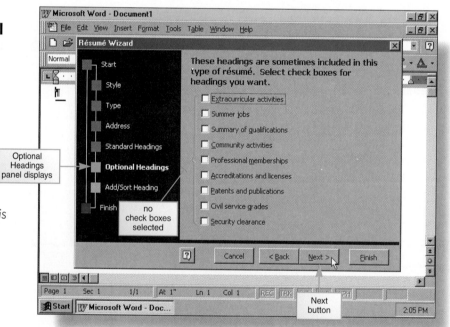

FIGURE 2-10

9 **Click the Next button. When the Add/Sort Heading panel displays in the Resume Wizard dialog box, type** Software experience **in the additional headings text box. Point to the Add button.**

*Word displays the **Add/Sort Heading panel** in the Resume Wizard dialog box, which allows you to enter any additional headings you want on your resume (Figure 2-11).*

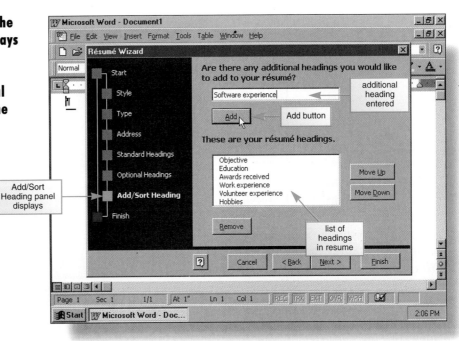

FIGURE 2-11

10 **Click the Add button. Scroll to the bottom of the list of resume headings and then click Software experience. Point to the Move Up button.**

*The Software experience heading is selected (Figure 2-12). You can rearrange the order of the headings on your resume by selecting a heading and then clicking the appropriate button (**Move Up button** or **Move Down button**). The headings will display on the resume in the order the names are displayed in this dialog box.*

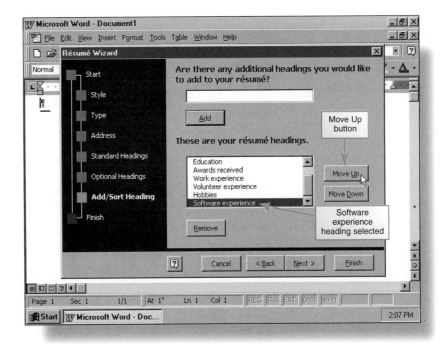

FIGURE 2-12

11 Click the Move Up button four times.

Word moves the heading, Software experience, up above the Awards received heading (Figure 2-13).

12 If the last person using the Resume Wizard added headings, you may have some additional unwanted headings. Your heading list should be as follows: Objective, Education, Software experience, Awards received, Work experience, Volunteer experience, and Hobbies. If you have an additional heading(s), click the unwanted heading and then click the Remove button in the Add/Sort Heading panel.

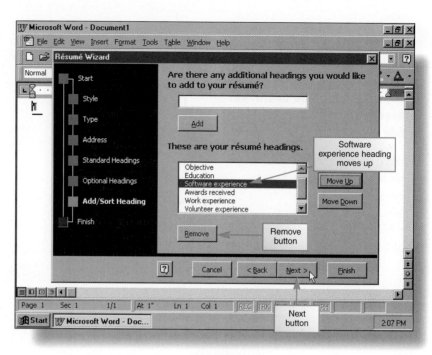

FIGURE 2-13

13 Click the Next button. When the Finish panel displays in the Resume Wizard dialog box, point to the Finish button.

Word displays the Finish panel in the Resume Wizard dialog box (Figure 2-14).

FIGURE 2-14

14 Click the Finish button. If the Office Assistant displays, click its Cancel button.

Word creates an entry-level professional style resume layout for you (Figure 2-15). You are to personalize the resume as indicated.

15 If the Word screen is not maximized, double-click its title bar to maximize it.

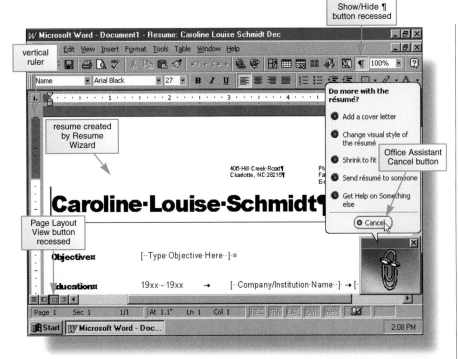

FIGURE 2-15

When you create a resume using the Resume Wizard, you can click the Back button in any panel of the Resume Wizard dialog box to change any of the previous options you selected. To exit the Resume Wizard and return to the document window without creating the resume, click the Cancel button in any panel of the Resume Wizard dialog box.

In addition to the Resume Wizard, Word provides many other wizards to assist you in creating documents: agenda for a meeting, award certificate, calendar, envelope, fax cover sheet, legal pleading, letter, mailing label, memorandum, newsletter, table, and Web page. These wizards either are installed with Word or may be downloaded from Microsoft's Web page.

When Word displays the resume in the document window, it switches from **normal view** to **page layout view**. The announcement you created in Project 1 was in normal view. In both normal and page layout views, you can type and edit text. The difference is that page layout view shows you exactly how the printed page will look.

You can tell you are in page layout view by looking at the Word screen (Figure 2-15). Notice that in page layout view, the **Page Layout View button** at the bottom of the Word screen is recessed. Also, notice that a **vertical ruler** now displays at the left edge of the document window, in addition to the horizontal ruler at the top of the window. In page layout view, the entire piece of paper is positioned in the document window, showing precisely the positioning of the text and margins on the printed page.

To see the entire resume created by the Resume Wizard, you should print the resume.

More *About* **Resumes**

Think of your resume as an advertisement about you. A good advertisement (and resume) doesn't tout negatives; rather it promotes positives. A resume should be accurate and truthful. It should also be up-to-date and customized for each job advertisement. List qualifications from most relevant to least, and be concise.

TO PRINT THE RESUME CREATED BY THE RESUME WIZARD

Step 1: Ready the printer and then click the Print button on the Standard toolbar.

Step 2: When the printer stops, retrieve the hard copy resume from the printer.

The printed resume is shown in Figure 2-16.

◆ **More** *About*
Resume Contents

Leave the following items off a resume: social security number, marital status, age, height, weight, gender, physical appearance, health, citizenship, references, reference of references, previous pay rates, reasons for leaving a prior job, current date, and high school information (if you are a college graduate).

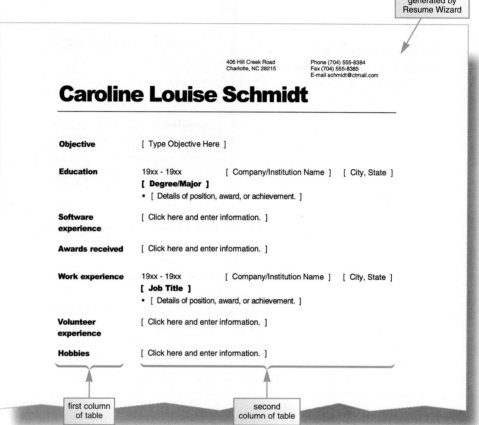

FIGURE 2-16

Personalizing the Resume

The next step is to **personalize the resume**. Where Word has indicated, you type the objective, education, software experience, awards received, work experience, volunteer experience, and hobbies next to the respective headings. In the education and work experience sections, you select and replace text to customize these sections. The following pages show how to personalize the resume generated by the Resume Wizard.

Displaying Nonprinting Characters

As discussed in Project 1, it is helpful to display **nonprinting characters** that indicate where in the document you pressed the ENTER key and SPACEBAR. If nonprinting characters do not already display on your screen, follow this step to display them.

TO DISPLAY NONPRINTING CHARACTERS

Step 1: If necessary, click the Show/Hide ¶ button on the Standard toolbar.

Word displays nonprinting characters in the document window, and the Show/Hide ¶ button on the Standard toolbar is recessed (Figure 2-15 on page WD 2.13).

Tables

When the Resume Wizard prepares a resume, it arranges the body of the resume as a table. A Word **table** is a collection of rows and columns. The section headings (Objective, Education, Software experience, Awards received, Work experience, Volunteer experience, and Hobbies) are placed in the first column of the table; and the detail for each of these sections is placed in the second column of the table (Figure 2-16). Thus, this table contains two columns. It also contains seven rows – one row for each section. To see clearly the rows and columns in a Word table, some users prefer to show gridlines. **Gridlines** are nonprinting characters; that is, they do not print in a hard copy. If you want to display gridlines in a table, position the insertion point somewhere in the table, click Table on the menu bar, and then click **Show Gridlines**. As illustrated in Figure 2-17, gridlines help identify the rows and columns in a table. The intersection of a row and a column is called a **cell**, and cells are filled with text. Each cell has an **end-of-cell mark**, which is another nonprinting character used to select and format cells. If you want to hide the gridlines, click somewhere in the table, click Table on the menu bar, and then click **Hide Gridlines**. Tables are discussed in more depth in a later project.

Styles

When you use a wizard to create a document, Word formats the document using styles. A **style** is a customized format applied to characters or paragraphs. The Style box on the Formatting toolbar displays the name of the style associated with the location of the insertion point. You can identify many of the characteristics assigned to a style by looking at the Formatting toolbar. In Figure 2-17, the insertion point is in a paragraph formatted with the Name style, which uses the 27-point Arial Black font for the characters.

If you click the Style box arrow on the Formatting toolbar, the list of styles associated with the current document displays. Paragraph styles affect an entire paragraph, whereas character styles affect only selected characters. In the Style list, **paragraph style** names are followed by a proofreader's paragraph mark (¶), and **character style** names are followed by a bold underlined letter a (**a**).

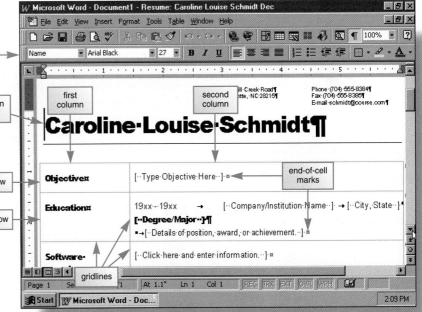

FIGURE 2-17

More *About*
Character Size

To adjust the size of the characters on the screen, you can increase or decrease the zoom percentage by clicking the Zoom box arrow on the Standard toolbar and then selecting the desired percentage. Zooming a document has no effect on the printed characters.

You can change a style applied to text. You also may select the appropriate style from the Style list box before entering the text so the text you type will be formatted according to the selected style.

Inserting a Blank Line above a Paragraph

The first step in formatting the resume is to insert a blank line between the e-mail address and the name. These two lines are too close to one another. Pressing the ENTER key will insert a 27-point blank line, which is too large. Perform the following step to insert a 12-point blank line above a paragraph.

Steps **To Insert a Blank Line above a Paragraph**

1 **If necessary, click somewhere in the name line of the resume. Press the CTRL+0 (zero) keys.**

Word inserts a blank line above the name in the resume (Figure 2-18). The shortcut CTRL+0 is a toggle; that is, the first time you press it, Word inserts a blank line, and the second time you press it, Word removes the blank line.

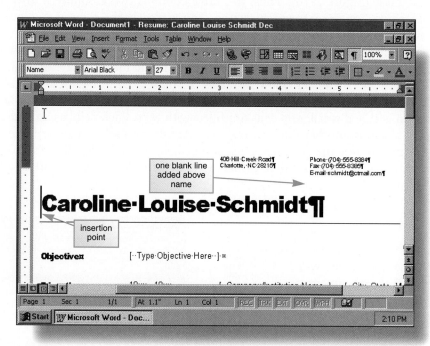

FIGURE 2-18

Other Ways

1. Right-click paragraph, click Paragraph on shortcut menu, click Indents and Spacing tab, type 12 in Spacing Before text box, click OK button
2. On Format menu click Paragraph, click Indents and Spacing tab, type 12 in Spacing Before text box, click OK button

Selecting and Replacing Text

The next step in personalizing the resume is to select the placeholder text that the Resume Wizard inserted into the resume and replace it with the personal information. The first heading on the resume is the objective. You enter the objective where the Resume Wizard inserted the words, Type Objective Here, which is called **placeholder text**. To do this, click the placeholder text, Type Objective Here, to select it. Then, you type the objective. As soon as you begin typing, the selected placeholder text is deleted; thus, you do not have to delete the selection before you begin typing. Perform the following steps to enter the objective into the resume.

Steps **To Select and Replace Placeholder Text**

1 **Click the placeholder text, Type Objective Here.**

Word highlights the placeholder text in the resume (Figure 2-19). Notice the new style is Objective in the Style box on the Formatting toolbar. The Objective style uses the 10-point Arial font for characters.

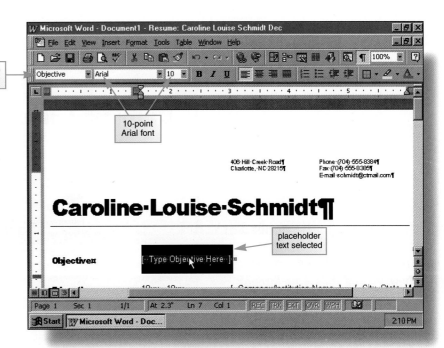

FIGURE 2-19

2 **Type** To obtain an entry-level proofreading position for computer software textbooks with a major publishing company.

Word replaces the highlighted placeholder text, Type Objective Here, with the objective you type (Figure 2-20). Your document may wordwrap on a different word depending on the type of printer you are using.

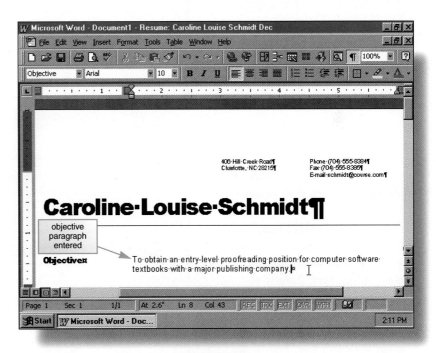

FIGURE 2-20

The next step in personalizing the resume is to replace the Wizard's words and phrases in the education section of the resume with your own words and phrases as shown in the steps on the next page.

Steps **To Select and Replace Resume Wizard Supplied Text**

1 **If necessary, scroll down to display the entire education section of the resume. Drag through the xx in the first 19xx in the education section.**

Word selects the xx in the first year (Figure 2-21).

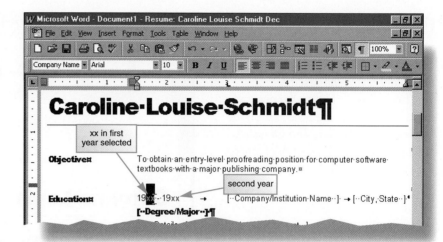

FIGURE 2-21

2 **Type** 94 **and then drag through the xx in the second year in the education section. Type** 98 **and then click the placeholder text, Company/Institution Name.**

Word highlights the placeholder text, Company/Institution Name (Figure 2-22). Notice the years now display as 1994 - 1998 in the education section.

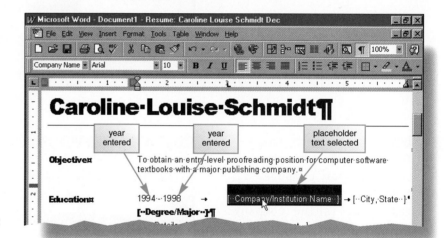

FIGURE 2-22

3 **Type** North Carolina University **and then click the placeholder text, City, State. Type** Charlotte, NC **and then click the placeholder text, Degree/Major. Type** Technical Writing **and then click the placeholder text, Details of position, award, or achievement. Type** B.A. in Technical Writing, May 1998 **and then press the ENTER key. Type** A.S. in Computer Technology, May 1996 **as the second item in the list.**

The university name, city, state, major and degrees are entered (Figure 2-23).

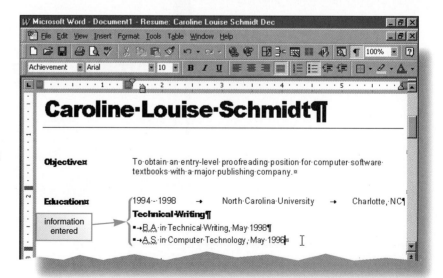

FIGURE 2-23

Entering a Line Break

The next step in personalizing the resume is to enter the software experience section. The style used for the characters in the software experience section is the same as for the objective section, that is, 10-point Arial font. A paragraph formatting characteristic of the Objective style is that when you press the ENTER key, the insertion point advances downward at least 11 points, which leaves nearly an entire blank line between each paragraph. Because you want the lines within the software experience section to be close to each other, you will not press the ENTER key between each type of software experience. Instead, you will create a **line break**, which advances the insertion point to the beginning of the next physical line – ignoring any paragraph formatting instructions. Perform the following steps to enter the software experience section using a line break, instead of a paragraph break, between each line.

More *About* **Styles**

To apply a different style to a paragraph, click the paragraph, click the Style box arrow on the Formatting toolbar, and then click the desired paragraph style. To apply a different character style, select the characters, click the Style box arrow on the Formatting toolbar, and then click the desired character style.

Steps **To Enter a Line Break**

1 **If necessary, scroll down to display the software experience section of the resume. In the software experience section, click the placeholder text, Click here and enter information. Type** Applications: Word, Excel, PowerPoint, Access, Outlook **and then press the SHIFT + ENTER keys.**

*Word inserts a **line break character** after the software product names and moves the insertion point to the beginning of the next physical line (Figure 2-24). Because the ENTER key would create a new paragraph and advance the insertion point down nearly two lines due to the paragraph formatting created by the Resume Wizard, you do not want to create a new paragraph. Thus, you enter a line break to start a new line. The line break character is a nonprinting character that displays on the screen each time you create a line break.*

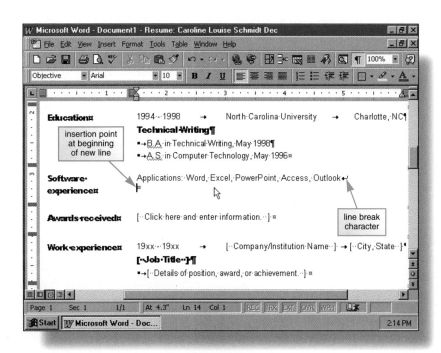

FIGURE 2-24

2 **Type** Programming: Visual Basic, C++, SQL, HTML **and then press the SHIFT+ENTER keys.** **Type** Operating Systems: Windows 95, DOS, UNIX **and then press the SHIFT+ENTER keys.** **Type** Other: Quicken, Project, Netscape, Internet Explorer **as the other software experience.**

The software experience section is entered (Figure 2-25).

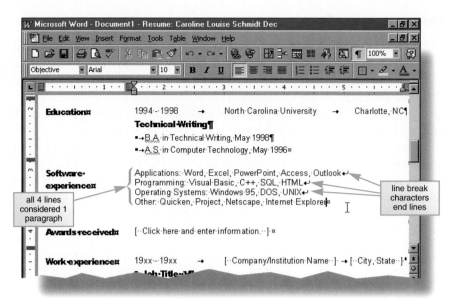

FIGURE 2-25

More *About* **As You Type**

Word has other As You Type features. For example, teh changes to the when you press the SPACEBAR. You can also add special symbols to your writing. For example, typing :) changes to ☺ when you press the SPACEBAR. To see a complete list, click Tools on the menu bar, click AutoCorrect, and then click the AutoCorrect tab.

AutoFormat As You Type

As you type text into a document, Word automatically formats it for you. Table 2-1 summarizes the types of AutoFormats available and their results. For the AutoFormat As You Type feature to work, it must be on. To check if AutoFormat is enabled, click Tools on the menu bar, click AutoCorrect, click the AutoFormat As You Type tab, select the appropriate check boxes, and then click the OK button.

Table 2-1

ENTRY	WORD AUTOFORMATTING	EXAMPLE
Number followed by a period, hyphen, or right parenthesis and then a space or tab followed by text	Creates a numbered list when you press the ENTER key	1. Numbered lists 2. are easy to 3. create with Word
Asterisk, hyphen, or dash and then a space or tab followed by text	Creates a bulleted list when you press the ENTER key	• Bulleted lists • make items • stand out
Three underscores, equal signs, or dashes and then press the ENTER key	Creates a border above the paragraph	_____ Underscores converted to a solid line
Fraction and then a space or hyphen	Converts the entry to a fraction-like notation	½
Ordinal and then a space or hyphen	Makes the ordinal a superscript	2nd
Web address	Formats it as a hyperlink	http://www.scseries.com
Two hyphens followed by text	Converts hyphens to an em dash	Em dash – two hyphens

In the awards received section of the resume, you use two of Word's AutoFormat As You Type features, as shown in the following steps.

Steps **To AutoFormat As You Type**

1 **If necessary, scroll down to display the awards received section of the resume. Click the placeholder text, Click here and enter information. Type** 1998 Outstanding Senior **and then press the SHIFT+ENTER keys. Type** 1st **as the beginning of the second award.**

The text and ordinal are entered (Figure 2-26).

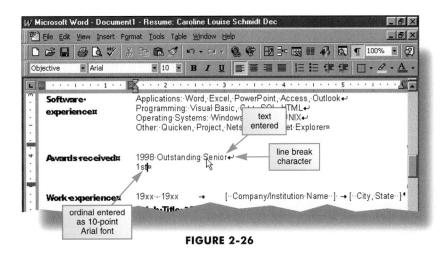

FIGURE 2-26

2 **Press the SPACEBAR. Type** Place **and then press the SPACEBAR. Type two hyphens (--).**

Word formats the ordinal as a superscript (Figure 2-27).

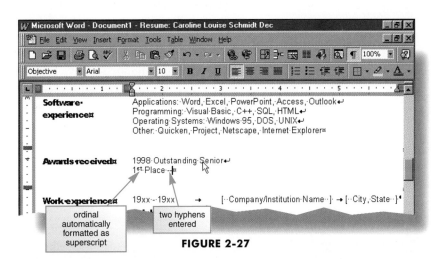

FIGURE 2-27

3 **Press the SPACEBAR. Type** 1998 Eli Rae Writing Contest **and then press the SHIFT+ENTER keys. Type** 1997 English Department Student of the Year **and then press the SHIFT+ENTER keys. Type** 1997 Scholarship Award, Technical Writing Association **as the last award in the list.**

Word converts the two hyphens to an em dash (Figure 2-28). The awards received section is complete.

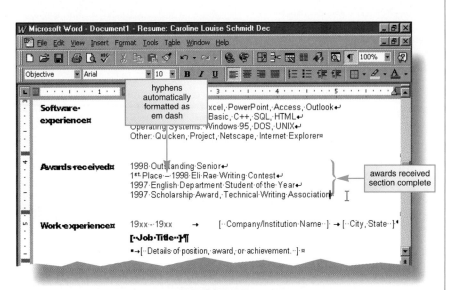

FIGURE 2-28

If, for some reason, you do not want Word to AutoFormat As You Type, you can turn off this feature. To do this, click Tools on the menu bar, click AutoCorrect, click the AutoFormat As You Type tab, turn off the check boxes, and then click the OK button.

Enter the remaining text for the resume as described in the following steps.

TO ENTER THE REMAINING SECTIONS OF THE RESUME

Step 1: If necessary, scroll down to display the work experience section of the resume. Drag through the xx in the first 19xx in the work experience section, type 96 and then drag through the xx in the second year. Type 98 as the year.

Step 2: Click the placeholder text, Company/Institution Name. Type North Carolina University as the college.

Step 3: Click the placeholder text, City, State. Type Charlotte, NC as the city and state.

Step 4: Click the placeholder text, Job Title. Type Student Assistant – Information Systems Department as the title.

Step 5: Click the placeholder text, Details of position, award, or achievement. Type Proofread documents for faculty, including grant proposals, research requests, course material, and meeting communications.

Step 6: Press the ENTER key. Type Maintain and update Web pages for Information Systems courses taught through the Internet.

Step 7: Press the ENTER key. Type Conduct classes for faculty, staff, and students on how to write technical publications effectively.

Step 8: If necessary, scroll down to display the volunteer experience section of the resume. Click the placeholder text, Click here and enter information. Type University Tutoring Center. Read student essays, assist students in correcting grammar errors, and suggest techniques for improving writing style.

Step 9: If necessary, scroll down to display the hobbies section of the resume. Click the placeholder text, Click here and enter information. Type Surfing the Internet and then press the SHIFT+ENTER keys. Type Digital photography and then press the SHIFT+ENTER keys. Type Camping as the last hobby.

The work experience, volunteer experience, and hobbies sections of the resume are complete (Figure 2-29).

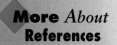

More *About* References

Do not state "References Available Upon Request" on your resume; nor should you list references on the resume. Employers assume you will give references, if asked, and this information simply clutters a resume. Often you are asked to list references on your application. Be sure to give your references a copy of your resume.

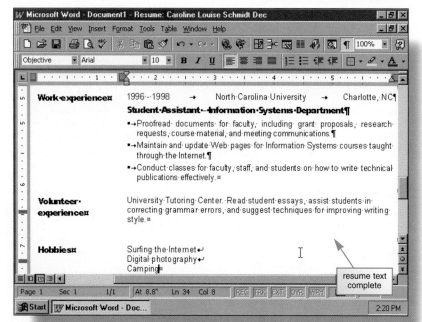

FIGURE 2-29

Changing the Font Size of Characters in the Resume

The next step in modifying the resume is to change the font size of all of the characters in the table of the resume, that is, all the text below the name. Currently, the characters are 10 point, which is difficult for most people to read comfortably. To change all the characters in the table to 11 point, you must select the entire table first and then change the font size as shown in the following steps.

 Steps **To Select a Table and Format Its Characters**

◆ **More** *About*
Tables

If you use the keyboard shortcut to select a table, ALT+NUM5, you must press the 5 on the numeric keypad. You cannot use the 5 on the keyboard area. Also, be sure that NUM LOCK is off; otherwise, the keyboard shortcut will not work.

1 ▸ **Be sure the insertion point is somewhere in the table. Click Table on the menu bar and then point to Select Table (Figure 2-30).**

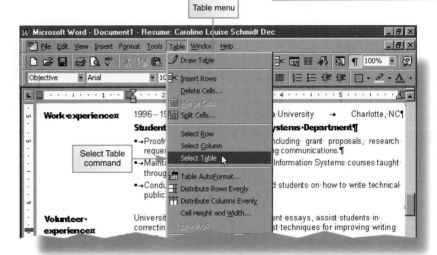

FIGURE 2-30

2 ▸ **Click Select Table.**

Word highlights all of the characters in the table (Figure 2-31).

3 ▸ **Click the Font Size box arrow on the Formatting toolbar and then point to 11.**

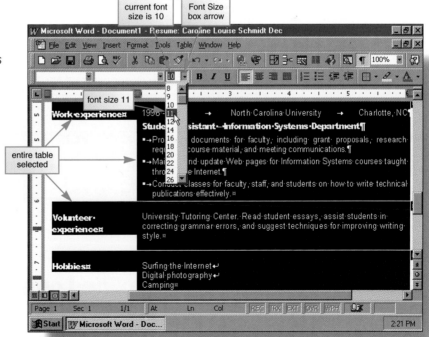

FIGURE 2-31

4 **Click 11.**

Word changes the font size of the selected text from 10 to 11 (Figure 2-32).

5 **Click anywhere in the document to remove the highlight.**

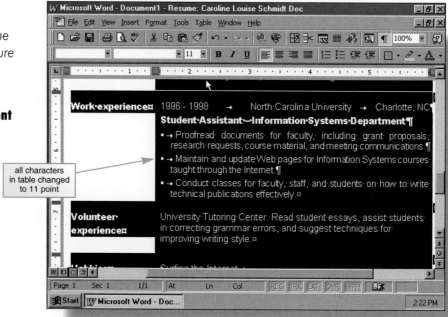

all characters in table changed to 11 point

FIGURE 2-32

The next step is to increase the font size of the address and telephone information that the Resume Wizard placed at the top of the resume. To allow for these items to be positioned anywhere on the resume, Word placed the address information in one frame and the telephone and e-mail address in another frame. Currently, the text in each of these frames is 7 point, which you increase by one point as shown in the following steps.

Steps **To Increase the Font Size by One Point**

1 **Press the CTRL+HOME keys to position the insertion point at the top of the document. Drag through the address above the name.**

Word surrounds the address information with a frame (Figure 2-33). A frame, indicated with the crosshatched border, is an invisible container for text or graphics that can be positioned anywhere on the page.

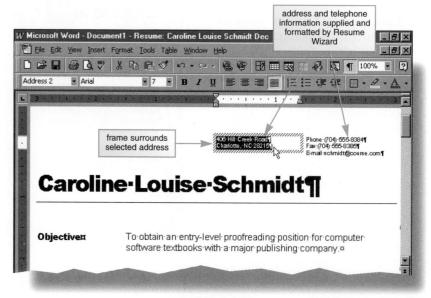

address and telephone information supplied and formatted by Resume Wizard

frame surrounds selected address

FIGURE 2-33

2 **Press the CTRL+] keys. Drag through the telephone and e-mail information to the right of the address.**

Word increases the font size of the selected text by one point, to 8 in this case (Figure 2-34). The telephone and e-mail information is surrounded by a frame.

3 **Press the CTRL+] keys. Click anywhere to remove the selection.**

Word increase the font size of the selected text by one point, to 8 in this case (see Figure 2-35).

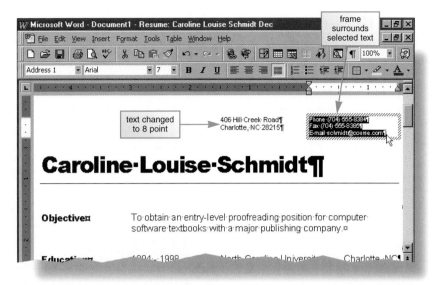

FIGURE 2-34

The resume is completely entered and formatted.

Viewing and Printing the Resume in Print Preview

To see exactly how a document will look when you print it, you should display it in **print preview**. Print preview displays the entire document in reduced size on the Word screen. In print preview, you can edit and format text, adjust margins, and view multiple pages. Once you preview the document, you can print it directly from within print preview. Perform the following steps to use print preview.

Other Ways

1. Click Font Size box arrow on Formatting toolbar, select desired point size in list

2. Right-click selected text, click Font on shortcut menu, click Font tab, select desired point size in Size list box, click OK button

3. On Format menu click Font, click Font tab, select desired point size in Size list box, click OK button

4. Press CTRL+SHIFT+P, type desired point size, press ENTER

Steps **To Print Preview a Document**

1 **Point to the Print Preview button on the Standard toolbar (Figure 2-35).**

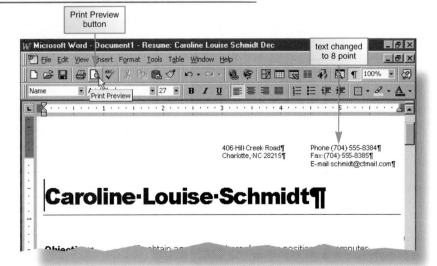

FIGURE 2-35

2 Click the Print Preview button. If your preview displays more than one page, click the One Page button on the Print Preview toolbar. Point to the Print button on the Print Preview toolbar.

Word displays the document in print preview (Figure 2-36). The **Print Preview toolbar** *displays below the menu bar; the Standard and Formatting toolbars have disappeared from the screen. You use the Print Preview toolbar to zoom and print the document.*

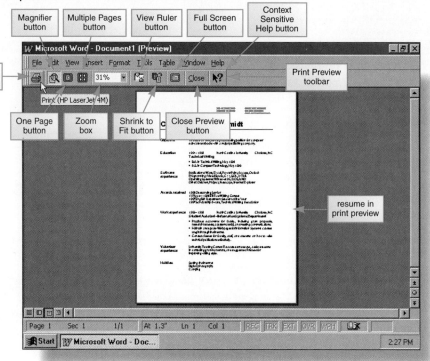

FIGURE 2-36

3 Ready the printer. Click the Print button on the Print Preview toolbar. When the printer stops, retrieve the printout.

Word prints the document on the printer (Figure 2-37).

4 Click the Close Preview button on the Print Preview toolbar.

Word returns to the document window (Figure 2-35 on the previous page).

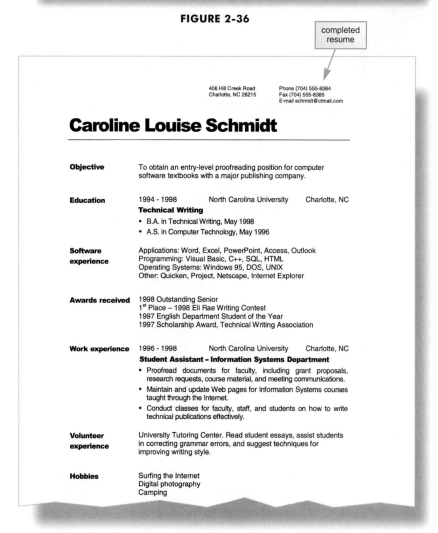

FIGURE 2-37

Saving the Resume

Because the resume is now complete, you should save it. For a detailed example of the procedure summarized below, refer to pages WD 1.25 through WD 1.27 in Project 1.

TO SAVE A DOCUMENT

Step 1: Insert your floppy disk into drive A.
Step 2: Click the Save button on the Standard toolbar.
Step 3: Type Schmidt Resume in the File name text box. Do not press the ENTER key.
Step 4: Click the Save in box arrow and then click 3½ Floppy (A:).
Step 5: Click the Save button in the Save As dialog box.

Word saves the document on a floppy disk in drive A with the file name Schmidt Resume.

The resume now is complete. The next step in Project 2 is to create a cover letter to send with the resume to a potential employer. Do not close the Schmidt Resume. You will use it again later in this project when you spell check it.

Creating a Cover Letter

You have created a personalized resume to send to prospective employers. Along with the resume, you will attach a cover letter. The following pages outline how to use Word to create and personalize a cover letter.

Components of a Business Letter

During your professional career, you will create many business letters. A **cover letter** is one type of a business letter. All business letters contain the same basic components. You should take care when preparing business letters to include all essential elements. **Essential business letter elements** include the date line, inside address, message, and signature block (Figure 2-38 on the next page). The **date line**, which consists of the month, day, and year, is positioned two to six lines below the letterhead. The **inside address**, placed three to eight lines below the date line, usually contains the addressee's courtesy title plus full name; business affiliation; and full geographical address. The **salutation**, if present, begins two lines below the last line of the inside address. The body of the letter, the **message**, begins two lines below the salutation. Within the message, paragraphs are single spaced with double-spacing between paragraphs. Two lines below the last line of the message, the **complimentary close** displays. You capitalize only the first word in a complimentary close. The **signature block** is typed at least four lines below the complimentary close, allowing room for the author to sign his or her name.

More *About*
Print Preview

If you want to read the contents of a page in print preview, you must magnify it. To magnify a page, be sure the Magnifier button is recessed on the Print Preview toolbar and then click in the document to zoom in or out. Magnifying a page has no effect on the printed document; it only changes the size of the characters on the screen.

More *About*
Cover Letters

You should always send a personalized cover letter with every resume. A cover letter should highlight aspects of your background relevant to the position. Because it is often difficult to recall past achievements and activities, you should keep a personal personnel file containing documents that outline your accomplishments.

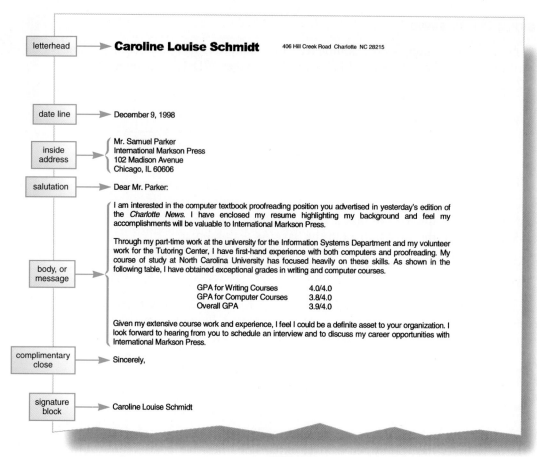

FIGURE 2-38

You can follow many different styles when you create business letters. The cover letter in this project (Figure 2-38) follows the **block style**. Table 2-2 outlines the differences between the common styles of business letters.

Table 2-2	
LETTER STYLES	FEATURES
Block	All components of the letter begin flush with the left margin.
Modified Block	The date, complimentary close, and signature block are positioned approximately five spaces to the right of center or at the right margin. All other components of the letter begin flush with the left margin.
Modified Semi-Block	The date, complimentary close, and signature block are positioned approximately five spaces to the right of center or at the right margin. The first line of each paragraph in the body of the letter is indented 5 or 10 spaces from the left margin. All other components of the letter begin flush with the left margin.

More *About*
Templates

When you create a new document by clicking the New button on the Standard toolbar, Word uses the Blank Document Template located on the General tab sheet in the New dialog box to format the document. If you want to use a different template or a wizard, you must use the New dialog box.

Using a Letter Template to Create a Resume Cover Letter

To create a resume cover letter, you can type a letter from scratch into a blank document window following the rules listed in the preceding paragraphs; you can use a wizard and let Word format the letter with appropriate spacing and layout as you did with the resume; or you can use a template. Recall that a template is like a blueprint; that is, Word prepares the requested document with text and/or formatting common to all documents of this nature. Then, you customize the letter by selecting and replacing text.

Recall that Word provides three styles, or families, of wizards and templates: Professional, Contemporary, and Elegant. If you want a related set of documents to have similar formatting, use wizards and templates from the same family. Because you used the Professional style for the resume, you should use the Professional style for the cover letter as shown in the following steps.

 Steps **To Create a Letter Using a Word Template**

1 **Click File on the menu bar and then point to New (Figure 2-39).**

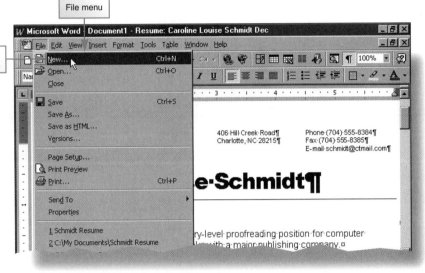

FIGURE 2-39

2 **Click New. If necessary, click the Letters & Faxes tab when the New dialog box first opens. Click the Professional Letter icon.**

Word displays the New dialog box (Figure 2-40). Recall that icons without the word, wizard, below them are templates. The Professional Letter icon is selected, and a preview of a professional letter displays in the Preview area. When you create a new document using the New button on the Standard toolbar, you use the **Blank Document template** *located on the General sheet in the New dialog box. If you want to use a different template or a wizard, you must use the New dialog box.*

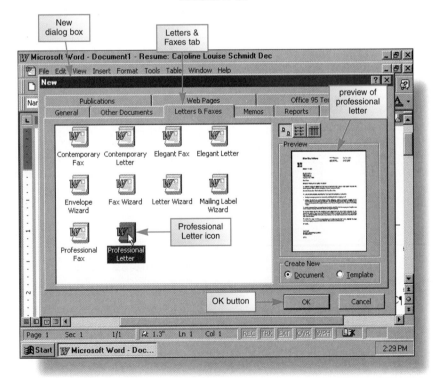

FIGURE 2-40

3 **Click the OK button.**

Word creates a Professional style letter layout for you and displays it in a document window (Figure 2-41). Because Word displays the current date in the letter, your date line probably will display a different date.

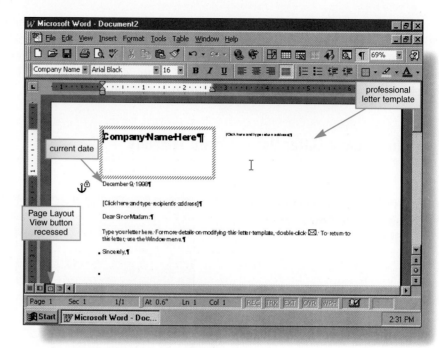

FIGURE 2-41

To see the entire letter created by Word, you should print it.

Printing the Cover Letter Generated Using Word's Professional Letter Template

To print the cover letter generated by Word, click the Print button on the Standard toolbar. The resulting printout is shown in Figure 2-42.

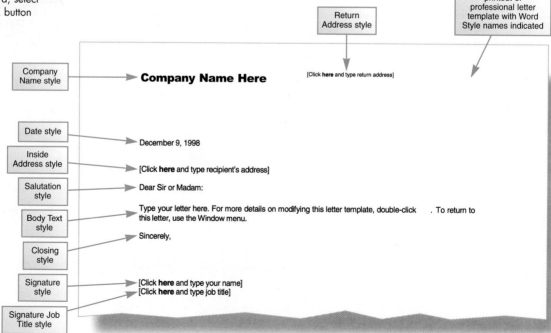

FIGURE 2-42

Recall that a **style** is a customized format Word applies to characters or paragraphs. The Style box on the Formatting toolbar displays the name of the style associated with the location of the insertion point. The styles used in the Professional Letter template are indicated in the printout of the cover letter in Figure 2-42. When you modify the cover letter, the style associated with the location of the insertion point will be applied to the text you type.

Personalizing the Cover Letter

If you compare the printout in Figure 2-42 to the cover letter in Figure 2-1 on page WD 2.5, you will notice several modifications are required. Notice how the template (Figure 2-42) creates the formatting for the business letter using the block style. The template uses proper spacing between lines for a business letter and indicates what you should type in the respective areas of the letter via placeholder text. You can see that using a template saves you formatting time when creating a business letter. The steps on the following pages illustrate how to personalize the cover letter.

Zooming a Document on the Screen

The document displayed in Figure 2-43 is displayed at 69% of its normal size. The characters and words are small and difficult to read. Depending on your settings, your zoom percentage may be different from that shown in Figure 2-43. To make the displayed characters larger or smaller on the screen, you change the zoom percentage, as shown in the following steps.

 Steps To Zoom a Document

1 **Click the Zoom box arrow on the Standard toolbar and then point to 100%.**

A list of magnification percentages displays (Figure 2-43). Any number greater than the current percentage will increase the size of the characters on the screen, and any number smaller will decrease the size of the characters on the screen.

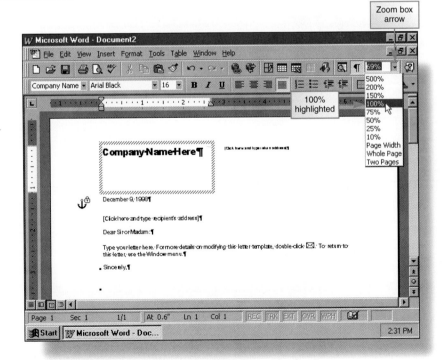

FIGURE 2-43

More *About*
Business Letters

A finished business letter should look like a symmetrically framed picture with even margins, all balanced below an attractive letterhead. In addition, the contents of the letter should contain proper grammar, correct spelling, logically constructed sentences, flowing paragraphs, and sound ideas.

More *About*
Frames

The crosshatched border surrounding the company name in Figure 2-43 is called a frame. A frame is an invisible container for text or graphics that can be positioned anywhere on the page. To change the contents of the frame, select the words as you would any other text and then type.

2 **Click 100%.**

The characters in the document window increase from 69% of their normal size to 100% (Figure 2-44). Notice that the characters are now easier to read. The larger the magnification, the easier the characters are to read.

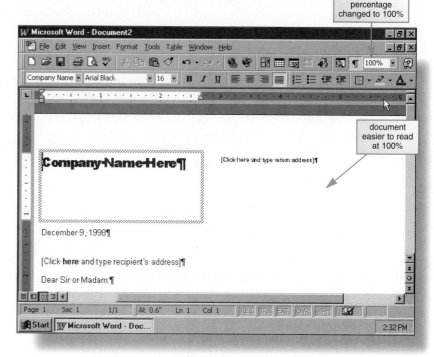

zoom percentage changed to 100%

document easier to read at 100%

FIGURE 2-44

OtherWays

1. On View menu click Zoom, select desired percentage, click OK button

Selecting and Replacing Template Placeholder Text

The next step in personalizing the cover letter is to select the placeholder text in the letter template and replace it with the personal information. The first placeholder text on the cover letter is in the letterhead, Company Name Here. Select and then replace this text as described below.

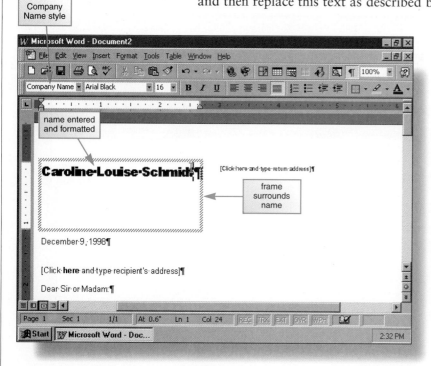

Company Name style

name entered and formatted

frame surrounds name

FIGURE 2-45

TO SELECT AND REPLACE PLACEHOLDER TEXT

Step 1: Drag through the placeholder text, Company Name Here.

Step 2: Type `Caroline Louise Schmidt` as the name.

The name displays surrounded by a frame on the first line of the letterhead (Figure 2-45). The Professional Letter template framed the name to provide flexibility in its location in the document. Notice the style is of this text is Company Name in the Style box. The Company Name style uses 16-point Arial Black font for characters.

The next step is to enter the return address to the right of the name as described in the steps below.

TO SELECT AND REPLACE MORE PLACEHOLDER TEXT

Step 1: Click the placeholder text, Click here and type return address, to select it.

Step 2: Type 406 Hill Creek Road, Charlotte, NC 28215 as the address.

The address displays surrounded by a frame to the right of the name (Figure 2-46). The Professional Letter template framed the return address to provide flexibility in its location in the document. Notice the style of this text is Return Address in the Style box. The Return Address style uses 7-point Arial font for characters.

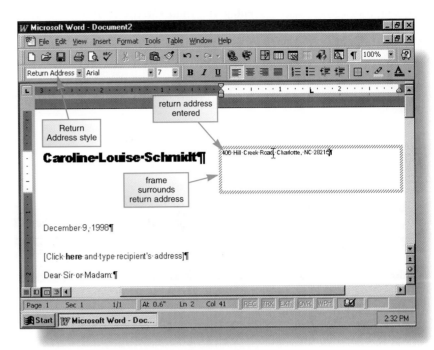

FIGURE 2-46

With the letterhead complete, the next step in personalizing the cover letter is to enter the recipient's address as described in the following steps.

TO SELECT AND REPLACE MORE PLACEHOLDER TEXT

Step 1: Click the placeholder text below the date, Click here and type recipient's address, to select it.

Step 2: Type Mr. Samuel Parker and then press the ENTER key.

Step 3: Type International Markson Press and then press the ENTER key.

Step 4: Type 102 Madison Avenue and then press the ENTER key.

Step 5: Type Chicago, IL 60606 as the city, state, and zip code.

The recipient's name, company, and address are entered (Figure 2-47). Notice the style is now Inside Address.

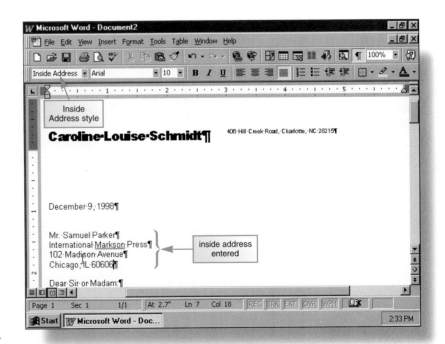

FIGURE 2-47

More *About* **the Inside Address**

Pay close attention to the spelling, punctuation, and official abbreviations of company names. For example, does the company name spell out the word and/or use the ampersand (&) character? Is the word Company spelled out?

Creating an AutoText Entry

If you use the same text frequently, you can store the text in an **AutoText entry** and then use the stored entry throughout this document, as well as future documents. That is, you need to type the entry only once, and for all future occurrences of the text, you access the stored entry as you need it. In this way, you avoid entering the text inconsistently or incorrectly in different places throughout the same document. Follow these steps to create an AutoText entry for the prospective employer's company name.

Steps **To Create an AutoText Entry**

1 **Drag through the text to be stored (International Markson Press, in this case). Be sure not to select the paragraph mark at the end of the text.**

Word highlights the company name, International Markson Press, in the inside address (Figure 2-48). Notice the paragraph mark is not part of the selection.

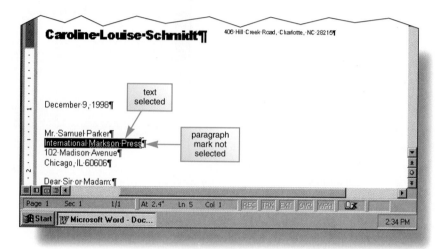

FIGURE 2-48

2 **Click Insert on the menu bar and then point to AutoText. Point to New on the AutoText submenu (Figure 2-49).**

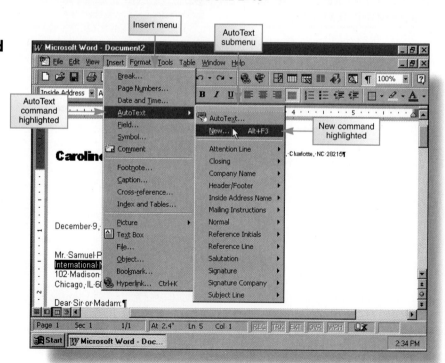

FIGURE 2-49

3 Click New on the AutoText submenu. When the Create AutoText dialog box displays, type `imp` and then point to the OK button.

Word displays the Create AutoText dialog box (Figure 2-50). In this dialog box, Word proposes a name for the AutoText entry, which usually is the first word(s) of the selection. In this case, the default AutoText entry's name is International. You change it to a shorter name, imp.

4 Click the OK button.

Word stores the entry, closes the AutoText dialog box, and returns to the document window.

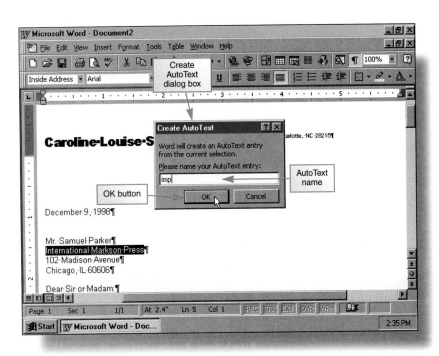

FIGURE 2-50

The name imp has been stored as an AutoText entry. Later in the project, you will use the AutoText entry (imp) instead of typing the company name (International Markson Press) again.

The next step is to enter the salutation as described in the steps below.

TO ENTER THE SALUTATION

Step 1: If necessary, scroll down to display the salutation.
Step 2: Drag through the text, Sir or Madam, in the salutation to select it.
Step 3: Type `Mr. Parker` as the recipient's name.

The salutation of the cover letter now displays as shown in Figure 2-51.

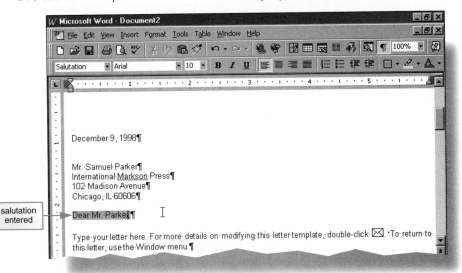

FIGURE 2-51

Saving the Cover Letter

Recall from Project 1 that it is prudent to save your work on disk at regular intervals. Because you have performed several tasks thus far, you should save your cover letter. For a detailed example of the procedure summarized below, refer to pages WD 1.25 through WD 1.27 in Project 1.

TO SAVE A DOCUMENT

Step 1: Insert your floppy disk into drive A.
Step 2: Click the Save button on the Standard toolbar.
Step 3: Type Schmidt Cover Letter in the File name text box. Do not press the ENTER key.
Step 4: Click the Save in box arrow and then click 3½ Floppy (A:).
Step 5: Click the Save button in the Save As dialog box.

Word saves the document on a floppy disk in drive A with the file name, Schmidt Cover Letter (Figure 2-52 below).

Applying Formatting Using Shortcut Keys

The next step is to type the message, or body, of the letter below the salutation. As you type paragraphs of text, you may want to format characters within the paragraph as you type them, instead of formatting them later. In Project 1, you typed all characters in the document and then selected the ones to be formatted and applied the desired formatting. In this section, you will use **shortcut keys** to format text as you type.

First, you will select the placeholder text below the salutation and then you will enter the text.

More *About* Formatting

Minimize strain on your wrist by switching between the mouse and keyboard as little as possible. If your fingers are already on the keyboard, then use shortcut keys on the keyboard to format text; if you fingers are already on the mouse, then use the mouse to format text.

Steps To Select a Paragraph

1 **If necessary, scroll down to display the body of the letter. Position the mouse pointer in the paragraph to be selected and then triple-click.**

Word selects the entire paragraph, which is placeholder text (Figure 2-52).

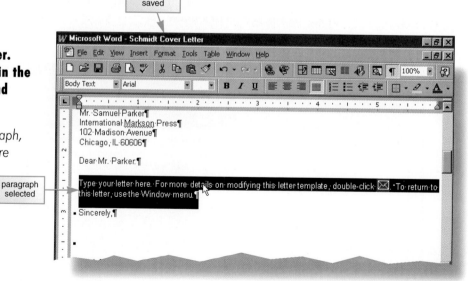

FIGURE 2-52

OtherWays
1. Double-click to left of paragraph to be selected

With the paragraph selected, you will begin typing the body of the letter. Recall that typing replaces selected text; thus, you do not have to delete the selected text. The following steps show how to format characters using the shortcut keys.

 Steps ## To Format Characters Using Shortcut Keys

1 **Type** I am interested in the computer textbook proofreading position you advertised in yesterday's edition of the **and then press the SPACEBAR. Press the CTRL+I keys.**

Word replaces the selection with the entered text (Figure 2-53). The next word to be typed is a newspaper name, which should be italicized. Because you pressed CTRL+I, the Italic button on the Formatting toolbar is recessed. When your fingers are on the keyboard, it sometimes is desirable to use a shortcut key to format text, instead of using the mouse to click a button.

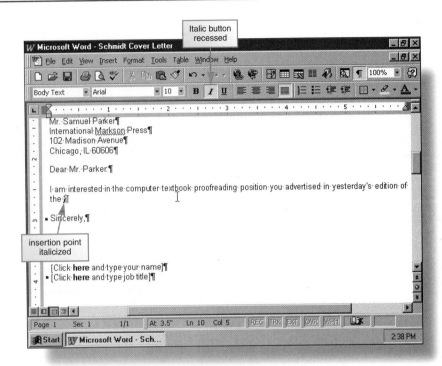

FIGURE 2-53

2 **Type** Charlotte News **and then press the CTRL+I keys. Type a period (.) and then press the SPACEBAR once.**

The newspaper name is entered in italics (Figure 2-54). The Italic button on the Formatting toolbar is no longer recessed. CTRL+I is a **toggle**; *that is, the shortcut key is used once to activate the button and used again to deactivate the button.*

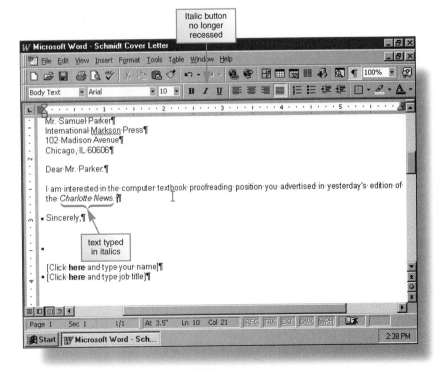

FIGURE 2-54

Many shortcut keys exist in Word for your convenience while typing. Table 2-3 lists the common shortcut keys used for formatting characters and their functions.

More *About* Shortcut Keys

To print a complete list of shortcut keys for formatting, click Help on the menu bar and then click Contents and Index, click the Index tab, type KEYS and then double-click shortcut keys. Click the Keys for formatting characters and paragraphs topic; right-click the Help window, click Print Topic on the shortcut menu, and then click the OK button.

Table 2-3	
FUNCTION	*SHORTCUT KEYS*
Bold	CTRL+B
Capitalize letters	CTRL+SHIFT+A
Decrease font size	CTRL+SHIFT+<
Decrease font size one point	CTRL+[
Double-underline	CTRL+SHIFT+D
Increase font size	CTRL+SHIFT+>
Increase font size one point	CTRL+]
Italicize	CTRL+I
Remove formatting (plain text)	CTRL+SPACEBAR
Small capitals	CTRL+SHIFT+K
Subscript	CTRL+=
Superscript	CTRL+SHIFT+PLUS SIGN
Underline	CTRL+U
Underline words, not spaces	CTRL+SHIFT+W

Inserting an AutoText Entry

At the end of the next sentence in the body of the cover letter, you want to put the company name, International Markson Press. Recall that earlier in this project, you stored an AutoText entry name of imp for International Markson Press. Thus, you will type the AutoText entry's name and then instruct Word to replace the AutoText entry's name with the stored entry of International Markson Press. Perform the following steps to insert an AutoText entry.

Steps **To Insert an AutoText Entry**

1 **Type** I have enclosed my resume highlighting my background and feel my accomplishments will be valuable to imp **as the beginning of the AutoText entry's name.**

The AutoText entry name displays (Figure 2-55).

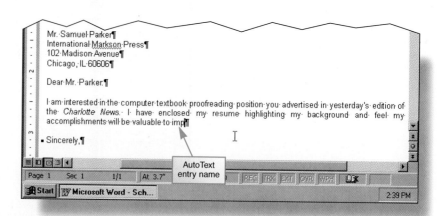

FIGURE 2-55

2 Press F3. Type a period (.) and then press the ENTER key.

Word replaces the characters, imp, in the cover letter with the stored AutoText entry, International Markson Press (Figure 2-56). Pressing F3 instructs Word to replace the AutoText entry name with the stored AutoText entry.

FIGURE 2-56

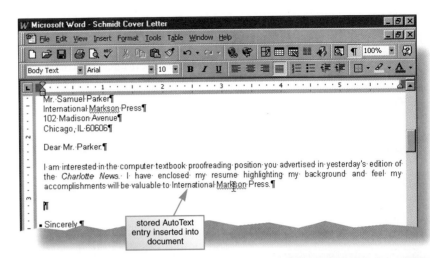

OtherWays

1. Type first few characters to display AutoComplete tip, press ENTER
2. On Insert menu point to AutoText, point to style linked to AutoText entry, click desired AutoText entry
3. On Insert menu point to AutoText, click AutoText, select desired AutoText entry name, click OK button

If you watch the screen as you type, you may discover that AutoComplete tips display on the screen. As you type, Word searches the list of AutoText entry names and if one matches your typing, Word displays its complete name above your typing as an **AutoComplete tip**. In addition to AutoText entries, Word proposes AutoComplete tips for the current date, a day of the week, a month, and so on. If your screen does not display AutoComplete tips, click Tools on the menu bar, click AutoCorrect, click the AutoText tab, click Show AutoComplete tip for AutoText and dates to select it, and then click the OK button. To view the complete list of entries, click Tools on the menu bar, click AutoCorrect, click the AutoText tab, and then scroll through the list of entries. To ignore an AutoComplete tip proposed by Word, simply continue typing to remove the AutoComplete tip from the screen.

Perform the following steps to enter the next paragraph into the cover letter.

TO ENTER A PARAGRAPH

Step 1: Type Through my part-time work at the university for the Information Systems Department and my volunteer work for the Tutoring Center, I have first-hand experience with both computers and proofreading.

Step 2: Press the SPACEBAR. Type As shown in the following table, I have obtained exceptional grades in writing and computer courses.

Step 3: Press the SPACEBAR. Type My course of study at North Carolina University has focused heavily on these skills.

The paragraph is entered (Figure 2-57).

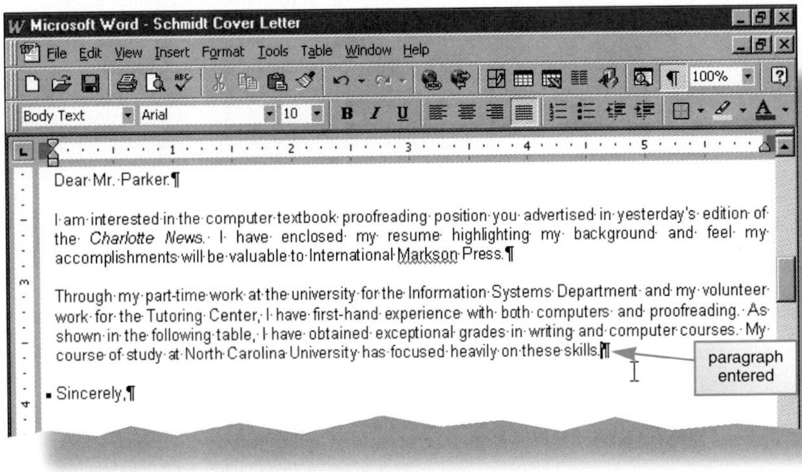

FIGURE 2-57

More *About*
Moving Text

When moving text a short distance, you should use the drag-and-drop technique. To move text a longer distance, like across multiple pages, use the cut-and-paste technique or print preview. In print preview, click the Magnifier button on the Print Preview toolbar and then drag and drop or cut and paste the text as you would in normal view.

Switching Two Sentences in the Resume

After proofreading the paragraph you just entered, you might realize that the second and third sentences in the paragraph would flow better if they were reversed. That is, you must move the second sentence so it is positioned at the end of the paragraph.

To move any items, such as sentences, you can **drag and drop** one of them or you can **cut and paste** one of them. Both techniques require that you first select the item to be moved. With **dragging and dropping**, you drag the selected item to its new location and then insert, or drop, it there. **Cutting** involves removing the selected item from the document and then placing it on the **Clipboard**, which is a temporary Windows storage area. **Pasting** is the process of copying an item from the Clipboard into the document at the location of the insertion point. When you paste text into a document, the contents of the Clipboard are not erased.

You should use the drag and drop technique to move an item a short distance. When you are moving between several pages or documents, however, the cut and paste technique is more efficient. Thus, use the drag and drop technique to switch the second and third sentences. To do this, you first must select the sentence to be moved as shown below.

Steps **To Select a Sentence**

1 **Position the mouse pointer (an I-beam) in the sentence to be moved. Press and hold the CTRL key. While holding the CTRL key, click the sentence. Release the CTRL key.**

Word selects the entire sentence (Figure 2-58). Notice the space after the period is included in the selection.

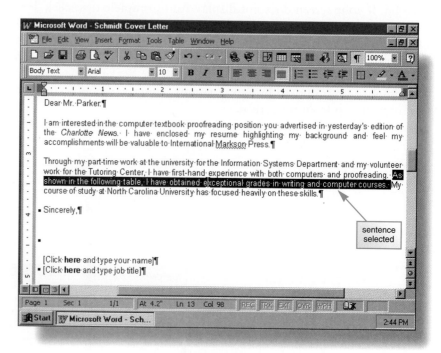

FIGURE 2-58

Throughout Projects 1 and 2, you have selected text and then formatted it. The text has ranged from characters to words to an entire document. Because selecting text is such a crucial function of Word, Table 2-4 summarizes the techniques used to select various forms of text with the mouse.

Table 2-4

ITEM TO SELECT	MOUSE ACTION
Block of text	Click at beginning of selection, scroll to end of selection, position mouse pointer at end of selection, hold down SHIFT key, then click
Character or Characters	Drag through character(s)
Document	Move mouse to left of paragraph until mouse pointer changes to a right-pointing arrow, then triple-click
Graphic	Click the graphic
Line	Move mouse to left of line until mouse pointer changes to a right-pointing arrow, then click
Lines	Move mouse to left of first line until mouse pointer changes to a right-pointing arrow, then drag up or down
Paragraph	Triple-click paragraph or move mouse to left of paragraph until mouse pointer changes to a right-pointing arrow, then double-click
Paragraphs	Move mouse to left of paragraph until mouse pointer changes direction, double-click, then drag
Sentence	Press and hold CTRL key, then click sentence
Word	Double-click the word
Words	Drag through words

With the sentence to be moved selected, you can drag and drop it as shown in the following steps.

 Steps To Drag and Drop Selected Text

1 **Move the mouse pointer into the selected text. Press and hold the mouse button.**

*When you begin to drag the selected text, the insertion point changes to a **dotted insertion point** and the mouse pointer has a small dotted box below it (Figure 2-59).*

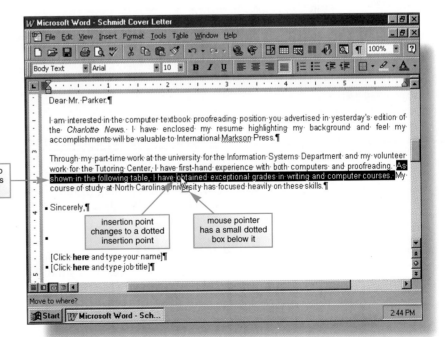

sentence to be moved is selected

insertion point changes to a dotted insertion point

mouse pointer has a small dotted box below it

FIGURE 2-59

2 **Drag the dotted insertion point to the location where the selected text is to be moved.**

The dotted insertion point is at the end of the paragraph (Figure 2-60).

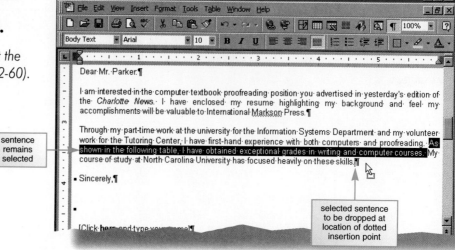

FIGURE 2-60

3 **Release the mouse button. Click outside the selection to remove the highlight.**

The selected text is moved to the location of the dotted insertion point in the document (Figure 2-61). The second and third sentences in the paragraph are switched.

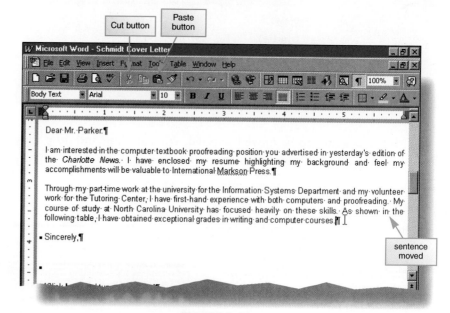

FIGURE 2-61

OtherWays

1. Click Cut button on Standard toolbar, position insertion point at location where text is to be pasted, click Paste button on Standard toolbar

2. On Edit menu click Cut, position insertion point at location where text is to be pasted, on Edit menu click Paste

3. Press CTRL+X, position insertion point at location where text is to be pasted, press CTRL+V

You can use the Undo button on the Standard toolbar if you accidentally drag and drop incorrectly or cut the wrong text.

You can use the drag and drop and cut and paste techniques to move any selected item. That is, you can move words, sentences, phrases, and graphics by selecting them and then dragging and dropping them or cutting and pasting them.

Using the TAB key

The next step is to create a small table to contain the GPAs you obtained. The table will contain two columns: one for a description and one for the GPA numbers. You want the GPA numbers to be aligned vertically; thus, you will use the TAB key to align the GPA numbers.

Word presets tab stops at every one-half inch. These preset, or **default**, tabs are indicated on the horizontal ruler by small **tick marks** (Figure 2-62). You want the first column of the table to begin at the 1.5-inch mark on the ruler and the second column to begin at the 3.5-inch mark. Instead of pressing the TAB key to move the insertion point from the 0-inch mark to the 1.5-inch mark, you will move the left margin inward to the 1.5-inch mark for this paragraph. Perform the following steps to increase the indent of the left margin.

More *About*
Aligning Text

You may be tempted to vertically-align text by pressing the SPACEBAR. The problem is that word processors use variable character fonts. Thus, when you use the SPACEBAR to vertically-align text, the column has a wavy look because each character does not begin at the same location.

Steps To Increase the Indent of the Left Margin

1 **Be sure the insertion point is at the end of the second paragraph in the body of the cover letter and then press the ENTER key. Point to the Increase Indent button on the Formatting toolbar.**

The insertion point is positioned at the 0-inch mark on the ruler (Figure 2-62).

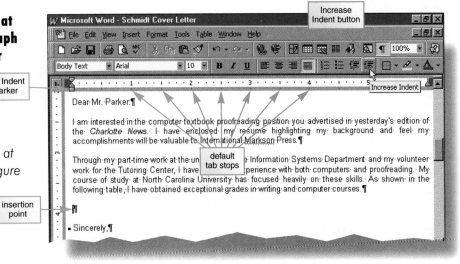

FIGURE 2-62

2 **Click the Increase Indent button three times.**

Word moves the Left Indent marker to the 1.5-inch mark on the ruler (Figure 2-63). That is, the Left Indent marker moves one-half inch to the right each time you click the Increase Indent button.

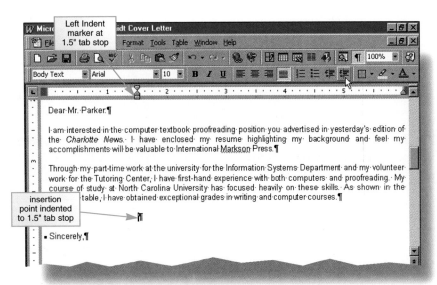

FIGURE 2-63

*Other***Ways**

1. Drag Left Indent marker to desired location on ruler

With the left margin set for the first column of the table, the next step is to enter the table text as shown in the steps on the next page.

Steps **To Align Information Vertically with the TAB Key**

1 **Type** GPA for Writing Courses **and then press the TAB key twice.**

*Word moves the insertion point two tab stops to the right (Figure 2-64). Thus, the GPA number will be entered at the 3.5-inch mark on the ruler. Notice the right-pointing arrows after the first column of text. A nonprinting character, the **right-pointing arrow**, displays each time you press the TAB key. Recall non-printing characters do not print; they only display in the document window*

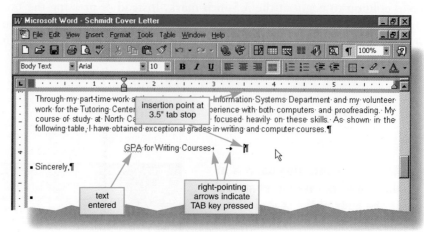

FIGURE 2-64

2 **Type** 4.0/4.0 **and then press the SHIFT+ENTER keys. Type** GPA for Computer Courses **and then press the TAB key. Type** 3.8/4.0 **and then press the SHIFT+ENTER keys.**

The first column of text is aligned at the 1.5-inch mark on the ruler, and the second column is aligned at the 3.5-inch mark (Figure 2-65).

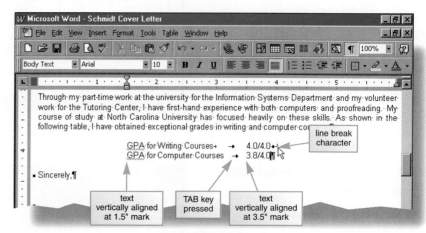

FIGURE 2-65

3 **Type** Overall GPA **and then press the TAB key three times. Type** 3.9/4.0 **as the last entry in the table.**

The table is complete (Figure 2-66).

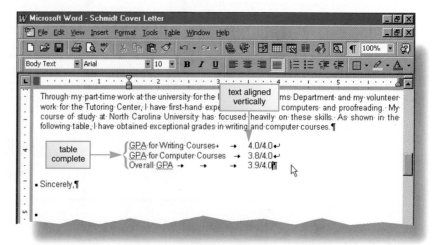

FIGURE 2-66

The next step is to enter the next paragraph in the cover letter. When you press the ENTER key to continue, however, the left margin will be indented 1.5 inches. Thus, you must reset the next paragraph to the left margin before you continue as shown in the following steps.

Steps To Decrease the Indent in a Paragraph

More *About*
Tab Stops

To set a custom tab, click the paragraph to contain the tab and then click the ruler at the desired tab stop location. To remove a custom tab stop, drag the tab stop marker down and out of the ruler.

1 **With the insertion point at the end of the table, press the ENTER key. Point to the Decrease Indent button on the Formatting toolbar.**

The insertion point is indented 1.5 inches from the left margin (Figure 2-67). Paragraph formatting is carried forward each time you press the ENTER key.

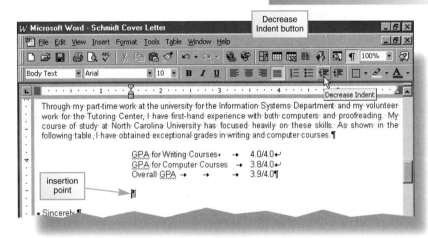

FIGURE 2-67

2 **Click the Decrease Indent button three times.**

Word positions the insertion point at the left margin.

3 **Type** Given my extensive course work and experience, I feel I could be a definite asset to your organization. I look forward to hearing from you to schedule an interview and to discuss my career opportunities with imp **and then press F3. Type a period.**

The paragraph is entered beginning at the left margin (Figure 2-68).

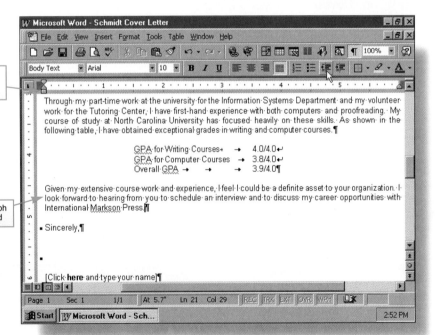

FIGURE 2-68

▶**Other**Ways

1. Drag Left Indent marker to desired location on ruler

The next step is to enter the signature block, which in this project contains just your name. Thus, you will delete the signature title line. Follow the steps on the next page to enter the signature block.

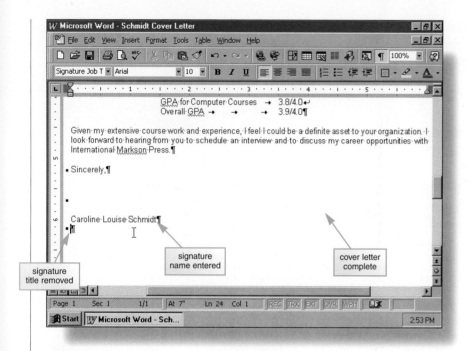

FIGURE 2-69

TO ENTER THE SIGNATURE BLOCK

Step 1: If necessary, scroll down to display the signature block.

Step 2: Click the first line of place-holder text in the signature block, Click here and type your name, to select it.

Step 3: Type `Caroline Louise Schmidt` as the name.

Step 4: Click the second line of place-holder text in the signature block, Click here and type job title, to select it.

Step 5: Right-click the selection to display a shortcut menu and then click Cut on the shortcut menu.

The signature block is entered (Figure 2-69).

More *About* Flagged Words

Recall that the commands in a shortcut menu differ depending on the object on which you right-click. If you select and then right-click a word, you can cut, copy, or paste it from the shortcut menu; however, if the selected word has a red wavy underline below it, you can only spell check it from the shortcut menu.

Checking Spelling at Once

As discussed in Project 1, Word checks your spelling and grammar as you type and places a wavy underline below possible spelling or grammar errors. You learned in Project 1 how to check these flagged words immediately. You also can wait and check the entire document for spelling or grammar errors at once.

The following steps illustrate how to spell check the Schmidt Cover Letter at once. Notice in the following example that the word, heavily, has been misspelled intentionally as heaviy to illustrate the use of Word's spell check at once feature. If you are doing this project on a personal computer, your cover letter may contain different misspelled words, depending on the accuracy of your typing.

Steps To Spell Check At Once

1 Press the CTRL+HOME keys to position the insertion point at the top of the document. Point to the Spelling and Grammar button on the Standard toolbar.

With the insertion point at line 1 and column 1, Word will begin the spelling and grammar check at the beginning of the document (Figure 2-70).

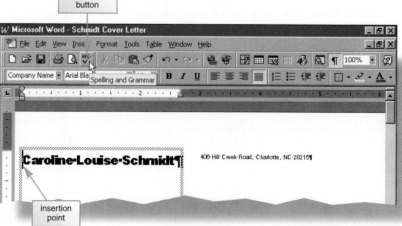

FIGURE 2-70

rrr1s1 1 111eeeeeeeeeeeeeeeeeeeeeeeeeeeeeeeeeeeeeeeeeeeeee

2 Click the Spelling and Grammar button.

Word displays the Spelling and Grammar: English (United States) dialog box (Figure 2-71). Word did not find Markson in its main dictionary because Markson is a company name. Markson is spelled correctly.

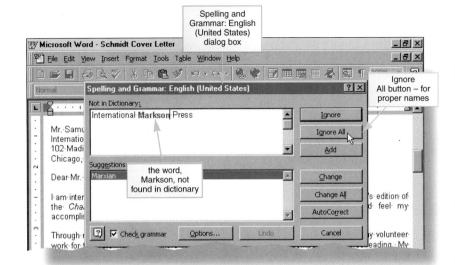

FIGURE 2-71

3 Click the Ignore All button.

The spelling and grammar check ignores all future occurrences of the word, Markson. Word continues the spelling and grammar check until it finds the next error or reaches the end of the document. The spelling and grammar check did not find the misspelled word, heaviy, in its main dictionary. The dialog box lists suggested corrections in the Suggestions list box, one of which you may select.

4 Click heavily in the list (Figure 2-72).

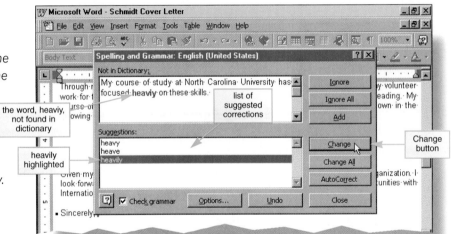

FIGURE 2-72

5 Click the Change button.

The spelling and grammar check changes the misspelled word (heaviy) to the selected word (heavily). Word continues to check spelling and grammar until it finds the next error or reaches the end of the document. Word did not find GPA in its main dictionary because it is an abbreviation (Figure 2-73).

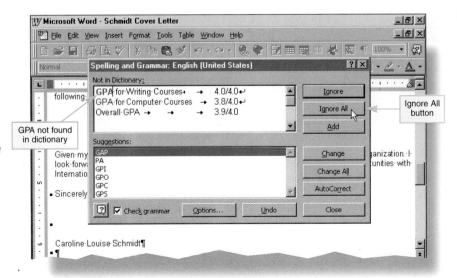

FIGURE 2-73

Click the Ignore All button.

Word continues to spell and grammar check until it finds the next error or reaches the end of the document. Word displays a message that is has checked the entire document (Figure 2-74).

 Click the OK button.

Word returns to your document. Your document no longer displays red and green wavy underlines below words and phrases. In addition, the red X on the Spelling and Grammar Status icon has returned to a red check mark.

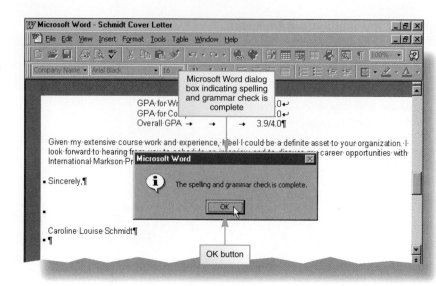

FIGURE 2-74

Saving Again and Printing the Cover Letter

The cover letter for the resume is now complete. Because you have performed several tasks since the last save, you should save the cover letter again by clicking the Save button on the Standard toolbar. Finally, you should print the cover letter by clicking the Print button on the Standard toolbar. When you remove the document from the printer, the printout displays the finished cover letter (Figure 2-75).

More *About*
Printing

Use a laser printer to print the resume and cover letter on standard letter-size white or ivory paper. Be sure to print a copy for yourself. And read it – especially before the interview. Most likely, the interviewer will have copies in hand, ready to ask you questions about the contents of both the resume and cover letter.

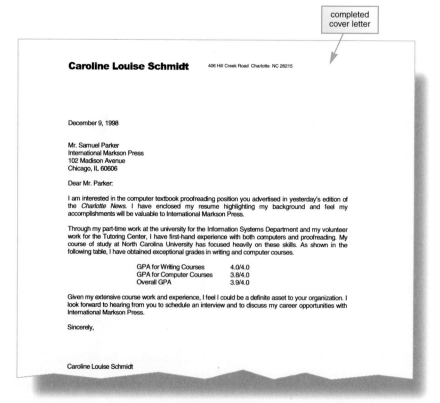

FIGURE 2-75

Working with Multiple Open Word Documents

You might realize at this time that you did not spell check the resume, or you might want to print another copy of the resume.

You currently have two documents open: the cover letter and the resume. Each is in a different document window. You can switch back and forth easily between the two documents. Perform the following steps to switch from the cover letter to the resume.

Steps **To Switch from One Open Word Document to Another**

1 **Click Window on the menu bar and then point to 1 Document1 – Resume: Caroline Louise Schmidt.**

Two Word documents currently are open: 1 Document1 – Resume: Caroline Louise Schmidt and 2 Schmidt Cover Letter (Figure 2-76). If you have closed and opened the resume during this project, the resume name will appear as 1 Schmidt Resume.

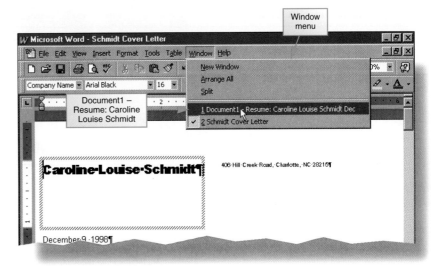

FIGURE 2-76

2 **Click 1 Document1 – Resume: Caroline Louise Schmidt.**

Word switches from the cover letter to the resume. The document window now displays the resume you created earlier in this project (Figure 2-77).

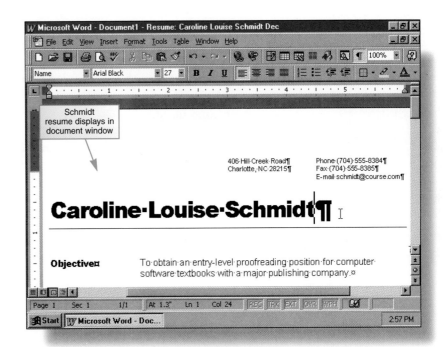

FIGURE 2-77

With the resume in the document window, you can spell and grammar check it, print it, or perform any other editing tasks you desire.

When you are finished with both documents, you may wish to close them. Instead of closing each one individually, you can close all open files at once as shown in these steps.

Steps **To Close All Open Word Documents**

1 **Press and hold the SHIFT key and then click File on the menu bar. Release the SHIFT key. Point to Close All on the File menu.**

Word displays the Close All command, instead of a Close command, on the File menu because you used the SHIFT key when clicking the menu name (Figure 2-78).

2 **Click Close All.**

Word closes all open documents and displays a blank document window. If at this point you wanted to begin a new document, you would click the New button on the Standard toolbar.

FIGURE 2-78

The final step in this project is to quit Word as described in the step below.

TO QUIT WORD

Step 1: Click the Close button in the Word window.

The Word window closes.

Project Summary

Project 2 introduced you to creating a cover letter and a resume using Word wizards and templates. You used the Resume Wizard to create a resume. Then, you used several formatting techniques to personalize the resume. You viewed and printed the resume in print preview. You used a letter template to create a cover letter and then personalized the cover letter. You created an AutoText entry, which you used when you personalized the cover letter. You learned how to move text using drag-and-drop editing. Finally, you learned how to switch between one open Word document to another and close multiple open Word documents.

What You Should Know

Having completed this project, you now should be able to perform the following tasks:

- Align Information Vertically with the TAB Key (WD 2.44)
- AutoFormat As You Type (WD 2.21)
- Close All Open Word Documents (WD 2.50)
- Create a Letter Using a Word Template (WD 2.29)
- Create a Resume Using Word's Resume Wizard (WD 2.7)
- Create an AutoText Entry (WD 2.34)
- Decrease the Indent in a Paragraph (WD 2.45)
- Display Nonprinting Characters (WD 2.15)
- Drag and Drop Selected Text (WD 2.41)
- Enter a Line Break (WD 2.19)
- Enter a Paragraph (WD 2.39)
- Enter the Remaining Sections of the Resume (WD 2.22)
- Enter the Salutation (WD 2.35)
- Enter the Signature Block (WD 2.46)
- Format Characters Using Shortcut Keys (WD 2.37)
- Increase the Indent of the Left Margin (WD 2.43)
- Increase the Font Size by One Point (WD 2.24)
- Insert a Blank Line above a Paragraph (WD 2.16)
- Insert an AutoText Entry (WD 2.38)
- Print Preview a Document (WD 2.25)
- Print the Resume Created by the Resume Wizard (WD 2.14)
- Quit Word (WD 2.50)
- Save a Document (WD 2.27, WD 2.36)
- Select a Paragraph (WD 2.36)
- Select a Sentence (WD 2.40)
- Select a Table and Format Its Characters (WD 2.23)
- Select and Replace Placeholder Text (WD 2.17, WD 2.32)
- Select and Replace Resume Wizard Supplied Text (WD 2.18)
- Spell and Grammar Check At Once (WD 2.46)
- Switch From One Open Word Document to Another (WD 2.49)
- Zoom a Document (WD 2.31)

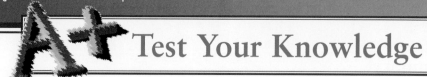

Test Your Knowledge

1 True/False

Instructions: Circle T if the statement is true or F if the statement is false.

T F 1. By asking you several basic questions, Word's templates prepare and format a document for you based on your responses.

T F 2. A cell is the intersection of a row and a column.

T F 3. Press the CTRL+B keys to insert a blank line above a paragraph.

T F 4. You can print a document from within print preview.

T F 5. Word provides three styles, or families, of wizards and templates: Gold, Silver, and Bronze.

T F 6. When you paste text into a document, the Clipboard contents are erased.

T F 7. The TAB key is used to align text vertically in a document.

T F 8. In Word, the default, or preset, tabs are spaced every inch on the ruler.

T F 9. To spell and grammar check at once, right-click the flagged word.

T F 10. To switch from one open Word document to another, click the Switch button on the Standard toolbar.

2 Multiple Choice

Instructions: Circle the correct response.

1. In the Style list box, style names followed by an underlined bold letter a (**a**) are called
_____.
   a. active styles
   b. inactive styles
   c. paragraph styles
   d. character styles

2. Press the _____ key(s) to create a line break.
   a. ENTER
   b. CTRL+ENTER
   c. SHIFT+ENTER
   d. ALT+ENTER

3. To increase the font size of selected text by one point, press the _____ keys.
   a. CTRL+]
   b. CTRL+>
   c. SHIFT+]
   d. SHIFT+>

4. In print preview, the Formatting toolbar _____.
   a. displays above the Print Preview toolbar
   b. displays below the Print Preview toolbar
   c. displays above the Formatting toolbar
   d. does not display

Test Your Knowledge

5. Which of the following is optional in a business letter?
   a. signature block   b. inside address   c. salutation   d. complimentary close
6. To insert an AutoText entry, press the _____ key(s) after you type the AutoText entry name.
   a. INSERT   b. ENTER   c. F3   d. CTRL+ENTER
7. To underline words, not spaces between words, press the _____ keys.
   a. CTRL+U
   b. CTRL+W
   c. CTRL+SHIFT+U
   d. CTRL+SHIFT+W
8. To select an entire paragraph, _____.
   a. double-click to the left of the paragraph
   b. triple-click the paragraph
   c. both a and b
   d. neither a nor b
9. When you press the TAB key, a _____ displays on the screen.
   a. raised dot
   b. paragraph mark
   c. right-pointing arrow
   d. letter T
10. To display the Close All command on the File menu, _____.
    a. double-click File on the menu bar
    b. right-click File on the menu bar
    c. press and hold the SHIFT key and then click File on the menu bar
    d. press and hold the ALT key and then click File on the menu bar

3 Understanding the Print Preview Toolbar

Instructions: In Figure 2-79, arrows point to several of the boxes and buttons on the Print Preview toolbar. In the spaces provided, briefly explain the purpose of each button or box.

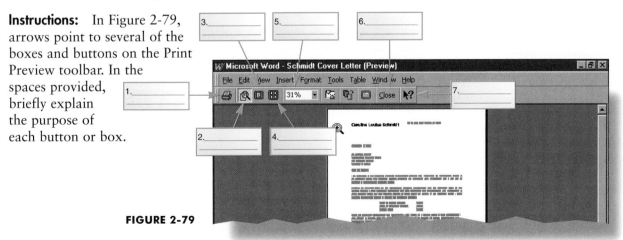

FIGURE 2-79

Test Your Knowledge

4 Understanding the Components of a Business Letter

Instructions: In Figure 2-80, arrows point to components a business letter. Identify the various elements of the letter in the spaces provided.

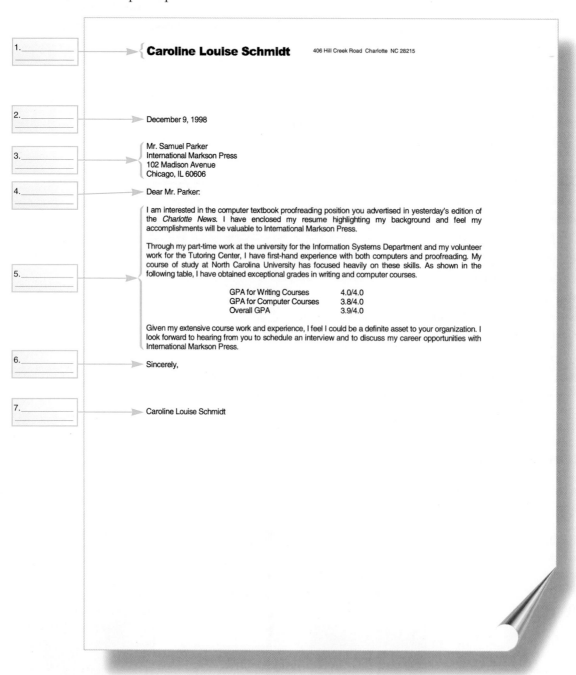

1. _____

Caroline Louise Schmidt   406 Hill Creek Road Charlotte NC 28215

2. _____

December 9, 1998

3. _____

Mr. Samuel Parker
International Markson Press
102 Madison Avenue
Chicago, IL 60606

4. _____

Dear Mr. Parker:

I am interested in the computer textbook proofreading position you advertised in yesterday's edition of the *Charlotte News*. I have enclosed my resume highlighting my background and feel my accomplishments will be valuable to International Markson Press.

Through my part-time work at the university for the Information Systems Department and my volunteer work for the Tutoring Center, I have first-hand experience with both computers and proofreading. My course of study at North Carolina University has focused heavily on these skills. As shown in the following table, I have obtained exceptional grades in writing and computer courses.

5. _____

GPA for Writing Courses	4.0/4.0
GPA for Computer Courses	3.8/4.0
Overall GPA	3.9/4.0

Given my extensive course work and experience, I feel I could be a definite asset to your organization. I look forward to hearing from you to schedule an interview and to discuss my career opportunities with International Markson Press.

6. _____

Sincerely,

7. _____

Caroline Louise Schmidt

FIGURE 2-80

? Use Help

1 Reviewing Project Activities

Instructions: Perform the following tasks using a computer.

1. Start Word. If the Office Assistant is on your screen, click it to display its balloon. If the Office Assistant is not on your screen, click the Office Assistant button on the Standard toolbar.
2. Type `templates and wizards` in the What would you like to do? text box. Click the Search button. Click the Quick ways to create letters, memos, and other documents link. Read the information. Use the shortcut menu or Options button to print the information.
3. Click the Help Topics button to display the Help Topics: Microsoft Word dialog box. Click the Contents tab. Double-click the Formatting book. Double-click the Formatting with Styles book. Double click the About styles topic. Read and print the information.
4. Click the Help Topics button. Click the Index tab. Type `AutoText` in the top box labeled 1 and then double-click the overview topic in the list box labeled 2. Double-click the Use shortcuts to insert frequently used text and graphics topic. Read and print the information.
5. Click the Help Topics button. Click the Find tab. Type `drag and drop` in the top box labeled 1 and then double-click the Move or copy text and graphics topic. Click the Move or copy text and graphics a short distance within a window link. Read and print the information.
6. Close any open Help dialog box or window by clicking its Close button. Close the Office Assistant.

2 Expanding on the Basics

Instructions: Use Word Help for a better understanding of the topics listed below. Answer the questions on your own paper or hand in the printed Help topic to your instructor.

1. In this project, you worked with a Word table in the resume. Use the Office Assistant to answer the following questions about Word tables.
    a. How do you create a simple Word table?
    b. How do you create a complex Word table?
    c. How to you convert existing text to a Word table?
2. In this project, you used print preview to view your document before printing it. Use the Contents tab in the Help Topics: Microsoft Word dialog box to answer the following questions about print preview.
    a. How do you edit text in print preview?
    b. In print preview, how can you prevent text from spilling onto a second page?
3. In this project, you used shortcut keys to format characters and paragraphs. Use the Index tab in the Help Topics: Microsoft Word dialog box to locate Help windows describing the keys used for the following tasks: editing and moving text and graphics, formatting characters and paragraphs, printing and previewing documents, and working with documents. Print each of the four Help topics.

(continued)

Use Help

Expanding on the Basics *(continued)*

4. In this project, you used the Professional Letter template to create the cover letter. Use the Find tab in the Help Topics: Microsoft Word dialog box to determine how to create a letter using the Letter Wizard, which is a command on a menu. Then, determine how to modify a letter created with the Letter Wizard.

5. Use the Microsoft on the Web command on the Help menu to connect to Microsoft's Free Stuff page on the Web. Print the pages associated with free items you may download that work with Word.

Apply Your Knowledge

1 Enhancing a Document

Instructions: Start Word. Open the document, apply-2, from the Word folder on the Data Disk that accompanies this book. The document, shown in Figure 2-81, is a cover letter for a resume. You are to switch two sentences and insert a table to the letter.

Jamie K. Rivers 101 Cedar Road, New Lenox, IL 60451

September 10, 1998

Ms. Karen Edwards
Tiger Photo Labs
100 Western Avenue
Chicago, IL 60605

Dear Ms. Edwards:

sentences to be switched

I am interested in the management trainee position you advertised in last Sunday's edition of the *Suburb Herald*. I have enclosed my resume highlighting my background and feel my accomplishments will be valuable to Tiger Photo Labs.

Many of the courses I have taken at Illinois State University are directly related to business and management. Through my part-time work at Rally Photo, I am extremely familiar with the film developing process and photography equipment. The following table summarizes my course work.

location for table to be inserted

Given my extensive course work and experience at Rally Photo, I feel I could be a definite asset to your organization. I look forward to hearing from you to schedule an interview and to discuss my career opportunities with Tiger Photo Labs.

Sincerely,

Jamie K. Rivers

FIGURE 2-81

Apply Your Knowledge

Perform the following tasks:

1. Position the mouse pointer in the sentence that begins, Through my part-time work at Rally ...
2. Press and hold the CTRL key while clicking the sentence. Release the CTRL key.
3. With the mouse pointer in the selected sentence, press and hold down the left mouse button. Drag the insertion point to the left of the M in the sentence beginning, Many of the courses I have taken, ... and then release the mouse button.
4. Position the insertion point at the end of the second paragraph and then press the ENTER key.
5. Click the Increase Indent button on the Formatting toolbar to move the Left Indent marker to the 0.5-inch mark on the ruler.
6. Click the Align Left button on the Formatting toolbar to left align the paragraphs in the table.
7. Type Business: and then press the TAB key. Type Accounting, Business Law, Finance, Marketing, Retailing, Sales and then press the SHIFT+ENTER keys.
8. Type Management: and then press the TAB key. Type Auditing, Forecasting, Information Systems, Investments, Operations as the end of the table.
9. Click File on the menu bar and then click Save As. Use the file name, Revised Rivers Letter, and then save the document on your floppy disk.
10. Click the Print Preview button on the Standard toolbar. Print the revised document in print preview.

In the Lab

1 Using Word's Resume Wizard to Create a Resume

Problem: You are a student at Wisconsin University expecting to receive your Bachelor of Science degree in Business Management this May. As the semester end is approaching quickly, you are beginning a search for full-time employment upon graduation. You prepare the resume shown in Figure 2-82 using Word's Resume Wizard.

Instructions:

1. Use the Resume Wizard to create a resume. Use the name and address information in Figure 2-82 when the Resume Wizard requests it.
2. Personalize the resume as shown in Figure 2-82. When entering multiple lines in the Awards received, Software experience, Interests and activities, and Hobbies sections, be sure to enter a line break at the end of each line, instead of a paragraph break. Add an extra blank line above the name at the top of the resume. Increase the font size of the text as indicated in Figure 2-82.
3. Check the spelling of the resume.
4. Save the resume on a floppy disk with Peterson Resume as the file name.
5. Print the resume from within print preview.

(continued)

In the Lab

Using Word's Resume Wizard to Create a Resume *(continued)*

8 point
for personal
information

54 Seventh Place	Phone (608) 555-1355
Monroe, WI 53566	Fax (608) 555-4436
	E-mail peterson@course.com

Mark Allan Peterson

11 point

Objective	To obtain an entry-level accountant position.
Education	1994 - 1998 Wisconsin University Madison, WI
	Business/Accounting
	▪ B.S. in Business Management, May 1998
	▪ A.S. in Business Practices, May 1996
Awards received	1st Place – 1998 Entrepreneur Society Challenge
	1998 Outstanding Senior
	1997 Top Student Award, Small Business Association
Relevant course work	Financial Accounting I and II, Intermediate Accounting, Cost Accounting, Tax Accounting, Auditing, Federal Income Taxes, Managerial Statistics, Management Information Systems
Work experience	1996 - 1998 West Accounting Services Madison, WI
	Accounting Assistant
	▪ Assist CPAs in tax preparation activities for individuals, small businesses, and large companies.
	▪ Post journal entries, prepare balance sheets and income statements, balance checkbook registers, generate payroll, pay bills for small businesses.
Software experience	Accounting: Quicken, Money
	Word Processing: Word, WordPerfect
	Spreadsheet: Excel, Quattro Pro
	Database: Access
	Other: PowerPoint, Internet Explorer
Interests and activities	Accounting Club, Treasurer, 1996-1998
	Student Government Association, President, 1997-1998
Hobbies	Surfing the Internet
	Hiking
	Antique Cars

FIGURE 2-82

In the Lab

2 Using the Letter Template to Create a Cover Letter

Problem: You have just prepared the resume shown in Figure 2-82 and now are ready to create a cover letter to send to a prospective employer. In yesterday's edition of the *Wisconsin Herald*, you noticed an advertisement for an entry-level accounting position at Lakeway Accounting. You prepare the cover letter shown in Figure 2-83 to send with your resume.

Instructions:

1. Create a professional style letter by clicking the Professional Letter icon on the Letters & Faxes sheet in the New dialog box.
2. Save the letter on a floppy disk with Peterson Cover Letter as the file name.
3. Enter the letterhead so it looks like the letterhead shown in Figure 2-83. Enter the inside address and then the salutation.
4. Create an AutoText entry for Lakeway Accounting that displays in the inside address.
5. Personalize the body of the cover letter so it matches Figure 2-83. Use the AutoText entry you created in Step 5 whenever you have to enter the company name, Lakeway Accounting. The first column of the table is indented 1.5-inches from the left margin, and the second column is positioned at the 3.5-inch mark on the ruler.
6. Enter the signature block as shown in Figure 2-83.
7. Check the spelling of the cover letter. Save the cover letter again with the same file name.
8. Print the cover letter.

Mark Allan Peterson   54 Seventh Place, Monroe, WI 53566

March 30, 1998

Ms. Rita Kramer
Lakeway Accounting
50 Randolph Street
Chicago, IL 60606

Dear Ms. Kramer:

I am interested in the entry-level accounting position you advertised in yesterday's edition of the *Wisconsin Herald*. I have enclosed my resume highlighting my background and feel my accomplishments will be valuable to Lakeway Accounting.

As a part-time employee at West Accounting Services and with my school club activities, I have first-hand experience with accounting practices. My course of study at Wisconsin University has focused heavily on accounting. As shown in the following table, I have obtained exceptional grades in my courses:

GPA for major courses	3.9/4.0
GPA for non-major courses	3.7/4.0
Total Accumulated GPA	3.8/4.0

With my extensive course work and experience, I feel I can be an asset to your organization. I look forward to hearing from you to schedule an interview and to discuss my career opportunities with Lakeway Accounting.

Sincerely,

Mark Allan Peterson

FIGURE 2-83

In the Lab

3 Using Word's Wizards to Compose a Cover Letter and Resume

Problem: You are looking for a new job and need to prepare a resume and cover letter.

Instructions: Obtain a copy of last Sunday's newspaper. Look through the classified section and cut out a want ad in an area of interest to you. Assume you are in the market for the position being advertised. Use the Resume Wizard to create a resume. Use the Letter Wizard to create the cover letter. Display the Letter Wizard by clicking Tools on the menu bar and then clicking Letter Wizard. You may need to refer to your Use Help 2 responses for assistance in using the Letter Wizard. Use the want ad for the inside address and your personal information for the return address. Try to be as accurate as possible when personalizing the resume and cover letter. Turn in the want ad with your cover letter and resume.

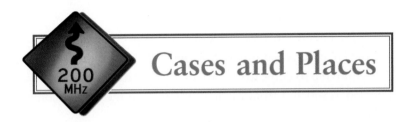

Cases and Places

The difficulty of these case studies varies: ▶ are the least difficult; ▶▶ are more difficult; and ▶▶▶ are the most difficult.

1 ▶ To keep on schedule, you post a large calendar for the current month on your door or wall. As the end of this month approaches, you begin preparation for next month's calendar. Next month is your birthday! Use the Calendar Wizard, together with the concepts and techniques presented in this project, to create a calendar for your birthday month (the calendar should have a clip art graphic on it). Be sure to delete the default graphic and insert an appropriate clip art file for your birthday month. If the Calendar Wizard is not installed on your system, click Help on the menu bar, point to Microsoft on the Web, click Free Stuff, and then follow the instructions to download more wizards from the Web.

2 ▶ You have just completed Word Project 2. Congratulations! Your instructor decides to present you with an award. You are the recipient of the award; your instructor will sign the award; the award is a Certificate of Completion presented by your school; and the accomplishment is Completing Word Project 2. Use today's date. Use the Award Wizard, together with the concepts and techniques presented in this project to create the Certificate of Completion. If the Award Wizard is not installed on your system, click Help on the menu bar, point to Microsoft on the Web, click Free Stuff, and then follow the instructions to download more wizards from the Web.

Cases and Places

3 ▶▶ As book reviewer for Jameson Publishers, you have just reviewed the word processing chapter in a computer concepts book. Your review is five pages long. It must be faxed to E. P. Harding at Jameson Publishers (145 Western Avenue, Hammond, IN 46323; telephone 219-555-2063; fax 219-555-2064), with a copy faxed to B. T. Andrews at the same number. In the fax, write a message informing E. P. Harding that your review of the word processing chapter is attached and if she has any questions, she can contact you. Use your own name, address, and telephone information in the fax. Use the Fax Wizard, together with the concepts and techniques presented in this project, to create and format a cover sheet for the facsimile transmission.

4 ▶▶ David Brandy, your boss at Grover Electric, has just received last month's telephone bill. He is extremely concerned about the increasing number of personal long-distance calls being made by company employees. Mr. Brandy does not mind an occasional telephone call home, but conversations ranging from 20 minutes to more than an hour are unacceptable. Not only does it take the employees away from their job duties, but also it is costing the company hundreds of dollars each month. Mr. Brandy has asked you to prepare a confidential memorandum regarding this matter for Sara Reynolds, a department head. The memorandum should explain the problem and solicit solutions. Copies of the memo also should be sent to Julie Adams and Ed West, the other department heads. Use the Memo Wizard, together with the concepts and techniques presented in this project, to create and format the interoffice memorandum.

5 ▶▶ Your credit report is maintained by one or more credit bureaus or credit reporting agencies. Obtain the name, address, and telephone number of a credit bureau that maintains your information. Find out how much they charge for a copy of a credit report. Using Word's Letter Wizard, prepare a credit report request. Apply the concepts and techniques presented in this project to personalize the credit report request.

6 ▶▶▶ Many organizations distribute brochures to promote their products and/or services. Brochures present prospective customers with more information than posted or published advertisements, as well as provide written material they can take with them and review at their leisure. Visit a local company and learn as much as you can about their product(s) and/or service(s). Find out how the product(s) and/or service(s) is unique, what features it offers, and why it would be valuable to potential buyers. Then, use Word's Newsletter Wizard, along with the concepts and techniques presented in this project, to design a newsletter advertising the product(s) and/or service(s). When the newsletter is complete, take it to the company and ask for its comments, suggestions, or recommendations.

Cases and Places

7 ▶▶▶ Everyone, at one time or another, has attended a meeting that was so disorganized that very little was accomplished. Meetings often can be more effective with an agenda, which is a written plan that states when and where the meeting will take place, the subject of the meeting, the participants and their responsibilities, and the topics that will be discussed. An agenda helps the chairperson keep a meeting on track and helps attendees prepare for the meeting. Find out about an upcoming meeting at your school, such as a club or student government meeting. Use Word's Agenda Wizard, and the concepts and techniques presented in this project, to prepare a thorough agenda for the meeting. Distribute the agenda to the relevant participants, and then attend the meeting to see if the agenda helps the meeting run more efficiently. If the Agenda Wizard is not installed on your system, click Help on the menu bar, point to Microsoft on the Web, click Free Stuff, and then follow the instructions to download more wizards from the Web.

Microsoft Word *97*

Creating a Research Paper with a Table

Objectives:

You will have mastered the material in this project when you can:

▶ Describe the MLA documentation style for research papers

▶ Change the margin settings in a document

▶ Adjust line spacing in a document

▶ Use a header to number pages of a document

▶ Indent paragraphs

▶ Use Word's AutoCorrect feature

▶ Add a footnote to a research paper

▶ Insert a Word table into a document

▶ Enter data into a Word table

▶ Format a Word table

▶ Insert a manual page break

▶ Create a hanging indent

▶ Create a text hyperlink

▶ Sort selected paragraphs

▶ Scroll by a page

▶ Find and replace text

▶ Use Word's thesaurus

▶ Display the number of words in a document

▶ Display the Web site associated with a hyperlink

Project 3

Researching, Writing, and Referencing

Citing Sources in Style

Throughout your collegiate career, adhering to one or more styles from a number of established guidelines, you will write research papers and other reports on a diversity of topics covered in your courses of study. After you have researched your subjects, found your reference materials, and written your essays, the crucial step of documenting these resources remains. The citation procedure may seem tedious, but it is the way your readers know how to find additional information on the subjects and the way you ethically give credit to the individuals who have researched these topics before you.

Depending on the course you are taking and the type of document that is assigned, your method of presenting these sources will vary. In academia, three major style systems for writers of research and scientific papers generally are recognized. Your instructors likely will direct you to the required style

Smith 1

Joe Smith

Professor J. Brown

History 421

December 1, 1998

The Copernican Revolution

In the sixteenth century, scientific thought on
ny was dominated by the ideas of the
such as Aristotle and Ptolemy. For
nicus, his ideas on a sun-centered system
challenged the popular belief and brought

MLA Handbook
for Writers of
Research Papers

Bibliog

citation

quotes

and appropriate handbooks as assignments are given. The research paper you are to create in this project with Microsoft Word 97 uses the Modern Language Association (MLA) style, which is used by scholars in the humanities fields. Another popular citation style developed by the American Psychological Association (APA) is used by researchers in the social sciences. The third style is the number system used by writers in the applied sciences.

These writers consult standard style manuals that describe, in detail, how to acknowledge reference sources in the body of the paper and in a general list at the end of the report. The MLA style is explained in the *MLA Handbook for Writers of Research Papers*, and the APA style is documented in the *Publication Manual of the American Psychological Association*. The researchers also consult other style guides, such as the University of Chicago's *The Chicago Manual of Style*, the *American Chemical Society Handbook for Authors*, and *The Microsoft Manual of Style for Technical Publications*.

Teams of instructors and scholars develop the style guidelines in each of these publications. The *MLA Handbook,* for example, originated in 1951 for MLA members. In 1977, it was expanded to become a guide for undergraduate students and renamed the *MLA Handbook for Writers of Research Papers*. Subsequent editions were published in 1984, 1988, and 1995. Keeping up with necessary revisions, however, is a never-ending task, especially with the evolution of online references on the Internet. Researchers are challenged continually to keep methods of style and citation accurate and current.

Until scholars agree on a universal style of documentation, you can familiarize yourself with the numerous citation systems and style guides available. Writers of virtually all types of commentary find the guides essential in preparation of essays, research papers, reports, and manuscripts of every kind. Attention to style and detail is evident in the finished product and just may make the difference in an excellent grade.

Raymond Chandler, U.S. author, stated in his 1947 *Letter*, "The most durable thing in writing is style, and style is the most valuable investment a writer can make with his time . . . the writer who puts his individual mark on the way he writes will always pay off."

Project 3

Microsoft
Word 97

Creating a Research Paper with a Table

Case Perspective

Anna L. Porter is a full-time student at Michigan State University, majoring in Information Systems and Computer Programming. The professor in one of her computer classes, CIS 201, has assigned a 500-word research paper. The paper must discuss some aspect of personal computers. Because Anna's computer at home recently was infected with a computer virus, Anna decides to write the research paper on computer viruses. The paper must be written according to the MLA documentation style, which specifies guidelines for report preparation. Professor Brown suggests students use the Internet to obtain the MLA guidelines. The paper also must contain one footnote, a table, and three references – one of which must be from the World Wide Web.

Anna will visit a library, surf the Internet, stop by a computer store, and interview the director of the Information Systems department at her school for information on computer viruses. She also plans to surf the Internet to obtain information and the guidelines for the MLA style of documentation.

Introduction

In both the academic and business environments, you will be asked to write reports. Business reports range from proposals to cost justifications to five-year plans to research findings. Academic reports focus mostly on research findings. Whether you are writing a business report or an academic report, you should follow a standard style when preparing it.

Many different styles of documentation exist for report preparation, depending on the nature of the report. Each style requires the same basic information; the differences among styles appear in the manner of presenting the information. For example, one documentation style may use the term *bibliography*, whereas another uses *references*, and yet a third prefers *works cited*. The **Modern Language Association (MLA)** presents a popular documentation style used today for research papers. Thus, this project uses the **MLA style of documentation**.

Project Three – Research Paper with a Table

Project 3 illustrates the creation of a short research paper describing computer viruses. A table at the end of the research paper outlines techniques for virus protection and system backup. As depicted in Figure 3-1, the paper follows the MLA style of documentation. The first two pages present the research paper and the third page lists the works cited alphabetically.

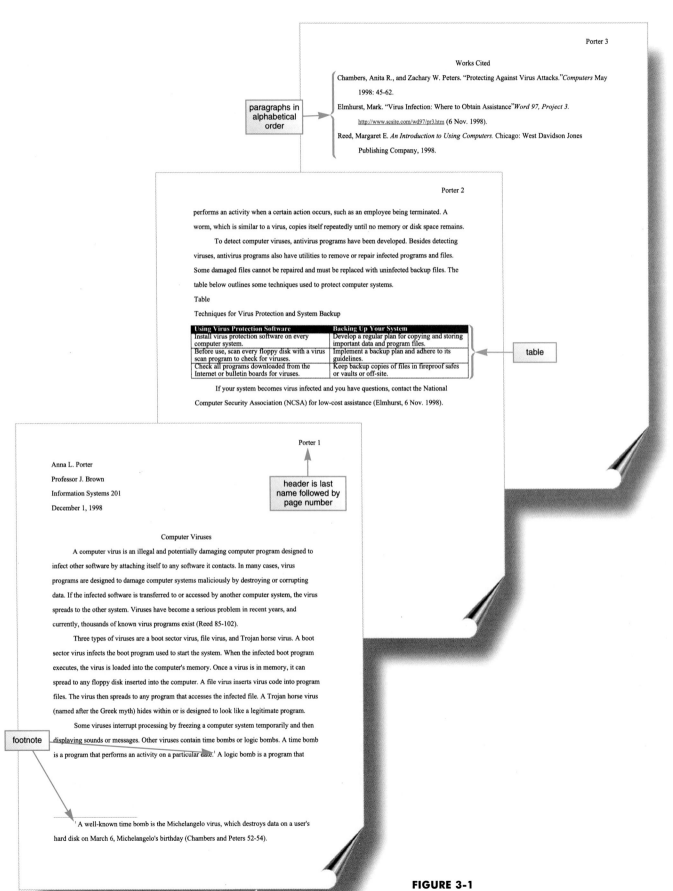

Porter 3

Works Cited

Chambers, Anita R., and Zachary W. Peters. "Protecting Against Virus Attacks." *Computers* May
        1998: 45-62.

Elmhurst, Mark. "Virus Infection: Where to Obtain Assistance" *Word 97, Project 3.*
        http://www.scsite.com/wd97/pr3.htm (6 Nov. 1998).

Reed, Margaret E. *An Introduction to Using Computers.* Chicago: West Davidson Jones
        Publishing Company, 1998.

paragraphs in alphabetical order

Porter 2

performs an activity when a certain action occurs, such as an employee being terminated. A
worm, which is similar to a virus, copies itself repeatedly until no memory or disk space remains.

To detect computer viruses, antivirus programs have been developed. Besides detecting
viruses, antivirus programs also have utilities to remove or repair infected programs and files.
Some damaged files cannot be repaired and must be replaced with uninfected backup files. The
table below outlines some techniques used to protect computer systems.

Table

Techniques for Virus Protection and System Backup

Using Virus Protection Software	Backing Up Your System
Install virus protection software on every computer system.	Develop a regular plan for copying and storing important data and program files.
Before use, scan every floppy disk with a virus scan program to check for viruses.	Implement a backup plan and adhere to its guidelines.
Check all programs downloaded from the Internet or bulletin boards for viruses.	Keep backup copies of files in fireproof safes or vaults or off-site.

table

If your system becomes virus infected and you have questions, contact the National
Computer Security Association (NCSA) for low-cost assistance (Elmhurst, 6 Nov. 1998).

Porter 1

Anna L. Porter

Professor J. Brown

Information Systems 201

December 1, 1998

header is last name followed by page number

Computer Viruses

A computer virus is an illegal and potentially damaging computer program designed to
infect other software by attaching itself to any software it contacts. In many cases, virus
programs are designed to damage computer systems maliciously by destroying or corrupting
data. If the infected software is transferred to or accessed by another computer system, the virus
spreads to the other system. Viruses have become a serious problem in recent years, and
currently, thousands of known virus programs exist (Reed 85-102).

Three types of viruses are a boot sector virus, file virus, and Trojan horse virus. A boot
sector virus infects the boot program used to start the system. When the infected boot program
executes, the virus is loaded into the computer's memory. Once a virus is in memory, it can
spread to any floppy disk inserted into the computer. A file virus inserts virus code into program
files. The virus then spreads to any program that accesses the infected file. A Trojan horse virus
(named after the Greek myth) hides within or is designed to look like a legitimate program.

Some viruses interrupt processing by freezing a computer system temporarily and then
displaying sounds or messages. Other viruses contain time bombs or logic bombs. A time bomb
is a program that performs an activity on a particular date. A logic bomb is a program that

footnote

A well-known time bomb is the Michelangelo virus, which destroys data on a user's
hard disk on March 6, Michelangelo's birthday (Chambers and Peters 52-54).

FIGURE 3-1

More *About* **Documentation Styles**

Another popular documentation style is by the American Psychological Association (APA). The MLA style is the standard in the humanities, whereas the APA style is preferred in the social sciences. Many differences exist between the two styles. For example, the APA style uses the term References for the bibliography.

MLA Documentation Style

When writing papers, you must be sure to adhere to some form of documentation style. The research paper in this project follows the guidelines presented by the MLA. To follow the MLA style, double-space all pages of the paper with one-inch top, bottom, left, and right margins. Indent the first word of each paragraph one-half inch from the left margin. At the right margin of each page, place a page number one-half inch from the top margin. On each page, precede the page number by your last name.

The MLA style does not require a title page; instead, it requires you to place your name and course information in a block at the left margin beginning one inch from the top of the page. Center the title two double-spaces below your name and course information. In the body of the paper, place author references in parentheses with the page number(s) where the referenced information is located. These in-text **parenthetical citations** are used instead of footnoting each source at the bottom of the page or at the end of the paper. In the MLA style, **footnotes** are used only for explanatory notes. In the body of the paper, use **superscripts** (raised numbers) to signal that an explanatory note exists.

According to the MLA style, explanatory notes are optional. **Explanatory notes** are used to elaborate on points discussed in the body of the paper. Explanatory notes may be placed either at the bottom of the page as footnotes or at the end of the paper as endnotes. Double-space the explanatory notes. Superscript each note's reference number, and indent it one-half inch from the left margin. Place one space following the note number before beginning the note text. At the end of the note text, you may list bibliographic information for further reference.

The MLA style uses the term **works cited** for the bibliographical references. The works cited page alphabetically lists works that are directly referenced in the paper by each author's last name. Place the works cited on a separate numbered page. Center the title, Works Cited, one inch from the top margin. Double-space all lines. Begin the first line of each work cited at the left margin; indent subsequent lines of the same work one-half inch from the left margin.

Document Preparation Steps

Document preparation steps give you an overview of how the research paper in Figure 3-1 will be developed. The following tasks will be completed in this project:

1. Start Word.
2. Change the margin settings for the document.
3. Adjust the line spacing for the document.
4. Create a header to number pages.
5. Change the font size to 12.
6. Enter your name and course information.
7. Center the paper title.
8. Save the research paper.
9. First-line indent paragraphs in the paper.
10. Enter the research paper with footnotes and a table.
11. Insert a manual page break.
12. Enter the works cited page.
13. Sort the paragraphs on the works cited page.
14. Save the document again.

More *About* **Paper Topics**

When you are assigned a research paper, you should be sure to select a topic that really interests you, as well as presents a thought that will appeal to your audience. To research your topic, use the following sources: library catalog, the Internet, periodical indexes, computer databases, magazines and journals, and books.

15. Use Word's thesaurus.
16. Check the number of words in the document.
17. Print the research paper.
18. Visit the Web site associated with a hyperlink in the document.
19. Quit Word.

The following pages contain a detailed explanation of each of these tasks.

Starting Word

Follow these steps to start Word or ask your instructor how to start Word for your system.

TO START WORD

Step 1: Click the Start button on the taskbar.
Step 2: Click New Office Document on the Start menu. If necessary, click the General tab when the New dialog box first opens.
Step 3: Double-click the Blank Document icon on the General sheet.
Step 4: If the Word screen is not maximized, double-click its title bar to maximize it.

Office starts Word. After a few moments, an empty document titled Document1 displays on the Word screen.

Displaying Nonprinting Characters

As discussed in the previous projects, it is helpful to display **nonprinting characters** that indicate where in the document you pressed the ENTER key, SPACEBAR, or TAB key. Follow this step to display nonprinting characters.

TO DISPLAY NONPRINTING CHARACTERS

Step 1: If the Show/Hide ¶ button on the Standard toolbar is not already recessed, click it.

Word displays nonprinting characters in the document window, and the Show/Hide ¶ button on the Standard toolbar is recessed (Figure 3-2 on the next page).

Changing the Margins

Word is preset to use standard 8.5-by-11-inch paper, with 1.25-inch left and right margins and 1-inch top and bottom margins. These margin settings affect every paragraph in the document. Often, you may want to change these default margin settings. For example, the MLA documentation style requires one-inch top, bottom, left, and right margins throughout the paper. The steps on the next page illustrate how to change the default margin settings for a document when your screen is in normal view.

More *About*
Changing Margins

In page layout view, you can change the margins using the ruler. The current margins are shaded in gray, and the margin boundary is positioned where the gray meets the white. You drag the margin boundary to change the margin. Hold down the ALT key while dragging the margin boundary to display the margin settings.

Steps To Change the Default Margin Settings

1 **Click File on the menu bar and then point to Page Setup (Figure 3-2).**

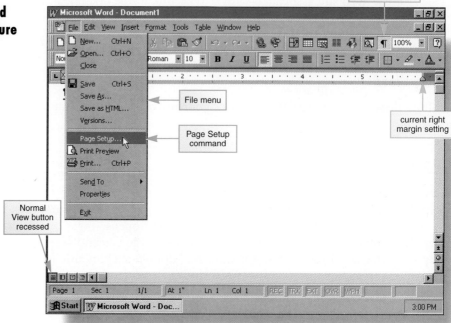

FIGURE 3-2

2 **Click Page Setup. If necessary, click the Margins tab when the Page Setup dialog box first opens.**

Word displays the Page Setup dialog box (Figure 3-3). Word lists the current margin settings in the respective text boxes and displays the settings graphically in the Preview area of the dialog box.

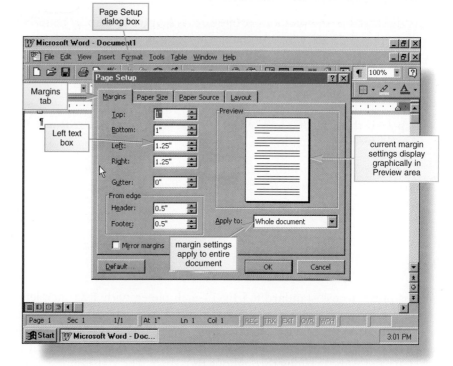

FIGURE 3-3

3 **Drag through the text in the Left text box to highlight 1.25". Type 1 and then press the TAB key. Type 1 and then point to the OK button.**

The new left and right margin settings are 1 inch (Figure 3-4). The Preview area in the Page Setup dialog box adjusts accordingly to reflect the new margin settings.

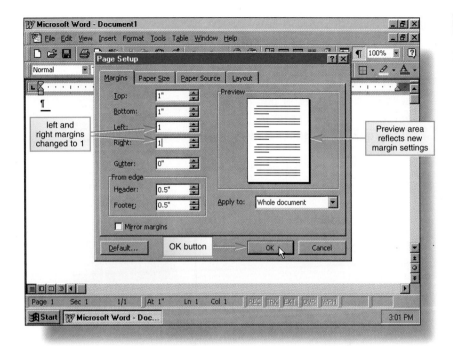

FIGURE 3-4

4 **Click the OK button.**

Word changes the left and right margins in the current document window (Figure 3-5).

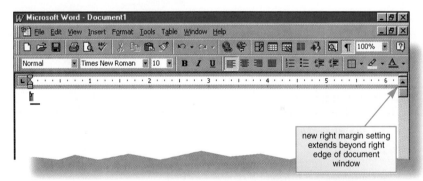

FIGURE 3-5

Compare Figure 3-2 to Figure 3-5. Notice that the right margin does not display in the document window in Figure 3-5, as it did in Figure 3-2, because you increased the width of your typing area when you changed the margins. The new margin settings take effect in the document immediately, and Word uses these margins for the entire document.

Adjusting Line Spacing

Word, by default, single-spaces between lines of text and automatically adjusts line height to accommodate various font sizes and graphics. The MLA documentation style requires that you double-space the entire paper; that is, one blank line should display between each line of text. Thus, you must adjust the line spacing from single to double as described in the steps on the next page.

OtherWays

1. In page layout view, drag margin boundary(s) on ruler

More *About* **Line Spacing**

Sometimes when you increase the font size of characters or import a graphic, the top of the characters or graphic is chopped off. If this happens, someone has set the line spacing in Word to Exactly. To correct it, change the line spacing to At least in the Paragraph dialog box, which accommodates the largest font or graphic.

Steps To Double-Space a Document

1 **Right-click the paragraph mark above the end mark in the document window. Point to Paragraph on the shortcut menu.**

Word displays a shortcut menu in the document window (Figure 3-6).

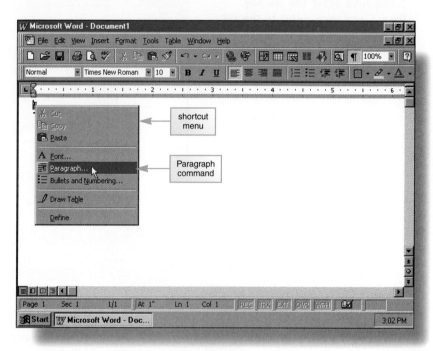

FIGURE 3-6

2 **Click Paragraph. If necessary, click the Indents and Spacing tab when the Paragraph dialog box first opens.**

Word displays the Paragraph dialog box, which lists the current settings in the text boxes and displays them graphically in the Preview area.

3 **Click the Line spacing box arrow and then point to Double.**

A list of available line spacing options displays (Figure 3-7).

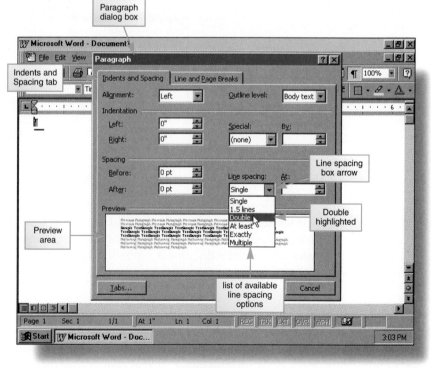

FIGURE 3-7

4 **Click Double. Point to the OK button.**

Word displays Double in the Line spacing text box and graphically portrays the new line spacing in the Preview area (Figure 3-8).

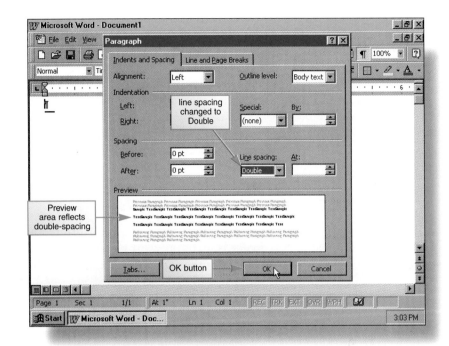

FIGURE 3-8

5 **Click the OK button.**

Word changes the line spacing to double in the current document (Figure 3-9). Notice that when line spacing is double, the end mark is positioned one blank line below the insertion point.

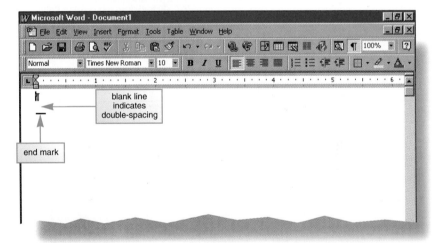

FIGURE 3-9

Other Ways

1. On Format menu click Paragraph, click Indents and Spacing tab, click Line spacing box arrow, click Double, click OK button
2. Press CTRL+2

The Line spacing list box contains a variety of settings for the line spacing (Figure 3-7). The default, Single, and the options 1.5 lines and Double instruct Word to adjust line spacing automatically to accommodate the largest font or graphic on a line. The next two options, At least and Exactly, enable you to specify a line spacing not provided in the first three options. The difference is that the At least option instructs Word to increase the designation if necessary; whereas, the Exactly option does not allow Word to increase the specification. With the last option, Multiple, you enter a multiple. For example, a multiple of 3 is the same as triple-spacing.

More *About* APA Guidelines

To follow the APA style, double-space all pages of the paper with 1.5" top, bottom, left, and right margins. Indent the first word of each paragraph one-half inch from the left margin. A running head is placed in the upper-right margin of each page; it consists of the page number double-spaced beneath a summary of the paper title.

Using a Header to Number Pages

In Word, you can number pages easily by clicking Insert on the menu bar and then clicking Page Numbers. Once you have clicked the Page Numbers command, it places page numbers on every page after the first. You cannot, however, place your name as required by the MLA style in front of the page number with the Page Numbers command. To place your name in front of the page number, you must create a header that contains the page number.

Headers and Footers

A **header** is text you want printed at the top of each page in the document. A **footer** is text you want printed at the bottom of every page. In Word, headers are printed in the top margin one-half inch from the top of every page, and footers are printed in the bottom margin one-half inch from the bottom of each page, which meets the MLA style. Headers and footers can include both text and graphics, as well as the page number, total number of pages, current date, and current time.

In this project, you are to precede the page number with your last name placed one-half inch from the top of each page. Your name and the page number should print **right-aligned**, that is, at the right margin. Use the procedures in the following steps to create the header with page numbers according to the MLA style.

Steps **To Create a Header**

1 Click View on the menu bar and then point to Header and Footer (Figure 3-10).

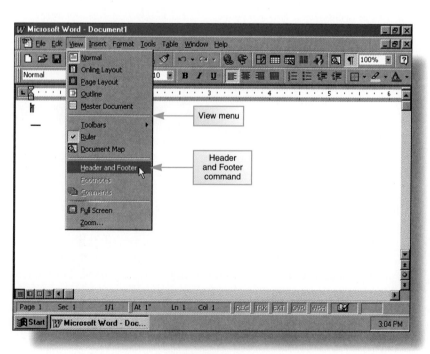

FIGURE 3-10

2 **Click Header and Footer. Point to the Align Right button on the Formatting toolbar.**

Word switches from normal view to page layout view and displays the **Header and Footer toolbar** *(Figure 3-11). The Header and Footer toolbar floats in the middle of the document window. You type header text in the* **header area,** *which displays enclosed by a nonprinting dashed rectangle above the Header and Footer toolbar. Notice that both the left and right margins display in the document window because Word switched to page layout view. Your zoom percentage may differ from this figure.*

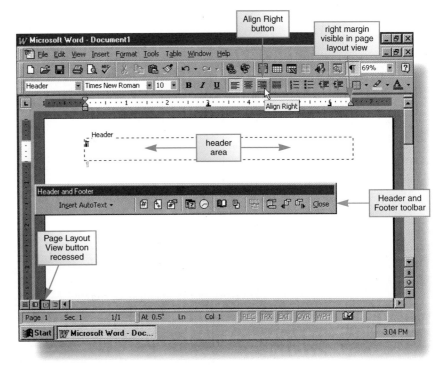

FIGURE 3-11

3 **Click the Align Right button on the Formatting toolbar. Type** Porter **and then press the** SPACEBAR. **Point to the Insert Page Number button on the Header and Footer toolbar.**

Word displays the last name, Porter, right-aligned in the header area (Figure 3-12). The Align Right button is recessed because the paragraph containing the insertion point is right-aligned.

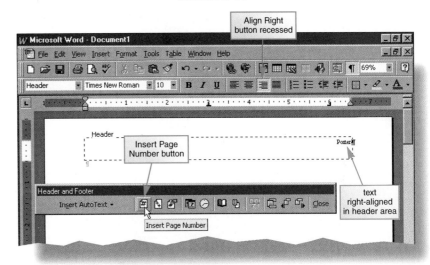

FIGURE 3-12

4 **Click the Insert Page Number button.**

Word displays the page number 1 in the header area (Figure 3-13). Notice that the header text is 10 point. You want all text in your research paper to be 12 point.

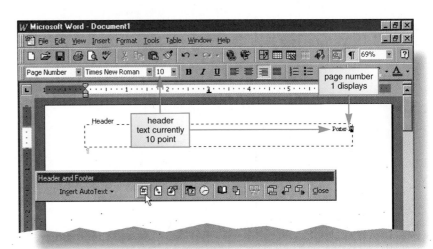

FIGURE 3-13

5 Select the text, Porter 1, by clicking to its left. Click the Font Size box arrow on the Formatting toolbar and then point to 12.

Word highlights the text, Porter 1, in the header area (Figure 3-14).

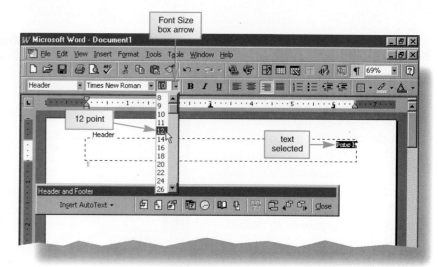

FIGURE 3-14

6 Click font size 12. Point to the Close Header and Footer button on the Header and Footer toolbar.

Word changes the font size of the selected text from 10 to 12 (Figure 3-15).

7 Click the Close Header and Footer button.

Word closes the Header and Footer toolbar and returns to normal view (Figure 3-16 on the opposite page).

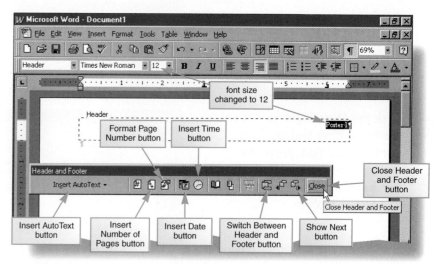

FIGURE 3-15

The header does not display on the screen when the document window is in normal view because it tends to clutter the screen. You will, however, want to verify that the header will print correctly. To see the header in the document window, you must switch to page layout view or display the document in print preview. These views display the header on the screen with the rest of the text. You can edit header text in both these views.

Just as the Insert Page Number button on the Header and Footer toolbar inserts the page number into the document, three other buttons on the Header and Footer toolbar (Figure 3-15 above) insert items into the document. The Insert Number of Pages button inserts the total number of pages in the document; the Insert Date button inserts the current date into the document; and the Insert Time button inserts the current time.

To edit an existing header, you can follow the same procedure that you use to create a new header. That is, click View on the menu bar and then click Header and Footer to display the Header and Footer toolbar; or switch to page layout view and then double-click the dimmed header. If you have multiple headers, click the Show Next button on the Header and Footer toolbar (Figure 3-15) until the appropriate header displays in the header area. Edit the header as you would any Word text and then click the Close Header and Footer button on the Header and Footer toolbar.

To create a footer, click View on the menu bar, click Header and Footer, click the Switch Between Header and Footer button on the Header and Footer toolbar, and then follow the same procedure as to create a header.

Notice that the Header and Footer toolbar initially floats in the middle of the document window. You can **dock**, or anchor, the floating toolbar below the Formatting toolbar by double-clicking its title bar. To move a docked toolbar, point between two buttons or boxes or to the edge of the toolbar and then drag it to the desired location. If you drag it to an edge of the window, the toolbar snaps to the edge of the window. If you drag it to the middle of the window, the toolbar floats in the Word window. If you double-click between two buttons or boxes or the edge of the toolbar, it floats in its original floating position.

Typing the Body of the Research Paper

The body of the research paper encompasses the first two pages in Figure 3-1 on page WD 3.5. The steps on the following pages illustrate how to enter the body of the research paper.

Changing the Default Font Size

As discussed in previous projects, a font size of 10 point is difficult for many people to read. In this project, all characters in all paragraphs should be a font size of 12. Perform the following steps to change the font size to 12.

TO CHANGE THE DEFAULT FONT SIZE

Step 1: Click the Font Size box arrow on the Formatting toolbar.
Step 2: Click font size 12.

Word changes the font size to 12 (Figure 3-16).

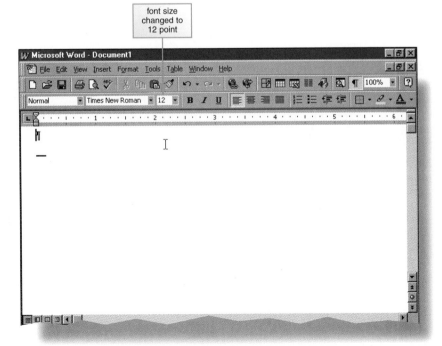

FIGURE 3-16

Entering Name and Course Information

Recall that the MLA style does not require a separate title page for research papers. Instead, you place your name and course information in a block at the top of the page at the left margin. Thus, follow the step below to begin the body of the research paper.

Steps To Enter Name and Course Information

1 **Type** Anna L. Porter **and then press the ENTER key. Type** Professor J. Brown **and then press the ENTER key. Type** Information Systems 201 **and then press the ENTER key. Type** December 1, 1998 **and then press the ENTER key twice.**

The student name displays on line 1, the professor name on line 2, the course name on line 3, and the paper due date on line 4 (Figure 3-17). Each time you press the ENTER key, Word advances two lines on the screen, but increments the line counter on the status bar by only one because earlier you set line spacing to double.

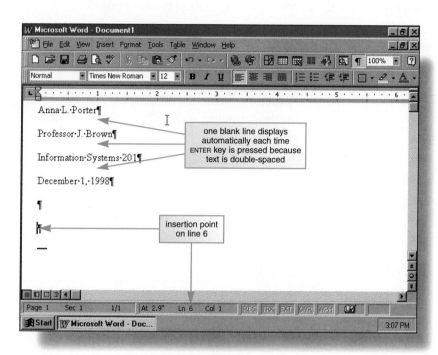

FIGURE 3-17

If you watch the screen as you type, you may have noticed that as you typed the first few characters, Dece, Word displayed the **AutoComplete tip**, December, above the characters. To save typing, you could press the ENTER key while the AutoComplete tip displays, which instructs Word to place the text of the AutoComplete tip at the location of your typing.

Centering a Paragraph Before Typing

In Project 1, you learned how to center a paragraph after you typed it. You also can center a paragraph before you type it. Because your fingers are already on the keyboard, you will use shortcut keys to format the paragraph as shown in the following steps.

Steps **To Center a Paragraph Before Typing**

1 **Position the insertion point on the paragraph mark to be centered and then press the CTRL+E keys. Type** Computer Viruses **and then press the ENTER key.**

Word centers the title between the left and right margins and the insertion point advances to line 7 (Figure 3-18). Notice that the paragraph mark and insertion point on line 7 are centered because the formatting specified in the prior paragraph (line 6) is carried forward to the next paragraph (line 7). Thus, the Center button on the Formatting toolbar remains recessed, indicating the next text you type will be centered. You do not, however, want the next line of text to be centered.

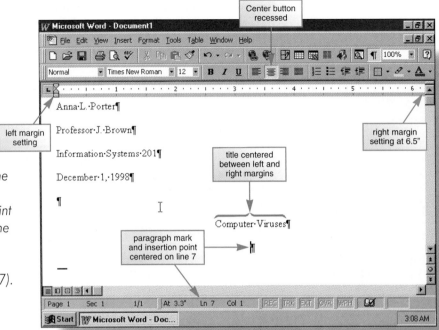

FIGURE 3-18

2 **Press the CTRL+L keys.**

Word positions the paragraph mark and the insertion point at the left margin (Figure 3-19). The next text you type will be left-aligned. CTRL+L is the keyboard shortcut to left-align a paragraph.

OtherWays

1. Click Center button
2. Right-click paragraph, click Paragraph on shortcut menu, click Indents and Spacing tab, click Alignment box arrow, click Centered, click OK button
3. On Format menu click Paragraph, click Indents and Spacing tab, click Alignment box arrow, click Centered, click OK button

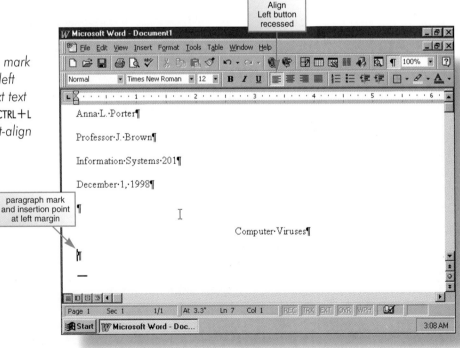

FIGURE 3-19

Saving the Research Paper

Recall that it is prudent to save your work on disk at regular intervals. Because you have performed several tasks thus far, you should save your research paper. For a detailed example of the procedure summarized below, refer to pages WD 1.25 through WD 1.27 in Project 1.

TO SAVE A DOCUMENT

Step 1: Insert your floppy disk into drive A.
Step 2: Click the Save button on the Standard toolbar.
Step 3: Type the file name Virus Research Paper in the File name text box. Do not press the ENTER key after typing the file name.
Step 4: Click the Save in box arrow and then click 3½ Floppy (A:).
Step 5: Click the Save button in the Save As dialog box.

Indenting Paragraphs

According to the MLA style, the first line of each paragraph in the research paper is to be indented one-half inch from the left margin. This procedure, called **first-line indent,** can be accomplished using the horizontal ruler as shown in the following steps.

Steps **To First-Line Indent Paragraphs**

1 **Point to the First Line Indent marker on the ruler.**

The First Line Indent marker is the top triangle at the 0" mark on the ruler (Figure 3-20). The small square at the 0" mark, called the Left Indent marker, is used to change the entire left margin, whereas the First Line Indent marker affects only the first line of the paragraph.

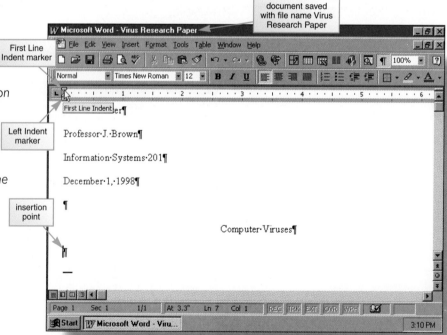

FIGURE 3-20

2 **Drag the First Line Indent marker to the .5" mark on the ruler.**

As you drag the mouse, a vertical dotted line displays in the document window, indicating the proposed location of the First Line Indent marker (Figure 3-21).

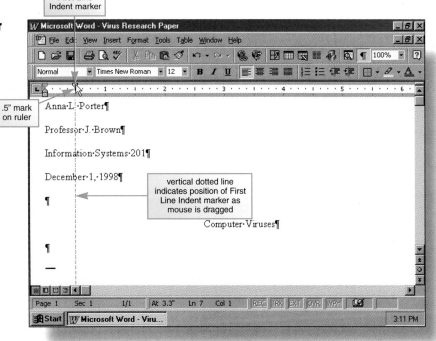

FIGURE 3-21

3 **Release the mouse button.**

The First Line Indent marker displays at the location of the first tab stop, which is one-half inch from the left margin (Figure 3-22). The paragraph mark containing the insertion point in the document window also moves one-half inch to the right.

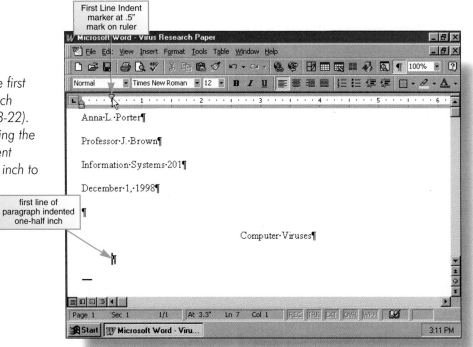

FIGURE 3-22

4 **Type the first paragraph of the research paragraph as shown in Figure 3-24 below. Press the ENTER key. Type the first sentence of the second paragraph:** `Three types of viruses are a boot sector virus, file virus, and Trojan horse virus.`

When you press the ENTER key at the end of the first paragraph of text, the insertion point automatically indents the first line of the second paragraph by one-half inch (Figure 3-23). Recall that each time you press the ENTER key, the paragraph formatting in the prior paragraph is carried forward to the next paragraph.

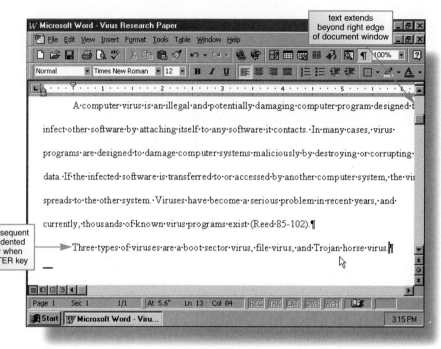

FIGURE 3-23

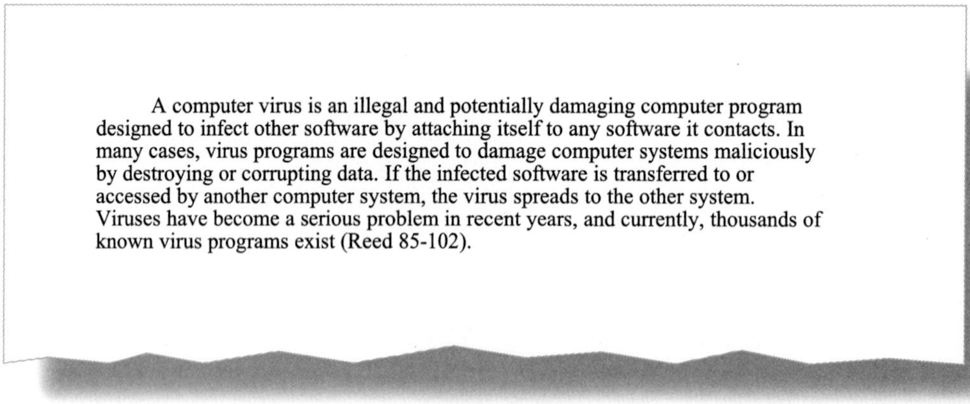

A computer virus is an illegal and potentially damaging computer program designed to infect other software by attaching itself to any software it contacts. In many cases, virus programs are designed to damage computer systems maliciously by destroying or corrupting data. If the infected software is transferred to or accessed by another computer system, the virus spreads to the other system. Viruses have become a serious problem in recent years, and currently, thousands of known virus programs exist (Reed 85-102).

FIGURE 3-24

OtherWays

1. Right-click paragraph, click Paragraph on shortcut menu, click Indents and Spacing tab, click Special box arrow, click First line, click OK button
2. On Format menu click Paragraph, click Indents and Spacing tab, click Special box arrow, click First line, click OK button

By setting the first-line indent with the ruler, the first-line indent format is carried automatically to each subsequent paragraph you type.

Zooming Page Width

When you changed the left and right margin settings earlier in this project, the right margin moved beyond the right edge of the document window. (Depending on your Word settings, your right margin may already display in the document window.) Thus, some of the text at the right edge of the document does not display in the document window (Figure 3-23 above). Recall in Project 2, you zoomed the cover letter and resume to make the characters appear larger on the screen. In this project, you want to make the characters smaller.

Because you often want to see both margins in the document window at the same time, Word provides a **page width zoom**, which brings both the left and right margins into view as shown in the following steps.

To Zoom Page Width

① **Click the Zoom box arrow on the Standard toolbar and then point to Page Width.**

Word displays a list of available zoom percentages, as well as the Page Width zoom option (Figure 3-25).

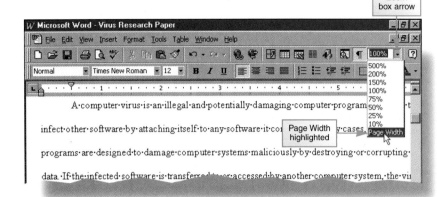

FIGURE 3-25

② **Click Page Width.**

Word brings both the left and right margins into view in the document window (Figure 3-26). The Zoom box now displays 92%, which Word computes based on your margin settings. Your percentage may be different depending on your system configuration.

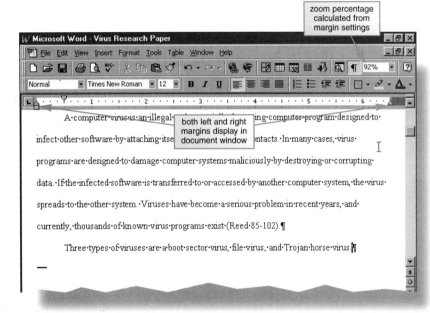

FIGURE 3-26

OtherWays

1. On View menu click Zoom, select desired zoom percentage, click OK button

If you want to zoom to a percentage not displayed in the Zoom list box, you can click View on the menu bar, click Zoom, and then enter any zoom percentage you desire.

Using Word's AutoCorrect Feature

Because you may often misspell words or phrases when you type, Word provides an **AutoCorrect** feature, which automatically corrects your misspelled words as you type them into the document. For example, if you type *adn*, Word automatically changes it to *and* for you. Word has predefined many commonly misspelled words, which it automatically corrects for you as shown on the next page.

More *About*
AutoCorrect

In addition to correcting misspelled words, the AutoCorrect feature fixes other mistakes. If you type two capital letters at the beginning of a sentence, Word makes the second letter lower case. If you forget to capitalize the first letter of a sentence, Word capitalizes it for you. Word also capitalizes names of days of the week, if you forget to.

Steps **To AutoCorrect As You Type**

1 **Press the SPACEBAR. Type the beginning of the second sentence in the second paragraph, and misspell the word, the, as follows:** A boot sector virus infects teh **(Figure 3-27).**

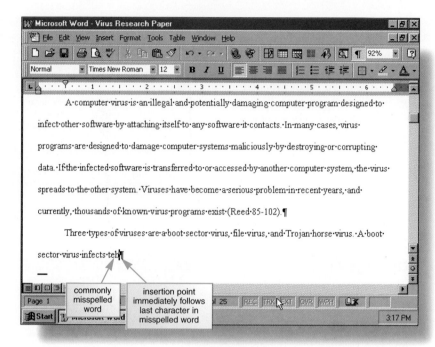

commonly misspelled word

insertion point immediately follows last character in misspelled word

FIGURE 3-27

2 **Press the SPACEBAR.**

As soon as you press the SPACEBAR, Word's AutoCorrect feature detects the misspelling and corrects the misspelled word for you (Figure 3-28).

3 **Type** boot program used to start the system. **and then press the SPACEBAR.**

The second sentence of the second paragraph is complete.

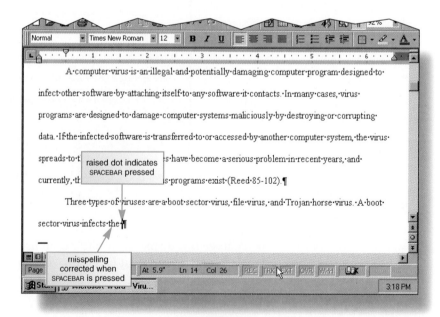

raised dot indicates SPACEBAR pressed

misspelling corrected when SPACEBAR is pressed

FIGURE 3-28

Word has a list of predefined misspelled words that AutoCorrect can detect and correct. In addition to the predefined list of commonly misspelled words, you can create your own AutoCorrect entries to add to the list. For example, if you often misspell the word *virus* as *vires*, you should make an AutoCorrect entry for it as shown in these steps.

Steps **To Create an AutoCorrect Entry**

1 **Click Tools on the menu bar and then point to AutoCorrect (Figure 3-29).**

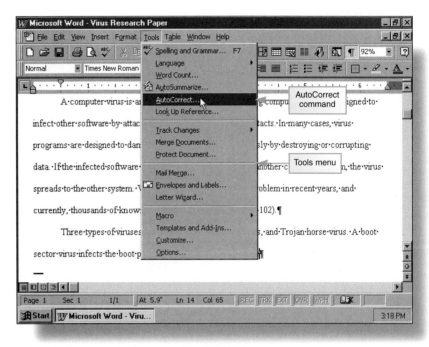

FIGURE 3-29

2 **Click AutoCorrect.**

Word displays the AutoCorrect dialog box (Figure 3-30). The insertion point blinks in the Replace text box, ready for you to create an AutoCorrect entry.

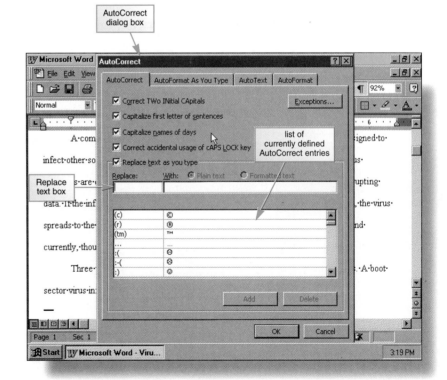

FIGURE 3-30

3 Type `vires` **in the Replace text box. Press the TAB key to advance to the With text box. Type** `virus` **in the With text box. Point to the Add button.**

The Replace text box contains the misspelled word, and the With text box contains its correct spelling (Figure 3-31).

4 **Click the Add button. (If your dialog box displays a Replace button instead, click it and then click the Yes button in the Microsoft Word dialog box.) Click the OK button.**

Word adds the entry alphabetically to the list of words to correct automatically as you type.

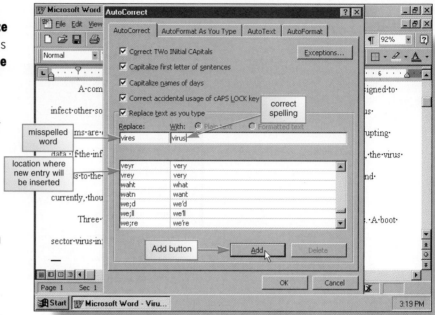

FIGURE 3-31

In addition to creating AutoCorrect entries for words you commonly misspell, you can create entries for abbreviations, codes, and so on. For example, you could create an AutoCorrect entry for *asap*, indicating that Word should replace this text with the phrase *as soon as possible*.

If you look at the list of AutoCorrect entries in the AutoCorrect dialog box (Figure 3-30 on the previous page), you will notice that Word also predefines commonly used symbols. For example, to insert a smiling face into a document, you type :) and word automatically changes it to ☺. Table 3-1 lists the characters you type to insert arrows, faces, and symbols into a Word document.

If, for some reason, you do not want Word to correct automatically as you type, you can turn off the replace as you type feature by clicking Tools on the menu bar, clicking AutoCorrect, clicking the AutoCorrect tab, clicking the Replace text as you type check box to deselect it, and then clicking the OK button.

The AutoCorrect sheet also contains four other check boxes that correct your typing if selected. If you type two capital letters in a row such as TH, Word will make the second letter lowercase, Th. If you begin a sentence with a lowercase letter, Word will capitalize the first letter of the sentence. If you type the name of a day in lowercase such as tuesday, Word will capitalize the first letter of the day, Tuesday. Finally, if you leave the CAPS LOCK key on and begin a new sentence such as aFTER, Word corrects the typing, After, and turns off the CAPS LOCK key.

In Project 2, you learned how to use the AutoText feature, which enables you to create entries (just as you did for the AutoCorrect feature) and then insert them into the document. The difference is that the AutoCorrect feature makes the corrections for you automatically as soon as you press the SPACEBAR, whereas you must press F3 or click the AutoText command before Word will make an AutoText correction.

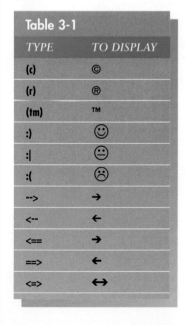

Table 3-1	
TYPE	TO DISPLAY
(c)	©
(r)	®
(tm)	™
:)	☺
:|	☻
:(	☹
-->	→
<--	←
<==	→
==>	←
<=>	↔

Adding Footnotes

Recall that **explanatory notes** are optional in the MLA documentation style. They are used primarily to elaborate on points discussed in the body of the paper. The style specifies to use superscripts (raised numbers) to signal that an explanatory note exists either at the bottom of the page as a **footnote** or at the end of the document as an **endnote**.

Word, by default, places notes at the bottom of each page. In Word, **note text** can be any length and format. Word automatically numbers notes sequentially for you by placing a **note reference mark** in the body of the document and in front of the note text. If you rearrange, insert, or remove notes, the remaining note text and reference marks are renumbered according to their new sequence in the document. Perform the following steps to add a footnote to the research paper.

More *About*
Footnotes

Both the MLA and APA guidelines suggest the use of in-text parenthetical citation, as opposed to footnoting each source of material in a paper. These parenthetical acknowledgments guide the reader to the end of the paper for complete information on the source, if the reader desires it.

 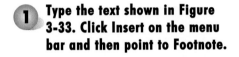

1 **Type the text shown in Figure 3-33. Click Insert on the menu bar and then point to Footnote.**

The insertion point is positioned immediately after the period following the word, date, in the research paper (Figure 3-32).

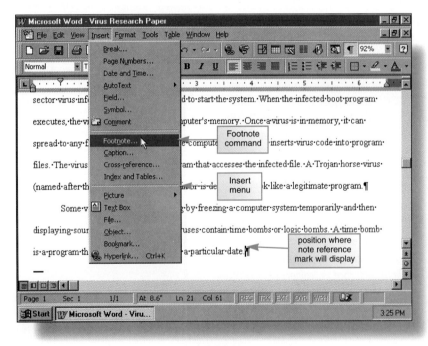

FIGURE 3-32

When the infected boot program executes, the virus is loaded into the computer's memory. Once a virus is in memory, it can spread to any floppy disk inserted into the computer. A file virus inserts virus code into program files. The virus then spreads to any program that accesses the infected file. A Trojan horse virus (named after the Greek myth) hides within or is designed to look like a legitimate program.

Some viruses interrupt processing by freezing a computer system temporarily and then displaying sounds or messages. Other viruses contain time bombs or logic bombs. A time bomb is a program that performs an activity on a particular date.

FIGURE 3-33

2 **Click Footnote. When the Footnote and Endnote dialog box displays, point to the OK button.**

Word displays the Footnote and Endnote dialog box (Figure 3-34). The selected Footnote option button indicates that footnotes are the default placement for notes.

FIGURE 3-34

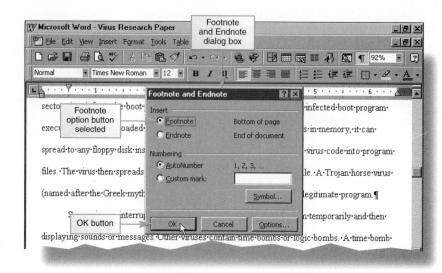

3 **Click the OK button.**

*Word opens a **note pane** in the lower portion of the window with the note reference mark (a super-scripted 1) positioned at the left margin of the pane (Figure 3-35). A **pane** is an area at the bottom of the screen, which contains an **option bar**, a **text area**, and a **scroll bar**. The note reference mark also displays in the document window at the location of the insertion point. Note **reference marks** are, by default, super-scripted; that is, raised above other letters. Notice that the default font size of footnote text is 10 point.*

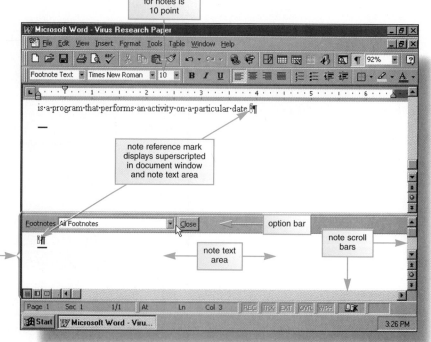

FIGURE 3-35

4 **Right-click to the right of the paragraph mark in the note pane. Point to Paragraph on the shortcut menu.**

Word displays a shortcut menu (Figure 3-36). Because you want to change both first-line indent and line spacing for the notes, you will use the Paragraph dialog box to perform both changes.

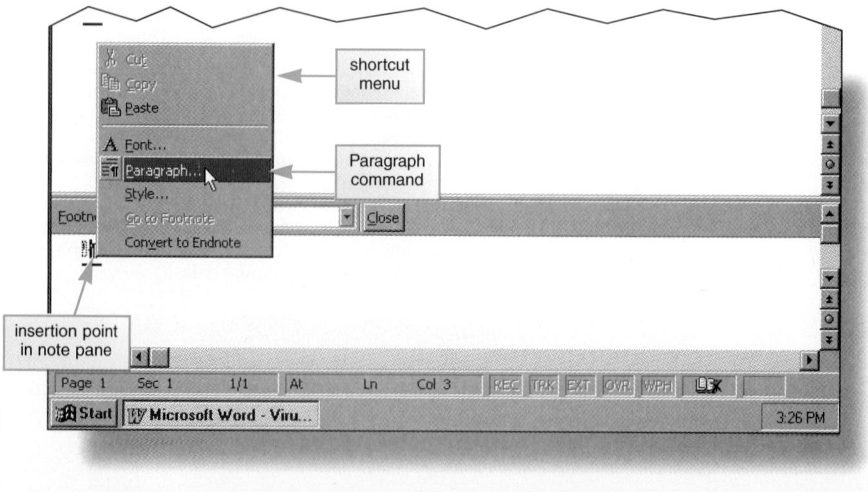

FIGURE 3-36

5 Click Paragraph. If necessary, click the Indents and Spacing tab when the Paragraph dialog box first opens. Click the Special box arrow and then point to First line.

Word displays the Paragraph dialog box (Figure 3-37). You can change the first-line indent in the Indents and Spacing sheet in the Paragraph dialog box.

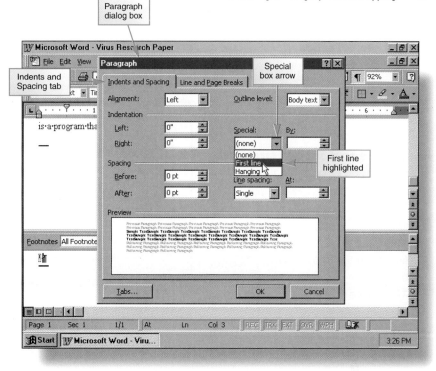

FIGURE 3-37

6 Click First line. Click the Line spacing box arrow and then click Double. Point to the OK button.

Word displays First line in the Special box and Double in the Line spacing box (Figure 3-38). The Preview area reflects the current settings in the Paragraph dialog box.

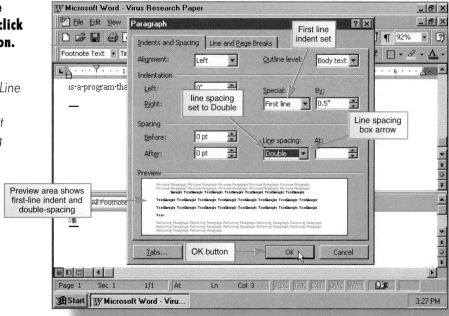

FIGURE 3-38

7 Click the OK button.

Word indents the first line of the note by one-half inch and sets the line spacing for the note to double.

8 Click the Font Size box arrow and then click 12. Type the note text:
A well-known time bomb is the Michelangelo virus, which destroys data on a user's hard disk on March 6, Michelangelo's birthday (Chambers and Peters 52-54).

The note text is entered in the note pane in 12-point font (Figure 3-39).

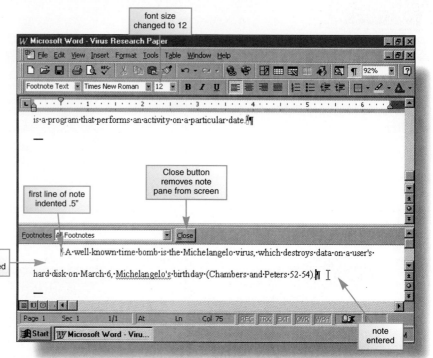

FIGURE 3-39

9 Click the Close button on the note pane option bar. Point to the note reference mark in the document window.

Word closes the note pane (Figure 3-40).

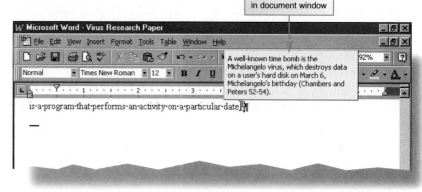

FIGURE 3-40

When Word closes the note pane and returns to the document, the note text disappears from the screen. Although the note text still exists, it is usually not visible as a footnote in normal view. If, however, you point to the note reference mark as shown in Figure 3-40, the note text appears above the note reference mark as a ScreenTip. To display footnotes in a note pane at the bottom of the screen, double-click the note reference mark in the document. If you want to verify that the note text is positioned correctly on the page, you must switch to page layout view or display the document in print preview.

To edit an existing footnote, click View on the menu bar and then click Footnotes or double-click the note reference mark in the document to display the note pane. Edit the footnote as you would any Word text and then click the Close button on the note pane option bar.

Automatic Page Breaks

As you type documents that exceed one page, Word automatically inserts page breaks, called **automatic page breaks** or **soft page breaks**, when it determines the text has filled one page according to paper size, margin settings, line spacing, and other settings. If you add text, delete text, or modify text on a page, Word recomputes the position of automatic page breaks and adjusts them accordingly. Word performs page recomputation between the keystrokes, that is, in between the pauses in your typing. Thus, Word refers to the automatic page break task as **background repagination**. In normal view, automatic page breaks appear on the Word screen as a single dotted horizontal line. Word's automatic page break feature is illustrated below.

More *About* **Background Repagination**

If background repagination has been deactivated on your system, Word stops all activities while repaginating the document. You can enable background repagination by clicking Tools on the menu bar, clicking Options, clicking the General tab, clicking the Background Repagination check box, and then clicking the OK button.

 Steps **To Page Break Automatically**

1 **Press the SPACEBAR and then type** A logic bomb is a program that performs an activity when a certain action occurs, such as an employee being terminated. A worm, which is similar to a virus, copies itself repeatedly until no memory or disk space remains. **Press the ENTER key and then type the next paragraph of the research paper, as shown in Figure 3-42 below.**

As you begin typing the paragraph, Word places an automatic page break above line containing the note reference mark. When Word detects an additional line at the end of the paragraph, it moves the automatic page break down one line, below the line with the note reference mark (Figure 3-41). The status bar now displays Page 2 as the current page.

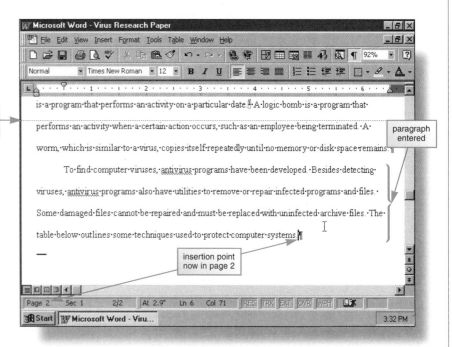

single dotted line indicates automatic page break

paragraph entered

insertion point now in page 2

FIGURE 3-41

To find computer viruses, antivirus programs have been developed. Besides detecting viruses, antivirus programs also have utilities to remove or repair infected programs and files. Some damaged files cannot be repaired and must be replaced with uninfected archive files. The table below outlines some techniques used to protect computer systems.

FIGURE 3-42

Word, by default, prevents widows and orphans from occurring in a document. A **widow** is created when the last line of a paragraph displays by itself at the top of a page, and an **orphan** occurs when the first line of a paragraph displays by itself at the bottom of a page. When you typed the end of the third paragraph, Word placed the automatic page break above the line with the note reference mark to ensure that the last two lines of the paragraph would be at the top of the next page (avoiding a widow). When you continued typing the paragraph, however, Word recognized the multiple lines at the end of the paragraph and moved the automatic page break. If, for some reason, you wanted to allow a widow or an orphan in a document, you would right-click the paragraph in question, click Paragraph on the shortcut menu, click the Line and Page Breaks tab in the Paragraph dialog box, click Widow/Orphan control to deselect the check box, and then click the OK button.

Creating a Table with the Insert Table Button

At the end of the fourth paragraph of the research paper, you are to place a table outlining the techniques for virus protection and system archive (Figure 3-1 on page WD 3.5). In Project 2, you created a table of GPAs in the cover letter for the resume using the TAB key. In this project, you create a table using Word's table feature. A Word **table** is a collection of rows and columns. The intersection of a row and a column is called a **cell**.

Within a Word table, you easily can rearrange rows and columns, change column widths, sort rows and columns, and sum the contents of rows and columns. You can use the Table AutoFormat dialog box to make the table display in a professional manner. You also can chart table data. For these reasons, many Word users create tables with the Insert Table button, rather than using tabs as discussed in the previous project.

The first step in creating a table is to insert an empty table into the document. When inserting a table, you must specify the total number of rows and columns in the table, called the **dimension** of the table. The table in this project has two columns. Because you often do not know the total number of rows in a table, many Word users create two rows initially and then add rows as they need them. The first number in a dimension is the number of rows, and the second is the number of columns. Perform the following steps to insert a 2 x 2 table, that is, a table with two rows and two columns.

Steps **To Insert an Empty Table**

1 **With the insertion point at the end of the document, press the SHIFT+ENTER keys. Type** Table **and then press the SHIFT+ENTER keys. Type** Techniques for Virus Protection and System Archive **as the table title. Point to the Insert Table button on the Standard toolbar.**

Word places a line break character at the end of each line entered (Figure 3-43). Recall that a line break causes Word to ignore paragraph formatting when advancing the insertion point to the next line. Thus, Word does not first-line indent the table caption or title.

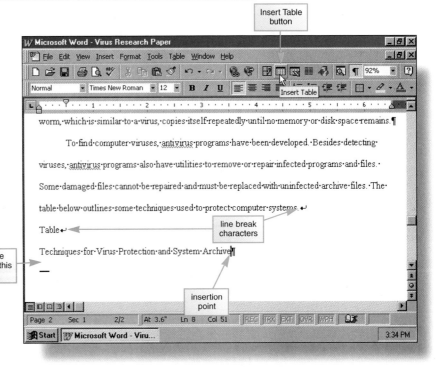

FIGURE 3-43

2 **Click the Insert Table button on the Standard toolbar. Point to the cell in the second row and second column of the grid.**

*Word displays a **grid** to define the dimensions of the desired table (Figure 3-44). The first two columns and first two rows in the grid are selected. The Insert Table button on the Standard toolbar is recessed. Word will insert the 2 × 2 table below the insertion point in the document window.*

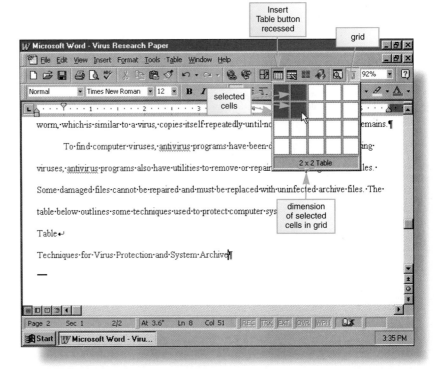

FIGURE 3-44

3 Click the cell in the second row and second column of the grid. If necessary, use the scroll bar to display the entire table in the document window.

Word inserts an empty 2 × 2 table into the document (Figure 3-45). The insertion point is in the first cell (row 1 and column 1) of the table.

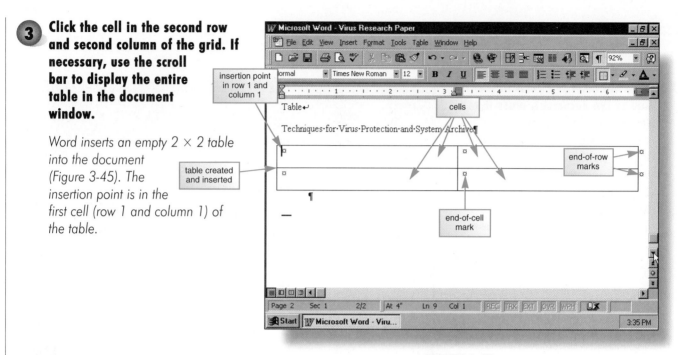

FIGURE 3-45

Each row has an **end-of-row mark**, which is used to add columns to the right of a table. Each cell has an **end-of-cell mark**, which is used to select a cell. Notice the end-of-cell marks are currently left-aligned within each cell, which indicates the data will be left-aligned within the cells.

For simple tables, such as the one just created, Word users click the Insert Table button to create a table. For more complex tables, such as one with a varying number of columns per row, Word has a new Draw Table feature that allows you to use a pen pointer to draw the table on the screen. The Draw Table feature is discussed in Project 4.

Entering Data into a Word Table

The next step is to enter data into the empty table. Cells are filled with data. The data you enter within a cell wordwraps just as text does between the margins of a document. To place data into a cell, you click the cell and then type. To advance rightward from one cell to the next, press the TAB key. When you are at the rightmost cell in a row, also press the TAB key to move to the first cell in the next row; do not press the ENTER key. The ENTER key is used to begin a new paragraph within a cell. Perform the following steps to enter the data into the table.

Steps **To Enter Data into a Table**

1 **With the insertion point in the upper-left cell of the table, type** Using Virus Protection Software **and then press the TAB key. Type** Backing Up Your System **and then press the TAB key. Type** Install virus protection software on every computer system. **Press the TAB key. Type** Develop a regular plan for copying and storing important data and program files.

*The table data is entered into the header row and the second row of the table (Figure 3-46). When the first row of a table contains column titles, it is called the **header row**.*

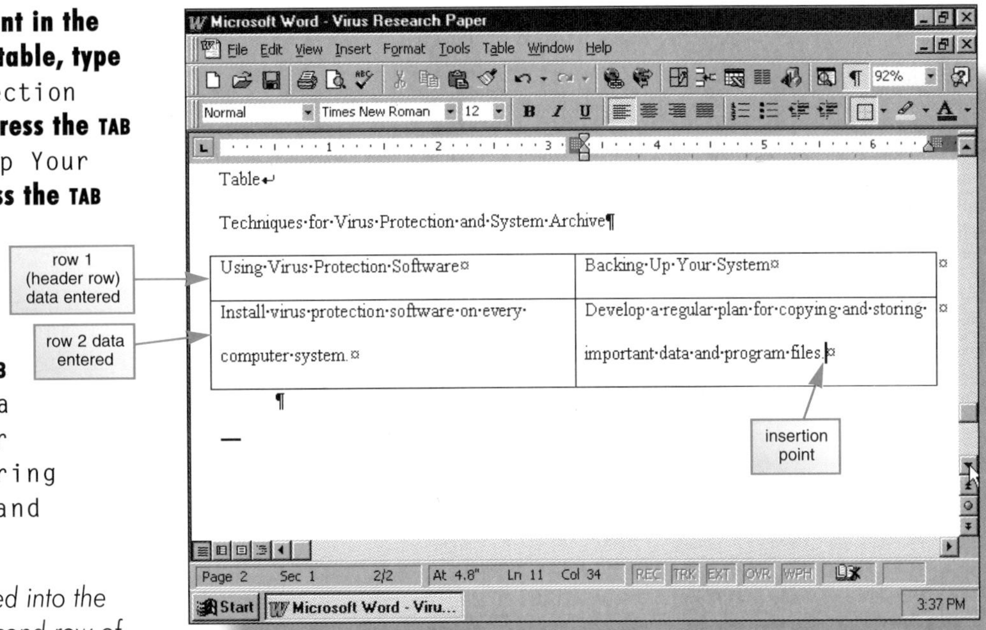

The insertion point currently is positioned at the cell intersecting row 2 and column 2. To create a new row at the bottom of a table, you press the TAB key while the insertion point is in the lower-right cell of the table.

FIGURE 3-46

2 **Press the TAB key. Type** Before use, scan every floppy disk with a virus scan program to check for viruses. **Press the TAB key. Type** Implement a backup plan and adhere to its guidelines. **Press the TAB key. Type** Check all programs downloaded from the Internet or bulletin boards for viruses. **Press the TAB key. Type** Keep backup copies of files in fireproof safes or vaults or off-site.

The table data is completely entered (Figure 3-47).

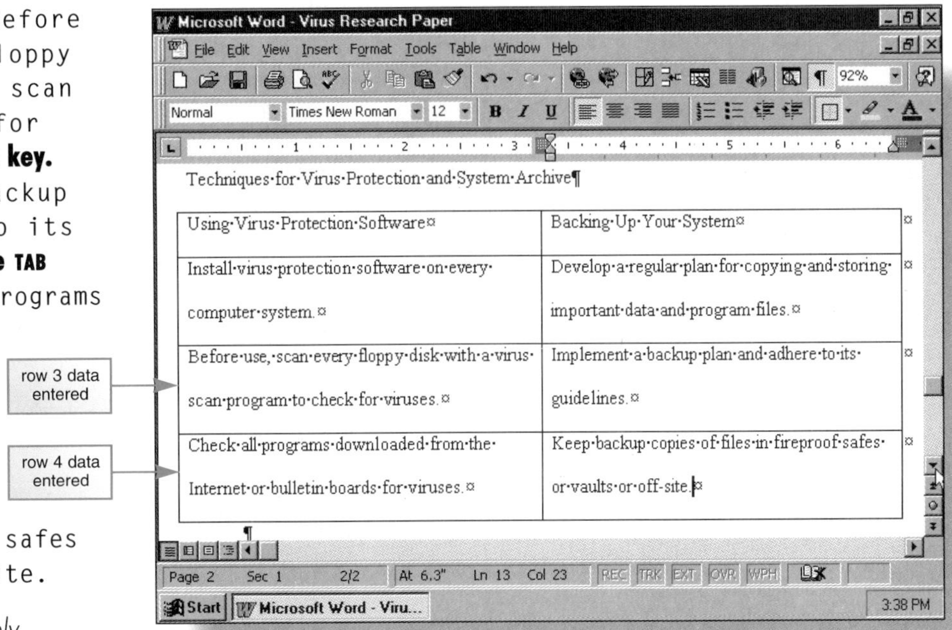

FIGURE 3-47

You modify the contents of cells just as you modify text in a document. To delete the contents of a cell, select the cell contents by pointing to the left edge of the cell and clicking when the mouse pointer changes direction, and then press the DELETE key. To modify text within a cell, click in the cell, and then correct the entry. You can double-click the OVR indicator on the status bar to toggle between insert and overtype modes. You also may drag and drop or cut and paste the contents of cells.

Because the TAB key advances you from one cell to the next in a table, press the CTRL+TAB keys to insert a tab character into a cell.

Formatting a Table

Although you can format each row, column, and cell of a table individually, Word provides a Table AutoFormat feature that contains predefined formats for tables. Perform the following steps to format the entire table using **Table AutoFormat**.

 Steps **To AutoFormat a Table**

1 **Right-click the table. Point to Table AutoFormat on the shortcut menu.**

Word displays a shortcut menu for tables (Figure 3-48).

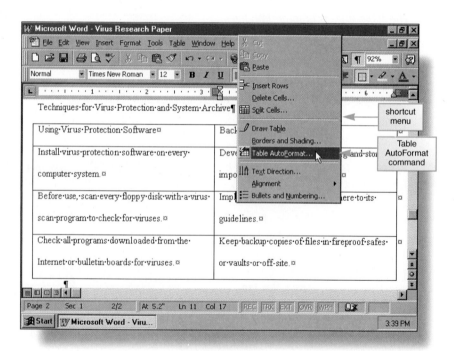

FIGURE 3-48

2 Click Table AutoFormat. When the Table AutoFormat dialog box displays, if necessary, click Color in the Formats to apply area to turn color on for the table. Scroll through the Formats list and then click Grid 8. Point to the OK button.

Word displays the Table AutoFormat dialog box (Figure 3-49). The Preview area shows the Grid 8 format. Because Heading rows is selected in the dialog box, the header row of the table has formatting different from the rest of the rows in the table.

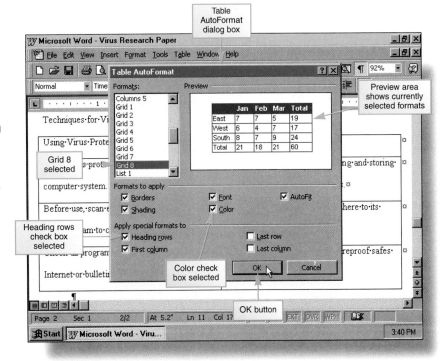

FIGURE 3-49

3 Click the OK button.

Word formats the table according to the Grid 8 format (Figure 3-50).

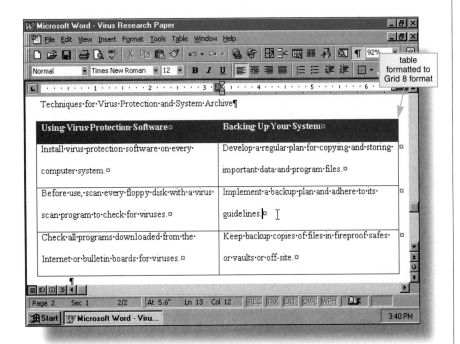

FIGURE 3-50

Other Ways

1. Click table, on Table menu click Table AutoFormat, click appropriate settings, click OK button

Changing the Line Spacing of the Table

Notice in Figure 3-50 that the cell contents are double-spaced; you want the paragraphs within the cells to be single-spaced. To change the line spacing of paragraphs in the table, you first must select the entire table and then format as shown in the steps on the next page.

Steps To Select an Entire Table

1 **With the insertion point somewhere in the table, click Table on the menu bar and then point to Select Table (Figure 3-51).**

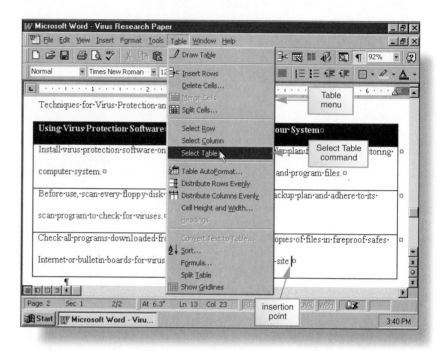

FIGURE 3-51

2 **Click Select Table.**

Word highlights the contents of the entire table.

3 **Press the CTRL+1 keys.**

Word single-spaces the contents of the table (Figure 3-52). CTRL+1 is the keyboard shortcut for single-spacing paragraphs; CTRL+2 is the keyboard shortcut for double-spacing paragraphs.

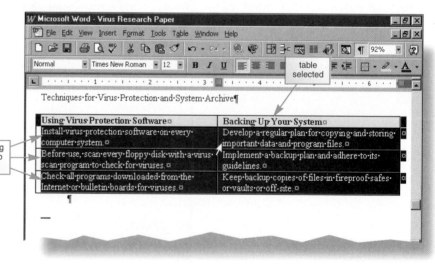

FIGURE 3-52

Changing Paragraph Formatting

When Word placed the table into the research paper, it placed a paragraph mark immediately below the table with no blank line between the paragraph mark and the table. Because the MLA style requires double-spacing of the entire document, you must change the line spacing above the paragraph mark. Perform the following step to insert a blank line above the paragraph mark below the table.

Steps To Insert a Blank Line above a Paragraph

1 Position the insertion point on the paragraph mark directly below the table (Figure 3-53).

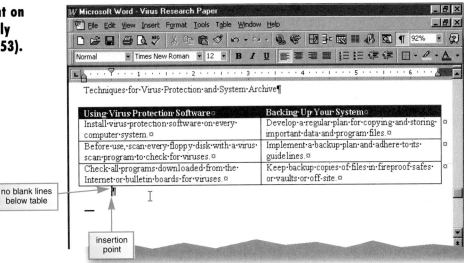

no blank lines below table

insertion point

FIGURE 3-53

2 Press the CTRL+0 (zero) keys.

Word inserts a blank line between the paragraph mark and the table.

3 Type the last sentence of the research paper: If your system becomes virus infected and you have questions, contact the National Computer Security Association (NCSA) for low-cost assistance (Elmhurst, 6 Nov. 1998).

The body of the research paper is complete (Figure 3-54).

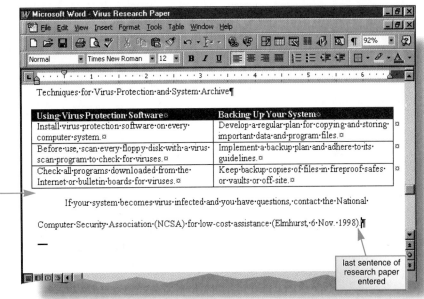

one blank line inserted below table

last sentence of research paper entered

FIGURE 3-54

Creating an Alphabetical Works Cited Page

According to the MLA style, the **works cited page** is a bibliographical list of works you reference directly in your paper. The list is placed on a separate page with the title, Works Cited, centered one inch from the top margin. The works are to be alphabetized by author's last name. The first line of each work begins at the left margin; subsequent lines of the same work are indented one-half inch from the left margin.

Other Ways

1. Right-click paragraph, click Paragraph on shortcut menu, click Indents and Spacing tab, type 12 in Spacing Before text box, click OK button

2. On Format menu click Paragraph, click Indents and Spacing tab, type 12 in Spacing Before text box, click OK button

The first step in creating the works cited page is to force a page break so the works display on a separate page.

Manual Page Breaks

Because the works cited are to display on a separate numbered page, you must insert a manual page break following the body of the research paper. A **manual page break** or **hard page break** is one that you force into the document at a specific location. Manual page breaks display on the screen as a horizontal dotted line, separated by the words, Page Break. Word never moves or adjusts manual page breaks; however, Word does adjust any automatic page breaks that follow in the document. Word inserts manual page breaks just before the location of the insertion point. Perform the following steps to insert a manual page break after the body of the research paper.

Steps To Page Break Manually

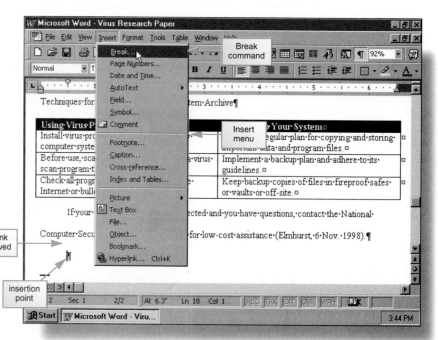

FIGURE 3-55

1 **With the insertion point at the end of the research paper, press the ENTER key. Press the CTRL+0 (zero) keys. Click Insert on the menu bar and then point to Break.**

Word removes the extra blank line above the paragraph mark (Figure 3-55). Recall that you inserted a blank line above the paragraph below the table. When you pressed the ENTER key, this paragraph formatting carried forward; thus, two blank lines displayed between these paragraphs (one for the double-spacing and one for the extra blank line). Pressing the CTRL+0 keys a second time removes one blank line from above a paragraph. The insertion point now is positioned one blank line below the body of the research paper.

2 **Click Break.**

Word displays the Break dialog box (Figure 3-56). The default option is Page Break.

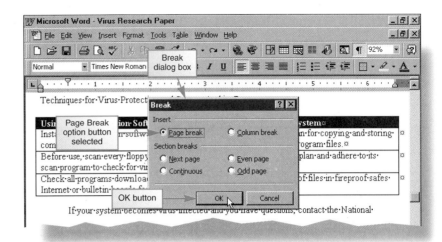

FIGURE 3-56

3 **Click the OK button.**

Word inserts a manual page break immediately above the insertion point and positions the insertion point immediately below the manual page break (Figure 3-57). The manual page break displays as a horizontal dotted line with the words, Page Break, in the middle of the line. The status bar indicates the insertion point is located on page 3.

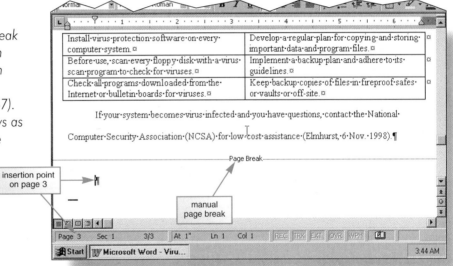

FIGURE 3-57

Other Ways

1. Press CTRL+ENTER

If, for some reason, you wanted to remove a manual page break from your document, you must first select it by double-clicking it. Then, right-click the selection and click Cut on the shortcut menu; or click the Cut button on the Standard toolbar; or press the DELETE key.

Centering the Title of the Works Cited Page

The works cited title is to be centered between the margins. If you simply click the Center button on the Formatting toolbar, the title will not be properly centered; instead, it will be one-half inch to the right of the center point because earlier you set first-line indent at the first tab stop. Thus, the first line of every paragraph is indented one-half inch. To properly center the title of the works cited page, you must move the First Line Indent marker back to the left margin before clicking the Center button as described on the next page.

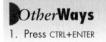

More *About*
Sources

When writing a research paper, you must acknowledge sources of information. Citing sources boils down to ethics and honesty. Caution must be used when summarizing or paraphrasing a source. Be sure to avoid plagiarism, which includes using someone else's words and ideas and claiming them as your own.

First Line Indent
marker moved
to left margin

Install·virus·protection·software·on·every·
computer·system.¤

Develop·a·regular·plan·for·copying·and·storing·
important·data·and·program·files.¤

Before·use,·scan·every·floppy·disk·with·a·virus·
scan·program·to·check·for·viruses.¤

Implement·a·backup·plan·and·adhere·to·its·
guidelines.¤

Check·all·programs·downloaded·from·the·
Internet·or·bulletin·boards·for·viruses.¤

Keep·backup·copies·of·files·in·fireproof·safes·
or·vaults·or·off-site.¤

If·your·system·becomes·virus·infected·and·you·have·questions,·contact·the·National·

Computer·Security·Association·(NCSA)·for·low-cost·assistance·(Elmhurst,·6·Nov.·1998).¶

―――――――Page Break―――――――

title centered
and typed → Works·Cited¶

Page 3   Sec 1   3/3   At 1"   Ln 1   Col 12   REC TRK EXT OVR WPH

Start   W Microsoft Word - Viru...   3:44 AM

FIGURE 3-58

TO CENTER THE TITLE OF THE WORKS CITED PAGE

Step 1: Drag the First Line Indent marker to the 0" mark on the ruler.

Step 2: Click the Center button on the Formatting toolbar.

Step 3: Type Works Cited as the title.

The title displays centered properly (Figure 3-58).

Creating a Hanging Indent

On the works cited page, the works begin at the left margin. Subsequent lines in the same paragraph are indented one-half inch from the left margin. In essence, the first line *hangs* to the left of the rest of the paragraph; thus, this type of paragraph formatting is called a **hanging indent**. Perform the following steps to create a hanging indent.

Steps To Create a Hanging Indent

1 **Press the ENTER key. Click the Align Left button on the Formatting toolbar. Point to the Hanging Indent marker on the ruler (Figure 3-59).**

Recall that the small square at the 0" mark, called the Left Indent marker, is used to change the entire left margin, whereas the Hanging Indent marker affects only the subsequent lines of the same paragraph.

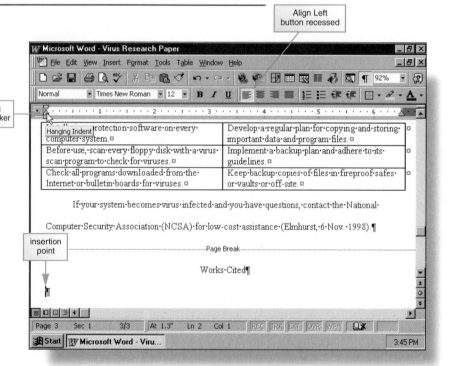

Align Left
button recessed

Hanging
Indent marker

insertion
point

FIGURE 3-59

2 **Drag the Hanging Indent marker to the .5-inch mark on the ruler.**

The Hanging Indent marker and Left Indent marker display at the location of the first tab stop, one-half inch from the left margin (Figure 3-60). When you drag the Hanging Indent marker, the Left Indent marker moves with it. The paragraph containing the insertion point in the document window is positioned at the left margin because only subsequent lines in the paragraph are to be indented.

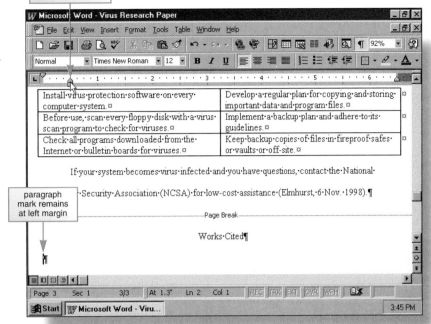

Hanging Indent marker positioned .5" from left margin

paragraph mark remains at left margin

FIGURE 3-60

To drag both the First Line Indent and Hanging Indent markers at the same time, you drag the Left Indent marker on the ruler.

Creating a Hyperlink

A **hyperlink** is a shortcut that allows a user to jump easily and quickly to other documents, objects, or pages. **Jumping** is the process of following a hyperlink to its destination. For example, by clicking hyperlink text on the Word screen, you jump to another document on your computer, on your network, or on the World Wide Web. When you close the hyperlink destination page or document, you return to the original location in your Word document. When the hyperlink text displays initially, it is underlined and colored blue. Once you click a hyperlink, the hyperlink text color changes to purple. When you create a Word document and wish to create a hyperlink to a Web page, you do not have to be connected to the Internet.

Recall from Project 2 that Word has an AutoFormat As You Type feature. Using this feature, you can create a hyperlink simply by typing the address of the file or Web page to which you want to jump. Be sure this feature is enabled by clicking Tools on the menu bar, clicking AutoCorrect, clicking the AutoFormat As You Type tab, clicking the Internet and network paths with hyperlinks, and then clicking the OK button.

In this project, one of the works is from a Web page on the Internet. When someone displays your research paper on the screen, you want him or her to be able to click the Web address in the work and jump to the site for more information. Perform the steps on the next page to create a hyperlink as you type.

More *About* **Citing Sources**

Information that is commonly known or accessible to the audience constitutes common knowledge and does not have to be listed as a parenthetical citation or in the bibliography. If, however, you question whether certain information is common knowledge, you should document it – just to be safe.

Steps | To Create a Hyperlink As You Type

1 **Type the Works Cited paragraphs as shown in Figure 3-62 below.**

When Word wraps the text in each works cited paragraph, it automatically indents the second line of the paragraph by one-half inch (Figure 3-61). When you press the ENTER key at the end of the first paragraph of text, the insertion point returns automatically to the left margin for the next paragraph. Recall that each time you press the ENTER key, the paragraph formatting in the prior paragraph is carried forward to the next paragraph. The insertion point is positioned to the right of the Web address.

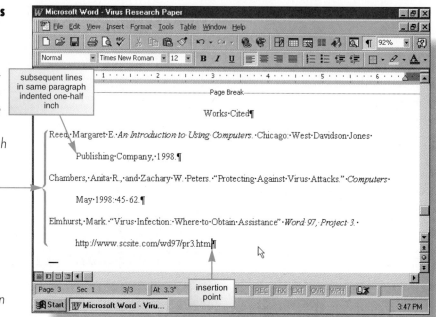

FIGURE 3-61

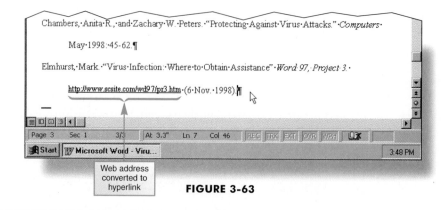

> Reed, Margaret E. *An Introduction to Using Computers.* Chicago: West Davidson Jones Publishing Company, 1998.
>
> Chambers, Anita R., and Zachary W. Peters. "Protecting Against Virus Attacks." *Computers* May 1998: 45-62.
>
> Elmhurst, Mark. "Virus Infection: Where to Obtain Assistance" *Word 97, Project 3.* http://www.scsite.com/wd97/pr3.htm

FIGURE 3-62

2 **Press the SPACEBAR and then type** (6 Nov. 1998).

As soon as you press the SPACEBAR after typing the Web address, the address formats as a hyperlink (Figure 3-63).

FIGURE 3-63

Later in this project, you will jump to the hyperlink destination.

Sorting Paragraphs

The MLA style requires that the works cited be listed in alphabetical order by author's last name. With Word, you can arrange paragraphs in alphabetic, numeric, or date order based on the first character in each paragraph. Ordering characters in this manner is called **sorting**. Arrange the works cited paragraphs in alphabetical order as illustrated in the following steps.

More *About*
Sorting

You can also sort the contents of a table. First, select the rows in the table to be sorted. Click Table on the menu bar, click Sort Text, click Ascending or Descending, and then click the OK button. Once a document has been saved with sorted paragraphs or tables, you cannot return to original order of the paragraphs or table.

 To Sort Paragraphs

1 Select all the works cited paragraphs by pointing to the left of the first paragraph and dragging down. Click Table on the menu bar and then point to Sort.

All of the paragraphs to be sorted are selected (Figure 3-64).

all paragraphs to be sorted are selected

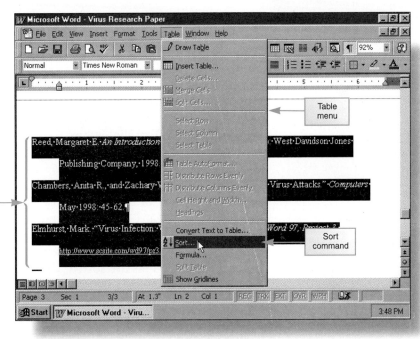

FIGURE 3-64

2 Click Sort.

Word displays the Sort Text dialog box (Figure 3-65). In the Sort by area, Ascending is selected. Ascending sorts in alphabetic or numeric order.

FIGURE 3-65

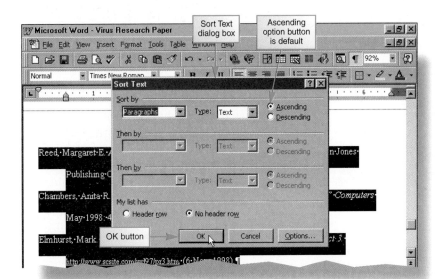

3 Click the OK button. Click outside of the selection to remove the highlight.

Word sorts the works cited paragraphs alphabetically (Figure 3-66).

paragraphs sorted alphabetically

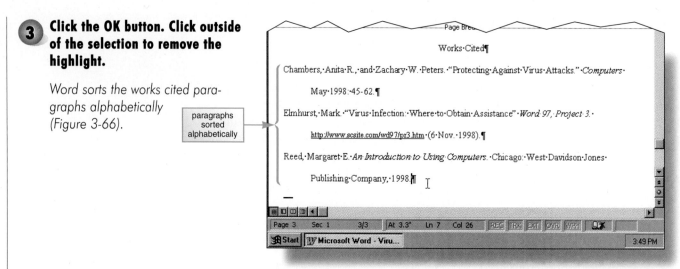

FIGURE 3-66

More *About*
APA Style

The APA style requires that the working bibliography be on a separate page, like the MLA; however, the title should be References, rather than Works Cited. The running head should appear on the References page. Guidelines for preparing reference list entries differ significantly from the MLA style. Refer to an APA handbook for specifics.

If you accidentally sort the wrong paragraphs, you can undo a sort by clicking the Undo button on the Standard toolbar.

In the Sort Text dialog box (Figure 3-65 on the previous page), the default sort order is Ascending. If the first character of each paragraph to be sorted is a letter, Word sorts alphabetically on the first letter of the paragraphs. If the first character of each paragraph to be sorted is a number, Word sorts numerically on the first number of the paragraphs. Word by default, orders in **ascending sort order**, which means from the beginning of the alphabet, lowest number, or earliest date. If the first character of the paragraphs to be sorted contains a mixture of letters, numbers, and dates, then the numbers appear first and letters appear last once the paragraphs are sorted. Uppercase letters appear before lowercase letters. In case of ties, Word looks to the first character with a nonidentical character and sorts on that character for the paragraphs where the tie occurs.

You also can sort in descending order by clicking Descending in the Sort Text dialog box. **Descending sort order** begins sorting from the end of the alphabet, the highest number, or the most recent date.

The research paper is now complete and ready for proofing.

Proofing and Revising the Research Paper

As discussed in Project 1, once you complete a document, you might find it necessary to make changes to it. Before submitting a paper to be graded, you should proofread it. While proofreading, you look for grammatical errors and spelling errors. You want to be sure the transitions between sentences flow smoothly and the sentences themselves make sense. Very often, you may count the words in a paper to meet minimum word guidelines specified by an instructor. To assist you in this proofreading effort, Word provides several tools. You already have used the spell checker and grammar checker in previous projects. Other helpful tools are discussed in the following pages.

Going to a Specific Location in a Document

Often, you would like to bring a certain page or footnote into view in the document window. To do this, you could scroll though the document to find the desired page or note. Instead of scrolling though the document, Word provides an easier method of going to a specific location via the **Select Browse Object menu**. Perform the following steps to go to the top of page two in the research paper.

Steps To Browse by Page

1 Click the Select Browse Object button on the vertical scroll bar. When the Select Browse Object menu displays, point to Browse by Page.

Word displays the Select Browse Object menu (Figure 3-67). As you point to various commands in the Select Browse Object menu, Word displays the command name at the bottom of the menu. For example, you could browse by footnote, endnote, table, and so on.

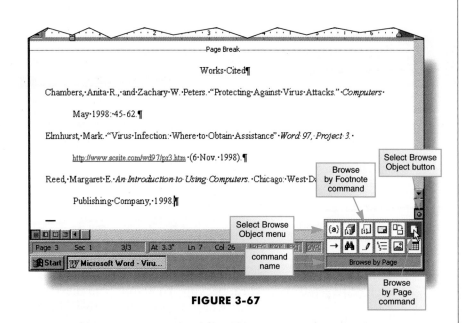

FIGURE 3-67

2 Click Browse by Page. Point to the Previous Page button on the vertical scroll bar.

Word closes the Select Browse Object menu (Figure 3-68). Depending on the command you select in the Select Browse Object menu, the function of the buttons above and below the Select Browse Object button on the vertical scroll bar changes. Because Browse by Page was selected, the buttons move to the previous or next page.

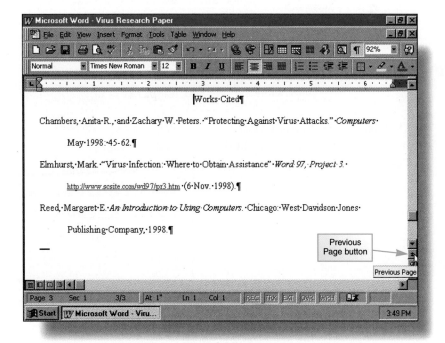

FIGURE 3-68

3 Click the Previous Page button.

Word places the top of page 2 (the previous page) at the top of the document window (Figure 3-69).

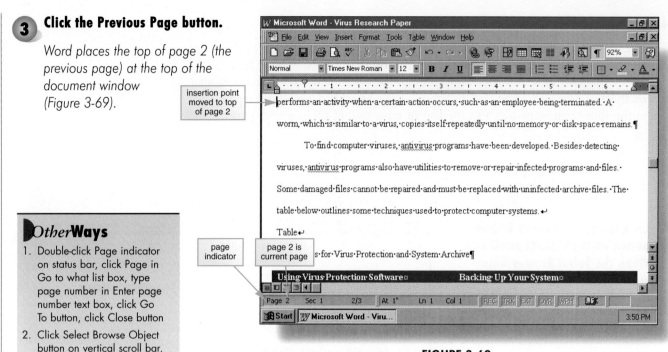

FIGURE 3-69

 OtherWays

1. Double-click Page indicator on status bar, click Page in Go to what list box, type page number in Enter page number text box, click Go To button, click Close button

2. Click Select Browse Object button on vertical scroll bar, click Go To, and then proceed starting with click Page in Go to what list box as described in 1 above

3. On Edit menu click Go To, and then proceed starting with click Page in Go to what list box as described in 1 above

4. Press CTRL+G, and then proceed starting with click Page in Go to what list box as described in 1 above

Finding and Replacing Text

While proofreading the paper, notice that it contains the word, archive, more than once in the document (see Figure 3-70 below); and you would rather use the word, backup. Therefore, you must change all occurrences of the word, archive, to the word, backup. To do this, you can use Word's find and replace feature, which automatically locates each occurrence of a specified word or phrase and then replaces it with specified text as shown in these steps.

Steps **To Find and Replace Text**

1 Click the Select Browse Object button on the vertical scroll bar. Point to Find.

Word displays the Select Browse Object menu (Figure 3-70). The Find command is highlighted.

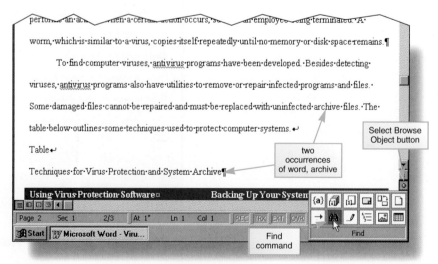

FIGURE 3-70

2 **Click Find. When the Find and Replace dialog box displays, click the Replace tab. Type** archive **in the Find what text box. Press the TAB key. Type** backup **in the Replace with text box. Point to the Replace All button.**

Word displays the Find and Replace dialog box (Figure 3-71). Clicking the Replace All button replaces all occurrences of the Find what text with the Replace with text.

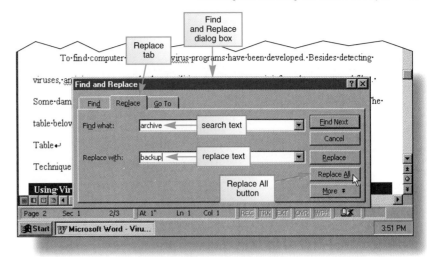

FIGURE 3-71

3 **Click the Replace All button.**

Word replaces all occurrences of the word, archive, with the word, backup, and then displays a Microsoft Word dialog box indicating the total number of replacements made (Figure 3-72).

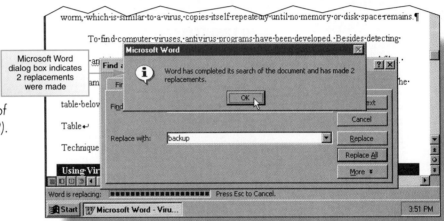

FIGURE 3-72

4 **Click the OK button in the Microsoft Word dialog box. Click the Close button in the Find and Replace dialog box.**

Word returns to the document window. The word, backup, now displays instead of the word, archive (Figure 3-73).

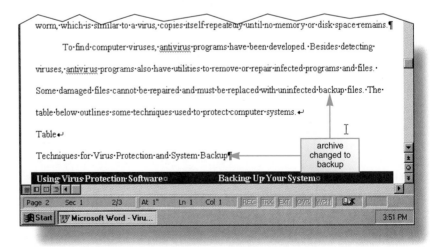

FIGURE 3-73

Other Ways

1. On Edit menu click Replace, type Find what text, type Replace with text, click Replace All button, click OK button, click Close button
2. Press CTRL+H, and then proceed starting with type Find what text as described in 1 above

In some cases, you may want to replace only certain occurrences of the text, not all of them. To instruct Word to confirm each change, click the Find Next button in the Find and Replace dialog box (Figure 3-71 on the previous page), instead of the Replace All button. When Word locates an occurrence of the text in the Find what text box, it pauses and waits for you to click either the Replace button or the Find Next button. Clicking the Replace button changes the text; clicking the Find Next button instructs Word to disregard the replacement and look for the next occurrence of the Find what text.

If you accidentally replace the wrong text, you can undo a replacement by clicking the Undo button on the Standard toolbar. If you used the Replace All button, Word undoes all replacements. If you used the Replace button, Word only undoes the most recent replacement.

Finding Text

Sometimes, you may want to only find text, instead of find and replace text. To search for just an occurrence of text, you would follow these steps.

TO FIND TEXT

Step 1: Click the Select Browse Object button on the vertical scroll bar.
Step 2: Click Find on the Select Browse Object menu.
Step 3: Type the text you want to locate in the Find what text box on the Find sheet.
Step 4: Click the Find Next button.
Step 5: To edit the text, click the Close button in the Find and Replace dialog box; to search for the next occurrence of the Find what text, click the Find Next button.

Using the Thesaurus

When writing papers, you may find that you used the same word in multiple locations or that a word you used was not quite appropriate. In these instances, you will want to look up a word similar in meaning to the duplicate or inappropriate word. These similar words are called **synonyms**. A book of synonyms is referred to as a **thesaurus**. Word provides its own thesaurus for your convenience. In this project, you need a synonym for the word, find, at the beginning of the fourth paragraph. Perform the following steps to use Word's thesaurus.

Steps **To Use Word's Thesaurus**

1 **Click the word for which you want to look up a synonym. Click Tools on the menu bar, point to Language on the Tools menu, and then point to Thesaurus on the Language submenu.**

The insertion point is positioned in the word, find, at the beginning of the fourth paragraph in the research paper (Figure 3-74).

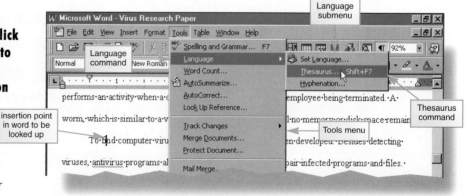

FIGURE 3-74

2 **Click Thesaurus. When the Thesaurus: English (United States) dialog box displays, click detect (verb) in the Meanings list box.**

Word displays the Thesaurus: English (United States) dialog box. The Meanings list box displays the different uses of the selected word, and the Replace with Synonym list box displays a variety of words with similar meanings. The Replace with Synonym list changes based on the meaning you select in the Meanings list.

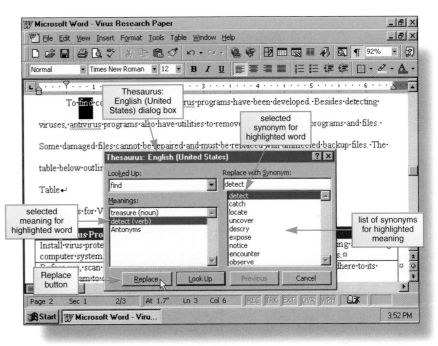

FIGURE 3-75

3 **Click the synonym you want (detect) and then point to the Replace button.**

The word, detect, is highlighted in the Replace with Synonym list (Figure 3-75).

4 **Click the Replace button.**

Word replaces the word, find, with detect and returns to the document window (Figure 3-76 below).

OtherWays

1. Press SHIFT+F7

Using Word Count

Often when you write papers, you are required to compose a paper with a specified number of words. The requirement for the research paper in this project was 500 words. For this reason, Word provides a command that displays the number of words, as well as the number of pages, characters, paragraphs, and lines in your document. Perform the following steps to use Word Count.

 **To Count Words**

1 **Click Tools on the menu bar and then point to Word Count (Figure 3-76).**

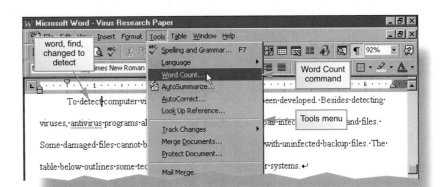

FIGURE 3-76

2 **Click Word Count. When the Word Count dialog box displays, if necessary, click Include footnotes and endnotes to select the check box.**

Word displays the Word Count dialog box (Figure 3-77). Word presents you with a variety of statistics on the current document, including number of pages, words, characters, paragraphs, and lines. You can choose to have note text included or not included in these statistics.

3 **Click Include footnotes and endnotes to deselect it. Click the Close button in the Word Count dialog box.**

Word deselects the Include footnotes and endnotes check box and then returns you to the document.

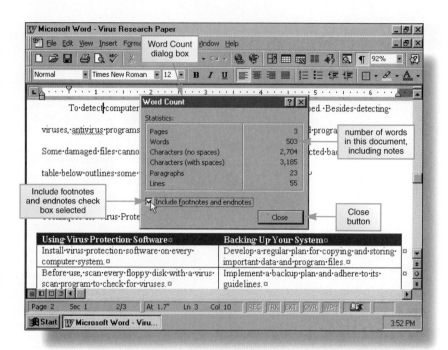

FIGURE 3-77

OtherWays

1. On File menu click Properties, click Statistics tab, click OK button

If you want statistics on only a section of your document, select the section before invoking the Word Count command.

You should change the zoom control back to 100% so the next person that uses Word will not have a reduced display.

TO ZOOM TO 100%

Step 1: Click the Zoom box arrow.
Step 2: Click 100% in the list of zoom percentages.

Word displays 100% in the Zoom box.

Checking Spelling, Saving Again, and Printing the Document

The document is now complete. After completing the document, you should check the spelling of the document by clicking the Spelling and Grammar button on the Standard toolbar. Because you have performed several tasks since the last save, you should save the research paper again by clicking the Save button on the Standard toolbar. Finally, you should print the research paper by clicking the Print button on the Standard toolbar. The completed research paper prints as shown in Figure 3-1 on page WD 3.5.

Navigating to a Hyperlink

Recall that one requirement of this research paper is that one of the works be a site on the Web. Your instructor, Professor J. Brown, has requested that you turn in a floppy disk with this research paper on it so he can verify information at the site. Perform the following steps to check your hyperlink.

 Steps **To Navigate to a Hyperlink**

1 **Display the third page of the research paper in the document window and then point to the hyperlink text.**

When you point to hyperlink text in a Word document, the mouse pointer shape changes to a pointing hand (Figure 3-78). To follow the link, click it.

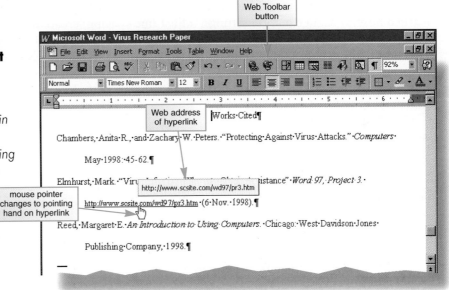

FIGURE 3-78

2 **Click the hyperlink text.**

If you currently are not connected to the Web, Word connects you using your default browser. After a few moments, the http://www.scsite.com/wd97/ pr3.htm Web page displays (Figure 3-79).

3 **Close the browser window.**

The Word screen redisplays.

4 **Click the Web Toolbar button on the Standard toolbar to remove the Web toolbar.**

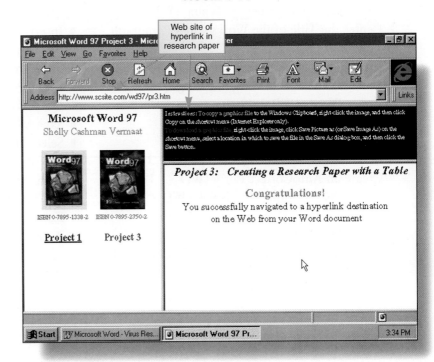

FIGURE 3-79

The final step in this project is to quit Word.

TO QUIT WORD

Step 1: Click the Close button in the Word window.

The Word window closes.

Project Summary

Project 3 introduced you to creating a research paper with a table using the MLA documentation style. You learned how to change margin settings, adjust line spacing, create headers with page numbers, and indent paragraphs. You learned how to use Word's AutoCorrect feature. Then, you added a footnote and created a table in the research paper. You alphabetized the works cited page by sorting its paragraphs and included a hyperlink to a Web page in one of the works. You learned how to browse through a Word document and find and replace text. Finally, you used Word's thesaurus to look up synonyms and saw how to display statistics about your document.

What You Should Know

Having completed this project, you now should be able to perform the following tasks:

▶ Add a Footnote (*WD 3.25*)
▶ AutoCorrect As You Type (*WD 3.22*)
▶ AutoFormat a Table (*WD 3.34*)
▶ Browse by Page (*WD 3.45*)
▶ Center a Paragraph before Typing (*WD 3.17*)
▶ Center the Title of the Works Cited Paragraph (*WD 3.40*)
▶ Change the Default Font Size (*WD 3.15*)
▶ Change the Default Margin Settings (*WD 3.8*)
▶ Count Words (*WD 3.49*)
▶ Create a Hanging Indent (*WD 3.40*)
▶ Create a Header (*WD 3.12*)
▶ Create a Hyperlink As You Type (*WD 3.42*)
▶ Create an AutoCorrect Entry (*WD 3.23*)
▶ Display Nonprinting Characters (*WD 3.7*)
▶ Double-Space a Document (*WD 3.10*)
▶ Enter Data into a Table (*WD 3.33*)
▶ Enter Name and Course Information (*WD 3.16*)

▶ Find and Replace Text (*WD 3.46*)
▶ Find Text (*WD 3.48*)
▶ First-Line Indent Paragraphs (*WD 3.18*)
▶ Insert a Blank Line above a Paragraph (*WD 3.37*)
▶ Insert an Empty Table (*WD 3.31*)
▶ Navigate to a Hyperlink (*WD 3.52*)
▶ Page Break Automatically (*WD 3.29*)
▶ Page Break Manually (*WD 3.38*)
▶ Quit Word (*WD 3.53*)
▶ Save a Document (*WD 3.18*)
▶ Select an Entire Table (*WD 3.36*)
▶ Sort Paragraphs (*WD 3.43*)
▶ Start Word (*WD 3.7*)
▶ Use Word's Thesaurus (*WD 3.48*)
▶ Zoom Page Width (*WD 3.21*)
▶ Zoom to 100% (*WD 3.50*)

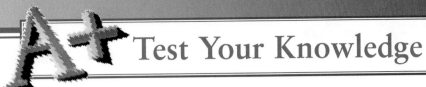 Test Your Knowledge

1 True/False

Instructions: Circle T if the statement is true or F if the statement is false.

T F 1. The MLA presents a popular documentation style used today for research papers.

T F 2. The MLA style uses the term works cited rather than bibliography.

T F 3. A footer is text you want to print at the bottom of each page in a document.

T F 4. Subscripted numbers are those that appear raised above other text in a document.

T F 5. An automatic page break displays on the screen as a single dotted horizontal line, separated by the words Page Break.

T F 6. A cell is the intersection of a row and a column in a Word table.

T F 7. To insert a tab character into a cell, press the TAB key.

T F 8. A hanging indent indents subsequent lines in the same paragraph one-half inch from the right margin.

T F 9. Word's thesaurus enables you to look up synonyms for a selected word.

T F 10. To jump to a hyperlink destination from a Word document, click the hyperlink text.

2 Multiple Choice

Instructions: Circle the correct response.

1. MLA stands for _____.
   a. Modern Language Abbreviation
   b. Modern Language Association
   c. Modern Lexical Abbreviation
   d. Modern Lexical Association

2. How can you edit header text?
   a. switch to page layout view
   b. display the document in print preview
   c. click View on the menu bar and then click Header and Footer
   d. all of the above

3. The AutoCorrect feature automatically fixes misspelled words when you _____ after entering the misspelled word.
   a. press the ESC key
   b. click the AutoCorrect button
   c. type a period
   d. press the SPACEBAR

4. If an AutoComplete tip displays on the screen, _____ to instruct Word to place the text of the AutoComplete tip at the location of your typing.
   a. press the ENTER key
   b. press the SHIFT+ENTER keys
   c. click the AutoComplete button
   d. either b or c

5. A(n) _____ occurs when the first line of a paragraph displays by itself at the bottom of a page.
   a. twin
   b. orphan
   c. sibling
   d. widow

6. A table with 7 rows and 4 columns is referred to as a(n) _____ table.
   a. 28
   b. 11
   c. 7 × 4
   d. 4 × 7

(continued)

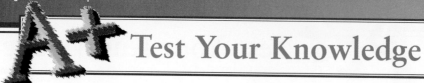

Test Your Knowledge

Multiple Choice *(continued)*

7. To insert a blank line above a paragraph, press the _____ keys.
   a. CTRL+0 (zero) b. CTRL+B c. ALT+0 (zero) d. ALT+B

8. To move both the First Line Indent marker and Hanging Indent marker on the ruler at the same time, you _____.
   a. drag the Left Indent marker c. right-drag the First Line Indent marker
   b. select both markers and then drag d. none of the above

9. A hyperlink is a shortcut that allows you to jump to _____.
   a. another document on your computer c. a page on the World Wide Web
   b. another document on your network d. all of the above

10. The Select Browse Object button is located on the _____.
    a. Standard toolbar c. vertical scroll bar
    b. Formatting toolbar d. horizontal scroll bar

3 Understanding the Ruler

FIGURE 3-80

Instructions: Answer the following questions concerning the ruler in Figure 3-80. The numbers in the figure correspond to the numbers of the questions below.

1. What is the name of the top triangle? What is the purpose of dragging this triangle?
2. What is the name of the bottom triangle? What is the purpose of dragging this triangle?
3. What is the name of the small square? What is the purpose of dragging this square?

4 Understanding the Note Pane

FIGURE 3-81

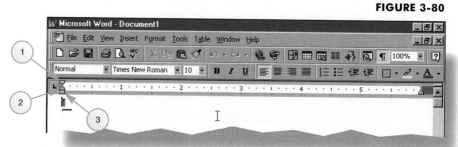

Instructions: In Figure 3-81, arrows point to major components of the note pane. Identify the various parts of the note pane in the spaces provided.

Use Help

1 Reviewing Project Activities

Instructions: Perform the following tasks using a computer.

1. Start Word.
2. If the Office Assistant is on your screen, click it to display its balloon. If the Office Assistant is not on your screen, click the Office Assistant button on the Standard toolbar.
3. Type `create a hyperlink` in the What would you like to do? text box. Click the Search button. Click the Create hyperlinks link. Read the information. Use the shortcut menu or Options button to print the information.
4. Click the Help Topics button to display the Help Topics: Microsoft Word dialog box. Click the Contents tab. Double-click the Working with Tables and Adding Borders book. Double-click the Parts of a table topic. Read and print the information.
5. Click the Help Topics button. Click the Index tab. Type `margins` and then double-click the overview topic. Double-click the Paragraph indenting vs. page margins topic. Read and print the information.
6. Click the Help Topics button. Click the Find tab. Type `header` and then double-click the Add page numbers topic. Read and print the information.
7. Close any open Help window(s) by clicking its Close button. Close the Office Assistant.

2 Expanding on the Basics

Instructions: Use Word Help to better understand the topics listed below. Answer the questions on your own paper or hand in the printed Help topic to your instructor.

1. In this project, you worked with a header. Use the Office Assistant to answer the following questions about headers and footers.
    a. What would cause the correct date, time, or other item to not appear in the header? When you locate the Help window containing this answer, the term, field, is used. What is a field?
    b. How do you create a unique header or footer for the first page of a document? When you locate the Help window containing the answer, the term, section, is used. What is a section?
    c. How do you delete a header or a footer?
2. In this project, you created a Word table. Use the Contents tab in the Help Topics: Microsoft Word dialog box to locate Help windows describing keys used for the following tasks: type and move around in a table and select items in a table. Print each of the two Help topics. Next, obtain answers to the following questions.
    a. How do you add a row to the end of a table? the middle of a table?
    b. How do you add a column to the right edge of a table? the middle of a table?
3. In this project, you inserted a hyperlink. Use the Index tab in the Help Topics: Microsoft Word dialog box to answer the following questions about hyperlinks.
    a. How do you change a hyperlink destination?
    b. How do you change existing hyperlink text?

(continued)

Use Help

Expanding on the Basics *(continued)*

    c. What is a Word publication?

    d. Assume when you click a hyperlink, an error message displays. Identify three reasons the error message might display.

4. In this project, you created an AutoCorrect entry. Use the Find tab in the Help Topics: Microsoft Word dialog box to answer the following questions about AutoCorrect entries.

    a. How do you change the contents of an AutoCorrect entry?

    b. How do you delete an AutoCorrect entry?

    c. How can you prevent AutoCorrect from correcting abbreviations or capitalized text?

    d. How can you add an AutoCorrect entry during a spelling check?

5. Click the Web Toolbar button on the Standard toolbar to display the Web toolbar. Use the What's This? command on the Help menu to display ScreenTips for each button on the Web toolbar. Print each ScreenTip by right-clicking it, clicking Print Topic on the shortcut menu, and then clicking the OK button.

Apply Your Knowledge

1 Working with a Table

Instructions: Start Word. Open the document, apply-3, from the Word folder on the Data Disk that accompanies this book. The document is a Word table that you are to edit and format. You may need to refer to your Use Help 2 responses for information on how to select items in the table and modify them. The revised table is shown in Figure 3-82.

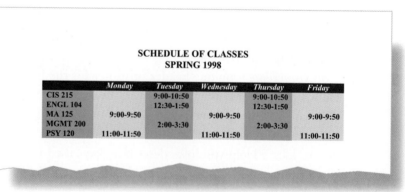

FIGURE 3-82

Perform the following tasks:

1. Right-click the table and then click Table AutoFormat on the shortcut menu. Click Columns 2 in the Formats area of the Table AutoFormat dialog box. Be sure all of the check boxes in the Formats to apply area are checked. Also, be sure that only the Heading rows check box is checked in the Apply special formats to area; you may need to deselect First column. Click the OK button.

Apply Your Knowledge

2. Add a new row to the table for ENGL 104, which meets on Tuesdays and Thursdays from 12:30-1:50.
3. Delete the Saturday column by selecting it, right-clicking the selection, and then clicking Delete Columns on the shortcut menu. You do not have any Saturday classes scheduled.
4. Click in the table, click Table on the menu bar, and then click Select Table.
5. Click Table on the menu bar and then click Cell Height and Width. If necessary, click the Row tab, click Center in the Alignment area, and then click the OK button to center the table between the left and right margins.
6. With the table still selected, click Table on the menu bar, click Sort, and then click the OK button. Click anywhere to remove the highlight from the table.
7. Select the header row and then click the Italic button on the Formatting toolbar.
8. Select the cells containing the class times and then click the Align Right button on the Formatting toolbar.
9. Click File on the menu bar and then click Save As. Use the file name Revised Class Schedule and then save the document on your floppy disk.
10. Print the revised table.

In the Lab

1 **Preparing a Research Paper with a Table**

Problem: You are a college student currently enrolled in an introductory computer class. Your assignment is to prepare a short research paper (400-450 words) about Computer Security. The requirements are that the paper be prepared according to the MLA documentation style, contain a table, and have three references – one of which must be from the Internet (Figure 3-83 on the next two pages).

Instructions:
1. If necessary, click the Show/Hide ¶ button on the Standard toolbar. Change all margins to one inch. Adjust line spacing to double. Create a header to number pages. Change the font size of all characters to 12 point. Type the name and course information at the left margin. Center and type the title. First-line indent all paragraphs in the paper.
2. Type the body of the paper as shown in Figure 3-83a and Figure 3-83b. The table is formatted in the Grid 8 format with the all check boxes selected except Last row and Last column. At the end of the body of the research paper, press the ENTER key and insert a manual page break.
3. Create the works cited page (Figure 3-83c).
4. Check the spelling of the paper.

(continued)

In the Lab

Preparing a Research Paper with a Table *(continued)*

5. Save the document on a floppy disk with Computer Security Research Paper as the file name.
6. Print the research paper. Above the title of your printed research paper, hand write the number of words in the research paper.

West 1

Jonathan Paul West

Professor M. Carter

Information Systems 200

September 9, 1998

Computer Security

Many commercial software packages are designed with computer security features that control who can access the computer. These types of access controls use a process called identification and authentication. Identification verifies that the user is a valid user, and authentication verifies that the user is who he or she claims to be. Three common methods of authentication are remembered information, possessed objects, and biometric devices.

With remembered information, a user is required to enter a word or series of characters that match an entry in a security file in the computer. Most multiuser operating systems provide for a logon code, a user ID, and a password (all forms of remembered information) that all must be entered correctly before a user is allowed to use an application program. A logon code usually identifies the application, and a user ID identifies the user. A password usually is confidential, often known only by the user and the system administrator (Baker and Danville 29-47).

A possessed object is any item that a user must carry to gain access to the computer facility. Examples of possessed objects are badges, cards, and keys. Possessed objects often are used in conjunction with a personal identification number (PIN), which is a numeric password (Price 40-68).

A biometric device is one that verifies personal characteristics to authenticate a user. Examples of personal characteristics are fingerprints, voice pattern, signature, hand size, and

FIGURE 3-83a

In the Lab

West 2

retinal (eye) patterns. A biometric device usually translates a user's personal characteristics into a digital code that is compared to a digital code stored in the computer (Victors 22-85). If the digital code in the computer does not match the user's code, access is denied.

Each of these authentication techniques has advantages and disadvantages. The table below outlines the major advantage and disadvantage of each technique.

Table

Advantages and Disadvantages of Authentication Techniques

	Remembered Information	Possessed Object	Biometric Device
Advantages	Inexpensive	Relatively inexpensive	Virtually foolproof
Disadvantages	Can be forgotten or guessed by a perpetrator	Can be lost or forgotten	Expensive

A computer system should implement one or more of these authentication techniques to secure it from accidental or intentional misuse. In addition, the organization should review the techniques in place regularly to determine if they are still appropriate.

FIGURE 3-83b

West 3

Works Cited

Baker, Jamie D. and Cynthia I. Danville. "Security, Ethics, and Privacy." Computers and Society Journal Feb. 1998: 29-47.

Price, Karen E. "Identification and Authentication Controls." Word 97, Project 3. http://www.scsite.com/wd97/pr3.htm (31 Aug. 1998).

Victors, Michael R. The Computer Auditor. St. Louis: Green Valley Publishing Company, 1998.

FIGURE 3-83c

2 Preparing a Research Report with a Footnote and a Table

Problem: You are a college student currently enrolled in an English class. Your assignment is to prepare a short research paper in any area of interest to you. The only requirements are that the paper be presented according to the MLA documentation style, contain a table, and have three references, one of which must be from the Internet. You decide to prepare a paper comparing word processing software and desktop publishing software (Figure 3-84 on the next two pages).

(continued)

In the Lab

Preparing a Research Report with a Footnote and a Table *(continued)*

Reed 1

Sally Reed

Professor P. Harmon

English 204

December 9, 1998

Word Processing vs. Desktop Publishing

Many organizations distribute brochures and newsletters to promote their products and/or

services. In the past, preparing these desktop publishing documents was best accomplished

through outside agencies. In the 1980s, however, word processors began including graphics and

different fonts as part of their standard software package (Larkin and Green, 8 Oct. 1998). That

is, many word processors were emerging with desktop publishing capabilities.

Desktop publishing software (DTP) allows users to design and produce professional

looking documents that contain both text and graphics. Examples of such documents include

newsletters, marketing literature, technical manuals, and annual reports. The common thread

among these packages is the ability to import graphic images, change fonts, draw lines, and

display in WYSIWYG mode (What You See Is What You Get).

Graphic images can be imported from previously created art, called clip art. Clip art may

be included with the software package being used or may be purchased.[1] Collections of clip art

contain several hundred to several thousand images grouped by type, such as holidays, vehicles,

or people. Input devices, called scanners, also can be used to import photographs and art into

[1] Winters found that nearly all of today's word processing software includes clip art,

which can be enlarged, reduced, moved, and altered in other ways.

FIGURE 3-84a

In the Lab

Reed 2

DTP documents (Brown 14-35). Regardless of how it is accomplished, once the image has been imported into the document, it can be enlarged, reduced, rotated, or moved.

Many word processing software packages today include features that previously were considered to be the domain of desktop publishing software. Conversely, many recent releases of DTP software contain enhanced word processing capabilities. The table below outlines the DTP features in word processing packages and features not yet in most word processing packages.

Table

DTP Features

DTP Features in Word Processing Packages	Additional DTP Features in DTP Software
Alters typefaces, styles, and point sizes	Includes color libraries
Adjusts margins, alignment, and spacing	Creates master pages, larger page sizes, and page grids
Includes columns, tables, graphics, borders, and shading	Stacks and overlaps multiple objects on a page and traps objects

With each release of word processing and DTP software, the differences between the two will decrease and their similarities will increase.

FIGURE 3-84b

Instructions: Perform the following tasks:

1. Change all margin settings to one inch. Adjust line spacing to double. Create a header to number pages. Change the font size of all characters to 12 point. Type the name and course information at the left margin. Center and type the title. First-line indent all paragraphs in the paper.

2. Type the body of the paper as shown in Figure 3-84a and Figure 3-84b. The table is formatted in the Grid 8 format with the all check boxes selected except Last row and Last column. At the end of the body of the research paper, press the ENTER key once and insert a manual page break.

3. Create the works cited page. Enter the works cited shown below as separate paragraphs and then alphabetize the paragraphs.

   a. Larkin, Henry P., and Janice A. Green. "Word Processing." *Word 97, Project 3.* http://www.scsite.com/wd97/pr3.htm (8 Oct. 1998).

   b. Winters, Jill. "Word Processing Software Packages Today." *Microcomputer Journal* Nov. 1998: 58-66.

   c. Brown, Robert. *Introductory Computer Concepts and Techniques.* Boston: International Publishing Company, 1998.

4. Check the spelling of the paper. Use Word's thesaurus to change the word, domain, in the last paragraph to a word of your choice.

5. Save the document on a floppy disk with Word Processing Paper as the file name.

6. Print the research paper. Above the title of your printed research paper, hand write the number of words, including the footnote, in the research paper.

In the Lab

3 Composing a Research Report with a Table and Footnotes

Problem: You have drafted the notes shown in Figure 3-85. Your assignment is to prepare a short research paper based on these notes. You are to review the notes and then rearrange and reword. Embellish the paper as you deem necessary. Add a footnote elaborating on a personal experience you have had. Create a table listing examples of peripherals. Present the paper according to the MLA documentation style.

Instructions: Perform the following tasks:

1. If necessary, click the Show/Hide ¶ button on the Standard toolbar. Change all margin settings to one inch. Adjust line spacing to double. Create a header to number pages. Change the font size of all characters to 12 point. Type the name and course information at the left margin. Center and type the title. First-line indent all paragraphs in the paper.

2. Compose the body of the paper from the notes in Figure 3-85 . Be sure to include a footnote and a table as specified above. At the end of the body of the research paper, press the ENTER key once and insert a manual page break.

3. Create the works cited page from the listed sources. Be sure to alphabetize the works.

4. Check the spelling and grammar of the paper.

5. Save the document on a floppy disk with YourName Research Paper as the file name (where Your-Name is your last name).

6. Print the research paper. Above the title of your printed research paper, hand write the number of words, including the footnote, in the research paper.

The five major categories of computers are (1) personal computers, (2) servers, (3) minicomputers, (4) mainframe computers, and (5) supercomputers.

Personal computers also are called micros, PCs, or microcomputers. Examples include hand-held, palmtop, notebook, subnotebook, laptop, pen, desktop, tower, and workstation. Hand-held, palmtop, notebook, subnotebook, laptop, and pen computers are considered portable computers. Prices range from several hundred to several thousand dollars. Source: Personal Computers, a book published by Windy City Publishing Company in Chicago, 1998, pages 15-45, author Jane A. Polson.

A server supports a computer network. A network allows multiple users to share files, application software, and hardware. Small servers range from $5,000 to $20,000; larger servers can cost as much as $150,000. Source: "Serving Networks," an article in Network World, September 1998 issue, pages 135-148, author Peter S. Thorn.

Minicomputers are more powerful than PCs and can support multiple users performing different tasks. Originally, they were developed to perform specific tasks such as engineering calculations. Many businesses use them today for information processing requirements. Costs range from $15,000 to several hundred thousand dollars. Source: "Evaluating Computers," an article in Computer Monthly, August 1998 issue, pages 98-105, authors Karen D. Samuels and Benjamin R. Edwards.

A mainframe computer is a large system that can handle hundreds of users, store large amounts of data, and process transactions at a very high rate. They usually require a specialized environment with separate air conditioning and electrical power. Raised flooring often is built to accommodate the many cables connecting the system components. Prices range from several hundred thousand to several million dollars. Source: Web page article "Mainframe Issues" on Web page Word 97, Project 3 at site http://www.scsite.com/wd97/pr3.htm on September 4, 1998.

Supercomputers are the most powerful computers. They process hundreds of millions of instructions per second and are used for applications such as weather forecasting and space exploration. The cost is several million dollars. Same source as for minicomputers.

FIGURE 3-85

Cases and Places

The difficulty of these case studies varies: ❿ are the least difficult; ❿❿ are more difficult; and ❿❿❿ are the most difficult.

1 ❿ Having completed three projects with Word 97, you should be comfortable with its capabilities. To reinforce your knowledge of Word, write a research paper that discusses its components and features (such as spell checking, grammar checking, wizards, AutoCorrect, and so on). Use your textbook, Word Help, and any other resources available. Explain why you think the component or feature is important and then explain exactly how to perform the task in Word. Include at least two references. Use the concepts and techniques presented in this project to format the paper.

2 ❿ Windows is a graphical user interface (GUI), which claims to be a much more user-friendly environment that DOS. Write a brief research paper that discusses the features of Windows. Use your textbook, Windows Help, and any other resources available. For each feature you identify, discuss whether or not you feel this feature is user-friendly and state your reason(s). Include at least two references. Use the concepts and techniques presented in this project to format the paper.

3 ❿❿ This project required the MLA style of documentation in the preparation of the research paper. Another popular documentation style is by the American Psychological Association (APA). The MLA style generally is used in the humanities, whereas the APA style is preferred in the social sciences. Many differences exist between the two styles. Using the school library or other resources (such as the Internet), research the APA style. Then, prepare a brief research paper that compares and contrasts the two styles. Include at least one explanatory note and three references, one of which must be a Web site on the Internet. Use the concepts and techniques presented in this project to format the paper.

4 ❿❿ When you install Windows, two accessories are provided: a word processor and a text editor. Although Windows supplies these two programs, most users purchase a separate word processing package, such as Word, for creating documents. Try creating the research paper from this project in the Windows word processor and also the text editor. Use Windows Help or any other resources to assist you with these documents. Then, prepare a brief research paper comparing and contrasting Word 97 to the word processor and text editor supplied with Windows. Include at least one explanatory note and two references. Use the concepts and techniques presented in this project to format the paper.

Cases and Places

5 ▶▶ Microsoft Word was introduced in 1983. Since then, it has experienced many version changes and upgrades. Using a school library or other resources (such as the Internet), learn how Microsoft Word has evolved to the product it is today. Identify when and how the first word processors came to be. Then, prepare a brief research paper on the evolution of Microsoft Word since the beginning of word processors through today. Include at least one explanatory note and three references, one of which must be a Web site on the Internet. Use the concepts and techniques presented in this project to format the paper.

6 ▶▶▶ Many different word processing packages are on the market, e.g., Word, WordPerfect, and so on. Using a school library or other resources (such as the Internet), determine the top three word processing packages and their features. Contact two businesses and ask which word processor they use; find out what they like and dislike about their word processor. Then, prepare a brief research paper comparing and contrasting the three word processing packages. At the end of the paper, identify the one you feel is the best. Include at least two explanatory notes and three references, one of which must be a Web site on the Internet. Use the concepts and techniques presented in this project to format the paper.

7 ▶▶▶ When you purchase a personal computer, the price often includes some installed software. Sometimes, it is more economical to buy the package; however, you may not receive the exact software you desire. Visit or call two computer stores. Obtain package prices for their latest personal computers. Also, obtain prices of the hardware and software individually. Ask why they chose the software they did for the package deals. Then, prepare a brief research paper on computer package deals; discuss whether you would buy a package deal or not at the present time. Include at least two explanatory notes and three references. Use the concepts and techniques presented in this project to format the paper.

Creating Web Pages

Case Perspective

Recall that in Project 2 Caroline Louise Schmidt created a resume (Figure 2-2 on page WD 2.6). Recently, Caroline has been *surfing the Internet* and has discovered that many people have their own personal Web pages with links to items such as resumes, schedules, and so on. These personal Web pages are very impressive. To make herself more attractive to a potential employer, Caroline has decided to create a personal Web page that contains a hyperlink to her resume. To do this, she will have to save her resume as an HTML file (Web page). She also plans to make her e-mail address a hyperlink to make it easy for a potential employer to send her a message.

To complete this Integration Feature, you will need the resume created in Project 2, so that you can save it as an HTML file and then use the resulting Web page as a hyperlink destination. (If you did not create the resume, see your instructor for a copy of it.)

Introduction

Word provides two techniques for creating Web pages. You can save any Word document as a **HyperText Markup Language (HTML)** file so that it can be posted on the Web and viewed by a Web browser, such as Internet Explorer. Or, you can start a new Web page by using a wizard or template.

If you have an existing Word document, you can convert it quickly to a Web page (HTML file). If you do not have an existing Word document to convert, you can create a new Web page by using the Web Page Wizard, which provides customized templates you can modify easily. In addition to these Web tools, Word has many other **Web page authoring** features. For example, you can include hyperlinks, sound, video, pictures, scrolling text, bullets, and horizontal lines on your Web pages.

Once complete, you want to make your Web page(s) available to others on your network, on an intranet, or on the World Wide Web. To post them on your network, simply save the Web page(s) and related files to the network server. If your company uses an **intranet**, which is a network that uses Internet technologies, you will have to copy your Web page(s) and related files to the Web server. To post your Web page(s) on the World Wide Web, you will need to locate an **Internet service provider (ISP)** that provides space for Web pages. Many ISPs allocate space for subscribers free of charge. What you need is an FTP (File Transfer Protocol) program so you can copy your Web page(s) and related files from your computer to your ISP's computer.

This Integration Feature illustrates saving the resume created in Project 2 as an HTML file (Figure 1c). Then, you use Word's Web Page Wizard to create a personal Web page (Figure 1a) that can be posted to a network, an intranet, or the World Wide Web (Figure 1b). The personal Web page contains a hyperlink to the resume (Figure 1c). It also contains a hyperlink to an e-mail address. When you click the e-mail address, Word opens your e-mail program automatically with the recipient's address already filled in (Figure 1d). You simply type your message and then click the Send button, which places the message in the Outbox or sends it if you are connected to an e-mail server.

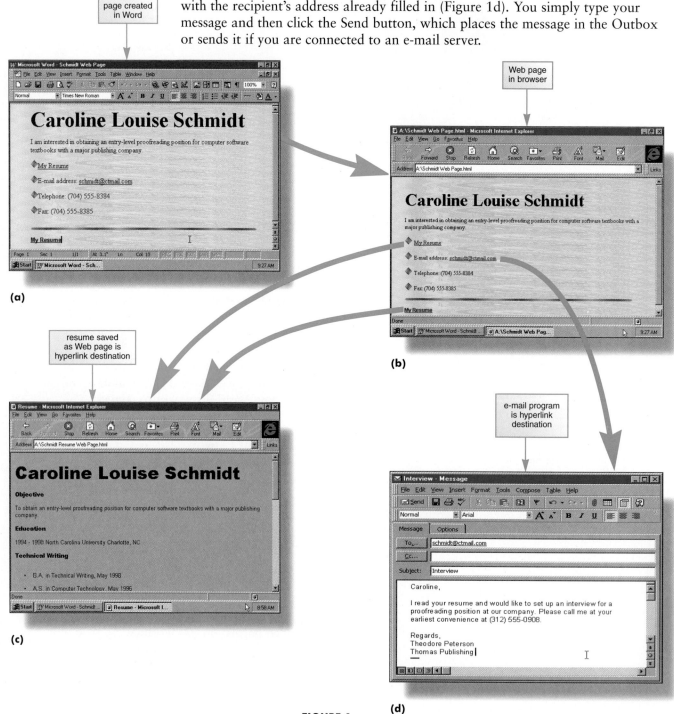

FIGURE 1

Saving a Word Document as a Web Page

Once you have created an existing Word document, you can save it easily as a HyperText Markup Language (HTML) file so it can be posted on the Web and viewed by a Web browser, such as Internet Explorer.

Some formatting in your Word document may not be supported by HTML. In this case, Word either changes the formatting or removes the text upon conversion. For example, certain table features are lost in the conversion. For this reason, it is recommended that you save the document as a Word file before converting it to HTML. In case you lose any information, you can reopen the original Word file and make the necessary adjustments.

Recall that the resume created in Project 2 contains a table. If you save the resume, as is, to an HTML format, the table will be removed (which is all the information below the heading). To preserve the table in the resume, you will convert the table to text; that is, remove the table formatting from the document. Then, you will save the revised resume as an HTML document.

Perform the following steps to convert the table in the Schmidt Resume to text.

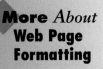

More *About* **Web Page Formatting**

Formatting not supported by HTML is unavailable while you are authoring a Web page in Word. For example, you cannot emboss, shadow, or engrave characters; and you cannot change line spacing, margins, or set tabs. You can, however, apply bold, italic, underline, and adjust font sizes of characters.

 Steps To Convert a Table to Text

1 **Start Word and then open the Schmidt Resume created in Project 2. (If you did not create the resume in Project 2, see your instructor for a copy of it.) If gridlines do not show on your resume's table, click Table on the menu bar, and then click Show Gridlines. Click anywhere in the table to position the insertion point in it. Click Table on the menu bar and then click Select Table. Click Table on the menu bar and then point to Convert Table to Text.**

Word selects the table in the resume (Figure 2). Gridlines are nonprinting characters that help you identify the rows and columns of a table. Your zoom percentage may differ from this figure.

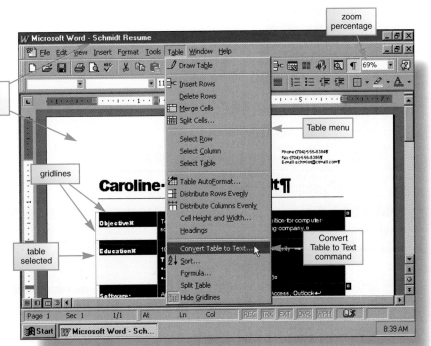

FIGURE 2

2 Click Convert Table to Text. When the Convert Table To Text dialog box displays, click Paragraph marks.

Word displays the Convert Table To Text dialog box (Figure 3). In this dialog box, you specify how Word should convert the columns to regular text; that is, every time a new column is encountered, what character should separate the text. Here you want each column to be treated as a new paragraph.

3 Click the OK button. Click anywhere in the document to remove the highlight.

Word converts the table in the resume to text (Figure 4 below). Notice the data originally in the second column of the table is formatted now as separate paragraphs in the resume.

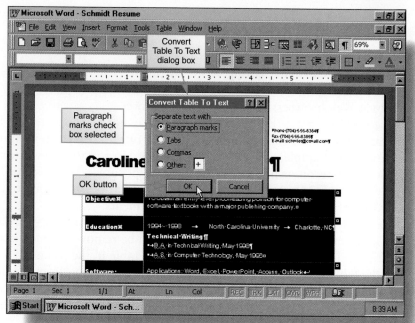

FIGURE 3

The next step is to save the resume as a Web page.

***Steps* To Save a Word Document as a Web Page**

1 Click File on the menu bar and then point to Save as HTML (Figure 4).

More *About* Web Page Paragraphs

Paragraphs created in Word automatically display a space before and after them on a Web page. Press CTRL+ENTER between paragraphs to eliminate the white space.

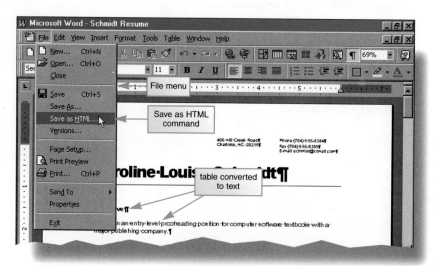

FIGURE 4

2 Click Save as HTML. When the Save As HTML dialog box displays, type Schmidt Resume Web Page in the File name text box and then, if necessary, change the Save in drive to 3½ Floppy (A:). Point to the Save button in the Save As HTML dialog box.

Word displays the Save As HTML dialog box (Figure 5).

3 Click the Save button. If Word displays a dialog box asking if you want to continue with the save, click the Yes button.

Word closes the Schmidt Resume Word document and then reopens the file in HTML format (Figure 1-6 on the next page). Word also changes some of the toolbar buttons and menu commands to provide Web page authoring features. The resume displays on the Word screen similarly to how it will appear in a Web browser.

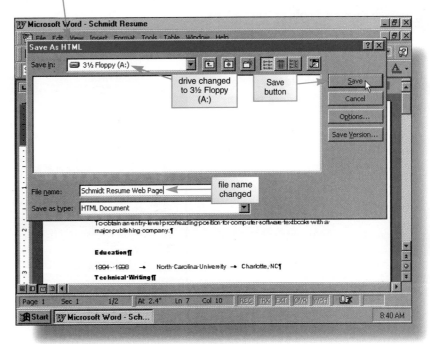

FIGURE 5

Recall that some of Word's formatting features are not supported by HTML; thus, your Web page may appear slightly different from the original Word document.

Viewing a Web Page Document

You may wish to view the Web page document in your default Web browser to see how it looks. Notice the Standard toolbar now has a **Web Page Preview button**. When you are working with a Web page, the buttons on the toolbars change to provide you with Web authoring features.

Perform the steps on the next page to view the Web page in your default browser.

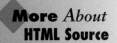

More *About*
HTML Source

If you wish to view the HTML source code associated with the Web page you have created, save the Web page in its current form, click View on the menu bar, and then click HTML Source. You can modify or print the HTML source. To return to the Web page, click the Exit HTML Source button on the Standard toolbar.

Steps   To View an HTML File in a Browser

1 Point to the Web Page Preview button on the Standard toolbar (Figure 6).

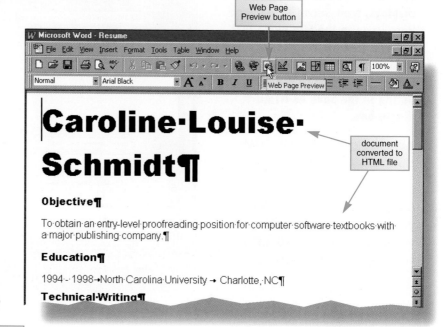

FIGURE 6

2 Click the Web Page Preview button on the Standard toolbar.

Word opens your Web browser in a separate window and displays the HTML file in the browser window (Figure 7).

3 Close the Web browser window. When the Word window redisplays, close the Schmidt Resume Web page file by clicking the Close button at the right edge of the menu bar. Leave Word open for the next steps.

The resume HTML files closes and the Word window redisplays.

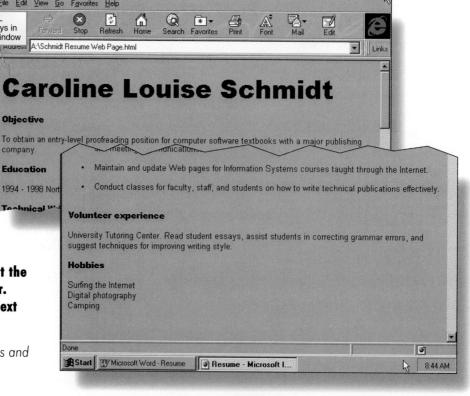

FIGURE 7

OtherWays

1. On File menu click Web Page Preview

Using Word's Web Page Wizard to Create a Web Page

In the previous section, you had an existing Word document you wanted to save as a Web page. Next, you want to create a brand new Web page. You can create a Web page from scratch using the Web page template or you can use the **Web Page Wizard**. Because this is your first experience creating a new Web page, you should use the Web Page Wizard as shown in the following steps.

Steps To Create a Web Page with the Web Page Wizard

1 **Click File on the menu bar and then click New. If necessary, click the Web Pages tab when the New dialog box first opens. Click the Web Page Wizard icon.**

Office displays several icons on the Web Pages sheet (Figure 8). The Blank Web Page icon is a Web page template. The Web Page Wizard icon is selected.

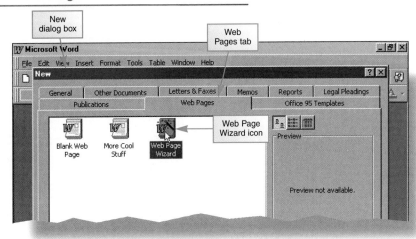

FIGURE 8

2 **Click the OK button. When the Web Page Wizard dialog box displays, click Simple Layout, if necessary, and then point to the Next button.**

After a few seconds, Word displays the first of two Web Page Wizard dialog boxes (Figure 9). This dialog box requests the type of Web page you wish to create. As you click the types in the list, the Web page in the background changes to reflect the selected type.

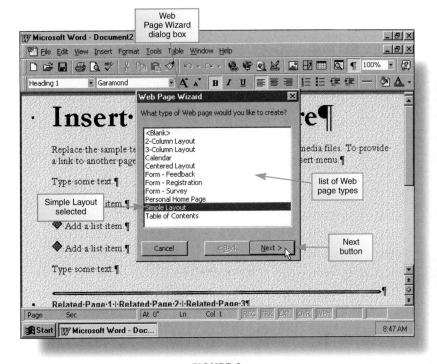

FIGURE 9

3 **Click the Next button. When the next Web Page Wizard dialog box displays, click Contemporary, if necessary, and then point to the Finish button.**

After a few seconds, Word displays the second, and final, Web Page Wizard dialog box (Figure 10). In this dialog box, you select the style of Web page you desire. As you click the styles in the list, the Web page in the background changes to reflect the selected style.

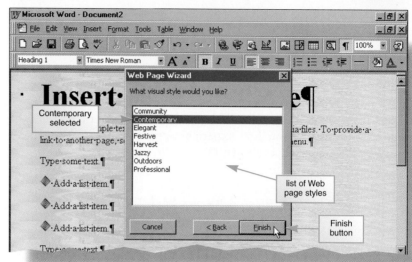

FIGURE 10

4 **Click the Finish button.**

Word creates a Web page layout for you (Figure 11). You are to personalize the Web page as indicated.

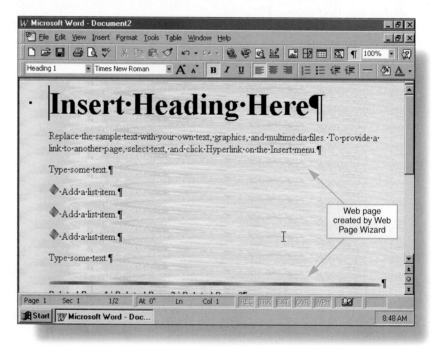

FIGURE 11

When you create a Web page using the Web Page Wizard, you can click the Back button in the second dialog box to change the Web page type, if you desire. To exit from the Web Page Wizard and return to the document window without creating the Web page, click the Cancel button in either of the Web Page Wizard dialog boxes.

Personalizing the Web Page with Hyperlinks

The next step is to personalize the Web page. First, you replace placeholder text with your own text. Next, you create hyperlinks, where necessary, to other documents, Web pages, or Internet sites. The following pages show how to personalize the Web page generated by the Web Page Wizard.

Recall from Project 3 that a **hyperlink** is colored and underlined text or a graphic that, when clicked, allows a user to jump easily and quickly to other documents, objects, or Web pages. If the AutoFormat As You Type feature is enabled, Word converts Internet and network paths to hyperlinks as you type them. In this Integration Feature, you want the e-mail address to be formatted as a hyperlink so that when someone clicks the e-mail address on your Web page, his or her e-mail program opens automatically with your e-mail address already filled in. Be sure this feature is enabled by clicking Tools on the menu bar, clicking AutoCorrect, clicking the AutoFormat As You Type tab, clicking Internet and network paths with hyperlinks, and then clicking the OK button.

Personalize the text on the Web page with e-mail address formatted as a hyperlink as described in the following steps.

TO SELECT AND REPLACE TEXT

Step 1: Select the text, Insert Heading Here, and then type `Caroline Louise Schmidt` as the title.

Step 2: Select the paragraph below the title by triple-clicking it, and then type `I am interested in obtaining an entry-level proofreading position for computer software textbooks with a major publishing company.`

Step 3: Select the paragraph with the text, Type some text. Right-click the selection and then click Cut on the shortcut menu.

Step 4: Select the first bulleted item by dragging through the text, Add a list item. Type `My Resume` as the first item.

Step 5: Select the second bulleted item and then type `E-mail address: schmidt@ctmail.com` and then press the SPACEBAR to convert the e-mail address to a hyperlink.

Step 6: Select the third bulleted item and then type `Telephone: (704) 555-8384` and then press the ENTER key. Type `Fax: (704) 555-8385` as the fourth bulleted item.

Step 7: Select the paragraph below the bulleted list, Type some text. Right-click the selection and then click Cut on the shortcut menu.

Step 8: Select the text, | Related Page 2 | Related Page 3, at the bottom of the Web page. Right-click the selection and then click Cut on the shortcut menu.

Step 9: Select the words, Related Page 1, at the bottom of the Web page, and then type `My Resume` as the text.

The Web page is personalized (Figure 12 on the next page). Notice the e-mail address is formatted as a hyperlink. Word formats it automatically when you press the SPACEBAR or the ENTER key after typing the address.

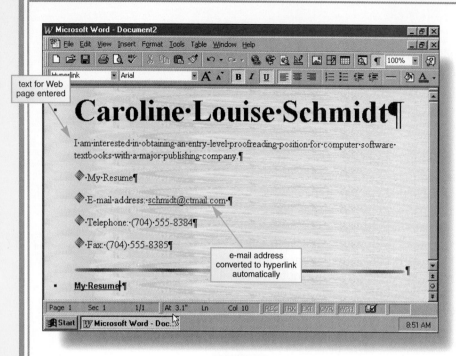

FIGURE 12

Save the Web page before proceeding to the next section.

TO SAVE THE WEB PAGE

Step 1: Insert your floppy disk into drive A.

Step 2: Click Save button on the Standard toolbar.

Step 3: Type the file name Schmidt Web Page in the File name text box. Do not press the ENTER key.

Step 4: If necessary, click the Save in box arrow and then click 3½ Floppy (A:).

Step 5: Click the Save button in the Save As dialog box.

Word saves the document on a floppy disk in drive A with the file name Schmidt Web Page.

Converting Text to a Hyperlink

In the previous example, the text you typed (the e-mail address) was an Internet or network path. Here, you want standard text (My Resume) to be a hyperlink. That is, when the user clicks My Resume, you want your resume page (Schmidt Web Page) to display on the screen. Perform the following steps to format existing text as a hyperlink.

Steps **To Format Existing Text as a Hyperlink**

1 Select the text in the first bulleted item, My Resume. Point to the Insert Hyperlink button on the Standard toolbar.

Word highlights the text, My Resume (Figure 13).

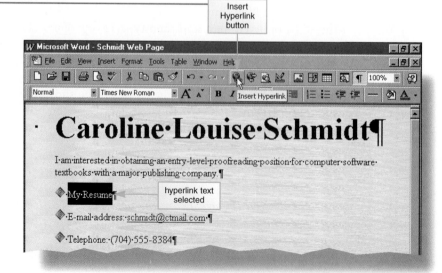

FIGURE 13

2 Click the Insert Hyperlink button. Insert the disk with the Schmidt Resume Web Page into drive A. When the Insert Hyperlink dialog box displays, type a:Schmidt Resume Web Page.html and then point to the OK button.

Word displays the Insert Hyperlink dialog box (Figure 14). If you are unable to remember the name of the Web page file, you can click the Browse button in this dialog box and find the desired file.

3 Click the OK button.

Word formats the selected text as a hyperlink (Figure 1a on page WDI 1.2).

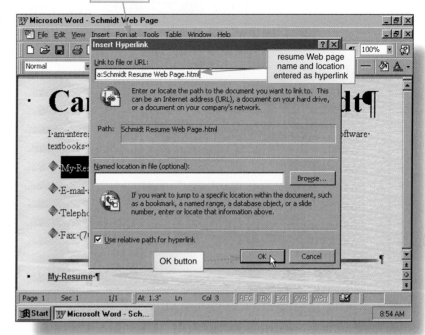

FIGURE 14

4 Repeat Steps 1 through 3 for the words, My Resume, at the bottom of the Web page to format it as a hyperlink also.

The Web page now is complete. You should save it again by clicking the Save button on the Standard toolbar.

To test the links, click the Web Page Preview button on the Standard toolbar. When the Schmidt Web Page displays in your browser window (Figure 1b on page WDI 1.2), click the My Resume link to display the Schmidt Resume Web Page in your browser window (Figure 1c on page WDI 1.2). Then, click the Back button to return to the Schmidt Web Page. Click the e-mail address to open your e-mail program with the address, schmidt@ctmail.com entered in the recipient's address box (Figure 1d on page WDI 1.2). Close any open windows.

The next step is to make your Web pages (Schmidt Web Page and Schmidt Resume Web Page) available to others on your network, an intranet, or the World Wide Web. Talk to your instructor about how you should do this for your system.

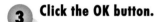

OtherWays

1. Select text, right-click selected text, click Hyperlink on shortcut menu, type address in Insert Hyperlink dialog box, click OK button

2. Select text, on Insert menu click Hyperlink, type address in Insert Hyperlink dialog box, click OK button

3. Select text, press CTRL+K, type address in Insert Hyperlink dialog box, click OK button

Summary

This Integration Feature introduced you to creating a Web page by saving an existing Word document as an HTML file. You also created a new Web page by using the Web Page Wizard and then personalized this Web page with your own text. On the personal Web page, you created a hyperlink to the resume Web page and a hyperlink to your e-mail program.

In the Lab

1 Use Help

Instructions: Start Word. If the Office Assistant is on your screen, click it to display its balloon. If the Office Assistant is not on your screen, click the Office Assistant button on the Standard toolbar. Type Web Page Wizard in the What would you like to do? text box. Click the Search button. Click the Create a Web Page link. Read and print the information. Click the Help Topics button to display the Help Topics: Microsoft Word window. Double-click the Creating and Working with Web Pages book. Double-click the Creating Web Pages book. Double-click the Items you can add to Web pages topic. Read and print the topic. Close any open Help windows. Close the Office Assistant.

2 Creating a Web Page with a Hyperlink to a Resume Web Page

Problem: You created the resume shown in Figure 2-82 on page WD 2.58 in Project 2. You decide to create a personal Web Page with a link to the Peterson Resume. Thus, you also must save the resume as a Web page.

Instructions:

1. Open the Peterson Resume shown in Figure 2-82. (If you did not create the resume, see your instructor for a copy of it.) Convert its table to text. Then, save the resume as a Web page.
2. Create a personal Web page using the Web Page Wizard. Use the Simple Layout and the Harvest style. The personal Web page should contain the following information in this order: name; objective; the words, My Resume, as first bulleted item, e-mail address as second bulleted item, telephone number as third bulleted item, and fax number as fourth bulleted item; and the words, My Resume, again at the bottom of the Web page. See Figure 2-82 for this information.
3. Save the Web page and then format the two occurrences of My Resume as hyperlinks to the Peterson Resume Web Page. Save the Web page again. Test your Web page links.
4. Ask your instructor for instructions on how to post your Web pages so others may have access to them.

3 Creating a Web Page with Hyperlinks

Problem: You have decided to create your own personal Web page using the Personal Home Page type in the Web Page Wizard.

Instructions:

1. Create your own personal Web page using the Web Page Wizard. Use the Personal Home Page type and the style you like best.
2. Personalize the Web page as indicated on the template. For each bullet in the hot list section, enter a URL of a site on the Web that interests you.
3. Save the Web page. Test your Web page links.
4. Ask your instructor for instructions on how to post your Web page so others may have access to it.

Microsoft Word 97

Microsoft Word 97

Project 4

Creating a Document with a Title Page and Tables

Objectives:

You will have mastered the material in this project when you can:

▶ Add color to characters

▶ Add an outside border with color to a paragraph

▶ Download clip art from the Microsoft Clip Gallery Live Web page

▶ Insert clip art into a document

▶ Change a floating picture to an inline picture

▶ Add a shadow to characters

▶ Insert a section break

▶ Return paragraph formatting to the Normal style

▶ Insert an existing document into an open document

▶ Save an active document with a new file name

▶ Set custom tabs

▶ Add an outside border to a table created with tabs

▶ Use the Draw Table feature to insert a table into a document

▶ Change alignment of data in table cells

▶ Change the direction of text in table cells

▶ Center a table between page margins

▶ Customize bullets in a list

▶ Create a header for a section

▶ Change the starting page number in a section

Charting a Course

Ancient Mapping,
Handwritten Computations,
and Contemporary Tables

S ea creatures — monstrous finned denizens of the ocean, lurking in the depths of the open seas, in readiness to pounce on and devour the unwary ships. The Seven Cities of Cibola — a tale that depicts an island far out into the Atlantic Ocean. Legend has it that, "there took ship seven Bishops, and went to Antilla, where each of them built a city; and lest their people should think to return to Spain, they set fire to their ships." Many who came to the island, never returned.

In the fourteenth and fifteenth centuries, these fanciful notions from the superstitious minds of medieval chartmakers embellished the first crude charts developed for seafaring explorers.

In a time when a sailor stood less than a fifty-fifty chance of returning home from a voyage, when ships were lost without a trace, few doubted that such charts told the truth. As more daring voyagers pushed beyond known limits, more accurate maps evolved with every journey. Soon, depth readings

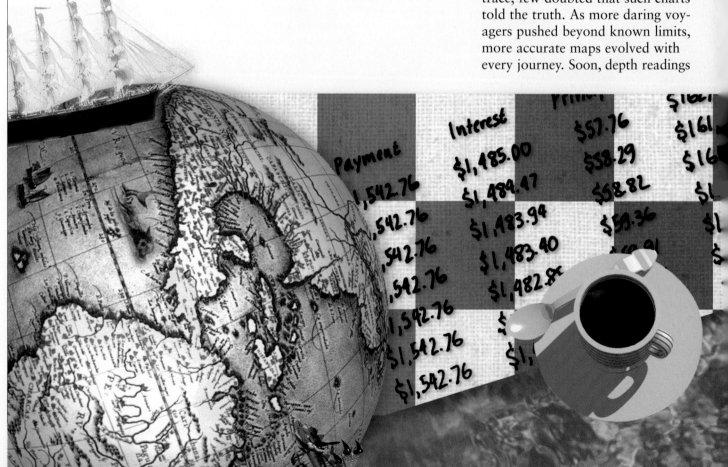

and ocean currents appeared on navigation maps. To this day, charting of the planet's land masses and oceans grows more sophisticated with modern technology to aid the effort.

Along with charts, various tables — especially tide tables that help ships avoid going aground — are important tools for the mariner, but another kind of table was just as important to early sailors as any scrap of paper. Looming mysteriously above Cape Town, South Africa is Table Mountain. With a top as flat as a football field, but vastly larger, its mystique is enhanced by frequent, sudden appearances of dense Antarctic fog on otherwise crystal-clear days, settling and spreading in a thin layer called the *Devil's tablecloth*. The mountain has served as beacon and inspiration to sailors, natives, and settlers for centuries. To the weary seafarer, Table Mountain meant a brief respite from the dangers of a daunting voyage, and ship captains gave lavish rewards to the first sailor to spy it.

From Latin *tabularis*, meaning board, the word, table, and its diminutive, tablet, have been used in varied contexts throughout human history. Medieval English accountants calculated sums on a checkered tablecloth, giving birth to the name Exchequer, Britain's royal treasury and the word cheque for bank drafts. Physicists consult the Periodic Table of Elements. Moses received the Ten Commandments on tablets of stone, while modern artists use digitized graphics tablets to enter drawings and sketches into a computer.

In the fast-paced '90s, you may not be required to chart the open seas. En route to a meeting via jet with laptop and mouse, however, the capability of creating tables and charts with ease and precision is a vital tool. Using Word 97 and the Draw Table feature in this project, you can create an attractive table, modify the structure, and enhance any document, proposal, or announcement you are asked to prepare. Apply borders and shading and add color for appeal.

The days of the drawing board are like ancient history. As we move into the twenty-first century, chart your course with the state-of-the-art business tools of Microsoft Word.

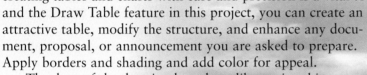

HOT AIR BALLOON RATES			
Passenger Types		Adult	Child
Peak Season	Sunrise	$120	$60
	Sunset	$130	$65
Off Season	Sunrise	$90	$45
	Sunset	$100	$50

Microsoft
Word 97

Creating a Document with a Title Page and Tables

Case Perspective

The owners of Fiesta Balloon Tours have hired you, a Marketing major in your senior year at Canyon University, to design a sales proposal. In your first meeting with the owners, William and Anita Hampton, you try to learn as much about Fiesta Balloon Tours as possible. The Hamptons give you a business card that outlines the schedules of balloon outings, as well as company telephone numbers. They tell you that Fiesta Balloon Tours has been in business since 1979 and has a perfect passenger safety record. All pilots are certified and have more than 300 hours of flying experience. The balloons, which are inspected regularly, accommodate four to eight passengers.

In addition to the two-hour flight, passengers receive a Fiesta Balloon Tours T-shirt, personalized flight certificate, flight pin, and a feast of food and beverages upon landing. Mrs. Hampton provides you with a rate sheet for balloon outings. She mentions that Fiesta Balloon Tours also offers for purchase other products and services, and these items are on the rate sheet. At the conclusion of your meeting, you inform the Hamptons that you will complete the proposal for their review within a week.

Introduction

In all probability, sometime during your professional life, you will find yourself placed in a sales role. You might be selling to a customer or client a tangible product such as plastic or a service such as interior decorating. Within an organization, you might be selling an idea, such as a benefits package to company employees or a budget plan to upper management. To sell an item, whether tangible or intangible, you often will find yourself writing a proposal. Proposals vary in length, style, and formality, but all are designed to elicit acceptance from the reader.

A proposal may be one of three types: planning, research, or sales. A **planning proposal** offers solutions to a problem or improvement to a situation. A **research proposal** usually requests funding for a research project. A **sales proposal** offers a product or service to existing or potential customers.

Project Four – Sales Proposal

Project 4 uses Word to produce the sales proposal shown in Figures 4-1, 4-2 and 4-3 on the next three pages. The sales proposal is designed to persuade the public to select Fiesta Balloon Tours for a hot air balloon outing. The proposal has a colorful title page to grasp the reader's attention. The body of the sales proposal uses tables to summarize data.

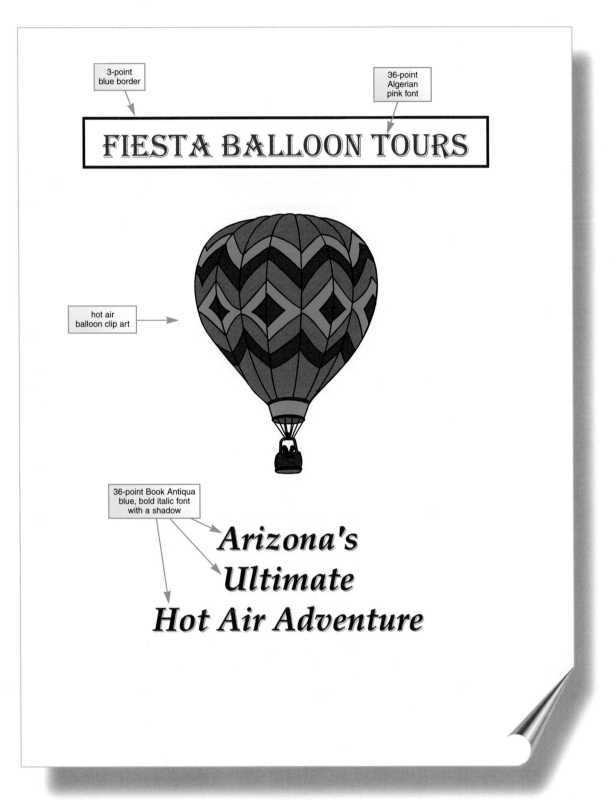

FIGURE 4-1

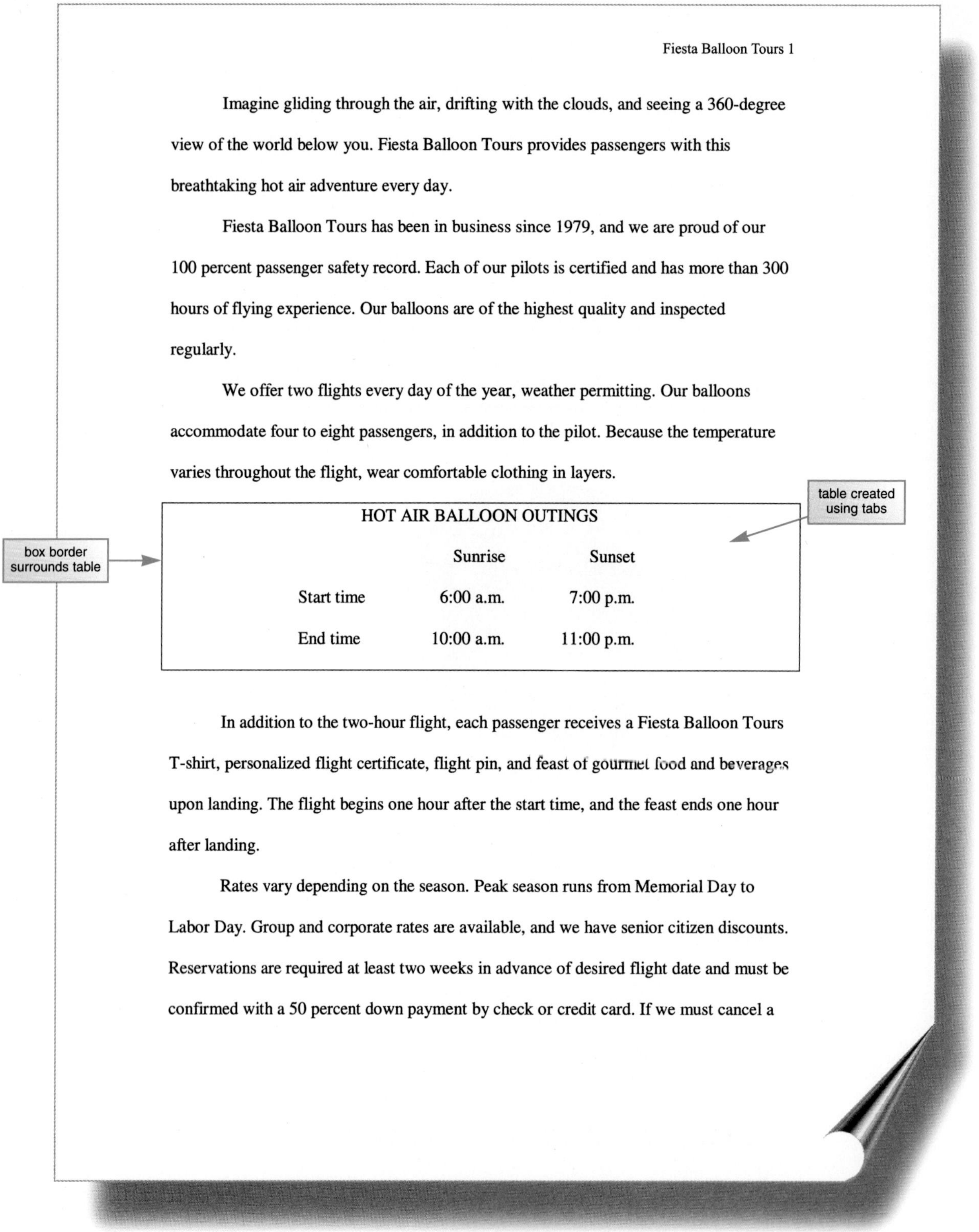

Fiesta Balloon Tours 1

Imagine gliding through the air, drifting with the clouds, and seeing a 360-degree view of the world below you. Fiesta Balloon Tours provides passengers with this breathtaking hot air adventure every day.

Fiesta Balloon Tours has been in business since 1979, and we are proud of our 100 percent passenger safety record. Each of our pilots is certified and has more than 300 hours of flying experience. Our balloons are of the highest quality and inspected regularly.

We offer two flights every day of the year, weather permitting. Our balloons accommodate four to eight passengers, in addition to the pilot. Because the temperature varies throughout the flight, wear comfortable clothing in layers.

table created using tabs

box border surrounds table

HOT AIR BALLOON OUTINGS		
	Sunrise	Sunset
Start time	6:00 a.m.	7:00 p.m.
End time	10:00 a.m.	11:00 p.m.

In addition to the two-hour flight, each passenger receives a Fiesta Balloon Tours T-shirt, personalized flight certificate, flight pin, and feast of gourmet food and beverages upon landing. The flight begins one hour after the start time, and the feast ends one hour after landing.

Rates vary depending on the season. Peak season runs from Memorial Day to Labor Day. Group and corporate rates are available, and we have senior citizen discounts. Reservations are required at least two weeks in advance of desired flight date and must be confirmed with a 50 percent down payment by check or credit card. If we must cancel a

FIGURE 4-2

flight due to weather conditions or other reasons, we will reschedule the outing on the

date of your choice or refund your money.

Each party must include at least one adult. Child rates apply to any person 14

years or younger.

table created using Draw Table feature →

HOT AIR BALLOON RATES			
Passenger Type		Adult	Child
Peak Season	Sunrise	$120	$60
	Sunset	$130	$65
Off Season	Sunrise	$90	$45
	Sunset	$100	$50

Fiesta Balloon Tours offers for purchase the following hot air balloon products

and services for your business or personal use.

new bullet format →

➢ Catalog of gift items, such as jewelry, clothing, windsocks, and mugs

➢ Gift certificates

➢ Decorations for parties, meetings, and conventions

➢ Pilot training

➢ Hot air balloons

Fiesta Balloon Tours invites you to enjoy *Arizona's Ultimate Hot Air Adventure*.

For reservations, call us at (520) 555-2928. For information on hot air balloon rides or

pilot training, talk to one of our captains at (520) 555-2927. To request a catalog or order

hot air balloon products, call our sales office at (520) 555-2929.

FIGURE 4-3

Document Preparation Steps

Document preparation steps give you an overview of how the sales proposal in Figures 4-1, 4-2, and 4-3 on the previous pages will be developed. The following tasks will be completed in this project.

1. Create a title page using an outside border, color, shadows, and clip art.
2. Save the title page.
3. Insert an existing document below the title page in a new section.
4. Save the active document with a new file name.
5. Add a table to the document using custom tab stops.
6. Add a table to the document using the Draw Table feature.
7. Customize bullets in a list.
8. Add a header to the second section of the document.
9. Print the document.

The following pages contain a detailed explanation of each of these tasks.

Starting Word

Follow these steps to start Word or ask your instructor how to start Word for your system.

TO START WORD

1. Click the Start button on the taskbar.
2. Click New Office Document on the Start menu. If necessary, click the General tab when the New Office Document dialog box first opens.
3. Double-click the Blank Document icon on the General sheet.
4. If the Word screen is not maximized, double-click its title bar to maximize it.

Office starts Word. After a few moments, an empty document titled Document1 displays on the Word screen.

Displaying Nonprinting Characters

You may recall that it is helpful to display nonprinting characters that indicate where in the document you pressed the ENTER key, SPACEBAR, or TAB key. Follow this step to display nonprinting characters.

TO DISPLAY NONPRINTING CHARACTERS

1. If the Show/Hide ¶ button on the Standard toolbar is not already recessed, click it.

Word displays nonprinting characters in the document window, and the Show/Hide ¶ button on the Standard toolbar is recessed (Figure 4-4).

Creating a Title Page

A **title page** should be designed to catch the reader's attention. Therefore, the title page of the sales proposal in Project 4 (Figure 4-1 on page WD 4.7) contains color, an outside border, shadowed text, clip art, and a variety of fonts and point sizes. The steps on the following pages discuss how to create the title page in Project 4.

Changing the Top Margin

The first step in creating the title page for the sales proposal is to change the top margin to 1.5 inches. Because the default in Word is 1 inch, perform the following steps to change the top margin to 1.5 inches.

TO CHANGE THE TOP MARGIN

1. Click File on the menu bar and then click Page Setup.
2. If necessary, click the Margins tab when the Page Setup dialog box first opens.
3. Type 1.5 in the Top text box (Figure 4-4).
4. Click the OK button.

The top margin is set at 1.5 inches.

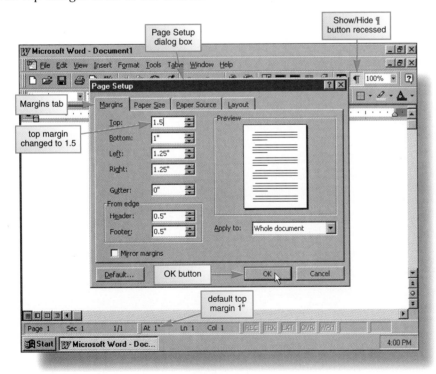

FIGURE 4-4

Adding Color to Characters

The next step in creating the title page is to enter the company name, centered using 36-point Algerian pink font. First, change the font, font size, and paragraph alignment. Then, use the Font Color button on the Formatting toolbar to add color to characters as shown on the next page.

TO FORMAT CHARACTERS

1 Click the Center button on the Formatting toolbar.
2 Click the Font box arrow on the Formatting toolbar and then click Algerian (or a similar font) from the list of available fonts.
3 Click the Font Size box arrow on the Formatting toolbar, scroll to and then click 36.

The font, font size, and paragraph alignment for the first line of the title are changed (Figure 4-5 below).

The next step is to change the color of the characters to pink.

Steps **To Color Characters**

1 **Point to the Font Color button arrow on the Formatting toolbar (Figure 4-5).**

The color that displays below the letter A on the Font Color button is the most recently used color for characters; thus, your color may differ from this figure.

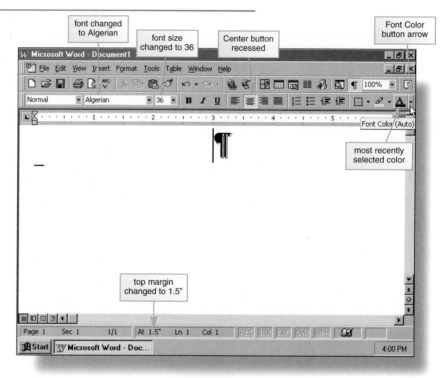

FIGURE 4-5

2 **Click the Font Color button arrow. When the color palette displays, point to the color Pink.**

Word displays a list of available colors for characters in the color palette (Figure 4-6). Automatic is the system default color, which usually is black.

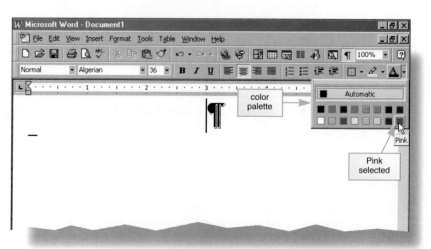

FIGURE 4-6

3 **Click the color Pink. Type** FIESTA BALLOON TOURS **and then press the ENTER key.**

Word displays the first line of the title page using the 36-point Algerian pink font (Figure 4-7). Notice the paragraph mark on line 2 also is pink. To ensure that the next characters you type are not pink, you should change the color back to automatic.

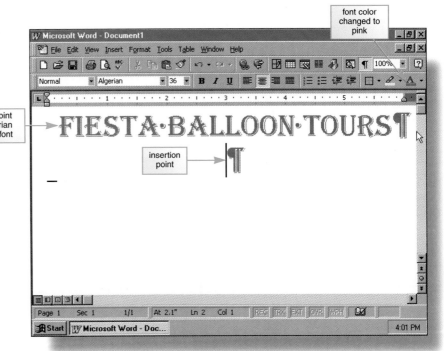

FIGURE 4-7

4 **Click the Font Color button arrow on the Formatting toolbar. When the color palette displays, point to Automatic (Figure 4-8).**

5 **Click Automatic.**

Word changes the font color to automatic (Figure 4-9 on the next page). The color of the paragraph mark on line 2 changes to black and so does the line on the Font Color button.

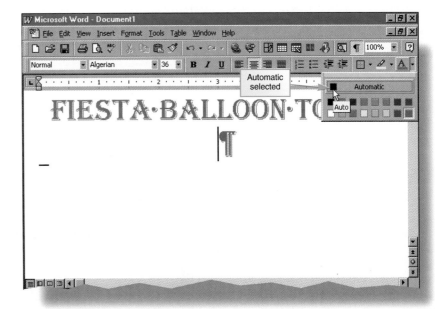

FIGURE 4-8

Adding a Shadow Box Border in Color with Shading

The next step is to surround the company name with a **border**. In Word, you can add a border, also called a **rule**, to any edge of a paragraph. That is, borders may be added above or below a paragraph, to the left or right of a paragraph, or any combination of these sides. You can add borders by clicking the **Tables and Borders button** on the Standard toolbar. When you click the Tables and Borders button, the Tables and Borders toolbar displays on the screen and the Tables and Borders button is recessed. Using the **Tables and Borders toolbar**, you also can add color to a border.

Other Ways

1. Right-click paragraph mark or selected text, click Font on shortcut menu, click Font tab, click Color box arrow, click desired color, click OK button

2. On Format menu click Font, click Font tab, click Color box arrow, click desired color, click OK button

Perform the following steps to add a blue outside border around the company name.

Steps   To Border a Paragraph

1 Click somewhere in line 1 to position the insertion point in the company name. Point to the Tables and Borders button on the Standard toolbar (Figure 4-9).

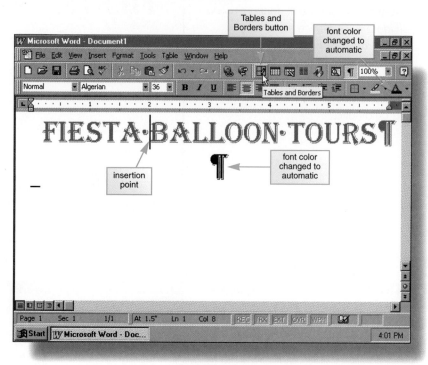

FIGURE 4-9

2 Click the Tables and Borders button. If the Tables and Borders toolbar is floating on the Word screen, point to the title bar of the Tables and Borders toolbar.

Word displays the Tables and Borders toolbar and switches to page layout view (Figure 4-10). Depending on the last position of this toolbar, it may be floating on the Word screen or it may be docked below the Formatting toolbar. You want it docked.

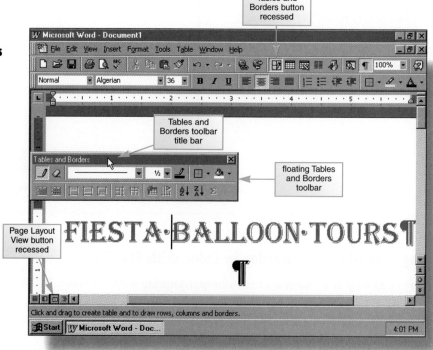

FIGURE 4-10

3 If the Tables and Borders toolbar is floating on the Word screen, double-click the title bar of the Tables and Borders toolbar.

Word docks the Tables and Borders toolbar below the Formatting toolbar.

FIGURE 4-11

4 Point to the Draw Table button on the Tables and Borders toolbar.

The Draw Table button is recessed when you first display the Tables and Borders toolbar (Figure 4-11). To border a paragraph, you do not want the Draw Table button recessed.

5 Click the Draw Table button. Click the Line Weight box arrow on the Tables and Borders toolbar and then point to 3 pt.

Word displays a list of available line weights (Figure 4-12). The Draw Table button is no longer recessed.

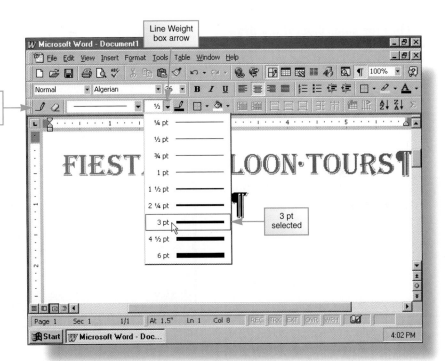

FIGURE 4-12

6 Click 3 pt. If the Draw Table button is recessed, click it to deselect it.

Word changes the line weight to 3 point.

7 Click the Border Color button on the Tables and Borders toolbar. When the color palette displays, point to the color Blue.

Word displays a color palette for border colors (Figure 4-13).

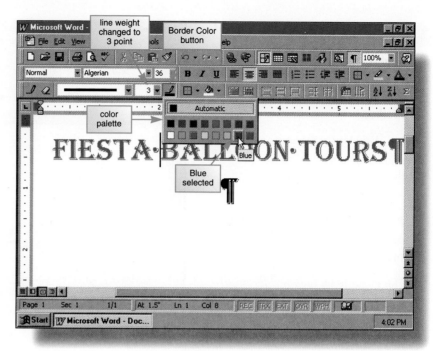

FIGURE 4-13

8 Click the color Blue. If the Draw Table button is recessed, click it to deselect it.

Word changes the color of the border lines to blue, as indicated in the Line Style box and the Border Color button.

9 Click the Outside Border button on the Tables and Borders toolbar.

Word places an outside border around the company name on the title page (Figure 4-14). The **Outside Border button** *on the Tables and Borders toolbar is recessed. Notice that the Outside Border button on the Formatting toolbar also is recessed. To ensure that the next border you draw is not 3-point blue, you should change the border line weight and color back to the default.*

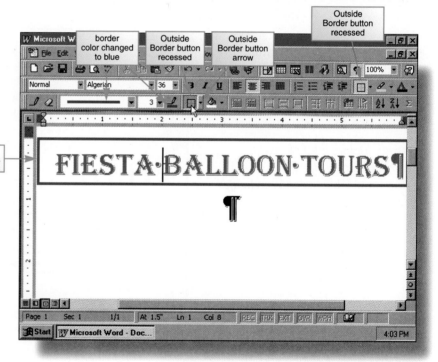

FIGURE 4-14

10 Click the Line Weight box arrow on the Tables and Borders toolbar and then click ½ pt. Click the Border Color button on the Tables and Borders toolbar and then click Automatic. Point to the Tables and Borders button on the Standard toolbar.

The line weight and border color are reset (Figure 4-15).

11 Click the Tables and Borders button.

The Tables and Borders toolbar no longer displays on the Word screen, and the Tables and Borders button is no longer recessed (Figure 4-16 on the next page).

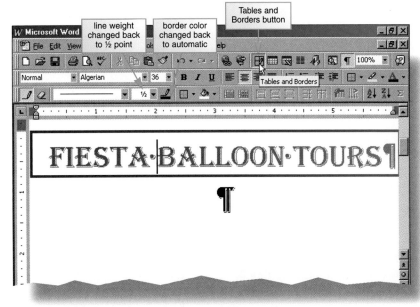

FIGURE 4-15

Other Ways

1. On Format menu click Borders and Shading, click Borders tab, click Box in Setting list, click desired style, color, and width, click OK button

When you click the Outside Border button on the Tables and Borders toolbar, Word places a border around the entire paragraph. You can add a border to any edge of a paragraph from the **borders palette**. To display the borders palette, click the Outside Border button arrow (Figure 4-14). For example, to add a border to the left edge of a paragraph, position the insertion point somewhere in the paragraph, click the Outside Border button arrow, and then click **Left Border** on the borders palette. To remove a border from a paragraph, position the insertion point somewhere in the paragraph, click the Outside Border button arrow, and then click **No Border** on the borders palette.

Notice in Figure 4-14 that the Outside Border button on the Formatting toolbar also is recessed. Word actually provides two Outside Border buttons. If you want to place a border using the same color and size as the most recently defined border, then you simply click the Outside Border button on the Formatting toolbar. If you want to change the size or color of the border, however, you have to use the Tables and Borders toolbar or the Borders and Shading dialog box.

If you have a black-and-white printer, the colors other than black or white will print in shades of gray.

Importing and Resizing a Graphic

You may recall that Word 97 includes a series of predefined graphics called **clip art files** or **Windows metafiles**. These clip art files are located in the **Clip Gallery**, which contains its own Help system to assist you in locating an image suited to your application. If you cannot locate an appropriate clip art file in the Clip Gallery, Microsoft provides a special Web page with additional clips. If you have access to the Web, you can download clip art files from the Web page into the Clip Gallery. You insert, or import, these clip art files from the Clip Gallery into a Word document by clicking **Picture** on the Insert menu.

The next series of steps in this project are to download a hot air balloon clip art file from Microsoft's Clip Gallery Live Web page and then import the clip art file into the Word document.

More *About* **Windows Metafiles**

You can edit a Windows metafile by clicking the Drawing button on the Standard toolbar to display the Drawing toolbar. To separate the graphic into individual parts, select the graphic, click the Draw button on the Drawing toolbar, and then click Group. When you are finished making changes, click the Draw button again and click Regroup.

Note: The following steps assume you are using Microsoft Internet Explorer as your browser and that you have access to the Web. If you are not using Internet Explorer or you do not have access to the Web, you will need to perform a different set of steps. Your browser's handling of pictures on the Web will be discovered in Step 6. If necessary, you may be directed to follow the steps on page WD 4.21 to install the picture from the Data Disk that accompanies this book. If you do not have access to the Web, go directly to the steps on page WD 4.21.

Steps ___ To Download Clip Art from Microsoft's Clip Gallery Live Web Page

1 **Click the paragraph mark below the company name to position the insertion point on line 2. Press the ENTER key to position the insertion point on line 3. Click Insert on the menu bar, point to Picture, and then point to Clip Art.**

The insertion point is on line 3 in the document (Figure 4-16). Because the submenu covers the insertion point, look on the status bar for the numeric location of the insertion point.

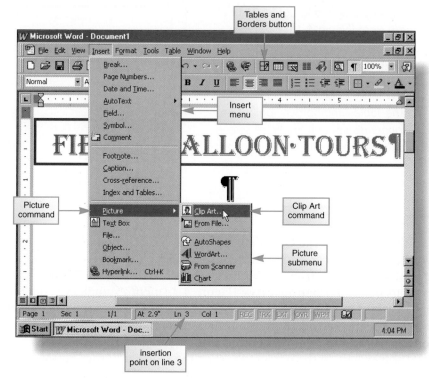

FIGURE 4-16

2 **Click Clip Art. If necessary, click the Clip Art tab when the Microsoft Clip Gallery dialog box first opens. Point to the Connect to Web for additional clips button.**

Word displays the Microsoft Clip Gallery dialog box (Figure 4-17). A list of clip art categories displays at the left of the dialog box. Clip art files associated with the selected category display to the right.

FIGURE 4-17

3 **Click the Connect to Web for additional clips button. If a Connect to Web for More Clip Art, Photos, Sounds dialog box displays, click its OK button.**

If you currently are not connected to the Web, Word connects you using your default browser. Microsoft Clip Gallery Live displays in a new window (Figure 4-18). The frame to the left of the window displays Microsoft's End-User License Agreement (EULA).

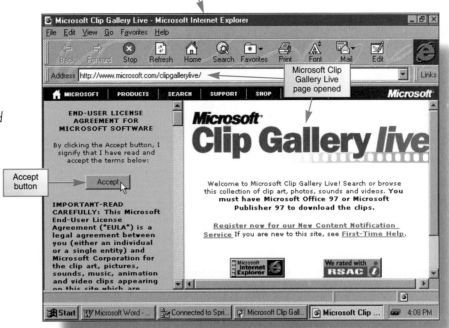

FIGURE 4-18

4 **Read the EULA and then click the Accept button. When the Browse and Search buttons display in the left frame, be sure the ClipArt button is recessed, click the Search button and then type** balloon **in the Enter keywords text box.**

Your browser replaces the EULA with buttons that enable you to locate clip art, pictures, sounds, and videos on the Web (Figure 4-19). The Browse button allows you to display categories similar to those in the Microsoft Clip Gallery dialog box. With the Search button, you type in a keyword and Microsoft searches through all the clips for matching images.

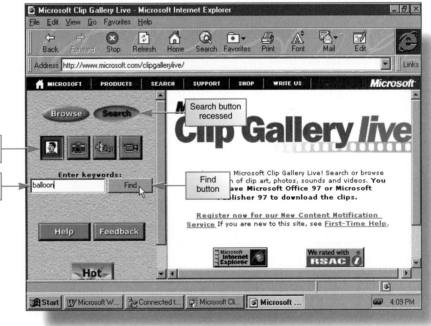

FIGURE 4-19

5 Click the Find button.

Your browser displays the clip art associated with keyword(s) you entered (Figure 4-20). The size of each clip art file displays below its name. To download a file into the Clip Gallery, you click the file name.

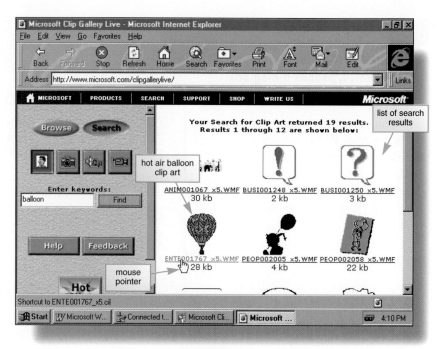

FIGURE 4-20

6 Click the file name ENTE001767_x5.WMF. (If your browser displays a dialog box asking whether you want to open the file or save the file, click Open and then click the OK button. If your browser displays a dialog box and Open is not an option, close your browser window, click the Cancel button in the Microsoft Clip Gallery dialog box, then go to the steps on page WD 4.21.)

Your browser downloads the file into your Microsoft Clip Gallery (Figure 4-21). If this is the first file downloaded, a new category called Downloaded Clips, is added to your category list.

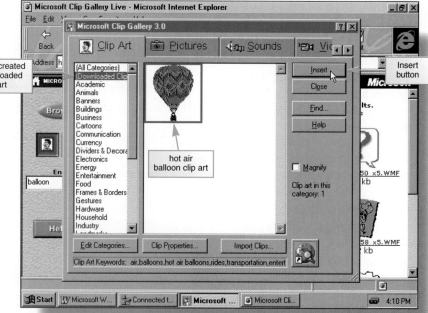

FIGURE 4-21

7 If it is not already selected, click the hot air balloon clip art image and then point to the Insert button.

8 Click the Insert button. If the Picture toolbar does not display, right-click the clip art image and then click Show Picture Toolbar on the shortcut menu.

Word inserts the hot air balloon clip art image into your document as a floating picture (Figure 4-22).

9 If necessary, close your Web browser window.

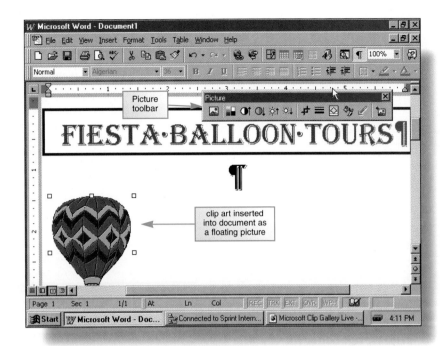

FIGURE 4-22

If you do not have access to the Web, you have to install the clip art file into the Microsoft Clip Gallery from the Data Disk that accompanies this book as described in the following steps.

TO INSTALL THE CLIP ART FROM THE DATA DISK

1 Click the paragraph mark below the company name to position the insertion point on line 2. Press the ENTER key to position the insertion point on line 3.

2 Click Insert on the menu bar, point to Picture on the Insert menu, and then point to Clip Art on the Picture submenu.

3 Click Clip Art. If necessary, click the Clip Art tab when the Microsoft Clip Gallery dialog box first opens.

4 Insert the Data Disk that accompanies this book into drive A.

5 Click the Start button on the taskbar, point to Programs on the Start menu, and then click Windows Explorer. When the Exploring window displays, scroll to the top of the All Folders side of the window and then click 3½ Floppy (A:) to select drive A. Double-click the Word folder in the Contents side of the window to display the contents of the Data Disk.

6 Double-click the file name ENTE001767_x5.CIL on the Data Disk. Close the Exploring window.

7 When the Microsoft Clip Gallery redisplays, click the balloon clip art and then click the Insert button.

Word inserts the hot air balloon clip art image into your document as a floating picture (see Figure 4-22 above).

More *About*
Toolbars

You can dock a floating toolbar by double-clicking its title bar. To float a docked toolbar, double-click its move handle (the double vertical bars at the toolbar's left edge). To move a toolbar, drag its move handle to the desired location.

Word imports a clip art file as a **floating picture**, which is a picture inserted in a layer over the text. An **inline picture**, on the other hand, is positioned directly in the text at the location of the insertion point. You change a floating picture to an inline picture using the **Format Picture dialog box**.

You may recall that you can resize a graphic by dragging its **sizing handles**. If you have a precise measurement for the graphic's dimensions, however, you can use the Format Picture dialog box to enter the exact width and height measurements.

Perform the following steps to change the clip art image from a floating picture to an inline picture and then resize it.

Steps **To Format a Picture**

1 **If it is not already selected, click the balloon clip art image. (If the Picture toolbar does not display, right-click the clip art image and then click Show Picture Toolbar on the shortcut menu.) Point to the Format Picture button on the Picture toolbar.**

Word displays the Picture toolbar when you select the clip art image (Figure 4-23). Recall that selected graphics display sizing handles at their corner and middle locations.

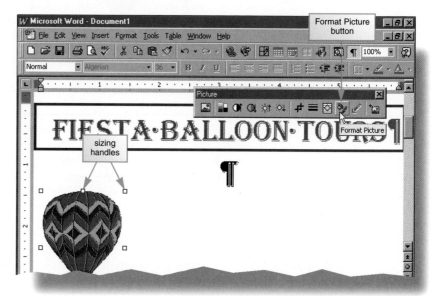

FIGURE 4-23

2 **Click the Format Picture button. When the Format Picture dialog box displays, click the Position tab and then click Float over text to clear the check box.**

Word displays the Format Picture dialog box (Figure 4-24). When the Float over text check box is selected, the image is a floating picture; when the check box is cleared, the image will be an inline picture.

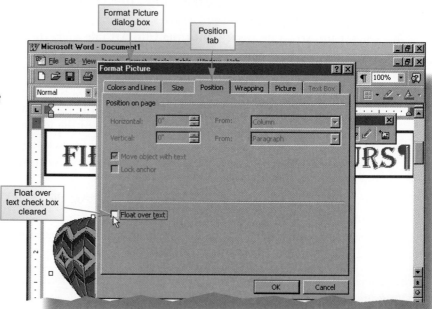

FIGURE 4-24

3 Click the Size tab. In the Size and rotate area, type 3 in the Height text box, type 3 in the Width text box, and then point to the OK button.

The numbers you enter in the Size and rotate area are in inches (Figure 4-25).

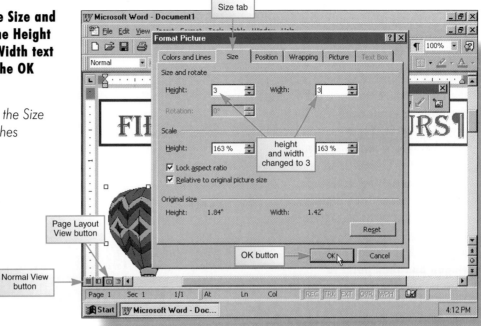

FIGURE 4-25

4 Click the OK button. Click outside the graphic to deselect it. Click the Normal View button at the bottom of the document window.

Word changes the graphic to an inline picture and resizes it to 3 inches by 3 inches (Figure 4-26). Notice the graphic is centered because the paragraph mark to which it is attached is centered. You switch to normal view to increase the work area in the Word window.

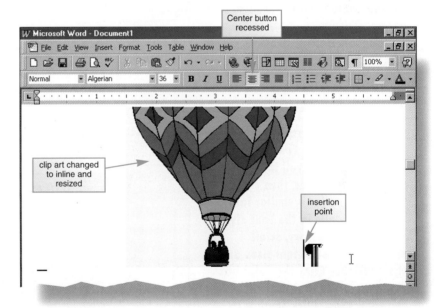

FIGURE 4-26

OtherWays
1. On Format menu click Picture, select desired settings, click OK button

Entering and Formatting the Company Slogan

The next step is to enter the company slogan below the graphic on the title page. The slogan is 36-point Book Antiqua blue, bold italic font. The characters also are formatted with a shadow. Because you need to display the Font dialog box to add a shadow to characters, you can change the font typeface, font style, and font size and color using the **Font dialog box** all at once, instead of using the Formatting toolbar. Perform the steps on the next page to enter the slogan and then format its characters using the Font dialog box.

Steps **To Enter and Format the Company Slogan**

1 **Position the insertion point at the end of the title page (after the balloon clip art). Press the ENTER key twice. Type** Arizona's **and then press the ENTER key. Type** Ultimate **and then press the ENTER key. Type** Hot Air Adventure **and then highlight the three paragraphs containing the company slogan. Right-click the selected slogan and then point to Font on the shortcut menu.**

All three lines of the company slogan are entered and selected (Figure 4-27). Notice when you type the slogan, it is formatted in all capital letters; this is because the Algerian font displays characters in uppercase.

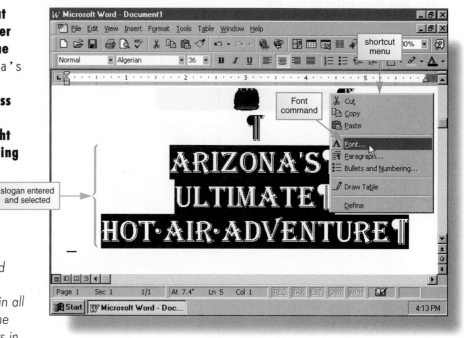

FIGURE 4-27

2 **Click Font. If necessary, click the Font tab when the Font dialog box first opens. Scroll through the list of fonts and then click Book Antiqua (or a similar font). Click Bold Italic in the Font style list box. If necessary, scroll through the list of font sizes and then click 36. Click the Color box arrow, scroll to and then click the color Blue. Click Shadow in the Effects area. Point to the OK button.**

The Preview area reflects the current selections (Figure 4-28).

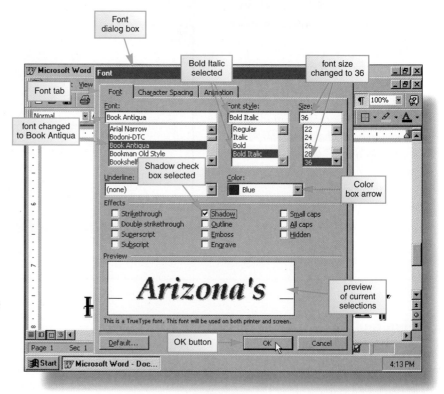

FIGURE 4-28

3 **Click the OK button. Click at the end of the slogan to remove the highlight.**

Word displays the company slogan formatted to 36-point Book Antiqua blue, bold italic font with a shadow (Figure 4-29).

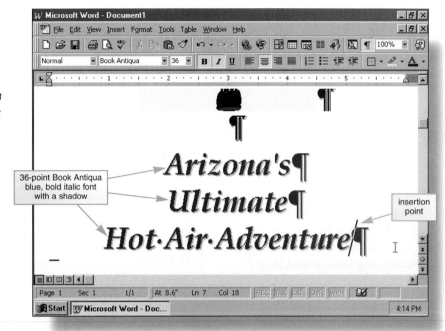

FIGURE 4-29

Saving the Title Page

Because you have finished the title page, you should save it by performing the following steps.

TO SAVE A DOCUMENT

1 Insert your floppy disk into drive A.
2 Click the Save button on the Standard toolbar.
3 Type `Fiesta Title Page` in the File name text box. Do not press the ENTER key after typing the file name.
4 Click the Save in box arrow and then click 3½ Floppy (A:).
5 Click the Save button in the Save As dialog box.

Word saves the document on a floppy disk in drive A with the file name Fiesta Title Page (Figure 4-30 on the next page).

The title page for the sales proposal is complete. The next step is to insert a draft of the proposal below the title page.

Inserting an Existing Document into an Open Document

Assume you already have prepared a draft of the body of the proposal and saved it with the file name Fiesta Balloon Tours Draft. You would like the draft to display on a separate page below the title page. Once the two documents display on the screen together as one document, you would like to save this active document with a new name so each of the original documents remains intact.

You want the inserted pages of the sales proposal to use the Times New Roman font and be left-aligned. That is, you want to return to the **Normal style**. Because the text to be entered at the insertion point currently is formatted for paragraphs to be centered using 36-point Book Antiqua blue, bold italic font, you should return to the Normal style as shown in the steps below.

Steps   To Return to the Normal Style

1 **Be sure the insertion point is on the paragraph mark on line 7 and then press the ENTER key. Click the Style box arrow on the Formatting toolbar and then point to Normal.**

Word displays the list of available styles (Figure 4-30). Notice the paragraph mark on line 8 is formatted the same as the slogan because when you press the ENTER key, formatting is carried forward to the next paragraph.

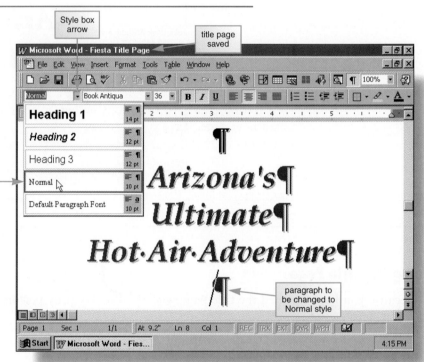

FIGURE 4-30

2 **Click Normal.**

Word returns the paragraph mark at the location of the insertion point to the Normal style (Figure 4-31). That is, the paragraph mark is left-aligned and the text to be entered is 10-point Times New Roman.

FIGURE 4-31

Inserting a Section Break

The draft of the sales proposal should appear on a separate page below the title page. The draft to be inserted requires different page formatting than the title page. Recall that you increased the top margin of the title page to 1.5 inches. The draft should have a top margin of 1 inch. To change margins for the draft of the proposal and retain the margins for the title page, you must create a new section in the document.

A Word document can be divided into any number of **sections**. All documents have at least one section. If during the course of creating a document, you would like to change the margins, paper size, page orientation, page number position, contents or position of headers, footers, or footnotes, you must create a new section. Each section may be formatted different from the others.

When you create a new section, a **section break** displays on the screen as a double dotted line separated by the words, Section Break. Section breaks do not print. When you create a section break, you specify whether or not the new section should begin on a new page. Perform the following steps to create a section break that begins on a new page.

◆ **More** *About*
Drafting a
Proposal

All proposals should have an introduction, body, and conclusion. The introduction could contain the subject, purpose, statement of problem, need, background, or scope. The body may include available or required facilities, cost, feasibility, methods, timetable, materials, or equipment. The conclusion summarizes key points or requests some action.

 Steps **To Create a Section Break**

① **Be sure the insertion point is positioned on the paragraph mark on line 8. Click Insert on the menu bar and then click Break. When the Break dialog box displays, click Next page in the Section breaks area. Point to the OK button.**

*Word displays the **Break dialog box** (Figure 4-32). The Next page option instructs Word to create a new page for the new section.*

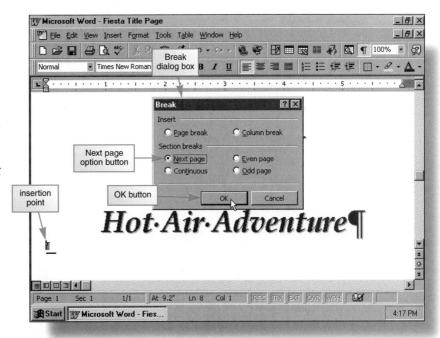

FIGURE 4-32

2 Click the OK button.

Word creates a section break in the document (Figure 4-33). The insertion point and paragraph mark are placed in the new section. Notice the status bar indicates the insertion point is on page 2 in section 2.

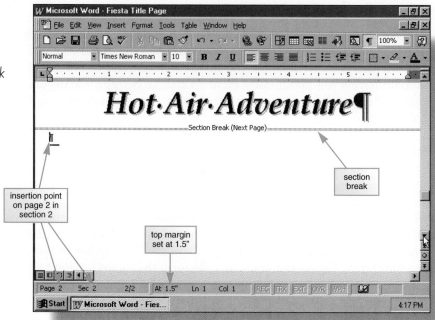

FIGURE 4-33

All section formatting is stored in the section break. You can delete a section break and all associated section formatting by selecting the section break, right-clicking the selection, and then clicking Cut on the shortcut menu. To select a section break, point to its left until the mouse pointer changes direction and then click. If you accidentally delete a section break, you can bring it back by clicking the Undo button on the Standard toolbar.

Notice in Figure 4-33 above that the top margin is set at 1.5 inches. Recall that the top margin of the new section containing the text of the draft of the sales proposal is to be set at 1 inch. Thus, follow these steps to change the top margin of section 2 to 1 inch.

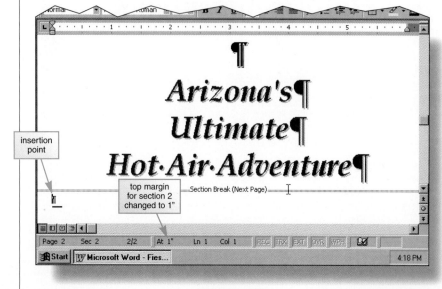

FIGURE 4-34

TO CHANGE THE TOP MARGIN

1. Be sure the insertion point is in section 2. Click File on the menu bar and then click Page Setup.
2. If necessary, click the Margins tab when the Page Setup dialog box first opens.
3. Type 1 in the Top text box.
4. Click the OK button.

The top margin is set at 1" (Figure 4-34).

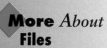
Inserting a Second Document into an Open Document

The next step is to insert the draft of the sales proposal below the section break. If you created the draft at an earlier time, you may have forgotten its name. Thus, you can display the contents of, or **preview**, any file before inserting it. Perform the following steps to insert the draft of the proposal into the open document.

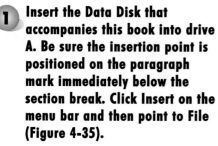

To Insert a Second Document into an Open Document

1 **Insert the Data Disk that accompanies this book into drive A. Be sure the insertion point is positioned on the paragraph mark immediately below the section break. Click Insert on the menu bar and then point to File (Figure 4-35).**

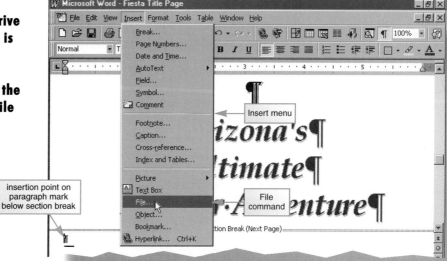

FIGURE 4-35

2 **Click File. When the Insert File dialog box displays, click the Look in box arrow and then click 3½ Floppy (A:). Double-click the Word folder. If it is not already recessed, click the Preview button. Click Fiesta Balloon Tours Draft and then point to the OK button.**

Word displays the Insert File dialog box (Figure 4-36). A list of available files in the Word folder on drive A displays. The contents of the selected file (Fiesta Balloon Tours Draft) display in the preview window.

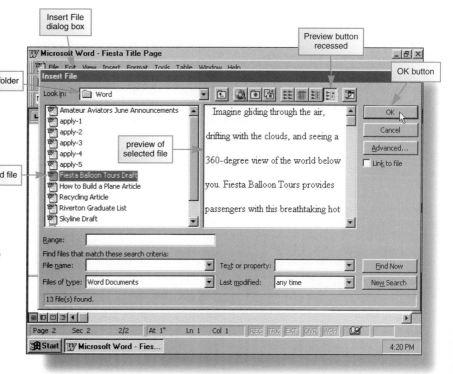

FIGURE 4-36

3 **Click the OK button. When Word returns to the document window, press the SHIFT+F5 keys.**

Word inserts the file, Fiesta Balloon Tours Draft, into the open document at the location of insertion point (Figure 4-37). The insertion point is positioned immediately below the section break, which was its location prior to inserting the new document. Pressing the SHIFT+F5 keys instructs Word to return the insertion point to your last editing location.

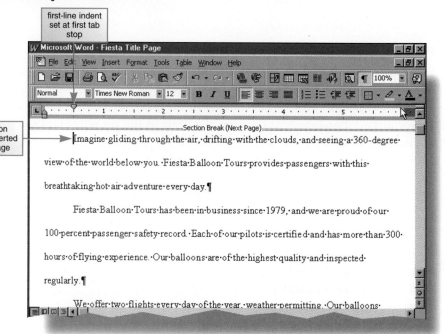

FIGURE 4-37

Word inserts the complete document immediately above the insertion point and positions the insertion point below the inserted document. Therefore, if the insertion point is positioned in the middle of the first document when you insert the second document, the first document continues after the end of the inserted document.

Previewing files before opening them is very useful if you have forgotten the name of a particular file. For this reason, you can preview files in both the Open and Insert File dialog boxes by clicking the **Preview button** in the respective dialog box.

Saving the Active Document with a New File Name

The current file name on the title bar is Fiesta Title Page, yet the active document contains both the title page and the draft of the sales proposal. Because you might want to keep the title page as a separate document called Fiesta Title Page, you should save the active document with a new file name. If you save the active document by clicking the Save button on the Standard toolbar, Word will assign it the current file name. Thus, use the following steps to save the active document with a new file name.

TO SAVE AN ACTIVE DOCUMENT WITH A NEW FILE NAME

1. Insert your floppy disk into drive A.
2. Click File on the menu bar and then click Save As.
3. Type Fiesta Proposal in the File name text box. Do not press the ENTER key.
4. If necessary, click the Save in box arrow and then click 3½ Floppy (A:).
5. Click the Save button in the Save As dialog box.

Word saves the document on a floppy disk in drive A with the file name Fiesta Proposal (Figure 4-39 on page WD 4.32).

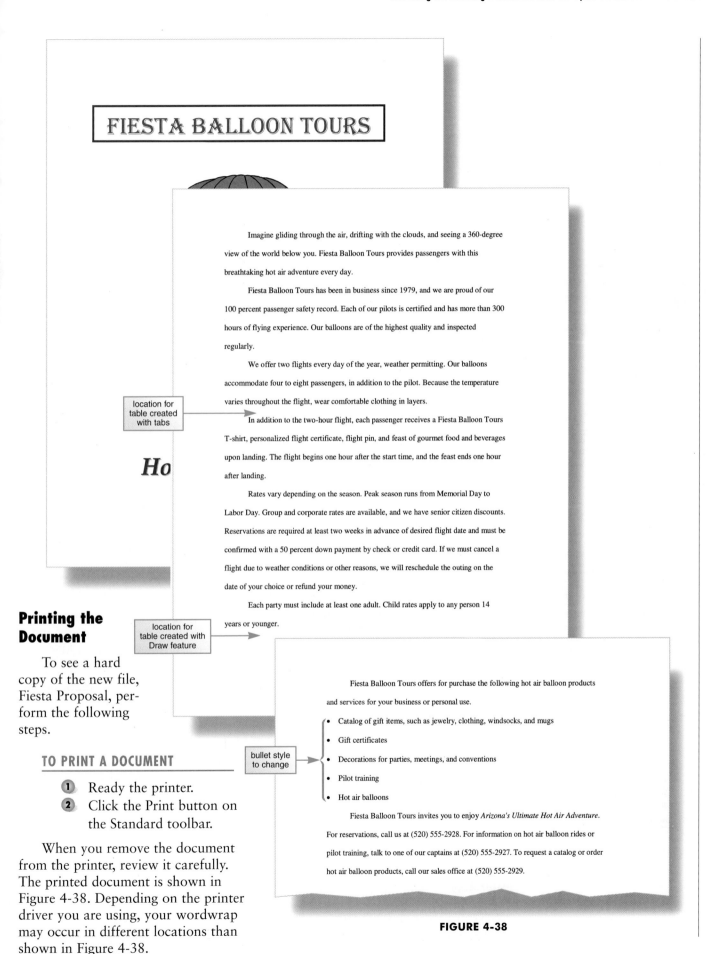

FIESTA BALLOON TOURS

Imagine gliding through the air, drifting with the clouds, and seeing a 360-degree view of the world below you. Fiesta Balloon Tours provides passengers with this breathtaking hot air adventure every day.

Fiesta Balloon Tours has been in business since 1979, and we are proud of our 100 percent passenger safety record. Each of our pilots is certified and has more than 300 hours of flying experience. Our balloons are of the highest quality and inspected regularly.

We offer two flights every day of the year, weather permitting. Our balloons accommodate four to eight passengers, in addition to the pilot. Because the temperature varies throughout the flight, wear comfortable clothing in layers.

location for table created with tabs →

In addition to the two-hour flight, each passenger receives a Fiesta Balloon Tours T-shirt, personalized flight certificate, flight pin, and feast of gourmet food and beverages upon landing. The flight begins one hour after the start time, and the feast ends one hour after landing.

Ho

Rates vary depending on the season. Peak season runs from Memorial Day to Labor Day. Group and corporate rates are available, and we have senior citizen discounts. Reservations are required at least two weeks in advance of desired flight date and must be confirmed with a 50 percent down payment by check or credit card. If we must cancel a flight due to weather conditions or other reasons, we will reschedule the outing on the date of your choice or refund your money.

Each party must include at least one adult. Child rates apply to any person 14 years or younger.

location for table created with Draw feature →

Printing the Document

To see a hard copy of the new file, Fiesta Proposal, perform the following steps.

Fiesta Balloon Tours offers for purchase the following hot air balloon products and services for your business or personal use.

bullet style to change →

- Catalog of gift items, such as jewelry, clothing, windsocks, and mugs
- Gift certificates
- Decorations for parties, meetings, and conventions
- Pilot training
- Hot air balloons

Fiesta Balloon Tours invites you to enjoy *Arizona's Ultimate Hot Air Adventure*. For reservations, call us at (520) 555-2928. For information on hot air balloon rides or pilot training, talk to one of our captains at (520) 555-2927. To request a catalog or order hot air balloon products, call our sales office at (520) 555-2929.

TO PRINT A DOCUMENT

1. Ready the printer.
2. Click the Print button on the Standard toolbar.

When you remove the document from the printer, review it carefully. The printed document is shown in Figure 4-38. Depending on the printer driver you are using, your wordwrap may occur in different locations than shown in Figure 4-38.

FIGURE 4-38

By adding two tables to the document and changing the bullet style, you can make the body of the proposal more pleasing to the eye. These enhancements to Project 4 are discussed in the following pages.

Setting and Using Tabs

Below the third paragraph of the sales proposal, you are to add a table that displays the starting and ending times of sunrise and sunset outings at Fiesta Balloon Tours. With Word, you can create tables by creating a Word table or by setting tab stops (as you would on a typewriter). In Project 3, you used the Insert Table button to create a Word table. For the first table in this project, you will set tab stops; for the second table that will be added later, you will draw a Word table.

Recall that Word, by default, places tab stops at every .5-inch mark on the ruler. You can use these default tab stops or set your own **custom tab stops**. When you set a custom tab stop, Word clears all default tab stops to the left of the custom tab stop. You also can specify how the text will align at a tab stop: left, centered, right, or decimal. Tab settings are stored in the paragraph mark at the end of each paragraph. Thus, each time you press the ENTER key, the custom tab stops are carried forward to the next paragraph.

The first step in creating this table is to center the title between the margins. If you simply click the Center button on the Formatting toolbar, the title will not be centered properly; instead, it will be one-half inch to the right of the center point because the first-line indent is set to the first tab stop (see Figure 4-37 on page WD 4.30). Thus, the first line of every paragraph is indented one-half inch. To properly center the title of the table, you must move the First Line Indent marker back to the left margin before clicking the Center button as described below.

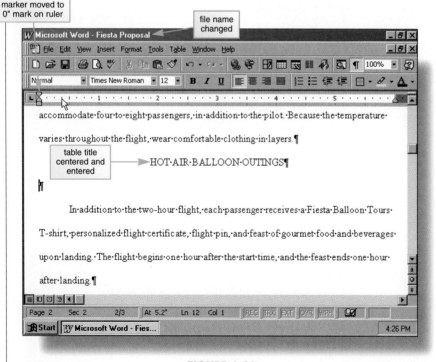

FIGURE 4-39

TO CENTER THE TITLE OF A TABLE

1 Position the insertion point at the end of the third paragraph (after the period following the word layers) and then press the ENTER key.

2 Drag the First Line Indent marker to the 0" mark on the ruler.

3 Click the Center button on the Formatting toolbar.

4 Type HOT AIR BALLOON OUTINGS and then press the ENTER key.

5 Press the CTRL+L keys.

The title displays centered properly (Figure 4-39).

The next step is to set custom tab stops for the data in the table. The text in the first tab stop should be left-aligned, the default; and the text in the last two tab stops should be right-aligned. Perform the following steps to set custom tab stops for the paragraph at the location of the insertion point.

 Steps **To Set Custom Tab Stops**

1 **Be sure the insertion point is on the paragraph mark below the title of the table. Point to the 1.25" mark on the ruler (Figure 4-40).**

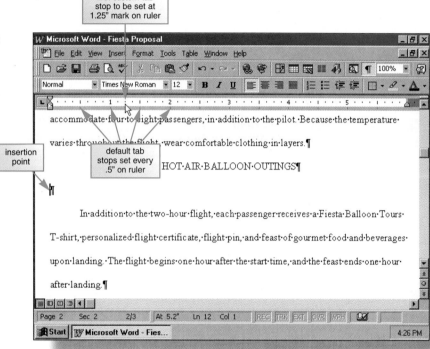

FIGURE 4-40

2 **Click the 1.25" mark on the ruler. Point to the Tab Alignment button at the left edge of the ruler.**

Word places a custom tab stop at the 1.25" mark on the ruler and removes the default tab stops at the .5" and 1" marks (Figure 4-41). A **tab marker** *displays on the ruler as a small dark capital L, the same symbol inside the* **Tab Alignment button**, *which indicates the text entered at the tab stop will be left-aligned. You want the next custom tab stop to be right-aligned.*

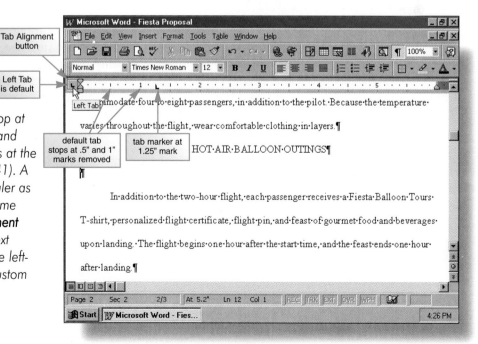

FIGURE 4-41

3 **Click the Tab Alignment button twice.**

The first time you click the Tab Alignment button, the symbol inside the Tab Alignment button changes to an upside down T, indicating a centered tab stop. The second click displays a mirror-image of a capital L, indicating the next custom tab stop set will be right-aligned (Figure 4-42).

4 **Click the 3.25" mark on the ruler and then click the 4.5" mark on the ruler.**

Word places custom tab stops at the 3.25" and 4.5" marks on the ruler and removes the default tab stops between the 1.25" and 3.25" marks and between the 3.25" and 4.5" marks. The tab markers display on the ruler as mirror-images of a capital L, indicating text typed at the tab stops will be right-aligned.

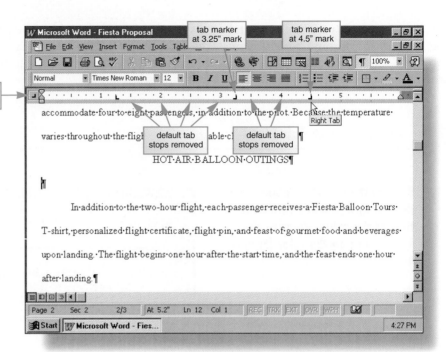

FIGURE 4-42

Other Ways

1. On Format menu click Tabs, enter tab stop position, click appropriate alignment, repeat if necessary, click OK button

More *About*
Tab Stops

You can use the Tabs dialog box to change an existing tab stop's alignment or position on the ruler. You can also place leader characters in the empty space occupied by the tab. Leader characters, such as a series of dots, often are used in a table of contents to precede the page number. To display the Tabs dialog box, click Tabs on the Format menu.

If necessary, to move a custom tab stop drag the tab marker to the desired location on the ruler. If you wanted to change the alignment of a custom tab stop, you could first remove the existing tab stop and then insert a new one as described in the steps above. To remove a custom tab stop, point to the tab marker on the ruler and then drag the tab marker down and out of the ruler. You could also use the **Tabs dialog box** to change an existing tab stop's alignment or position. To display the Tabs dialog box, click Format on the menu bar and then click Tabs.

The next step in creating the table with tabs is to enter the text in the table.

Entering Text Using Custom Tab Stops

To move from one tab stop to another, you press the **TAB key**. A tab character displays in the empty space between tab stops and the insertion point moves to the next custom tab stop. Perform the following steps to enter text using custom tab stops.

TO ENTER TEXT USING CUSTOM TAB STOPS

1 Be sure the insertion point is positioned on the paragraph mark on line 12 in the sales proposal. Press the TAB key twice. Type Sunrise and then press the TAB key. Type Sunset and then press the ENTER key.

2 Press the TAB key. Type Start time and then press the TAB key. Type 6:00 a.m. and then press the TAB key. Type 7:00 p.m. and then press the ENTER key.

3 Press the TAB key. Type End time and then press the TAB key. Type 10:00 a.m. and then press the TAB key. Type 11:00 p.m. and then press the ENTER key.

The first table in the sales proposal displays as shown in Figure 4-43.

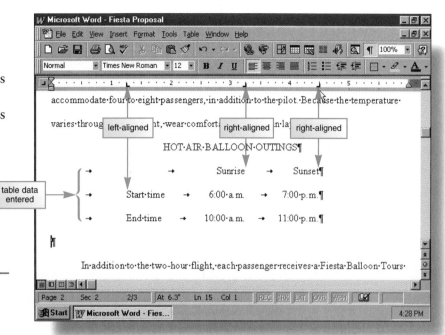

FIGURE 4-43

Adding a Border to a Table

To emphasize the table, you want to add an outside border around it. Recall that you place borders around a paragraph(s). Earlier in this project, you used the Tables and Borders toolbar to add a 3-point blue border to a paragraph on the title page and then changed the border back to its default size and color. Because this border is to be the current border size and color, you can use the Outside Border button on the Formatting toolbar. Because the table consists of four separate paragraphs, including the title, you first select the paragraphs and then add the border as shown in the following steps.

More *About* **Borders**

If you don't want the border of the current paragraph to extend to the margins, drag the right or left indent markers to the desired location on the ruler.

 Steps **To Border a Table**

1 **Select the four paragraphs in the table and then point to the Outside Border button on the Formatting toolbar.**

Word highlights the entire table (Figure 4-44).

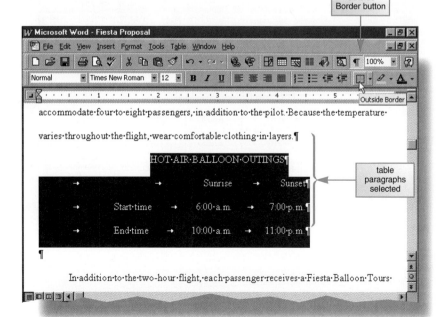

FIGURE 4-44

2 **Click the Outside Border button. Click outside the selection to remove the highlight.**

Word places a border around the selected paragraphs that extends from the left margin to the right margin of the document (Figure 4-45).

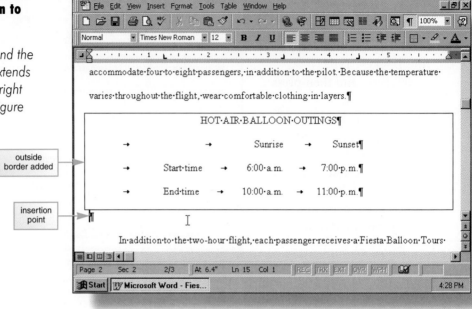

FIGURE 4-45

Creating a Table Using the Draw Table Feature

Below the sixth paragraph of the sales proposal draft (Figure 4-38 on page WD 4.31), you are to add another table. This table is more complicated than the previous one, so you are to create a Word table. In Project 3, you created a Word table using the Insert Table button on the Standard toolbar. When you have a simple table, one with the same number of rows and columns, use the Insert Table button to create a Word table. This table, however, is more complex (Figure 4-46). It contains a varying number of columns per row. To create a complex Word table, use the **Draw Table feature**.

You may recall that a Word table is a collection of rows and columns and that the intersection of a row and a column is called a **cell**. Cells are filled with data.

Within a table, you can easily rearrange rows and columns, change column widths, sort rows and columns, and sum the contents of rows and columns. You can use the Table AutoFormat dialog box to make the table display in a professional manner. You can also chart table data. For these reasons, many Word users create tables with the Insert Table button or the Draw Table feature, rather than using tabs as discussed in the previous section.

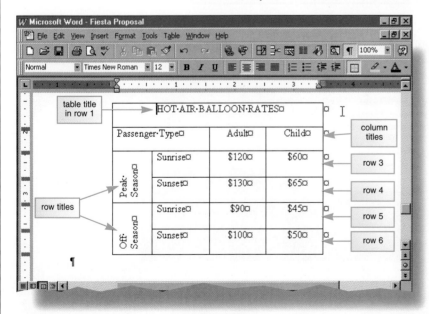

FIGURE 4-46

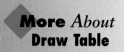
Drawing a Table

The first step is to draw an empty table in the document. To do this, you use the **Draw Table button** on the Tables and Borders toolbar. Perform the following steps to draw the table shown in Figure 4-46.

 To Draw a Table

More *About*
Draw Table

If you make a mistake while drawing a table, remember you can always click the Undo button to undo your most recent action.

1 **Position the insertion point at the end of the sixth paragraph (after the period following the word younger) and then press the ENTER key. If necessary, click the Tables and Borders button on the Standard toolbar to display the Tables and Borders toolbar. If it is not already recessed, click the Draw Table button on the Tables and Borders toolbar. Move the mouse pointer into the document window to the location shown in Figure 4-47.**

Word displays the Tables and Borders toolbar and switches to page layout view (Figure 4-47). The

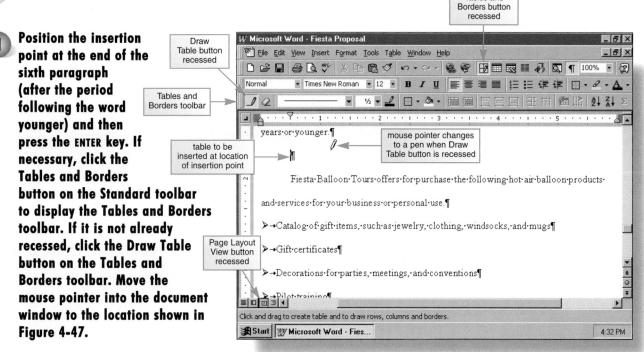

FIGURE 4-47

mouse pointer shape changes to a pen when the Draw Table button is recessed. To draw the outside boundary of the table, you drag the pen pointer from one corner to the opposite diagonal corner of the desired table.

2 **Drag the pen pointer downward and to the right until the dotted rectangle is positioned similarly to the one shown in Figure 4-48.**

Word displays a dotted rectangle that shows the table's size (Figure 4-48).

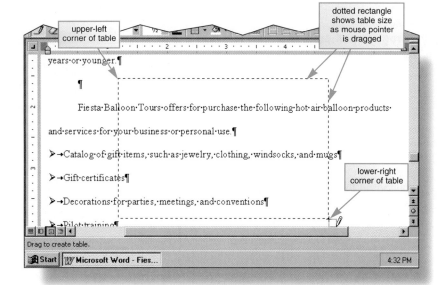

FIGURE 4-48

3 **Release the mouse button. If necessary, scroll to display the entire table in the document window. (If the table is positioned in the wrong paragraph mark, click Table on the menu bar, click Select Table, and then drag the selected table to the correct paragraph mark.)**

Word draws a table (Figure 4-49). If you wanted to redraw the table, you could click the Undo button on the Standard toolbar. If you wanted to resize the table, you would click the Draw Table button to turn off the Draw Table feature and then drag the table boundaries to their new locations. The next step is to begin drawing the rows and columns in the table.

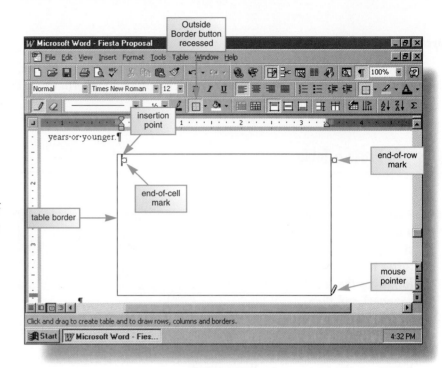

FIGURE 4-49

4 **Be sure the Draw Table button is still recessed. Position the pen pointer as shown in Figure 4-50.**

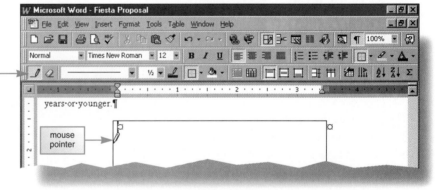

FIGURE 4-50

5 **Drag the pen pointer to the right to draw a horizontal line.**

*Word draws a horizontal line, which forms the bottom border of the first row in the table (Figure 4-51). If, while drawing rows and columns in the table, you want to remove and redraw a line, click the **Eraser button** on the Tables and Borders toolbar and then drag the eraser pointer through the line to erase. Click the Eraser button again to turn it off.*

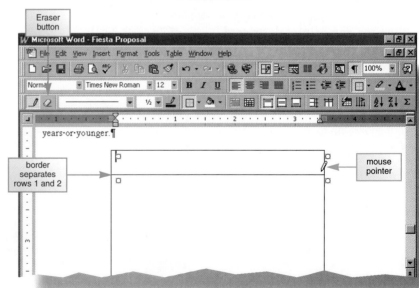

FIGURE 4-51

6 Be sure the Draw Table button is still recessed. Draw another horizontal line below the first as shown in Figure 4-52. Then, position the pen pointer as shown in Figure 4-52.

Word draws a second horizontal line to form the bottom border of the second row in the table (Figure 4-52). The pen pointer is positioned to draw the first column.

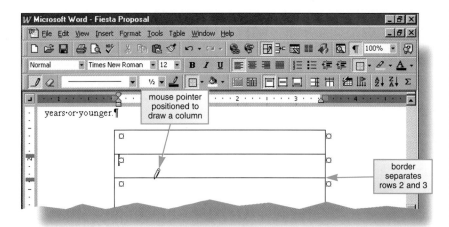

FIGURE 4-52

7 Draw three vertical lines to form the column borders as shown in Figure 4-53.

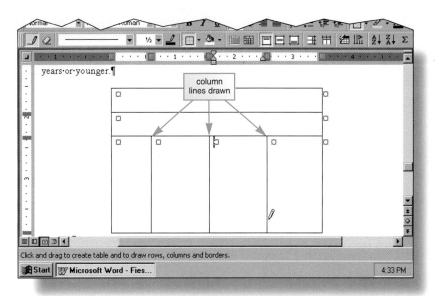

FIGURE 4-53

8 Draw four horizontal lines to form the row borders as shown in Figure 4-54.

The table displays as shown in Figure 4-54.

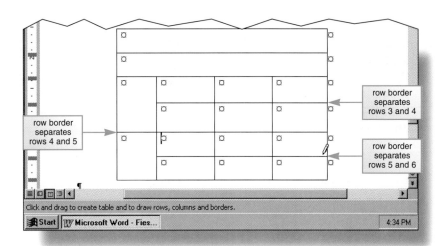

FIGURE 4-54

Other Ways

1. On Table menu click Draw Table, use pen pointer to draw table

More *About*
Table Columns

Column markers are located on the ruler and indicate the beginning and end of columns. A column boundary is the vertical gridline immediately to the right of a column in the table itself. To resize a column width, you drag the column boundary in the table or column marker on the ruler. Holding down the ALT key while dragging markers displays column width measurements.

All Word tables have a .5-point border. To change this border, you can use the Tables and Borders toolbar as described earlier in this project.

Recall that each row has an **end-of-row mark** (Figure 4-55 below), which is used to add columns to the right of a table, and each cell has an **end-of-cell mark**, which is used to select a cell. Notice the end-of-cell marks currently are **left-aligned** within each cell, which indicates the data will be left-aligned within the cells.

To format a table or data within a table, first you must select the cell(s) and then apply the appropriate formats. Because selecting table text is such a crucial function of Word tables, techniques to select these items are described in Table 4-1.

TABLE 4-1

ITEM TO SELECT	ACTION
Cell	Click the left edge of the cell.
Row	Click to the left of the row.
Column	Click the column's top gridline or border.
Contiguous cells, rows, or columns	Drag through the cells, rows, or columns.
Text in next cell	Press the TAB key.
Text in previous cell	Press the SHIFT+TAB keys.
Entire table	Click the table, click Table on the menu bar, then click Select Table.

If you look at the table drawn in Figure 4-54 on the previous page, the height of the rows varies and the width of the columns appears uneven. Perform the following steps to make the spacing between the columns and the rows even.

Steps ## To Distribute Rows and Columns Evenly

1 **If the Draw Table button on the Tables and Borders toolbar is recessed, click it to deselect it. Point to the left of the cell shown in Figure 4-55 until the mouse pointer changes direction.**

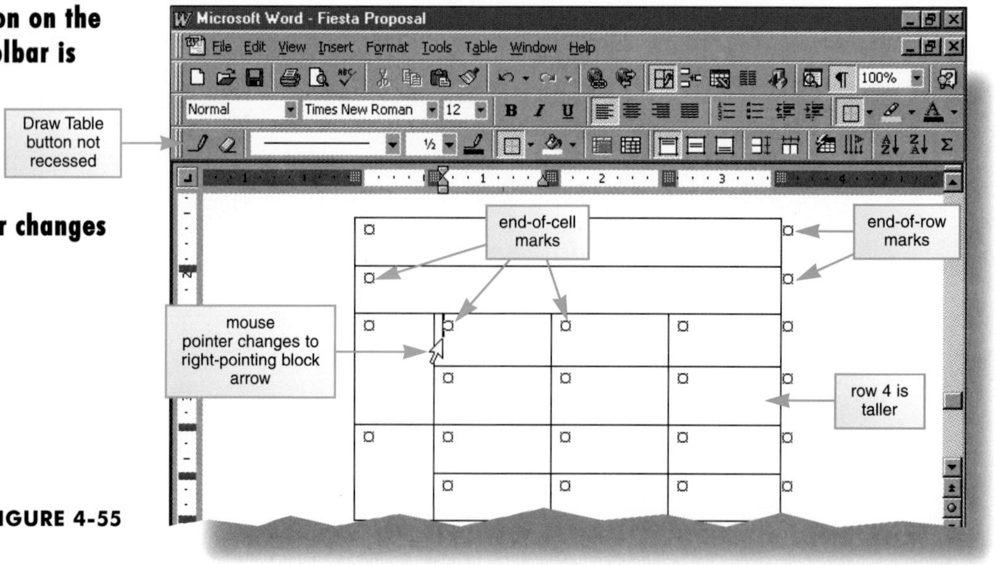

FIGURE 4-55

2 Drag through the cells to highlight the 12 cells shown in Figure 4-56.

The cells to be evenly distributed are selected (Figure 4-56).

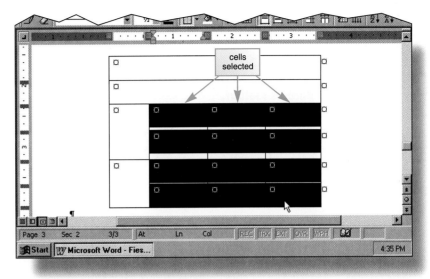

FIGURE 4-56

3 Click the Distribute Rows Evenly button on the Tables and Borders toolbar. Click the Distribute Columns Evenly button on the Tables and Borders toolbar. Click in the table to remove the highlight.

Word makes the height of the selected rows and the width of the selected columns uniform (Figure 4-57).

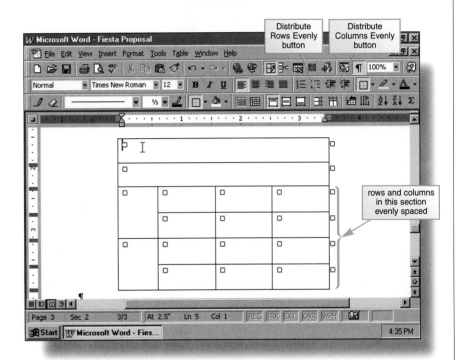

FIGURE 4-57

You notice you want to add two additional lines for column headings in the table. Perform the steps on the next page to continue drawing the table.

Other Ways

1. Select cells, on Table menu click Distribute Rows Evenly or Distribute Columns Evenly

2. Drag row or column boundaries (borders) on table

3. Drag row markers on vertical ruler or drag Move Table Column markers on horizontal ruler

4. On Table menu click Cell Height and Width, click appropriate tab, enter desired width or height, click OK button

Steps **To Draw More Table Lines**

1 Click the Draw Table button on the Tables and Borders toolbar. Position the mouse pointer as shown in Figure 4-58.

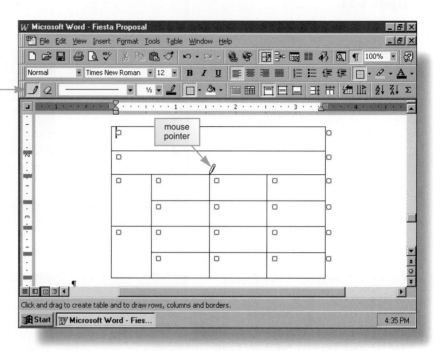

FIGURE 4-58

2 Draw a line upward extending the column border up. Draw a second line as shown in Figure 4-59. Click the Draw Table button on the Tables and Borders toolbar to deselect it.

The table is completely drawn (Figure 4-59).

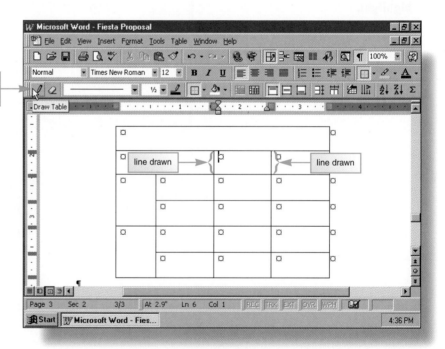

FIGURE 4-59

Entering the Data into the Table

The next step is to enter the data into the table. To advance from one column to the next, press the TAB key. To advance from one row to the next, also press the TAB key; do not press the ENTER key. The ENTER key is used to begin new paragraphs within a cell. Perform the following steps to enter the data into the table.

TO ENTER DATA INTO A TABLE

1 Click in the first cell of the table. Click the Center button on the Formatting toolbar. Type HOT AIR BALLOON RATES and then press the TAB key.

2 Type Passenger Type and then press the TAB key. Type Adult and then press the TAB key. Type Child and then press the TAB key.

3 Type Peak Season and then press the TAB key. Type Sunrise and then press the TAB key. Type $120 and then press the TAB key. Type $60 and then press the TAB key twice. Type Sunset and then press the TAB key. Type $130 and then press the TAB key. Type $65 and then press the TAB key.

4 Type Off Season and then press the TAB key. Type Sunrise and then press the TAB key. Type $90 and then press the TAB key. Type $45 and then press the TAB key twice. Type Sunset and then press the TAB key. Type $100 and then press the TAB key. Type $50 as the last entry.

The table data is entered (Figure 4-60).

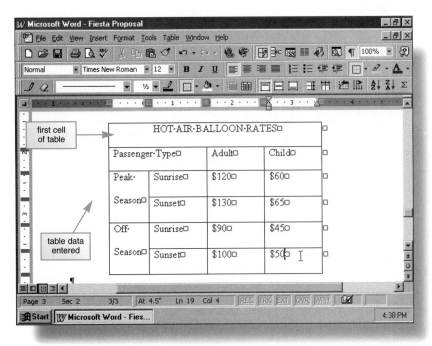

FIGURE 4-60

More *About* Table Contents

You can sum a column or row of numbers in a table. First, click the cell where you want the sum to appear. Then, click Formula on the Table menu. If you agree with the formula Word proposes in the Formula dialog box, click the OK button; otherwise, delete the formula and then build your own formula through the Paste Function list box.

Just as with paragraphs, you can left-align, center, or right-align the end-of-cell marks in a table. The next step is to center the rates and respective column headings in the cells as shown on the next page.

Changing the Alignment of Data within Cells

The data you enter into the cells is by default left-aligned. You can change the alignment just as you would for a paragraph. Before changing the alignment, you must select the cell(s). Perform the following steps to center the end-of-cell marks for cells in the second and third columns below the title.

Steps **To Center Cell Contents**

1 **Drag through the cells to center as shown in Figure 4-61. Point to the Center button on the Formatting toolbar.**

The cells to center are selected (Figure 4-61).

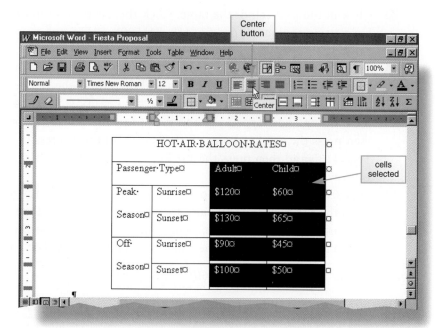

FIGURE 4-61

2 **Click the Center button. Click the selection to remove the highlight.**

Word centers the end-of-cell marks in the selected area (Figure 4-62). The Center button on the Formatting toolbar is recessed.

OtherWays

1. Select cells, click Paragraph on shortcut menu, click Indents and Spacing tab, click Alignment box arrow, click Centered, click OK button
2. Select cells, on Format menu click Paragraph, click Indents and Spacing tab, click Alignment box arrow, click Centered, click OK button
3. Select cells, press CTRL+E

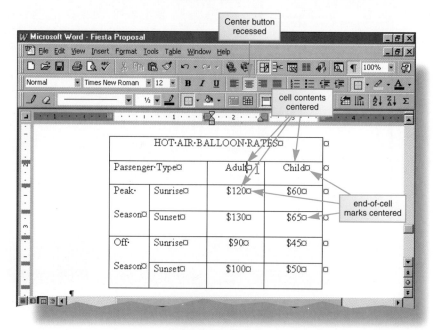

FIGURE 4-62

The next step is to **rotate** the row heading text, Peak Season and Off Season, so it displays vertically instead of horizontally.

Changing the Direction of Text in Cells

The data you enter in cells is, by default, displayed horizontally. You can change the text so it displays vertically. Changing the direction of text adds variety to your tables. Perform the following steps to display the row heading text vertically.

 Steps To Vertically Display Text in a Cell

1 **Select the row heading text cells containing the words, Peak Season and Off Season. Point to the Change Text Direction button on the Tables and Borders toolbar.**

The cells to be formatted are selected (Figure 4-63).

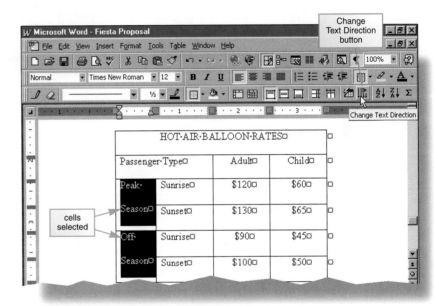

FIGURE 4-63

2 **Click the Change Text Direction button.**

The text displays vertically, top-to-bottom, in the selected cells (Figure 4-64). The first time you click the Change Text Direction button, the words display vertically so you read them from top to bottom.

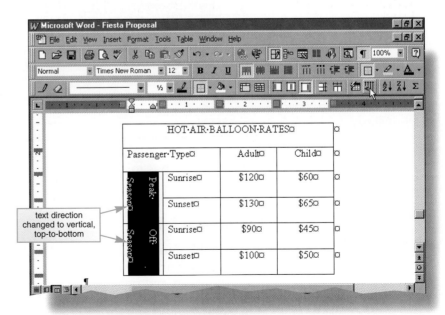

FIGURE 4-64

3 **With the cells still selected, click the Change Text Direction button again.**

The text displays vertically, bottom-to-top, in the selected cells (Figure 4-65). The second time you click the Change Text Direction button, the words display vertically so you read them from bottom to top. If you click the button a third time, the text would display horizontally again.

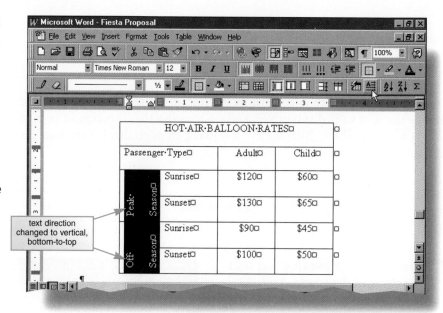

FIGURE 4-65

4 **Press the CTRL+1 keys. Click inside the selection to remove the highlight.**

Word formats the text in the selected cells to single-spacing (Figure 4-66). Recall that CTRL+1 is the keyboard shortcut for single-spacing paragraphs.

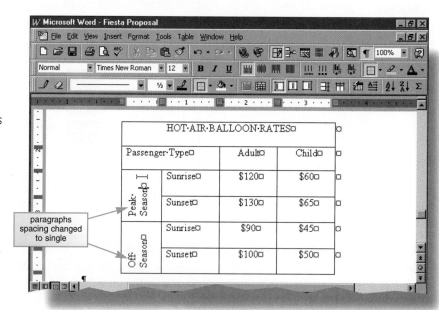

FIGURE 4-66

The next step is to center the table between the left and right margins of the document.

Centering a Table

The table currently is positioned on the screen where you drew it. Although it appears to be fairly close to the center point, you want it to be centered precisely between the left and right margins. To center the entire table, you first select the entire table and then click the Center button on the Formatting toolbar as shown in the following steps.

Steps **To Center a Table**

1 Make sure the insertion point is positioned somewhere inside the table. Click Table on the menu bar and then point to Select Table (Figure 4-67).

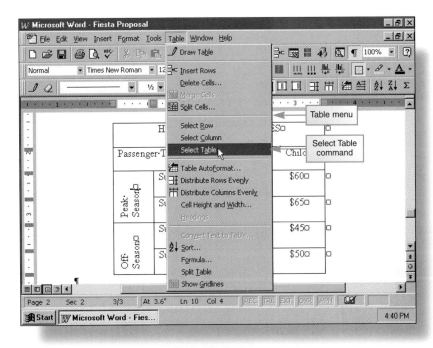

FIGURE 4-67

2 Click Select Table. Click the Center button on the Formatting toolbar. Click in the selection to remove the highlight. Click the Tables and Borders button on the Standard toolbar.

Word centers the table between the margins (Figure 4-68). Because the table is complete, you remove the Tables and Borders toolbar from the screen.

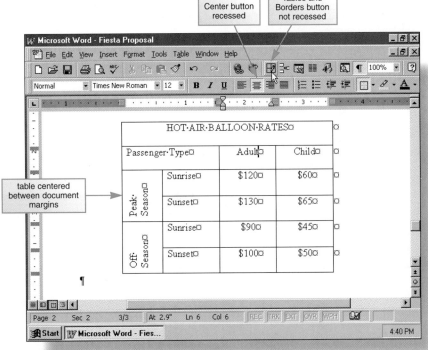

FIGURE 4-68

OtherWays

1. Select table, on Table menu click Cell Height and Width, click Row tab, click Center in Alignment area, click OK button

Working with Tables

At times you might want to add additional rows or columns to a table. To add a row to the end of a table, position the insertion point in the bottom right corner cell and then press the TAB key. Depending on the task you want to perform in a table, the function of the **Table button** on the Standard toolbar changes and the commands change on the Table menu and associated shortcut menu. To **add rows** in the middle of a table, select the row below where you want to insert a row and then click the **Insert Rows button** (the same button you clicked to insert a table) or click the **Insert Rows command** on the Table or shortcut menu. To **add a column** in the middle of a table, select the column to the right of where you want to insert a column and then click the **Insert Columns button** (the same button you clicked to insert a table) or click the **Insert Columns command** on the Table or shortcut menu. To add a column to the right of a table, select the end-of-row marks at the right edge of the table, then click the Insert Columns button or click the Insert Columns command on the Table or shortcut menu.

If you want to **delete row(s)** or **delete column(s)** from a table, select the row(s) or column(s) to delete and then click **Delete Rows** or **Delete Columns** on the Table or shortcut menu.

Adding Finishing Touches to the Document

The document requires two more enhancements: change the bullet type in the list of products and services for sale and add a header to the document.

Customizing Bullets in a List

You can add the default bullets, which are small circles, to a list by selecting the list and then clicking the **Bullets button** on the Formatting toolbar. In this project, you want the bullets to be arrow shaped. To change the bullet style, use the **Bullets and Numbering command** as shown in the following steps.

Steps To Customize Bullets in a List

1 Scroll to and then select the paragraphs in the list. Right-click the selection. Point to Bullets and Numbering on the shortcut menu.

A shortcut menu displays (Figure 4-69).

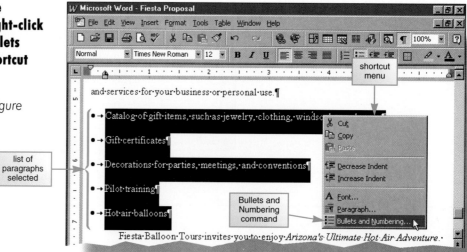

FIGURE 4-69

2 **Click Bullets and Numbering. If necessary, click the Bulleted tab when the Bullets and Numbering dialog box first opens. Click the arrow shaped bullets and then point to the OK button.**

Word displays the Bullets and Numbering dialog box (Figure 4-70). The arrow shaped bulleted list sample has a box around it, indicating it is selected.

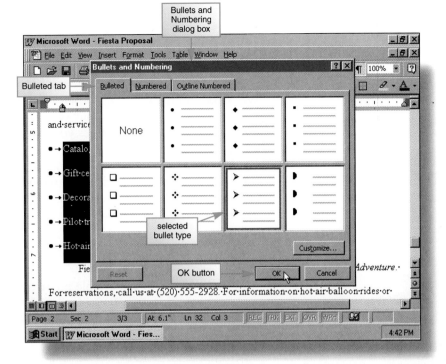

FIGURE 4-70

3 **Click the OK button. Click outside the selection to remove the highlight.**

Word places arrow shaped bullets to the left of each paragraph (Figure 4-71).

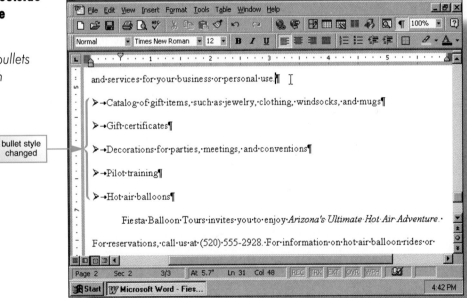

FIGURE 4-71

The next step is to add a header to the sales proposal.

Other Ways

1. Select the list, on Format menu click Bullets and Numbering, click Bullets tab, click desired bullet style, click OK button

Adding a Header to the Sales Proposal

You want the company name and page number to display on the sales proposal; you do not, however, want this header on the title page. Recall that the title page and the body of the sales proposal are in separate sections. You do not want a header in section 1, but you do want one in section 2. When you initially create a header, Word assumes you want it in all sections. Thus, when you create the header in section 2, you must instruct Word to not place it in section 1.

Currently, the insertion point is located in page 3 of the document. To illustrate creating the header, you will move the insertion point to the top of page 2. Follow these steps to display page 2 in the document window and then create the header for section 2.

TO DISPLAY THE PREVIOUS PAGE

1. Point to the double up arrow button above the Select Browse Object button on the vertical scroll bar. If the ScreenTip, Previous Page, displays below the double up arrow button, then click the button; otherwise, proceed with Step 2.

If you edited your document or table recently, the ScreenTip on the double up arrow button will not be Previous Page and the double up arrows will display in the color blue.

2. Click the Select Browse Object button on the vertical scroll bar. Point to the Browse by Page command (Figure 4-72).
3. Click the Browse by Page command. Click the Previous Page button.

Word displays page 2 at the top of the document window (Figure 4-73).

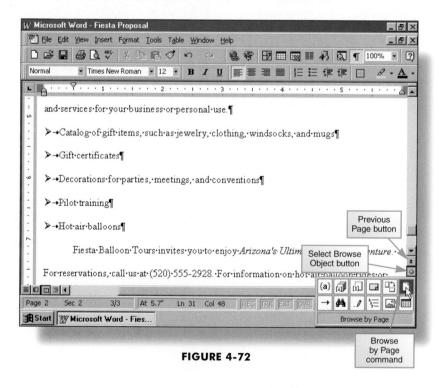

FIGURE 4-72

The next step is to create the header for section 2 of the document.

Steps **To Add a Header to the Sales Proposal**

1 **Click View on the menu bar and then click Header and Footer. Point to the Same as Previous button on the Header and Footer toolbar.**

Word displays the Header and Footer toolbar (Figure 4-73). Notice the Same as Previous button is recessed, which instructs Word to place the header in the previous section also. Because you do not want this header in section 1, you do not want the Same as Previous button to be recessed.

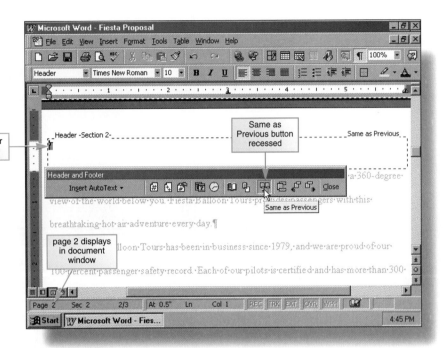

FIGURE 4-73

2 **Click the Same as Previous button. Click the Align Right button on the Formatting toolbar to right-align the header. Type** Fiesta Balloon Tours **and then press the SPACEBAR. Click the Insert Page Number button on the Header and Footer toolbar.**

Word displays the header for section 2 (Figure 4-74). The Same as Previous button no longer is recessed. Because Word begins numbering pages from the beginning of the document, the page number 2 displays in the header.

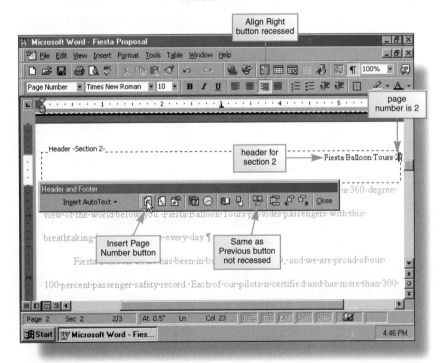

FIGURE 4-74

Notice in Figure 4-74 that the page number is a 2. You want to begin numbering the body of the sales proposal with a number 1. Thus, you need to instruct Word to begin numbering the pages in section 2 with a 1 as shown in the steps on the next page.

Steps To Page Number Differently in a Section

1 **Click Insert on the menu bar and then point to Page Numbers (Figure 4-75).**

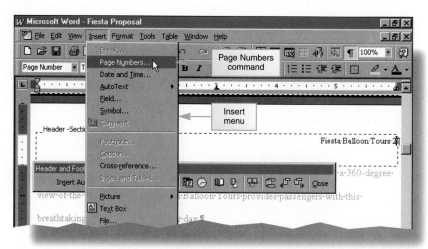

FIGURE 4-75

2 **Click Page Numbers. When the Page Numbers dialog box displays, point to the Format button.**

Word displays the Page Numbers dialog box (Figure 4-76).

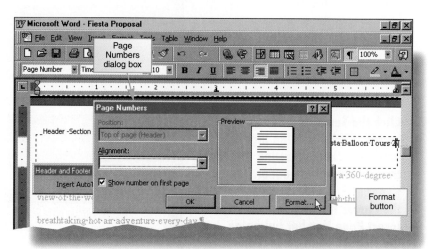

FIGURE 4-76

3 **Click the Format button. When the Page Number Format dialog box displays, click Start at in the Page numbering area and then point to the OK button.**

Word displays the Page Number Format dialog box (Figure 4-77). The number 1 displays in the Start at box, by default.

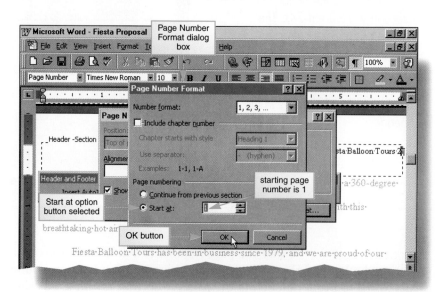

FIGURE 4-77

4 Click the OK button in the Page Number Format dialog box. When the Page Numbers dialog box redisplays, point to its Close button.

Word closes the Page Number Format dialog box and returns to the Page Numbers dialog box (Figure 4-78). This dialog box displays both an OK button and a Close button. Be sure to click the Close button, instead of the OK button, in the Page Numbers dialog box; otherwise, you will have another set of page numbers in the document.

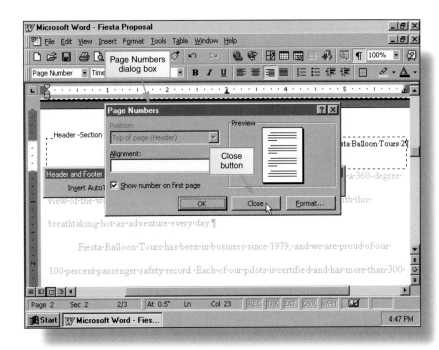

FIGURE 4-78

5 Click the Close button.

Word changes the starting page number for section 2 to the number 1 (Figure 4-79).

6 Click the Close Header and Footer button on the Header and Footer toolbar. If necessary, click the Normal View button at the bottom of the document window.

Word closes the Header and Footer toolbar and returns to normal view. Recall that headers and footers do not display on the screen in normal view.

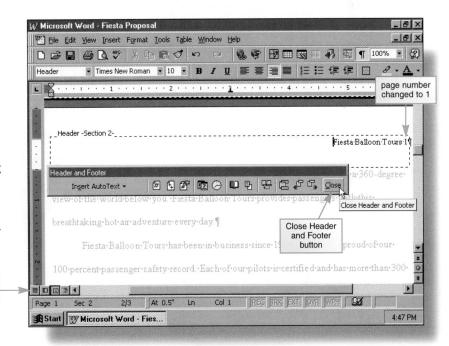

FIGURE 4-79

Check the spelling of the document by clicking the **Spelling and Grammar button** on the Standard toolbar. Save the document one final time by clicking the Save button on the Standard toolbar, and then print the sales proposal by clicking the Print button. The printed document displays as shown in Figure 4-80 on the next page.

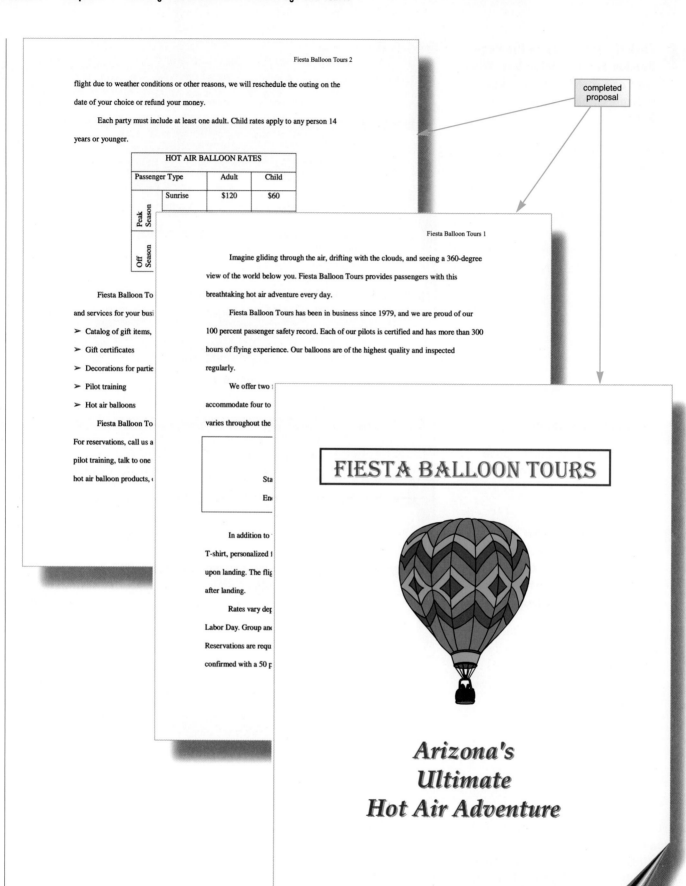

completed proposal

Fiesta Balloon Tours 2

flight due to weather conditions or other reasons, we will reschedule the outing on the

date of your choice or refund your money.

Each party must include at least one adult. Child rates apply to any person 14

years or younger.

HOT AIR BALLOON RATES		
Passenger Type	Adult	Child
Sunrise	$120	$60

Peak Season

Off Season

Fiesta Balloon To

and services for your busi

➤ Catalog of gift items,

➤ Gift certificates

➤ Decorations for partie

➤ Pilot training

➤ Hot air balloons

Fiesta Balloon To

For reservations, call us a

pilot training, talk to one

hot air balloon products, o

Fiesta Balloon Tours 1

Imagine gliding through the air, drifting with the clouds, and seeing a 360-degree

view of the world below you. Fiesta Balloon Tours provides passengers with this

breathtaking hot air adventure every day.

Fiesta Balloon Tours has been in business since 1979, and we are proud of our

100 percent passenger safety record. Each of our pilots is certified and has more than 300

hours of flying experience. Our balloons are of the highest quality and inspected

regularly.

We offer two

accommodate four to

varies throughout the

Sta

En

In addition to

T-shirt, personalized f

upon landing. The flig

after landing.

Rates vary dep

Labor Day. Group and

Reservations are requ

confirmed with a 50 p

FIESTA BALLOON TOURS

Arizona's
Ultimate
Hot Air Adventure

FIGURE 4-80

You have now finished Project 4. Follow this step to quit Word.

TO QUIT WORD

① Click the Close button in the Word window.

The Word window closes.

Project Summary

Project 4 introduced you to creating a proposal with a title page and tables. First, you created a title page with a graphic, outside border, color, and characters in a variety of fonts and styles. You learned how to insert an existing document into the active document. Then, you saved the active document with a new file name. Next, you set custom tabs and used them to create a table. Then, you used the Draw Table feature to create a second table. Finally, you changed the bullet style in the list of items and created a header for the second section of the document.

What You Should Know

Having completed this project, you now should be able to perform the following tasks:

▶ Add a Header to the Sales Proposal *(WD 4.51)*

▶ Border a Paragraph *(WD 4.14)*

▶ Border a Table *(WD 4.35)*

▶ Center a Table *(WD 4.47)*

▶ Center Cell Contents *(WD 4.44)*

▶ Center the Title of a Table *(WD 4.32)*

▶ Change the Top Margin *(WD 4.11 and WD 4.28)*

▶ Color Characters *(WD 4.12)*

▶ Create a Section Break *(WD 4.27)*

▶ Customize Bullets in a List *(WD 4.48)*

▶ Display Nonprinting Characters *(WD 4.10)*

▶ Display the Previous Page *(WD 4.50)*

▶ Distribute Rows and Columns Evenly *(WD 4.40)*

▶ Download Clip Art from Microsoft's Clip Gallery Live Web Page *(WD 4.18)*

▶ Draw a Table *(WD 4.37)*

▶ Draw More Table Lines *(WD 4.42)*

▶ Enter and Format the Company Slogan *(WD 4.24)*

▶ Enter Data into a Table *(WD 4.43)*

▶ Enter Text Using Custom Tab Stops *(WD 4.34)*

▶ Format a Picture *(WD 4.22)*

▶ Format Characters *(WD 4.12)*

▶ Insert a Second Document into an Open Document *(WD 4.29)*

▶ Install Clip Art from the Data Disk *(WD 4.21)*

▶ Page Number Differently in a Section *(WD 4.52)*

▶ Print a Document *(WD 4.31)*

▶ Quit Word *(WD 4.55)*

▶ Return to the Normal Style *(WD 4.26)*

▶ Save a Document *(WD 4.25)*

▶ Save an Active Document with a New File Name *(WD 4.30)*

▶ Set Custom Tab Stops *(WD 4.33)*

▶ Start Word *(WD 4.10)*

▶ Vertically Display Text in a Cell *(WD 4.45)*

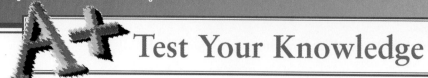

Test Your Knowledge

1 True/False

Instructions: Circle T if the statement is true or F if the statement is false.

T F 1. A research proposal offers a product or service to existing or potential customers.
T F 2. When Word displays the Tables and Borders toolbar, it switches to page layout view.
T F 3. One way to dock a floating toolbar is to click the title bar of the floating toolbar.
T F 4. If you have access to the Web, you can download clip art files from Microsoft's Clip Gallery Live Web page into the Clip Gallery.
T F 5. All documents have at least two sections.
T F 6. To save an active document with a new file name, click Save As on the File menu.
T F 7. To move a custom tab stop, drag the tab marker along the ruler.
T F 8. To create a complex table, use Word's Draw Table feature.
T F 9. By default, all Word tables have a 3-point border.
T F 10. To center a table, select the entire table and then click the Center button on the Formatting toolbar.

2 Multiple Choice

Instructions: Circle the correct response.

1. The Font Color button is located on the _____.
   a. menu bar
   b. Standard toolbar
   c. Formatting toolbar
   d. vertical scroll bar
2. In Word, you can add a border _____ a paragraph.
   a. above or below
   b. to the left or right of
   c. both a and b
   d. neither a nor b
3. To return the insertion point to your last editing location, press the _____ key(s).
   a. F5
   b. CTRL+F5
   c. SHIFT+F5
   d. ALT+F5

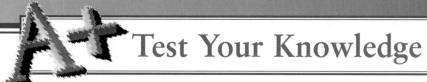

Test Your Knowledge

4. Word, by default, places tab stops at every _____-inch mark on the ruler.
   a. .25
   b. .5
   c. 1
   d. none of the above
5. The Tab Alignment button is located on the _____.
   a. Standard toolbar
   b. Formatting toolbar
   c. vertical ruler
   d. horizontal ruler
6. The Outside Border button is located on the _____.
   a. Formatting toolbar
   b. Tables and Borders toolbar
   c. both a and b
   d. neither a nor b
7. When the Draw Table button is recessed, the mouse pointer shape changes to a(n) _____.
   a. pen
   b. eraser
   c. table
   d. letter D
8. To select noncontiguous cells, select the first cell, then press and hold down the _____ key while clicking the second cell.
   a. TAB
   b. CTRL
   c. ALT
   d. none of the above
9. The Change Text Direction button is located on the _____.
   a. Formatting toolbar
   b. Tables and Borders toolbar
   c. both a and b
   d. neither a nor b
10. To change the style of bullets on a list, _____.
   a. click the Bullets button on the Formatting toolbar
   b. click Bullets and Numbering on the Format menu
   c. press the CTRL+B keys
   d. both b and c

Test Your Knowledge

3 Understanding the Tables and Borders Toolbar

Instructions: In Figure 4-81, arrows point to several of the boxes and buttons on the Tables and Borders toolbar. In the spaces provided, briefly explain the purpose of each button or box.

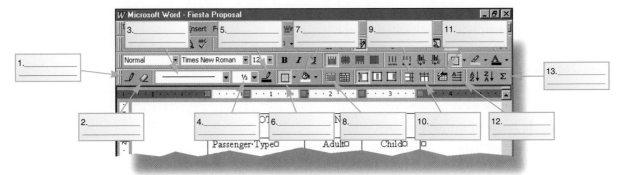

FIGURE 4-81

4 Understanding Custom Tab Stops

Instructions: Answer the questions below concerning Figure 4-82. The numbers in the figure correspond to question numbers below.

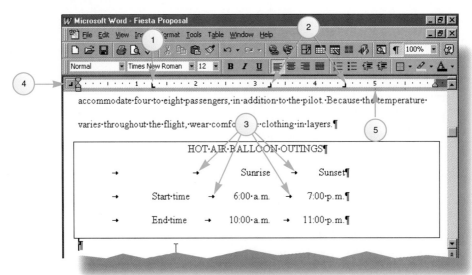

FIGURE 4-82

1. What is the alignment of the tab stop at the 1.25" mark?
2. What is the alignment of the tab stops at the 3.25" and 4.5" marks?
3. Why do the dark, right-pointing arrows display between the tab stops in the table?
4. What is the purpose of this button?
5. Why is a default tick mark at the 5" mark on the ruler?

Use Help

1 Reviewing Project Activities

Instructions: Perform the following tasks using a computer.

1. Start Word. If the Office Assistant is on your screen, click it to display its balloon. If the Office Assistant is not on your screen, click the Office Assistant button on the Standard toolbar.
2. Type `floating picture` in the What would you like to do? text box. Click the Search button. Click the Change a floating picture to an inline picture and vice-versa link. Read the information. Use the shortcut menu or Options button to print the information.
3. Click the Help Topics button to display the Help Topics: Microsoft Word dialog box. Click the Contents tab. Double-click the Changing the Appearance of Your Page book. Double-click the Inserting Page Breaks and Section Breaks book. Double-click the Types of section breaks topic. Read and print the information.
4. Click the Help Topics button. Click the Index tab. Type `colors` and then double-click the formatting topic. Read and print the information.
5. Click the Help Topics button. Click the Find tab. Type `complex tables` and then double-click the Create a complex table topic. Read and print the information.
6. Close any open Help window(s) by clicking its Close button. Close the Office Assistant.

2 Expanding on the Basics

Instructions: Use Word Help for a better understanding of the topics listed below. Answer the questions on your own paper or hand in the printed Help topic to your instructor.

1. In this project, you created a table using the Draw Table button on the Tables and Borders toolbar. Use the Office Assistant to answer the following questions about Word tables.
   a. What are the five new table features of Word 97?
   b. How do you sum a row or column of numbers in a table?
   c. How do you reference cells in a table in a formula?
   d. How do you split a single cell into multiple cells?
2. In this project, you added a border around a paragraph. Use the Contents tab in the Help Topics: Microsoft Word dialog box to answer the following questions about borders.
   a. How do you place a border around an entire page?
   b. How do you change a table's border?
   c. How do you add a box border around a single word?
3. In this project, you used tabs to create a table. Use the Index tab in the Help Topics: Microsoft Word dialog box to answer the following questions about tabs.
   a. How do you change the spacing between default tab stops?
   b. What are leader characters? How do you insert them in tab stops?
4. In this project, you created one table using tabs and another using the Draw Table feature. Word has three other types of tables: table of authorities, table of contents, and table of figures. For each of these three types of tables, (1) identify their purpose and (2) explain how to create them.

Apply Your Knowledge

1 Working with Tables

Instructions: Start Word. Open the document, apply-4, from the Word folder on the Data Disk that accompanies this book. The document is a table created with the Draw Table feature. You are to color the title lines, merge the cells of the column headings, change the direction of the row heading text, sum the columns, and format the data. The completed table is shown in Figure 4-83. You may need to refer to your Use Help 2 responses for assistance on tables.

Aquatics Unlimited									
Two-Year Comparison (in millions)									
		This Year				Last Year			
		1Q	2Q	3Q	4Q	1Q	2Q	3Q	4Q
Revenue	Sales	1650	1724	1850	1335	1425	1590	1765	1227
	Other	123	288	367	101	105	216	304	100
	Total	1773	2012	2217	1436	1530	1806	2069	1327
Expenses	Manufacturing	682	1150	1482	555	590	805	1298	413
	Research	157	265	339	112	135	207	313	98
	Administrative	222	314	356	141	214	300	316	133
	Total	1061	1729	2177	808	939	1312	1927	644

cell C8

cell C10

FIGURE 4-83

Apply Your Knowledge

Perform the following tasks.

1. Select the cell containing the title, Aquatics Unlimited. Center it and change its font size to 26. If necessary, click the Tables and Borders button on the Standard toolbar to display the Tables and Borders toolbar. Click the Shading Color button arrow on the Tables and Borders toolbar and then click the color Teal. Click the Font Color button arrow on the Formatting toolbar and then click the color White.

2. Select the cell containing the subtitle. Center it. Click the Font Color button arrow on the Formatting toolbar and then click the color Teal.

3. Select the cell containing the column heading, This Year, and the next three cells to its right. Click the Merge Cells button on the Tables and Borders toolbar to merge these four cells into one. Click the Center button to center the column heading over the four quarters. Repeat this procedure for the column heading Last Year.

4. Select the cells containing the 1Q, 2Q, 3Q, and 4Q headings. Center them.

5. Select the cells containing the row headings, Revenue and Expenses. Click the Change Text Direction button on the Tables and Borders toolbar twice. Drag the border line to the right of these cells until the width of the row headings' cells looks like Figure 4-83.

6. You cannot use the AutoSum button for the total revenue cells because this function sums all cells above the current cell; here, you want to sum the two revenue cells. AutoSum will include the 1Q, 2Q, 3Q, and so on, in the sums. Click the cell to contain the total revenue for the 1Q of this year. Click Table on the menu bar and then click Formula. Enter the following formula in the Formula text box: =SUM(C5:C6) and then click the OK button. Click the cell to contain the total revenue for the 2Q of this year. Click Table on the menu bar and then click Formula. Enter the following formula in the Formula text box: =SUM(D5:D6) and then click the OK button. Repeat this process for each total revenue cell – increasing the letter in the sum function by one each time you move one column to the right.

7. You cannot use AutoSum for the total expenses because this function sums all cells above the current cell; here, you want to sum only the three expense cells. Click the cell to contain the total expenses for the first quarter (1Q) of this year. Click Table on the menu bar and then click Formula. Enter the following formula in the Formula text box: =SUM(C8:C10) and then click the OK button. Click the cell to contain the total expenses for the second quarter (2Q) of this year. Click Table on the menu bar and then click Formula. Enter the following formula in the Formula text box: =SUM(D8:D10) and then click the OK button. Repeat this process for each total expense cell, increasing the letter in the sum function by one each time you move one column to the right.

8. Bold the cells containing This Year, Last Year, Revenue, Expenses, Total, and all total figures.

9. Select all the cells containing numbers and then click the Align Top button on the Formatting toolbar.

10. Click File on the menu bar and then click Save As. Use the file name Revised Aquatics Report to save the document on your Data Disk.

11. Print the revised document.

In the Lab

1 Creating a Proposal Using Tabs

Problem: The LakeView Sports Car Club is preparing for its Tenth Annual Car Show. As a member of the club and the resident computer expert, you have been asked to prepare the informal sales proposal announcing the event (Figures 4-84 and 4-85), which will be sent to all community residents.

Instructions:

1. Create the title page as shown in Figure 4-84. The sports car is located in the Transportation category of the Clip Gallery. Change the clip art to an inline picture and change its size to 75% of the original size (1.4" height by 5.4" width), if necessary.

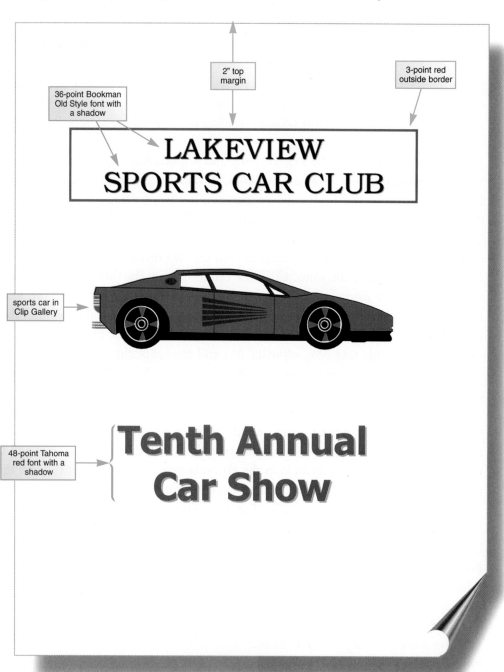

36-point Bookman Old Style font with a shadow

2" top margin

3-point red outside border

LAKEVIEW SPORTS CAR CLUB

sports car in Clip Gallery

48-point Tahoma red font with a shadow

Tenth Annual Car Show

FIGURE 4-84

In the Lab

2. Insert a section break. Return to the normal style. Change the top margin to 1" for section 2. Adjust line spacing to double. Change the font size to 12 for the body of the proposal.
3. Enter the body of the proposal as shown in Figure 4-85. The body of the proposal has a list with square shaped bullets and a table created with tabs. The tabs are set at 1" (left-aligned), 3.5" and 4.5" (both centered).
4. Spell check the document. Save the document with LakeView Proposal as the file name.
5. View the document in print preview. Print the document from within print preview.

LakeView Sports Car Club invites you to join us for our *Tenth Annual Car Show*, the hottest auto event of the decade, on the weekend of October 10-11 in LakeView.

Bring the entire family! LakeView Sports Car Club has scheduled events for everyone. Admission is $2.00 per day for adults, and children under 12 are admitted free to all activities.

❑ More than 150 sports cars

❑ Parts Swap Meet

❑ Arts and crafts displays

❑ Carnival and children's games

❑ Live music, featuring the Nifty Fifties band

If you have a sports car that you would like to enter in the show or want to rent an arts and crafts booth, you still have time! Advance reservations must be made by Friday, October 2, by calling 555-4838.

VENDOR FEES		
	In Advance	At the Gate
Sports Car Vendor	$30	$35
Arts and Crafts Vendor	$20	$25

All participants are eligible for door prizes and commemorative T-shirts. Spectators at the car show will cast ballots for the *People's Choice Awards*. The Parts Swap Meet will have a *Name the Car Part* contest.

The car show and activities start at 9:00 a.m. and end at 7:00 p.m. each day. For more information, call 555-4838.

FIGURE 4-85

2 Creating a Proposal Using Downloaded Clip Art and the Draw Table Feature

Problem: You are manager of Spooky Treats, a Halloween store. To promote business, you decide to compose a sales proposal outlining your products. You develop the proposal shown in Figures 4-86 and 4-87.

Instructions:

1. Create the title page as shown in Figure 4-86. You are to download the clip art files from Microsoft's Clip Gallery Live Web page with the file names SPEC002182_x5, SPEC002183_x5, and SPEC002184_x5. To reach these files, type Halloween celebration in the Search text box. If you do not have access to the Web, you can install these files from the Data Disk that accompanies this book. Change the clip art images to inline pictures and change their sizes as indicated in Figure 4-86.

FIGURE 4-86

In the Lab

2. Insert a section break. Return to the normal style. Change the top margin to 1" for section 2. Adjust line spacing to double.

3. Create the body of the proposal as shown in Figure 4-87. The body of the proposal has a table created with the Draw Table button. Use the AutoSum button for the Clown Totals. The formulas for the Pirate Totals of adult, teen, and child outfits are as follows: =SUM(C6:C7), =SUM(D6:D7), and =SUM(E6:E7), respectively. Center the table between the page margins.

4. Spell check the document. Save the document with Spooky Treats Proposal as the file name.

5. View the document in print preview. Print the document from within print preview.

Spooky Treats is a full-service Halloween store offering a huge selection of Halloween merchandise. We stock a complete line of high-quality costumes, masks, makeup, and accessories for adults, teens, and children at very reasonable prices.

Sample Price List		Adult	Teen	Child
Clown	Costume	28.99	15.99	13.99
	Accessories	16.99	14.99	7.99
	Total	45.98	30.98	21.98
Pirate	Costume	21.99	14.99	13.99
	Accessories	14.99	12.99	8.99
	Total	36.98	27.98	22.98

Costumes and accessories are sold separately. For example, the clown costume consists of a one-piece, multicolored suit with matching collar and hat. The accessories include a rainbow wig, red nose, white gloves, striped socks, and makeup.

Our salespeople are professional and courteous and are trained in makeup application techniques to answer any questions you have or provide you with any instruction you may require.

Spooky Treats has supplied the best in Halloween attire and accessories from our same location for the past 10 years at 104 Southwestern Avenue, Chicago, Illinois. Let us outfit you this Halloween. Come by and see us or place your order by telephone and request a catalog at 312-555-0826.

FIGURE 4-87

In the Lab

3 Enhancing a Draft of a Proposal

Problem: You are the owner of Skyline Office Rentals. One of your employees has drafted an informal sales proposal to be sent to prospective clients around the country (Figure 4-89). You decide to add pizzazz to the proposal by creating a title page (Figure 4-88). You also add a couple of tables to the body of the proposal.

Instructions:

1. Create the title page as shown in Figure 4-88. The office buildings clip art is located in the Buildings category of the Clip Gallery. Change the clip art to an inline picture.

FIGURE 4-88

In the Lab

2. Insert the draft of the body of the proposal below the title page using the File command on the Insert menu. The draft is called Skyline Draft in the Word folder on the Data Disk that accompanies this book. The draft of the body of the proposal is shown in Figure 4-89. Be sure to change the top margin to 1" for section 2.

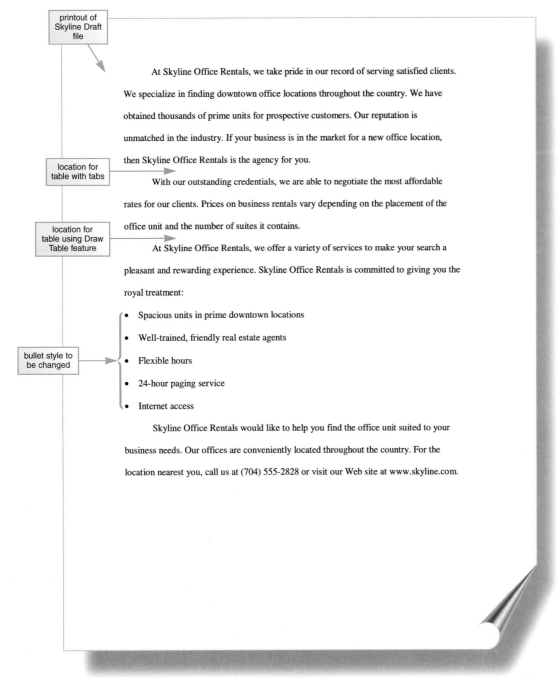

printout of Skyline Draft file

At Skyline Office Rentals, we take pride in our record of serving satisfied clients. We specialize in finding downtown office locations throughout the country. We have obtained thousands of prime units for prospective customers. Our reputation is unmatched in the industry. If your business is in the market for a new office location, then Skyline Office Rentals is the agency for you.

location for table with tabs

With our outstanding credentials, we are able to negotiate the most affordable rates for our clients. Prices on business rentals vary depending on the placement of the office unit and the number of suites it contains.

location for table using Draw Table feature

At Skyline Office Rentals, we offer a variety of services to make your search a pleasant and rewarding experience. Skyline Office Rentals is committed to giving you the royal treatment:

- Spacious units in prime downtown locations
- Well-trained, friendly real estate agents

bullet style to be changed

- Flexible hours
- 24-hour paging service
- Internet access

Skyline Office Rentals would like to help you find the office unit suited to your business needs. Our offices are conveniently located throughout the country. For the location nearest you, call us at (704) 555-2828 or visit our Web site at www.skyline.com.

FIGURE 4-89

(continued)

In the Lab

Enhancing a Draft of a Proposal *(continued)*

3. Add the following table, created with tabs, below the first paragraph in the proposal. Double-space the table and set custom tab stops at 1", 3", and 4.5". Draw an outside border around the table. Above the table, center and bold the title, Skyline Track Record.

	# OF CLIENTS	# OF UNITS RENTED
This Year	5692	5109
Last Year	4998	4514

4. Use the Draw Table button to create the following table below the second paragraph in the proposal. Double-space the table. Center the table between the page margins. Above the table, center and bold the title, Average Monthly Rental Prices.

Average Monthly Rental Prices				
		2-ROOM	3-ROOM	4-ROOM
Lower Floors	Window Unit	1025	1245	1475
	Inside Unit	895	1035	1275
Upper Floors	Window Unit	1445	1665	1895
	Inside Unit	1265	1465	1675

5. Change the style of the bullet characters in the list.
6. Add a header to section 2 of the proposal.
7. Save the active document with the file name Skyline Proposal using the Save As command on the File menu.
8. View the document in print preview. Print the document from within print preview.

Cases and Places

The difficulty of these case studies varies: ❿ are the least difficult; ❿❿ are more difficult; and ❿❿❿ are the most difficult.

1 ❿ Your school probably has one or more facilities open to both students and the general public; e.g., a day-care center, a fitness center, a cafeteria, or the library. Select one of these facilities that interests you. Obtain information about the facility using one or more of these fact-gathering techniques: visit the facility and use its resources; collect brochures and other literature about the facility; interview an employee of the facility; interview a visitor to the facility. Then, draft a sales proposal for the facility to send to the general public as a marketing tool. Be sure the proposal includes at least one table and has a creative cover page with appropriate color and graphics.

2 ❿ Hobbies can be exciting and interesting, ranging from snow skiing to photography to making crafts. Pick a hobby of your own, a family member, or friend and then acquire as much information about it as possible. Assume you are the chairperson of a club that meets monthly to discuss this hobby; the club also sponsors a variety of social events. You want to recruit new members to the club. Draft a sales proposal for the club to send to the general public as a marketing tool. Be sure the proposal includes at least one table and has a creative cover page with appropriate color and graphics.

3 ❿❿ Assume you are president of the Student Government Organization at your school and that you have concerns about an issue on campus, such as security, computer availability, facilities for the disabled, or student advising/registration. Select an item from this list, or one of your own, that you feel needs improvement at your school. Investigate how other schools locally and nationally handle the same issue. Visit the library or *surf* the Internet for guidelines on preparing a planning proposal. Draft a planning proposal for the Student Government Organization to submit to your school's Board of Directors that recommends some action the school should take to improve the situation you investigated. Be sure the proposal includes at least one table and has an appropriate cover page.

4 ❿❿ As a concerned resident, you have a suggestion(s) for improving the quality of life in your neighborhood. Such suggestions might include initiating a recycling program, creating a bike lane or path on main roads, or placing speed bumps or a stop sign at an area populated with young children. Select an item from this list, or one of your own, that you feel would benefit your neighborhood. Investigate how other communities have implemented the same type of program successfully. Visit the library or *surf* the Internet for guidelines on preparing a planning proposal. Draft a planning proposal that recommends some action to be taken to improve the situation you investigated. Be sure the proposal includes at least one table and has an appropriate cover page.

Cases and Places

5 ▶▶ Assume you have graduated recently from your school with a degree in your field of study. The department head of your major has contacted you for suggestions on improving the abilities and skills of students in your major. She wants your recommendation(s) on changing the curriculum. Obtain evidence to support your recommendation(s) such as interviewing local businesses that hire your school's graduates, using the Internet to discover how other school's curricula are organized, or surveying recent alumni of your program. Visit the library or *surf* the Internet for guidelines on preparing a planning proposal. Draft a planning proposal that recommends your suggestions to the department head. Be sure the proposal includes at least one table and has an appropriate cover page.

6 ▶▶▶ As chair of the Resources and Planning Committee for your school, you have been assigned the task of writing a proposal to acquire new hardware and/or software for your school. The proposal must contain figures on the current hardware and/or software configurations on campus, as well as the proposed configurations. A minimum of two proposed cost quotations must be provided, with sources of the quotations cited. Obtain evidence to support your proposal such as current industry trends in the computer field. Visit the library or *surf* the Internet for guidelines on preparing a research proposal. Draft a research proposal that presents your findings, suggests two alternatives, and then recommends your suggested configuration to your school's decision-making body. Be sure the proposal includes at least one table and has an appropriate cover page.

7 ▶▶▶ As director of the outside sales force at a local company, you are responsible for providing each salesperson with a company car. Each year you must submit a proposal to the president for approval. Your recommended vehicle must meet current safety regulations. You also must provide figures on leasing, renting, and purchasing each of three different makes of vehicles. The quotations must list the dealer from which the figures were obtained or the Internet address, if obtained via the Internet. Visit the library or *surf* the Internet for guidelines on preparing a research proposal. Draft a research proposal that presents your safety findings; suggests purchase, lease, and rent alternatives for three different makes; and then recommends your suggestion. Be sure the proposal includes at least one table and has an appropriate cover page.

Microsoft *Word 97*

Generating Form Letters, Mailing Labels, and Envelopes

Objectives:

You will have mastered the material in this project when you can:

- ▶ Explain the merge process
- ▶ Create a letterhead
- ▶ Explain the terms, data field and data record
- ▶ Create a data source
- ▶ Switch from a data source to the main document
- ▶ Insert merge fields into the main document
- ▶ Use an IF field in the main document
- ▶ Merge and print form letters
- ▶ Selectively merge and print form letters
- ▶ Sort a data source
- ▶ Address and print mailing labels
- ▶ Address and print envelopes

Pharaoh's Favorite

A Man of Letters

As the sun sets in the west to begin its nightly journey into day, a barge crosses the mythic Nile, bearing an ornate stone coffin. On the western bank, the burial chamber is transferred to an ox-drawn sledge. Priests clad in leopard skins, chanting ritual prayers and wafting incense, lead a solemn procession of mourners. Finally, they reach a splendid mortuary tabernacle next to the royal temples of ancient Thebes and inter the mummy of a man who lived to be eighty.

The last rites of a powerful Pharaoh or some regal personage?

No. It is the funeral of a commoner, a scribe, who rose to become vizier to Pharaoh Amenhotep III, who reigned during Egypt's New Kingdom. Next to the Pharaoh himself, scribes were the most important officials in ancient Egypt. As people of letters, they supervised virtually all public activity, from tallying harvests to levying taxes.

Since the first cuneiform alphabet enabled mankind to preserve thoughts on clay tablets, the world has respected, even revered, its writers. History owes much to those who recorded their wisdom in letters. One of the more prolific letter writers of all time was Thomas Jefferson. Fortunately for historians, he was also a dedicated scientist and used a patented duplicating machine — called a polygraph — to make a copy of each letter he wrote. As he moved a quill pen attached to the machine, a complex system of gears and pulleys moved a second quill in unison with his movements, even dipping the second pen in an inkwell when he dipped his. Not exactly *form* letters, but "formed letters," for sure.

Early popular novelists used collections of letters to tell their stories. In the modern novel, *The Color Purple*, Alice Walker continues this tradition, using "Dear God" letters to tell a poignant story. Walker and other writers sometimes are called *belletrists*, practitioners of the fine art of *belles-lettres*, a literary style so highly regarded for its aesthetic value, that content becomes secondary.

Today, letters are the principal feature of modern enterprise, with form letters ranking foremost in the order of business. Most of us receive dozens of them every year. Though usually considered "junk mail," they serve a vital function, helping businesses reach potential customers.

You are a correspondent of sorts when you are required to demonstrate your creative writing skills. You may be asked to organize a school bazaar and recruit your fellow classmates to assist during the event. A family reunion might require your expertise in the form of an announcement to all your relatives, or at some time soon, you may seek an employment position in your field of study. All these tasks can be simplified using the many Word features presented in this project to create form letters. With Word 97, you can design custom letterheads, create a data source, and generate mailing labels or envelopes. Then, pull it all together using the Mail Merge feature, and you are off to the post office.

As a man or woman of letters, take your aspirations to the limits. Apply your creative talents and succeed.

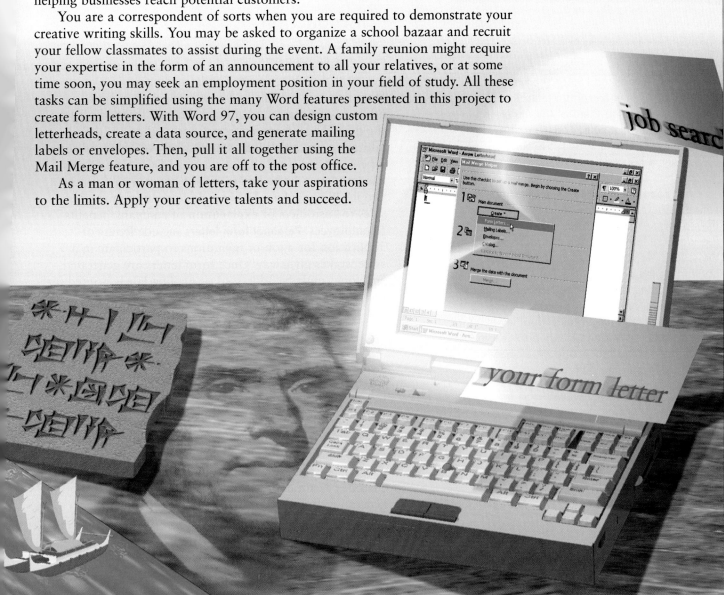

Microsoft
Word 97

Generating Form Letters, Mailing Labels, and Envelopes

Case Perspective

Connie L. Peterson, president of Arrow Electronics, has asked Henry Thomas in the Information Center to send a letter to all customers informing them of the upcoming year-end clearance sale. The letter should arrive in the customers' hands around December 8 because the sale is to run for the last two weeks of the year. Instead of typing a separate letter to each customer, which could be very time consuming, Henry uses a form letter. The form letter contains the identical information that is to be in all the letters. He also creates a separate file containing the names and addresses of each customer; this file is called a data source. Then, he merges the data source with the form letter so an individual letter prints for each customer. Henry also creates and prints mailing labels and envelopes for each customer in the data source.

This year, Connie has indicated she wants to have two separate discount rates: one for VIP Club members and another, lower discount, for regular customers. That is, VIP Club members are to receive a 25 percent discount and all other customers are to receive a 10 percent discount.

Introduction

Form letters are used regularly in both business and personal correspondence. The basic content of a group of form letters is similar; however, items such as name, address, city, state, and zip code change from one letter to the next. Thus, form letters are personalized to the addressee. An individual is more likely to open and read a personalized letter than a standard Dear Sir or Dear Madam letter. Form letters usually are sent to a group of people. **Business form letters** include announcements of sales to customers or explanation of company benefits to employees. **Personal form letters** include letters of application for a job or invitations to participate in a sweepstakes giveaway. Once form letters are generated, envelopes must be addressed or mailing labels printed for the envelopes.

Project Five – Form Letters, Mailing Labels, and Envelopes

Project 5 illustrates the generation of a business form letter and corresponding mailing labels and envelopes. The form letter is sent to all current customers, informing them of the year-end clearance sale. The discount percentage rate varies, depending on whether or not the customer is a member of the VIP Club. The process of generating form letters involves creating a main document for the form letter and a data source, and then merging, or *blending*, the two together into a series of individual letters as shown in Figure 5-1.

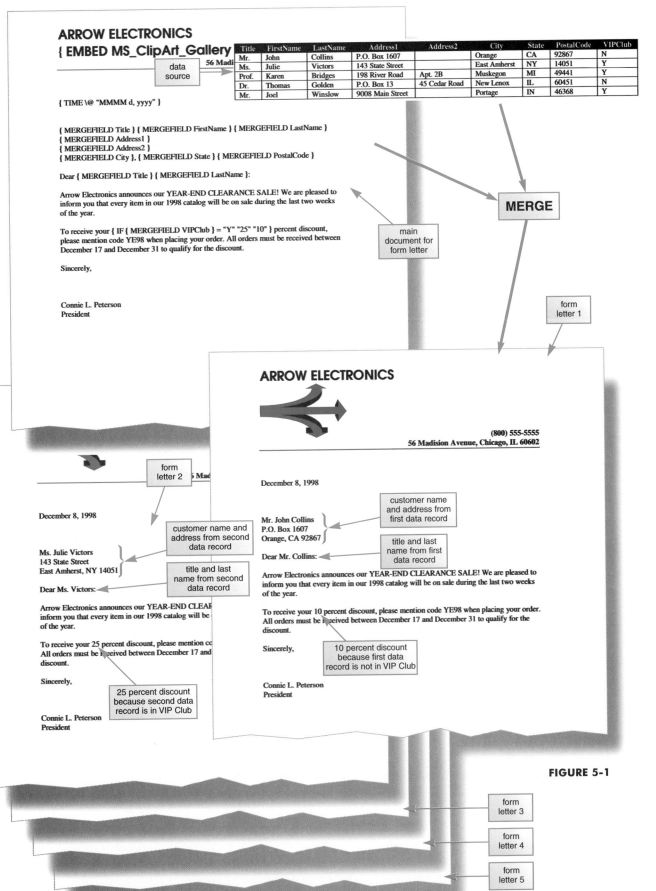

FIGURE 5-1

Merging

Merging is the process of combining the contents of a data source with a main document. The **main document** contains the constant, or unchanging, text, punctuation, spaces, and graphics. In Figure 5-1 on the previous page, the main document represents the portion of the form letters that is identical from one merged letter to the next. Conversely, the **data source** contains the variable, or changing, values in each letter. In Figure 5-1, the data source contains five different customers. One form letter is generated for each customer listed in the data source.

Document Preparation Steps

Document preparation steps give you an overview of how the main document, data source, and form letters in Figure 5-1 and corresponding mailing labels and envelopes will be developed. The following tasks will be completed in this project.

1. Create a letterhead for Arrow Electronics correspondence.
2. Identify the main document as a form letter.
3. Create a data source.
4. Create the main document for the form letter.
5. Merge and print the form letters.
6. Create and print mailing labels.
7. Create and print envelopes.

The following pages contain a detailed explanation of each of these tasks.

Starting Word

Follow these steps to start Word or ask your instructor how to start Word for your system.

TO START WORD

1. Click the Start button on the taskbar.
2. Click New Office Document on the Start menu. If necessary, click the General tab when the New Office Document dialog box first opens.
3. Double-click the Blank Document icon in the General sheet.
4. If the Word screen is not maximized, double-click its title bar to maximize it.

Office starts Word. After a few moments, an empty document titled Document1 displays.

Displaying Nonprinting Characters

It is helpful to display nonprinting characters that indicate where in the document you pressed the ENTER key, SPACEBAR, or TAB key. Follow this step to display the nonprinting characters.

TO DISPLAY NONPRINTING CHARACTERS

① If the Show/Hide ¶ button on the Standard toolbar is not recessed, click it.

Word displays nonprinting characters in the document window, and the Show/Hide ¶ button on the Standard toolbar is recessed (Figure 5-2 on the next page).

Creating Company Letterhead

In many businesses, letterhead is preprinted on stationery that is used by everyone throughout the corporation. In some organizations, however, preprinted letterhead may not be purchased because of its expense. An alternative for these companies is to create their own letterhead and save it in a file. Then, company employees can open the letterhead file when they begin a document, create their document on the letterhead file, and then save their document with a new name – to preserve the original letterhead file.

In Project 5, the letterhead at the top of the main document is created with a header as described in the steps below.

TO CREATE COMPANY LETTERHEAD

① Click View on the menu bar and then click Header and Footer. Click the Font box arrow on the Formatting toolbar and then click Albertus Extra Bold (or a similar font). Click the Font Size box arrow on the Formatting toolbar and then click 20. Click the Bold button on the Formatting toolbar. Click the Font Color button arrow and then click Dark Blue. Type ARROW ELECTRONICS and then press the ENTER key.

② Click Insert on the menu bar, point to Picture, and then click Clip Art. If necessary, click the Clip Art tab when the Microsoft Clip Gallery dialog box first opens. Scroll through the list of categories and then click Shapes. Scroll through the shapes and then click the three-way arrow with the keywords, Alternative Options Disagreement Change. Click the Insert button to insert the floating picture into the header.

③ If the Picture toolbar does not display, right-click the clip art image and then click Show Picture Toolbar on the shortcut menu. Click the Format Picture button on the Picture toolbar. When the Format Picture dialog box displays, click the Position tab and then click Float over text to clear the check box. Click the Size tab. In the Scale area, type 25 in the Height and Width text boxes and then click the OK button. Click the paragraph mark to the right of the clip art image.

④ Press the TAB key twice. Click the Font box arrow on the Formatting toolbar and then click Times New Roman. Click the Font Size box arrow on the Formatting toolbar and then click 12. Type (800) 555-5555 and then press the ENTER key. Press the TAB key twice. Type 56 Madison Avenue, Chicago, IL 60602 and then press the ENTER key three times. Click the Font Color button arrow and then click Automatic.

The letterhead displays in the header area (Figure 5-2 on the next page).

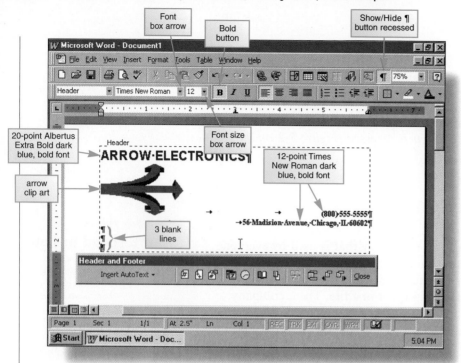

FIGURE 5-2

Adding a Bottom Border to a Paragraph

To add more professionalism to the letterhead, you would like to draw a horizontal line from the left margin to the right margin immediately below the address line. Recall that in Word, you can draw a solid line, called a **border**, to any edge of a paragraph. That is, borders may be added above or below a paragraph, to the left or right of a paragraph, or any combination of these sides. In Project 4, you added an outside border to the company name on the title page of the sales proposal. Here, you will add a bottom border to a paragraph. Perform the following steps to add a 1½-point red bottom border to a paragraph.

Steps To Bottom Border a Paragraph

1 Position the insertion point in the address line of the header. If necessary, click the Tables and Borders button on the Standard toolbar to display the Tables and Borders toolbar. Click the Line Weight box arrow on the Tables and Borders toolbar and then click 1 ½ pt. Click the Border Color button on the Tables and Borders toolbar and then click the color Red on the color palette. Click the Outside Border button arrow on the Tables and Borders toolbar, then point to the Bottom Border button on the border palette.

Word displays the border palette (Figure 5-3). Using the ***border palette****, you can add a border to any edge(s) of a paragraph(s).*

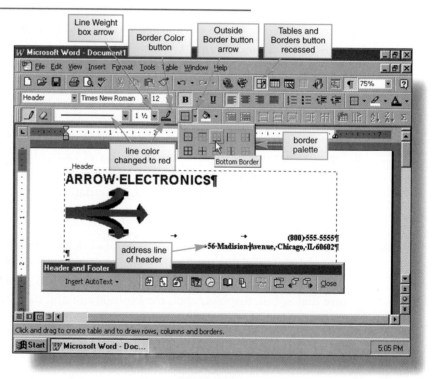

FIGURE 5-3

2 Click the Bottom Border button on the border palette.

Word places a 1½-point red bottom border below the paragraph containing the insertion point (Figure 5-4).

3 Click the Tables and Borders button on the Standard toolbar to remove the Tables and Borders toolbar from the Word window. Click the Close Header and Footer button on the Header and Footer toolbar.

Word returns to the document window (Figure 5-5 on the next page). Recall that a header does not display on the screen in normal view.

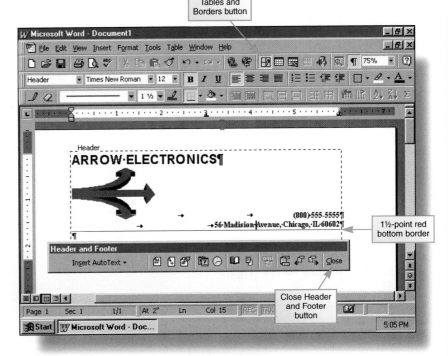

FIGURE 5-4

Now that you have created the company letterhead, the next step is to save it in a file.

TO SAVE THE COMPANY LETTERHEAD IN A FILE

1 Insert your floppy disk into drive A.

2 Click the Save button on the Standard toolbar.

3 Type the file name `Arrow Letterhead` in the File name text box. Do not press the ENTER key after typing the file name.

4 If necessary, click the Save in box arrow and then click 3½ Floppy (A:).

5 Click the Save button in the Save As dialog box.

Word saves the document on a floppy disk on drive A with the file name, Arrow Letterhead (Figure 5-5 on the next page).

Identifying the Main Document and Creating the Data Source

Creating form letters requires merging a main document with a data source. To create form letters using Word's mail merge, first, you identify the main document and then create or specify the data source; next, create the main document; and finally, merge the data source with the main document to generate and print the form letters.

Identifying the Main Document

The first step in the mail merge process it to open the document you will use as the main document. If it is a new document, click the New button on the Standard toolbar. Because the main document in this project is to contain Arrow Electronics' letterhead, you should leave the file Arrow Letterhead open in the document window. Once the main document file is open, you must identify it as such to Word's mail merge as shown in these steps.

Steps **To Identify the Main Document**

1 **Click Tools on the menu bar and then point to Mail Merge (Figure 5-5).**

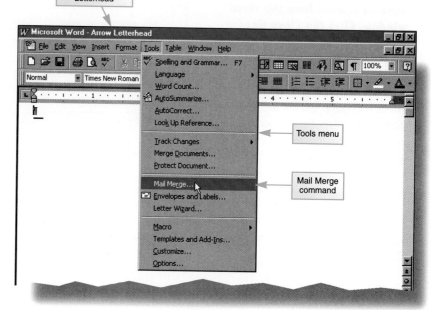

letterhead saved with name, Arrow Letterhead

Tools menu

Mail Merge command

FIGURE 5-5

2 **Click Mail Merge. When the Mail Merge Helper dialog box displays, point to the Create button.**

Word displays the Mail Merge Helper dialog box (Figure 5-6). Using this dialog box, you can identify the main document and create the data source. Notice the instructions at the top of this dialog box.

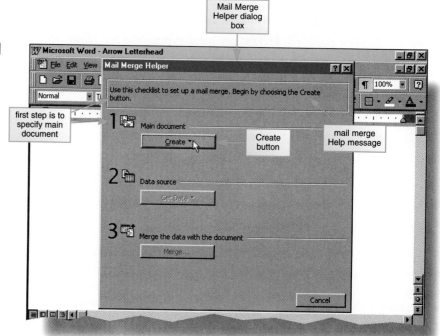

Mail Merge Helper dialog box

first step is to specify main document

Create button

mail merge Help message

FIGURE 5-6

3 **Click the Create button. Point to Form Letters.**

Word displays a list of main document types (Figure 5-7).

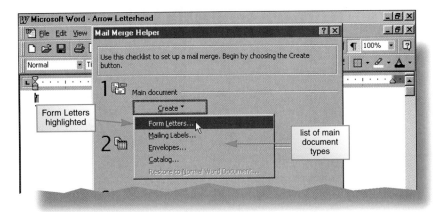

FIGURE 5-7

4 **Click Form Letters.**

Word displays a Microsoft Word dialog box asking if you want to use the active document window for the form letters (Figure 5-8). The current active document window is Arrow Letterhead. The Active Window button uses Arrow Letterhead as the main document, whereas the New Main Document button creates a new document window for the main document – a procedure similar to clicking the New button on the Standard toolbar.

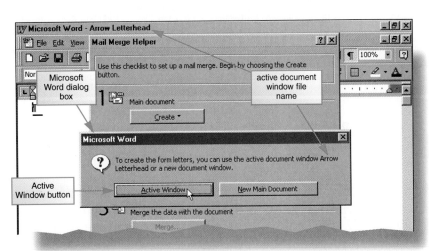

FIGURE 5-8

5 **Click the Active Window button.**

Word returns to the Mail Merge Helper dialog box (Figure 5-9). The merge type is identified as Form Letters and the main document is A:\Arrow Letterhead.doc, the letterhead for Arrow Electronics. An Edit button now displays in the Mail Merge Helper dialog box so you can modify the contents of the main document.

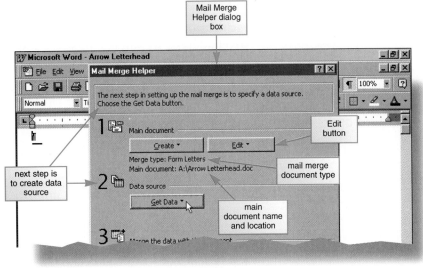

FIGURE 5-9

At this point, you do not create the main document; you simply identify it. As indicated in the Mail Merge Helper dialog box, the next step is to create the data source. After you create the data source, you will enter the main document text.

Creating the Data Source

A data source is a Word table (Figure 5-10). Recall that a **Word table** is a series of rows and columns. The first row of the data source is called the **header row**. Each row below the header row is called a **data record**. Data records contain the text that varies from one merged document to the next. The data source for this project contains five data records. In this project, each data record identifies a different customer. Thus, five form letters will be generated from this data source.

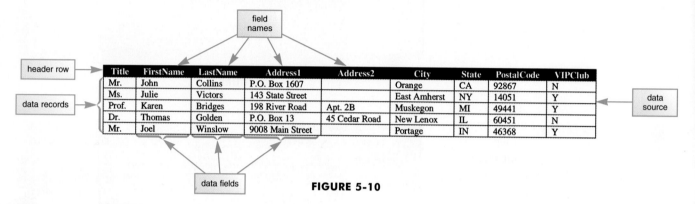

	Title	FirstName	LastName	Address1	Address2	City	State	PostalCode	VIPClub
	Mr.	John	Collins	P.O. Box 1607		Orange	CA	92867	N
	Ms.	Julie	Victors	143 State Street		East Amherst	NY	14051	Y
	Prof.	Karen	Bridges	198 River Road	Apt. 2B	Muskegon	MI	49441	Y
	Dr.	Thomas	Golden	P.O. Box 13	45 Cedar Road	New Lenox	IL	60451	N
	Mr.	Joel	Winslow	9008 Main Street		Portage	IN	46368	Y

FIGURE 5-10

header row
data records
field names
data source
data fields

Each column in the data source is called a **data field**. A data field represents a group of similar data. In this project, the data source contains nine data fields: Title, FirstName, LastName, Address1, Address2, City, State, PostalCode, and VIPClub.

In a data source, each data field must be uniquely identified with a name, called a **field name**. For example, the name FirstName represents the field (column) containing the first names of the customers. Field names are placed in the header row of the data source to identify the name of each column.

The first step in creating a data source is to decide which fields it will contain. That is, you must identify the information that will vary from one merged document to the next. In Project 5, each record contains up to nine different fields for each customer: a courtesy title (e.g., Mrs.), first name, last name, first line of street address, second line of street address (optional), city, state, zip code, and VIP Club. The field VIPClub is either the value, Y, for Yes or the value, N, for No depending on whether the customer is a member of the VIP Club. The discount percent is determined based on the value of the VIPClub field.

For each field, you must decide on a field name. Field names must be unique. That is, no two field names may be the same. Field names may be up to 40 characters in length, can contain only letters, numbers, and the underscore (_), and must begin with a letter. Field names cannot contain spaces. Because data sources often contain the same fields, Word provides you with a list of thirteen commonly used field names. To improve the readability of field names, Word uses a mixture of uppercase and lowercase letters to separate words within the field (remember spaces are not allowed). You will use eight of the thirteen field names supplied by Word: Title, FirstName, LastName, Address1, Address2, City, State, and PostalCode. You will delete the other five field names from the list supplied by Word. That is, you will delete JobTitle, Company, Country, HomePhone, and WorkPhone. In this project, the only field that Word does not supply is the VIPClub field. Thus, you will add a field name called VIPClub.

Fields and related field names may be listed in any order in the data source. The order of fields has no effect on the order they will print in the main document.

Perform the following steps to create a new data source.

Steps To Create a Data Source in Word

1 **In the Mail Merge Helper dialog box, click the Get Data button and then point to Create Data Source.**

Word displays a list of data source options (Figure 5-11). You can create your own data source in Word, use a data source already created in Word, or use files from Access or Excel as a data source.

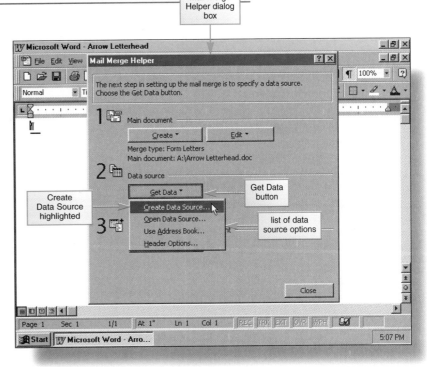

FIGURE 5-11

2 **Click Create Data Source. When the Create Data Source dialog box displays, click JobTitle in the Field names in header row list box.**

Word displays the Create Data Source dialog box (Figure 5-12). In the Field names in header row list box, Word displays a list of commonly used field names. You can remove a field name from this list if you do not want it to be in the header row of your data source. JobTitle is highlighted for removal.

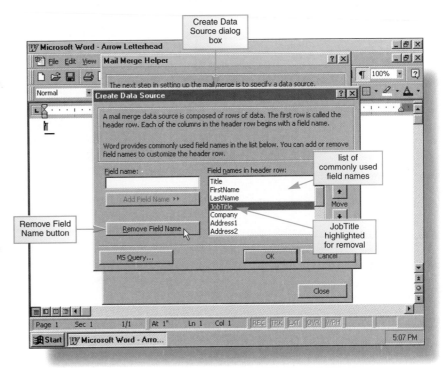

FIGURE 5-12

3 **Click the Remove Field Name button. With the Company field highlighted, click the Remove Field Name button. Scroll to the bottom of the Field names in header row list box. Click Country in the Field names in header row list box. Click the Remove Field Name button. With HomePhone highlighted, click the Remove Field Name button. With WorkPhone highlighted, click the Remove Field Name button.**

Word removes five field names from the Field names in header row list (Figure 5-13). The remaining fields in the Field names in header row list box are to be included in the data source. The last field name removed, WorkPhone, displays in the Field name text box.

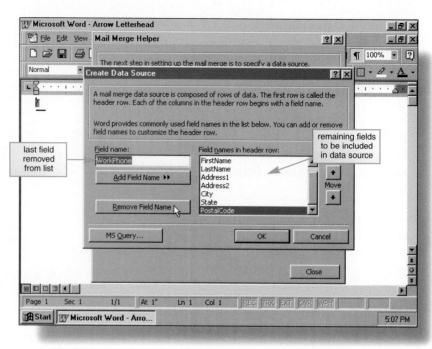

FIGURE 5-13

4 **Type** VIPClub **in the Field name text box and then point to the Add Field Name button (Figure 5-14).**

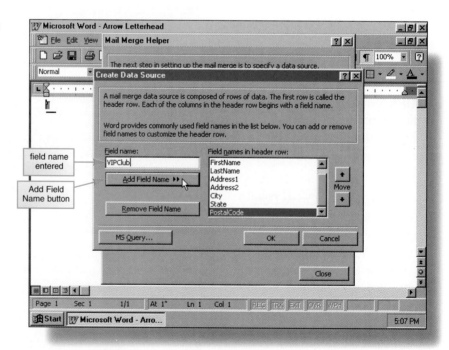

FIGURE 5-14

5 Click the Add Field Name button. Point to the OK button.

Word adds the VIPClub field name to the bottom of the Field names in header row list box (Figure 5-15).

FIGURE 5-15

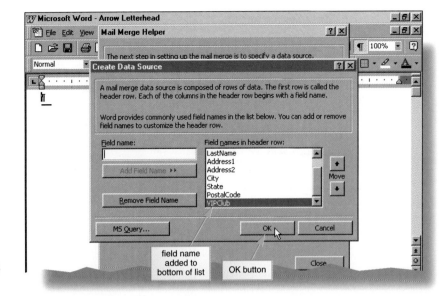

6 Click the OK button.

Word displays the Save As dialog box. You assign a file name to the data source in this dialog box.

7 **Type** Arrow Customer List **and, if necessary, change the drive to 3½ Floppy (A:). Point to the Save button in the Save As dialog box.**

Word displays the file name, Arrow Customer List, in the File name text box (Figure 5-16). The data source for Project 5 will be saved with the file name, Arrow Customer List.

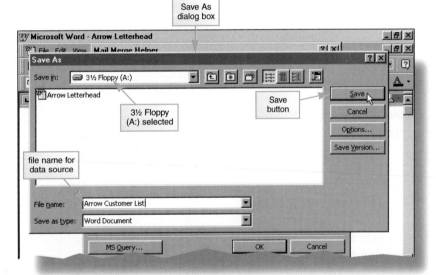

FIGURE 5-16

8 Click the Save button.

Word displays a Microsoft Word dialog box asking if you would like to edit the data source or edit the main document at this point (Figure 5-17). Because you want to add data records to the data source, you will edit the data source now.

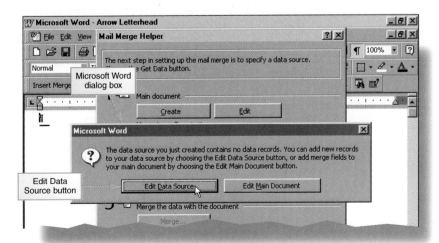

FIGURE 5-17

9 **Click the Edit Data Source button.**

*Word displays a **Data Form dialog box** (Figure 5-18). You can use this dialog box to enter the data records into the data source. Notice the field names from the header row are displayed along the left edge of the dialog box with an empty text box to the right of each field name. The insertion point is in the first text box.*

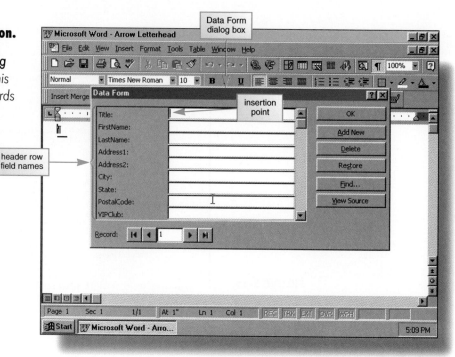

FIGURE 5-18

10 **Type** Mr. **and then press the TAB key. Type** John **and then press the TAB key. Type** Collins **and then press the TAB key. Type** P.O. Box 1607 **and then press the TAB key twice. Type** Orange **and then press the TAB key. Type** CA **and then press the TAB key. Type** 92867 **and then press the TAB key. Type** N **and then point to the Add New button.**

The first data record values are entered in the Data Form dialog box (Figure 5-19). Notice you press the TAB key to advance from one text box to the next. If you notice an error in a text box, click the text box and then correct the error as you would in the document window. Clicking the Add New button displays another blank form, which you can use to add another data record.

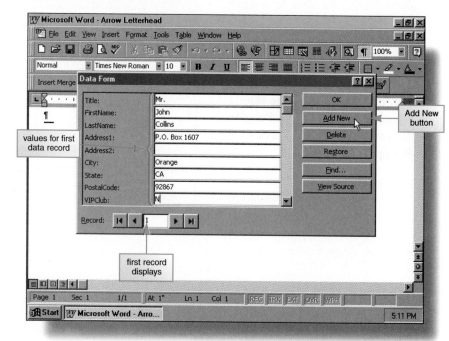

FIGURE 5-19

11 **Click the Add New button. Type** Ms. **and then press the TAB key. Type** Julie **and then press the TAB key. Type** Victors **and then press the TAB key. Type** 143 State Street **and then press the TAB key twice. Type** East Amherst **and then press the TAB key. Type** NY **and then press the TAB key. Type** 14051 **and then press the TAB key. Type** Y **and then point to the Add New button.**

The second data record is entered (Figure 5-20).

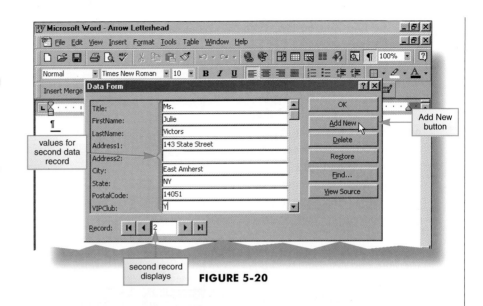

FIGURE 5-20

12 **Click the Add New button. Type** Prof. **and then press the TAB key. Type** Karen **and then press the TAB key. Type** Bridges **and then press the TAB key. Type** 198 River Road **and then press the TAB key. Type** Apt. 2B **and then press the TAB key. Type** Muskegon **and then press the TAB key. Type** MI **and then press the TAB key. Type** 49441 **and then press the TAB key. Type** Y **and then point to the Add New button.**

The third data record is entered (Figure 5-21).

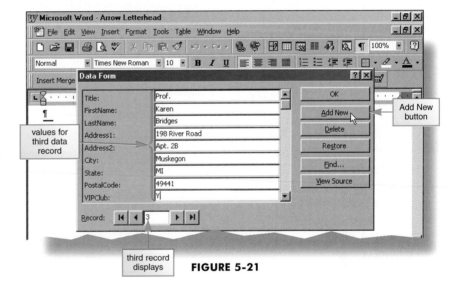

FIGURE 5-21

13 **Click the Add New button. Type** Dr. **and then press the TAB key. Type** Thomas **and then press the TAB key. Type** Golden **and then press the TAB key. Type** P.O. Box 13 **and then press the TAB key. Type** 45 Cedar Road **and then press the TAB key. Type** New Lenox **and then press the TAB key. Type** IL **and then press the TAB key. Type** 60451 **and then press the TAB key. Type** N **and then point to the Add New button.**

The fourth data record is entered (Figure 5-22).

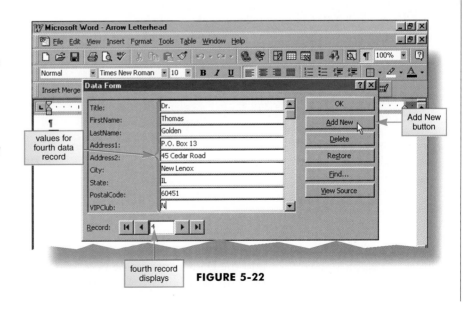

FIGURE 5-22

14 Click the Add New button. Type Mr. and then press the TAB key. Type Joel and then press the TAB key. Type Winslow and then press the TAB key. Type 9008 Main Street and then press the TAB key twice. Type Portage and then press the TAB key. Type IN and then press the TAB key. Type 46368 and then press the TAB key. Type Y and then point to the View Source button.

The fifth, and last, data record is entered (Figure 5-23). All of the data records have been entered into the data source, but Word has not saved the records in the file, Arrow Customer List.

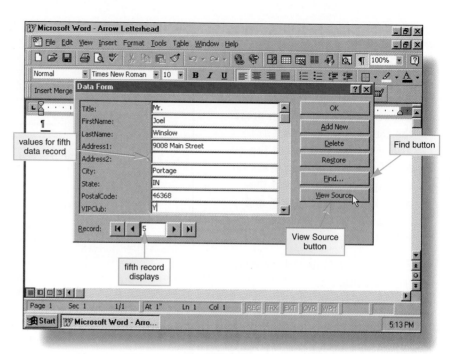

FIGURE 5-23

15 Click the View Source button. Click the Save button on the Standard toolbar. If gridlines do not display in your table, click Table on the menu bar and then click Show Gridlines.

*Word displays the data records in table form (Figure 5-24). Because the data records are not saved in the data source file when you fill in the Data Form dialog box, you must save them here. The **Database toolbar** displays below the Formatting toolbar.*

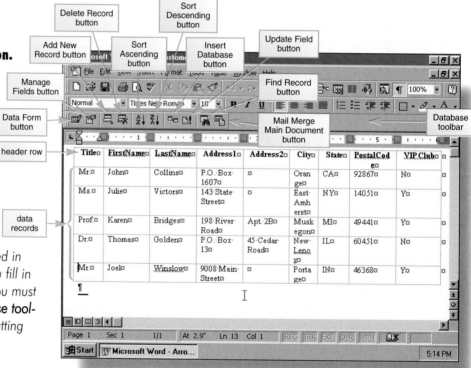

FIGURE 5-24

More *About* Data Sources

The data source is a table. Thus, you can format it using the Table AutoFormat dialog box. If the printed data source is too wide for the paper, change to landscape orientation by clicking Page Setup on the File menu, clicking the Paper Size tab, clicking Landscape, then clicking the OK button.

All of the data records have been entered into the data source and saved with the file name, Arrow Customer List. If, when you are entering your data records into the Data Form dialog box, you accidentally click the OK button instead of the Add New button, Word will return to the main document. To return to the

Data Form dialog box and continue adding data records, click the Edit Data Source button on the Mail Merge toolbar shown in Figure 5-26 on page WD 5.20.

Editing Records in the Data Source

In the **Data Form dialog box**, you can add, change, or delete data records. To **add a new record**, click the Add New button as shown in the previous steps. To **change an existing record**, display it in the Data Form dialog box by clicking the appropriate Record button(s) or using the Find button to locate a particular data item (see Figure 5-23). For example, to find Karen Bridges, you could click the Find button, enter her title, Prof., in the Find What text box and then click the OK button. Once you have changed an existing record's data, click the OK button in the Data Form dialog box. To **delete a record**, display it in the Data Form dialog box, and then click the Delete button. If you accidentally delete a data record, click the Restore button to bring it back.

You also can add, change, and delete data records when you are viewing the source in table form as shown in Figure 5-24. Click the Add New Record button on the Database toolbar to **add a blank row** to the bottom of the table and then fill in the field values. To **delete a row**, click somewhere in the row and then click the Delete Record button on the Database toolbar. Because the data source is a Word table, you also can add and delete records the same way you add and delete rows in a Word table, which was discussed in Project 4.

The data source is complete. If you wish, you can print the data source by clicking the Print button on the Standard toolbar. The next step is to switch from the data source to the main document so you can enter the contents of the form letter into the main document.

More *About*
Organizing Data

Organize the information in a data source so it is reusable. For example, you may want to print a person's title, first, middle, and last name (e.g., Ms. Jane L. Verlow) in the inside address but only the title and last name in the salutation (Dear Ms. Verlow). Thus, you should break the name into separate fields: title, first name, middle initial, and last name.

Steps **To Switch from the Data Source to the Main Document**

1 **Point to the Mail Merge Main Document button on the Database toolbar (Figure 5-25).**

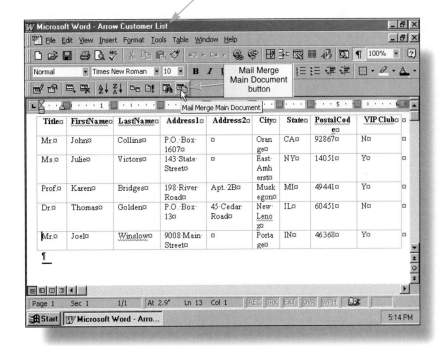

FIGURE 5-25

2 **Click the Mail Merge Main Document button.**

Word opens the main document (Figure 5-26). The **Mail Merge toolbar** *displays below the Formatting toolbar in place of the Database toolbar. When you are viewing the data source, the Database toolbar displays; and when you are viewing the main document, the Mail Merge toolbar displays. The title bar displays the file name Arrow Letterhead because Arrow Electronics' letterhead currently is the main document.*

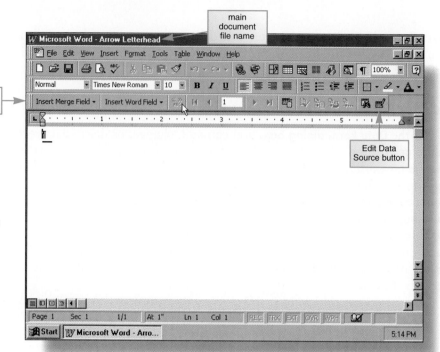

FIGURE 5-26

Creating the Main Document for the Form Letter

The next step is to create the **main document**, which is the form letter (see Figure 5-1 on page WD 5.5). The form letter is based on a **block style** letter. That is, all paragraphs are left-aligned. The current date displays in the left corner of the form letter below the letterhead. Keep in mind that you created the letterhead earlier as a header and saved it in a file called Arrow Letterhead.

You may recall that all business letters have common elements such as a date line, inside address, message, complimentary close, and signature block. The form letter in this project is a business letter that follows these guidelines:

- Inside address is three blank lines below the date line
- Salutation is one blank line below the inside address
- Letter message is one blank line below the salutation
- Paragraphs within the message are separated by one blank line
- Complimentary close is one blank line below the message
- Signature block is three blank lines below the complimentary close

The steps on the following pages illustrate how to create the main document for the form letter.

Saving the Main Document with a New File Name

The main document currently has the name Arrow Letterhead, the name of the letterhead for Arrow Electronics. Because you want the letterhead to remain unchanged, you should save the main document with a new file name as described in these steps.

TO SAVE THE MAIN DOCUMENT WITH A NEW FILE NAME

1. If necessary, insert your floppy disk into drive A.
2. Click File on the menu bar and then click Save As.
3. Type `Arrow Form Letter` in the File name text box. Do not press the ENTER key.
4. If necessary, click the Save in box arrow and then click 3½ Floppy (A:).
5. Click the Save button in the Save As dialog box.

Word saves the main document on a floppy disk in drive A with the file name, Arrow Form Letter (Figure 5-27 below).

Redefining the Normal Style

When you enter a document, its text and paragraphs are based on the Normal style. The **Normal style** is defined as single-spaced, left-aligned paragraphs containing characters in 10-point Times New Roman font. In this project, you want all of the characters to be in 12 point. You can change the font size of all characters you type from 10 to 12 by clicking the Font Size box arrow and then clicking 12 in the list. If you use this procedure, however, the current date and the discount percent will be in 10 point because they are Word fields, and Word fields are inserted based on the Normal style. Thus, you have to redefine the Normal style to 12 point.

Perform the following steps to redefine the Normal style to 12 point for this document.

Steps To Redefine the Normal Style

1. **Click Format on the menu bar and then point to Style (Figure 5-27).**

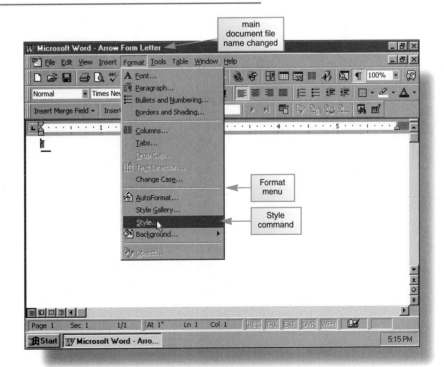

FIGURE 5-27

2 Click Style. When the Style dialog box displays, point to the Modify button.

*Word displays the **Style dialog box** (Figure 5-28). You can modify any of the styles listed in the Styles list box.*

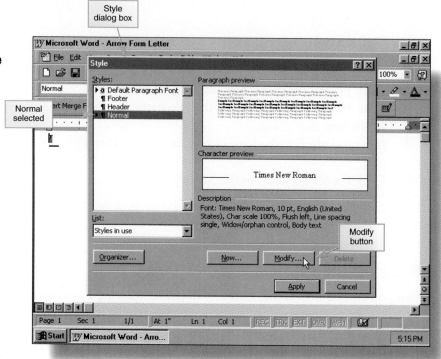

FIGURE 5-28

3 Be sure Normal is selected in the Styles list box and then click the Modify button. When the Modify Style dialog box displays, click the Format button and then point to Font.

*Word displays the **Modify Style dialog box** (Figure 5-29). Using this dialog box, you can change characteristics about a style's characters (font), paragraphs, tabs, borders, language, frames, and numbering.*

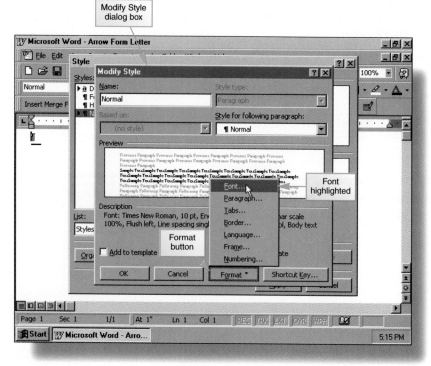

FIGURE 5-29

4 Click Font. When the Font dialog box displays, click 12 in the Size list box and the point to the OK button.

Word displays the Font dialog box (Figure 5-30). Using this dialog box, you can change characteristics of a style's font.

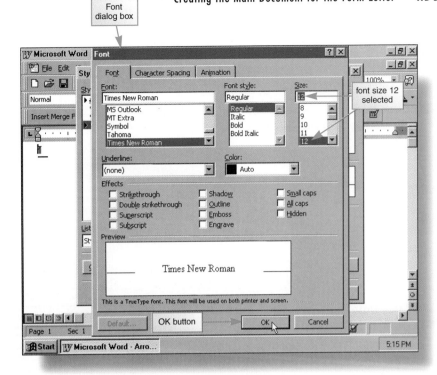

FIGURE 5-30

5 Click the OK button in the Font dialog box. When the Modify Style dialog box redisplays, click the OK button. When the Style dialog box redisplays, click the Apply button.

Word redefines the Normal style to 12 point (Figure 5-31).

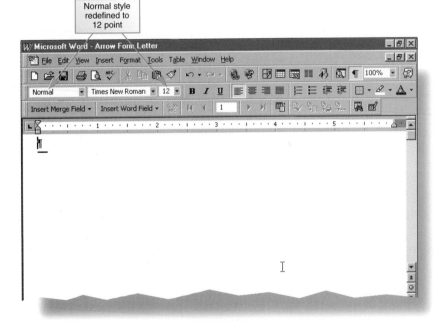

FIGURE 5-31

Inserting the Current Date in the Form Letter

When sending letters to the customers, you want the current date to print below the letterhead. Word provides a method of inserting the computer's system date into a document. In this way, if you type the letter today and print it at a later date, it will print the current date. Follow the steps on the next page to insert the current date in the main document.

More *About* **Dates**

If you do not want the date to change to the current date each time you print a document, do not make it a field. That is, do not click the Update automatically check box in the Date and Time dialog box when you insert the current date.

Steps **To Insert the Current Date into a Document**

1 **Click Insert on the menu bar and then point to Date and Time (Figure 5-32).**

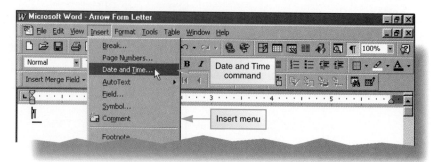

FIGURE 5-32

2 **Click Date and Time. When the Date and Time dialog box displays, click the format December 8, 1998 (the current date on your screen). If it is not selected, click Update automatically.**

Word displays the **Date and Time** *dialog box (Figure 5-33). A list of available formats for showing the current date and time displays. Your screen will not show December 8, 1998; instead, it will display the current system date stored in your computer. The current date will display in the main document according to the highlighted format.*

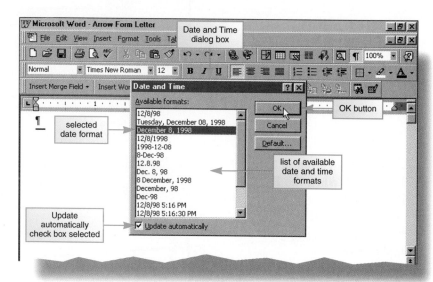

FIGURE 5-33

3 **Click the OK button. Press the ENTER key four times. If your date is shaded, click Tools on the menu bar, click Options, click the View tab, click the Field shading box arrow, click When selected, then click the OK button.**

Word displays the current date in the main document (Figure 5-34). The insertion point is on line 5 with three blank lines above it.

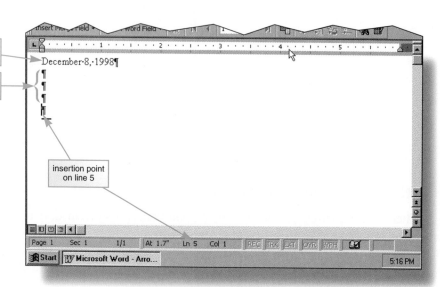

FIGURE 5-34

The current date is actually a field that Word updates when it prints the document. If you open the document at a later date, Word will not update the date on the screen until you print the document. If you would like to update the field on the screen prior to printing, click the date and then press the F9 key. If, for some reason, you want to delete the date field from the main document, double-click it, right-click the selection, and then click Cut on the shortcut menu.

The next step is to enter the inside address on the letter. The contents of the inside address are located in the data source. Thus, you insert fields from the data source into the main document.

Inserting Merge Fields into the Main Document

Earlier in this project, you created the data source for the form letter. The first record in the data source, the header row, contains the field names of each field in the data source. To link the data source to the main document, you must insert these field names into the main document. In the main document, these field names are called **merge fields** because they merge, or combine, the main document with the contents of the data source. When a field is inserted into the main document from the data source, Word surrounds the field name with **chevrons**. These chevrons mark the beginning and ending of a merge field. Chevrons are not on the keyboard; therefore, you cannot type them directly into the document. They display as a result of inserting a merge field with the **Insert Merge Field button** on the Mail Merge toolbar.

Perform the following steps to create the inside address and salutation using fields from the data source.

> ### More *About* Fields
>
> When you position the insertion point in a field, the entire field is shaded gray. The shading displays on the screen only to help you identify fields; the shading does not print on a hard copy. Thus, the date and merge fields appear shaded when you click them. To select an entire field, you must double-click it.

 Steps To Insert Merge Fields into the Main Document

1 Be sure the insertion point is on line 5 in the main document. Click the Insert Merge Field button on the Mail Merge toolbar. In the list of fields, point to Title.

Word displays a list of fields from the data source (Figure 5-35). The field you select will be entered at the location of the insertion point in the main document.

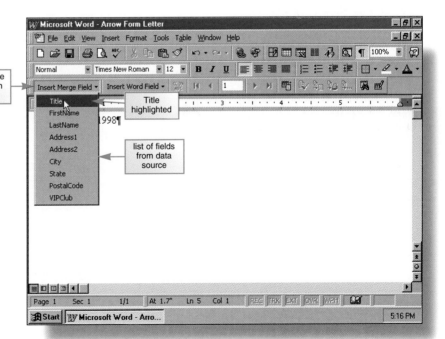

FIGURE 5-35

2 **Click Title. When the list of fields disappears from the screen, press the SPACEBAR.**

Word displays the field name, Title, surrounded with chevrons in the main document (Figure 5-36). When you merge the data source with the main document, the customer's title (e.g., Mr. or Ms.) will print at the location of the merge field Title. One space follows the ending chevron after the Title merge field.

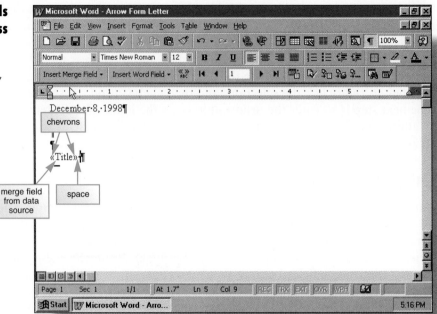

FIGURE 5-36

3 **Click the Insert Merge Field button on the Mail Merge toolbar and then click FirstName. Press the SPACEBAR. Click the Insert Merge Field button and then click LastName. Press the ENTER key. Click the Insert Merge Field button and then click Address1. Press the ENTER key. Click the Insert Merge Field button and then click Address2. Press the ENTER key. Click the Insert Merge Field button and then click City. Type , (a comma) and then press the SPACEBAR. Click the Insert Merge Field button and then click State. Press the SPACEBAR. Click the Insert Merge Field button and then click PostalCode.**

The inside address is complete (Figure 5-37).

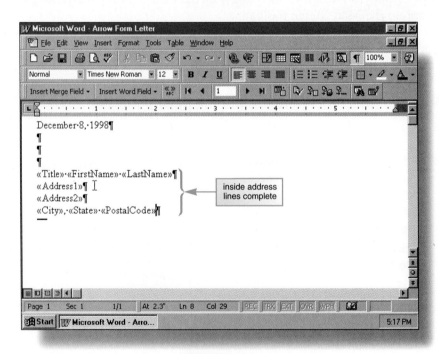

FIGURE 5-37

Entering the Salutation and Body of the Form Letter

The next step is to enter the salutation and then the first paragraph in the body of the form letter. The first paragraph contains *constant*, or unchanging, text to be printed in each form letter. Perform the following steps to enter the salutation and the first paragraph in the body of the form letter.

TO ENTER THE SALUTATION AND FIRST PARAGRAPH IN THE FORM LETTER

1 Press the ENTER key twice. Type Dear and then press the SPACEBAR. Click the Insert Merge Field button and then click Title. Press the SPACEBAR. Click the Insert Merge Field button and then click LastName. Type : (a colon).

2 Press the ENTER key twice. If the Office Assistant displays, click its Cancel button. Type Arrow Electronics announces our YEAR-END CLEARANCE SALE!

3 Press the SPACEBAR. Type We are pleased to inform you that every item in our 1998 catalog will be on sale during the last two weeks of the year.

The salutation and body of the form letter display as shown in Figure 5-38. Depending on your printer driver, your wordwrap may occur in different locations.

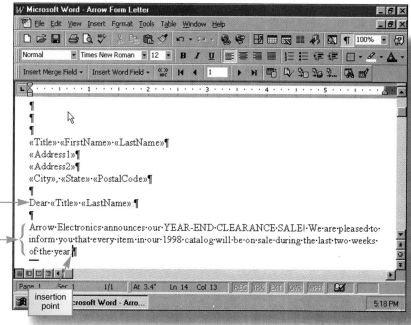

FIGURE 5-38

Using an IF Field to Conditionally Print Text in a Form Letter

In addition to merge fields, you can insert other types of fields in your main document. One type of field is called an **IF field**. One form of the IF field is: If a condition is true, then perform an action. For example, If Mary is a student, then inform her of the good student discount program for car insurance. This type of IF field is called **If...Then**. Another form of the IF field is: If a condition is true, then perform an action; else perform a different action. For example, If the weather is sunny, we will go to the beach; else we will go the movies. This type of IF field is called **If...Then...Else**.

In Project 5, the form letter checks whether the customer is a member of the VIP Club. If the customer is a member, then the discount is 25 percent. If the customer is not a member of the VIP Club, then the discount is 10 percent. For Word to determine which discount percent to use, you must enter an If...Then...Else: If VIP Club is equal to Y (for Yes), then print 25 percent as the discount, else print 10 percent as the discount.

The phrase that appears after the word If is called a **condition**. A condition is comprised of an expression, followed by a comparison operator, followed by a final expression.

EXPRESSIONS The **expression** in a condition can be a merge field, a number, a string of characters, or a mathematical formula. Word surrounds a string of characters with quotation marks ("). Place two quotation marks together ("") to indicate an empty, or **null**, expression.

More *About*
Field Codes

If, when you insert fields into a document, the field displays surrounded by braces instead of chevrons and extra instructions appear between the braces, then field codes have been turned on. To turn off field codes and display the field results, press ALT+F9, which toggles between field codes and field results.

More *About*
Word Fields

In addition to the IF field, Word provides other fields that may be used in form letters. For example, the ASK and FILLIN fields prompt the user to enter data for each record in the data source. The SKIP RECORD IF field instructs the mail merge to not generate a form letter for a data record if a specific condition is met.

More *About*
IF Fields

The term, IF field, comes from computer programming. Don't be intimidated by the terminology. An IF field simply specifies a decision. Some programmers refer to it as an IF statement. An IF field can be quite simple or complex. Complex IF fields include nested IF fields, which is a second IF field inside true or false text of the first IF field.

COMPARISON OPERATORS The **comparison operator** in a condition must be one of six characters: = (equal to or matches the text), <> (not equal to or does not match text), < (less than), <= (less than or equal to), > (greater than), >= (greater than or equal to).

If the result of a condition is true, then the **true text** is evaluated; otherwise, if the result of the condition is false, the **false text** is evaluated. In Project 5, the first expression in the condition is a merge field (VIPClub); the comparison operator is an equal sign (=); and the second expression is the text "Y". The true text is "25" and the false text is "10". That is, the complete IF field is as follows:

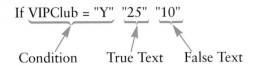

If VIPClub = "Y"   "25"   "10"

Condition   True Text   False Text

Perform the following steps to insert the IF field into the form letter.

Steps **To Insert an IF Field into the Main Document**

1 **Press the ENTER key twice. Type** To receive your **and then press the SPACEBAR. Click the Insert Word Field button on the Mail Merge toolbar. When the list of Word fields displays, point to If...Then...Else.**

A list of Word fields that may be inserted into the main document displays (Figure 5-39).

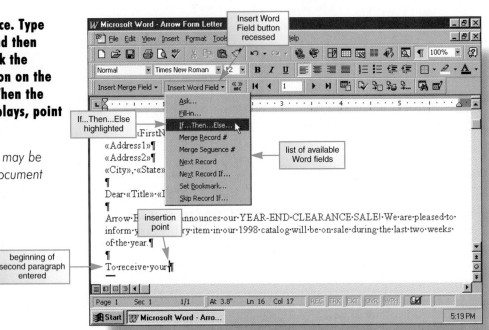

FIGURE 5-39

2 Click If...Then...Else. When the Insert Word Field: IF dialog box displays, point to the Field name box arrow.

Word displays the Insert Word Field: IF dialog box (Figure 5-40). You can specify the condition in the IF area of this dialog box.

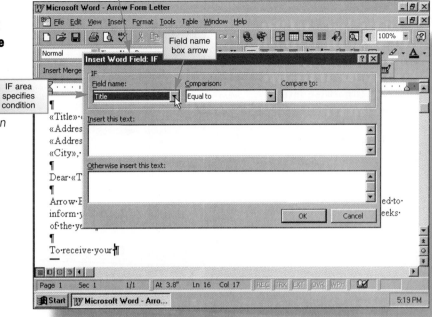

FIGURE 5-40

3 Click the Field name box arrow. Scroll through the list of fields and then point to VIPClub.

Word displays a list of fields from the data source (Figure 5-41).

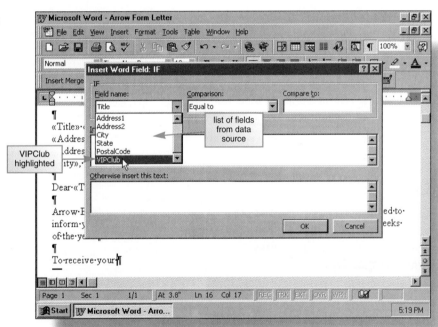

FIGURE 5-41

4 Click VIPClub. Click the Compare to text box. Type Y and then press the TAB key. In the Insert this text text box, type 25 and then press the TAB key. Type 10 in the Otherwise insert this text text box.

The entries in the Insert Word Field: IF dialog box are complete (Figure 5-42).

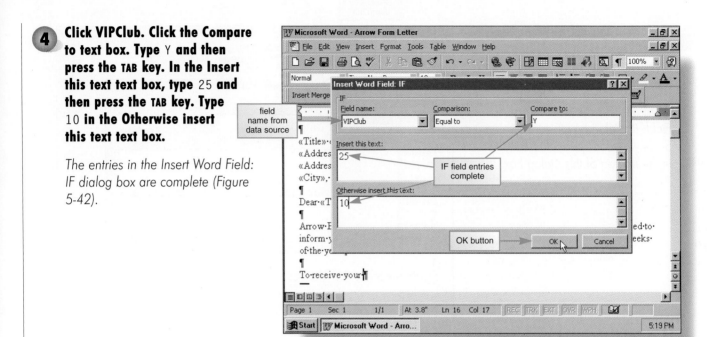

FIGURE 5-42

5 Click the OK button.

Word returns to the document. The discount percent, 10, displays at the location of the insertion point because the first record in the data source is not a member of the VIP Club.

6 Press the SPACEBAR. Type percent discount, please mention code YE98 when placing your order. Press the SPACEBAR. Type All orders must be received between December 17 and December 31 to qualify for the discount. Press the ENTER key twice. Type Sincerely, and then press the ENTER key four times. Type Connie L. Peterson and then press the ENTER key. Type President in the signature block.

The form letter is complete (Figure 5-43).

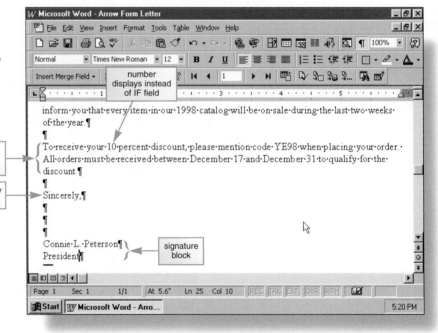

FIGURE 5-43

The main document for the form letter is complete. You should save it again by clicking the Save button on the Standard toolbar.

Displaying Field Codes

Notice that the IF field does not display in the document window; instead, the value of the IF field, called the **field results,** displays. That is, the number 10 displays because the first data record contains a customer that is not a member of the VIP Club.

The IF field is referred to as a **field code,** and the default mode for Word is field codes off. Thus, field codes will not print or display unless you turn them on. You use one procedure to display field codes on the screen and a different procedure to print them on a hard copy. Whether field codes are on or off on your screen has no effect on the print merge process. The following steps illustrate how to turn on field codes so you may see them on the screen. Most Word users turn on field codes only to verify their accuracy. Because field codes tend to clutter the screen, you may want to turn them off after checking their accuracy.

> **More** *About*
> **Fields**
>
> If you wanted to lock a field so that its field results cannot be changed, click the field and then press CTRL+F11. To subsequently unlock a field so that it may be updated, click the field and then press CTRL+SHIFT+F11.

 Steps **To Turn Field Codes On or Off for Display**

1 **Press the ALT+F9 keys. Scroll up the document to view the field codes.**

Word displays the main document with field codes on (Figure 5-44). With field codes on, the term, MERGEFIELD, appears before each field from the data source. The IF field also displays. With field codes on, braces surround the fields instead of chevrons.

2 **Press the ALT+F9 keys again.**

Word turns field codes off in the main document.

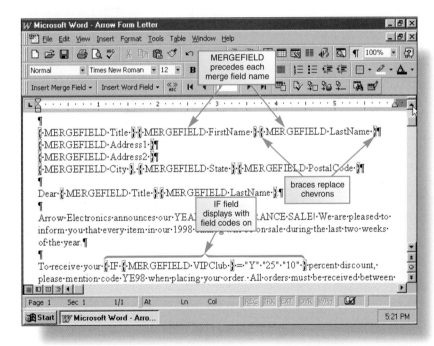

FIGURE 5-44

> *Other***Ways**
> 1. On Tools menu click Options, click View tab, click Field Codes, click OK button

Printing Field Codes

You also may want to print the field codes version of the form letter so you have a hard copy of the fields for future reference (see Figure 5-47). Field codes can be printed using the Print dialog box. When you print field codes, you must remember to turn off the field codes option so future documents print field results rather than field codes. For example, with field codes on, merged form letters will display field codes instead of data. Perform the following steps to print the field codes in the main document and then turn off the field codes print option for future printing.

Steps To Print Field Codes in the Main Document

① Click File on the menu bar and then click Print. When the Print dialog box displays, point to the Options button.

Word displays the Print dialog box (Figure 5-45).

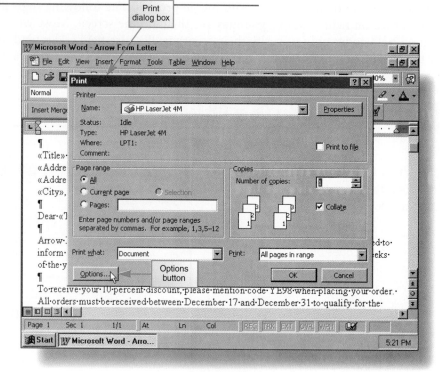

FIGURE 5-45

2 **Click the Options button. When the next Print dialog box displays, click Field codes in the Include with document area.**

Word displays another Print dialog box (Figure 5-46). The Field codes check box is selected.

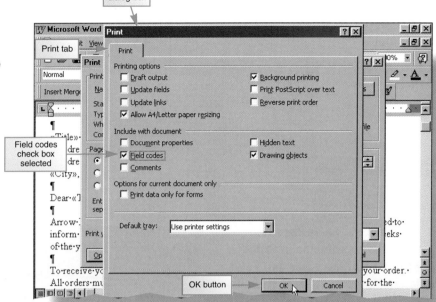

FIGURE 5-46

3 **Click the OK button in the active Print dialog box. When Word returns to the first Print dialog box, click the OK button.**

Word sends the main document with field codes to the printer (Figure 5-47). Notice the date field and IF field display on the printout.

4 **Click File on the menu bar and then click Print. Click the Options button. Turn off field codes by clicking Field codes. Click the OK button in the active Print dialog box and then click the Close button in the Print dialog box.**

The field codes have been turned off. No future documents will print field codes. If you accidentally click the Print button, instead of the Close button, in the Print dialog box, you will print the main document again – without field codes.

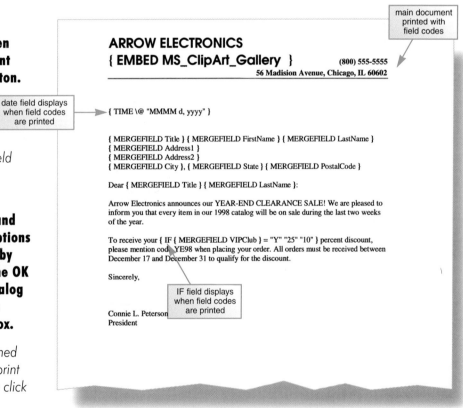

FIGURE 5-47

Other Ways

1. Press CTRL+P, click Options button, click Field codes, click OK button in Print dialog box, click OK button

2. On Tools menu click Options, click Print tab, click Field codes, click OK button, click Print button on Standard toolbar

Merging the Documents and Printing the Letters

The data source and main document for the form letter are complete. The next step is to merge them together to generate the individual form letters as shown in the following steps.

Steps To Merge the Documents and Print the Form Letters

1 Press the CTRL+HOME keys to move the insertion point to the beginning of the document. Point to the Merge to Printer button on the Mail Merge toolbar (Figure 5-48).

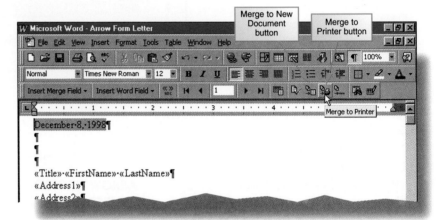

FIGURE 5-48

2 Click the Merge to Printer button. When the Print dialog box displays, click the OK button.

Word displays the Print dialog box and then sends the form letters to the printer. Form letters for five customers print (Figure 5-49).

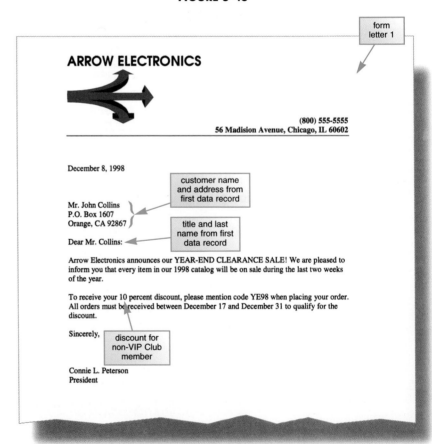

FIGURE 5-49

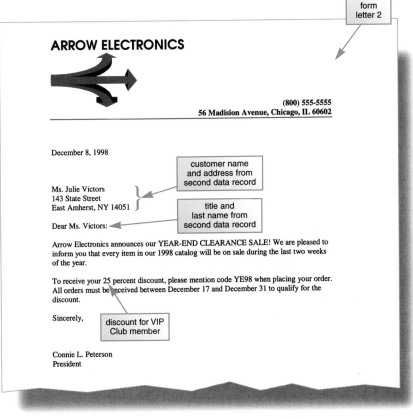

FIGURE 5-49 (continued)

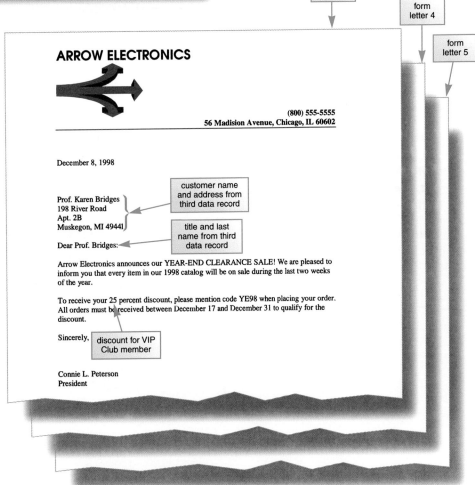

The contents of the data source merge with the merge fields in the main document to generate the form letters. One form letter for each customer is generated because each customer is a separate record in the data source. Notice that the address lines *suppress* blanks. That is, customers without a second address line begin the city on the line immediately below the first address line. Also notice that the discount percent changes from one letter to the next based on whether or not the customer is a member of the VIP Club.

If you notice errors in your form letters, you can edit the main document the same way you edit any other document. Then, you can save your changes and merge again.

Instead of printing the form letters, you could send them into a new document window by clicking the **Merge to New Document button** on the Mail Merge toolbar (Figure 5-48 on page WD 5.34). With this button, you view the merged form letters to verify their accuracy before sending them to the printer. When you are finished viewing the merged form letters, close the document window by clicking the Close button at the right edge of the menu bar and then click the No button to not save the document. In addition, you could save the merged form letters into a file and then print the file containing the letters at a later time using the Print button on the Standard toolbar.

Selecting Data Records to Merge and Print

Instead of merging and printing all of the records in the data source, you can choose which records will merge, based on a condition you specify. For example, to merge and print only those customers who are not a member of the VIP Club, perform the following steps.

Steps **To Selectively Merge and Print Records**

1 Click the Mail Merge button on the Mail Merge toolbar. When Word displays the Merge dialog box, point to the Query Options button.

Word displays the Merge dialog box (Figure 5-50).

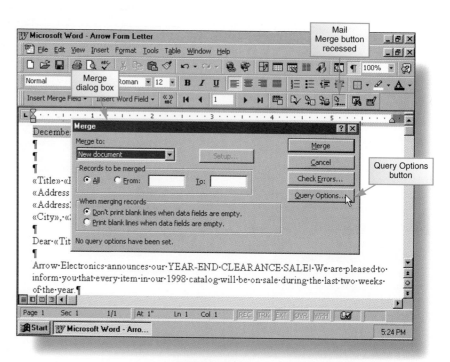

FIGURE 5-50

2 **Click the Query Options button. If necessary, click the Filter Records tab when the Query Options dialog box first opens. Click the Field box arrow to display a list of fields from the data source. Scroll to the bottom of the list and then click VIPClub. In the Compare to text box, type** N **and then point to the OK button.**

Word displays the Query Options *dialog box (Figure 5-51). VIPClub displays in the Field box, Equal to displays in the Comparison box, and N displays in the Compare to text box.*

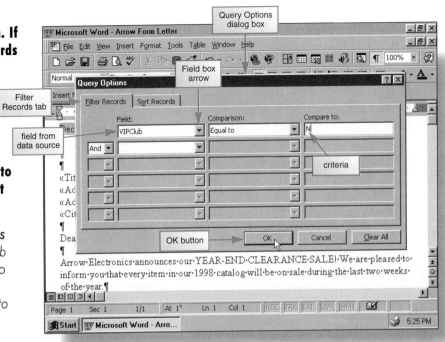

FIGURE 5-51

3 **Click the OK button. When the Merge dialog box redisplays, click the Merge to box arrow and then click Printer. Point to the Merge button in the Merge dialog box.**

Word returns to the Merge dialog box (Figure 5-52). You can merge to the printer or to a new document window using this dialog box.

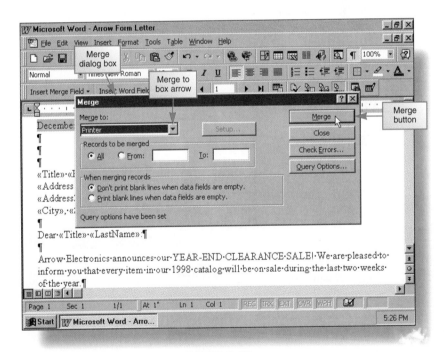

FIGURE 5-52

4 **Click the Merge button. When Word displays the Print dialog box, click the OK button.**

Word prints the form letters that match the specified condition: VIPClub is Equal to N (Figure 5-53). Two form letters print because two customers are not members of the VIP Club.

5 **Click the Mail Merge button on the Mail Merge toolbar. Click the Query Options button in the Merge dialog box. Click the Clear All button. Click the OK button. Click the Close button in the Merge dialog box.**

Word removes the specified condition so that future merges will not be restricted to VIPClub is Equal to N.

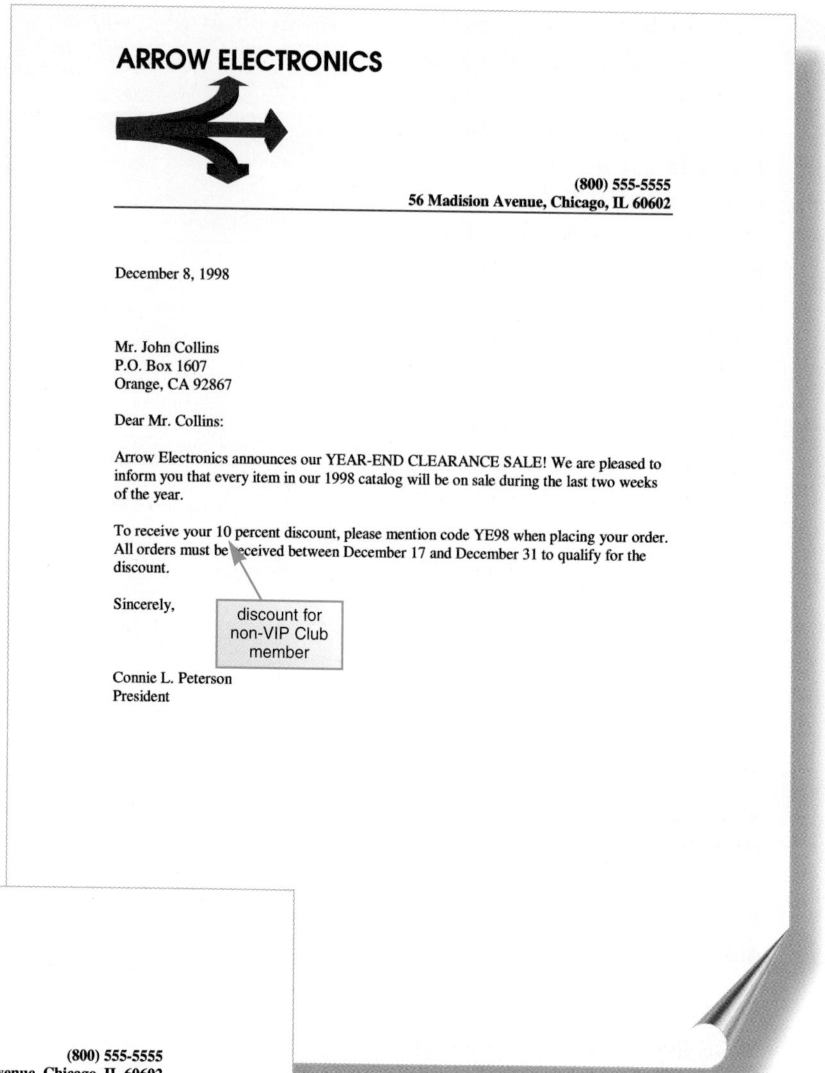

ARROW ELECTRONICS

(800) 555-5555
56 Madision Avenue, Chicago, IL 60602

December 8, 1998

Mr. John Collins
P.O. Box 1607
Orange, CA 92867

Dear Mr. Collins:

Arrow Electronics announces our YEAR-END CLEARANCE SALE! We are pleased to inform you that every item in our 1998 catalog will be on sale during the last two weeks of the year.

To receive your 10 percent discount, please mention code YE98 when placing your order. All orders must be received between December 17 and December 31 to qualify for the discount.

Sincerely,

discount for
non-VIP Club
member

Connie L. Peterson
President

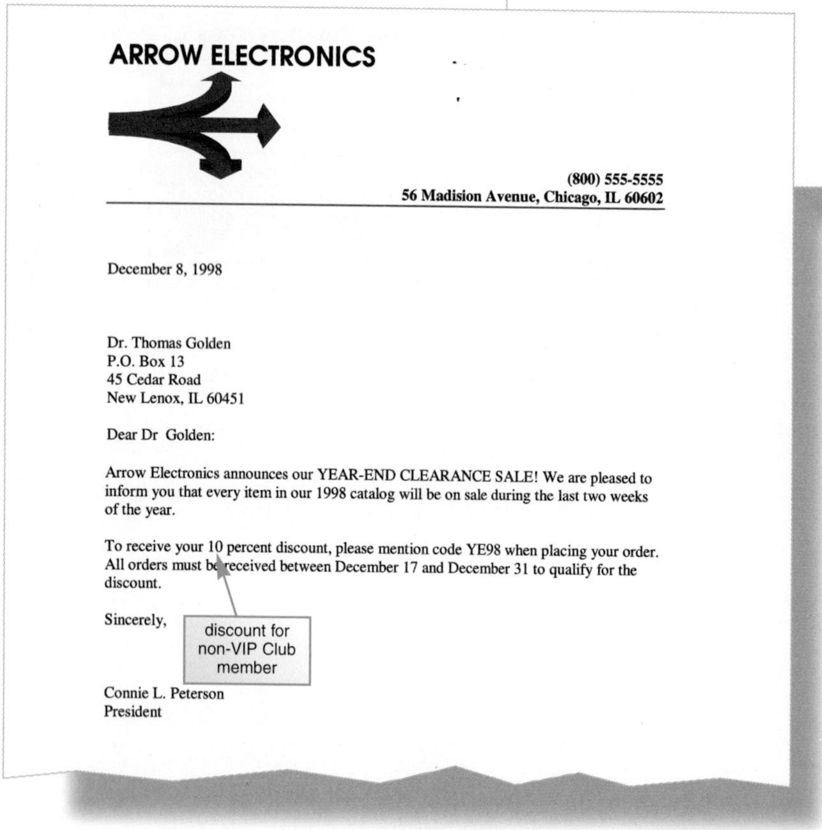

ARROW ELECTRONICS

(800) 555-5555
56 Madision Avenue, Chicago, IL 60602

December 8, 1998

Dr. Thomas Golden
P.O. Box 13
45 Cedar Road
New Lenox, IL 60451

Dear Dr Golden:

Arrow Electronics announces our YEAR-END CLEARANCE SALE! We are pleased to inform you that every item in our 1998 catalog will be on sale during the last two weeks of the year.

To receive your 10 percent discount, please mention code YE98 when placing your order. All orders must be received between December 17 and December 31 to qualify for the discount.

Sincerely,

discount for
non-VIP Club
member

Connie L. Peterson
President

FIGURE 5-53

▶*Other*Ways

1. Click Mail Merge Helper button on Mail Merge toolbar, click Merge button, click Query Options button, enter condition, click OK button, click Merge to box arrow, click Printer in list box, click Merge button in Merge dialog box, click Close button

Sorting Data Records to Merge and Print

If you mail your form letters using the U.S. Postal Service's bulk rate mailing service, the post office requires you to sort and group the form letters by zip code. Thus, follow these steps to sort the data records by zip code.

 Steps **To Sort the Data Records**

① **Click the Mail Merge button on the Mail Merge toolbar. When Word displays the Merge dialog box, click the Query Options button. If necessary, click the Sort Records tab when the Query Options dialog box first opens. Point to the Sort by box arrow.**

Word displays the Query Options dialog box (Figure 5-54). You can order the data source records by any of its fields. For example, you could alphabetize by LastName or order by PostalCode.

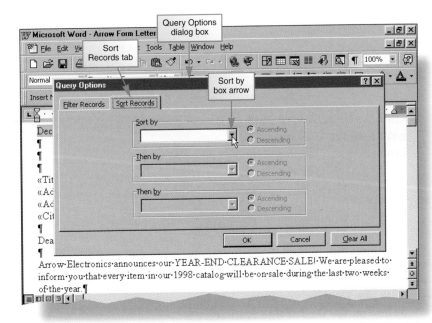

FIGURE 5-54

② **Click the Sort by box arrow to display a list of fields from the data source. Scroll to the bottom of the list and then click PostalCode.**

Word displays PostalCode in the Sort by box (Figure 5-55). The Ascending option button is selected. Thus, the smallest zip code (those beginning with zero) will be at the top of the data source and the largest will be at the bottom.

③ **Click the OK button. When the Merge dialog box redisplays, click the Close button.**

The data records are sorted by zip code.

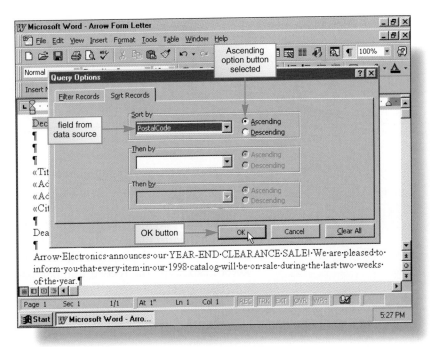

FIGURE 5-55

If you chose to merge the form letters again at this point, Word would print them in order of zip code; that is, the letter to Julie Victors would print first and the letter to John Collins would print last.

Because you want the mailing labels and envelopes to print in order of zip code, leave the sort condition set in the Query Options dialog box.

Viewing Merged Data

You can verify the order of the data records without printing them by using the **View Merged Data button** on the Mail Merge toolbar as shown below.

Steps To View Merged Data in the Main Document

1 **Click the View Merged Data button on the Mail Merge toolbar.**

Word displays the contents of the first data record in the main document, instead of the merge fields (Figure 5-56). The View Merged Data button is recessed.

2 **Click the View Merged Data button on the Mail Merge toolbar again.**

Word displays the merge fields in the main document, instead of the field values.

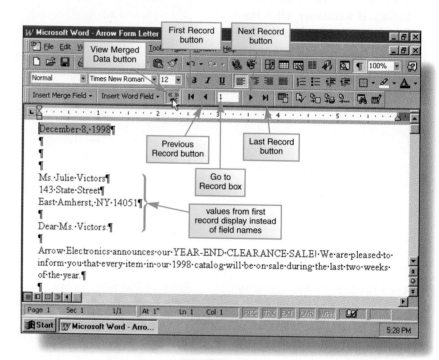

FIGURE 5-56

More *About* Opening Main Documents

When you open a main document, Word automatically looks for the associated data source and attempts to open it, too. If the data source is not in exactly the same location (i.e., drive and folder) as when it was originally saved, Word displays a dialog box indicating that it couldn't find the data source. If this happens, click the Find Data Source button to display the Open Data Source dialog box.

When you are viewing merged data in the main document (the View Merged Data button is recessed), you can click the **Last Record button** on the Mail Merge toolbar to display the values in the last record in the data source, the **Next Record button** to display the values in the next consecutive record number, the **Previous Record button** to display the values in the previous record number, or the **First Record button** to display the values in record one. You also can click in the **Go to Record box**, type the record number you want to display in the main document, and then press the ENTER key.

Addressing and Printing Mailing Labels

Now that you have printed the form letters, the next step is to address **mailing labels** for the envelopes of the form letters. The mailing labels will use the same data source as the form letter, Arrow Customer List. The format and content of the mailing labels will be exactly the same as the inside address in the main document for the form letter. That is, the first line will contain the customer's title, followed by the first name, followed by the last name. The second line will contain the customer's street address, and so on.

If your printer can print graphics, you can add a **POSTNET delivery-point bar code**, usually referred to as simply a **bar code**, above the address on each mailing label. Using a bar code speeds up the delivery service by the U.S. Postal Service. A bar code represents the addressee's zip code and first street address.

Follow the same basic steps as you did to create the main document for the form letters when you create the main document for the mailing labels. The major difference is that the data source already exists because you created it earlier in this project. The following pages illustrate how to address and print mailing labels from an existing data source.

 Steps **To Address and Print Mailing Labels from an Existing Data Source**

1 **Point to the New button on the Standard toolbar (Figure 5-57).**

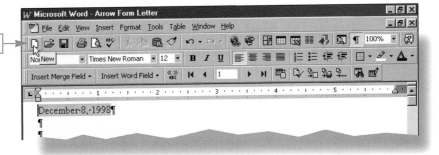

FIGURE 5-57

2 **Click the New button. Click File on the menu bar and then click Save As. Type** Arrow Mailing Labels **in the File name text box. If necessary, click the Save in box arrow and then click 3½ Floppy (A:). Click the Save button in the Save As dialog box. Click Tools on the menu bar and then click Mail Merge. When the Mail Merge Helper dialog box displays, click the Create button. Point to Mailing Labels.**

Word displays a new document window for the mailing labels (Figure 5-58). The file name of the new document is Arrow Mailing Labels.

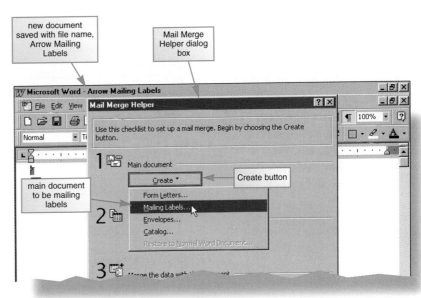

FIGURE 5-58

3 **Click Mailing Labels.**

A Microsoft Word dialog box displays asking if you want to use the active window for the mailing labels (Figure 5-59). The active window is Arrow Mailing Labels, which is the one you want.

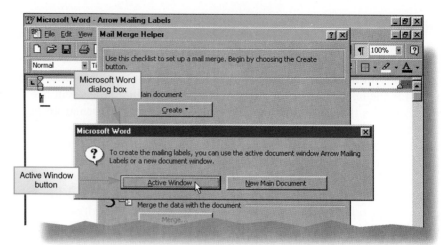

FIGURE 5-59

4 **Click the Active Window button. When the Mail Merge Helper dialog box displays, click the Get Data button and then point to Open Data Source.**

Word returns to the Mail Merge Helper dialog box (Figure 5-60). The merge type is identified as mailing labels for the main document. Because you will use the same data source as you did for the form letters, you will open a data source instead of creating one.

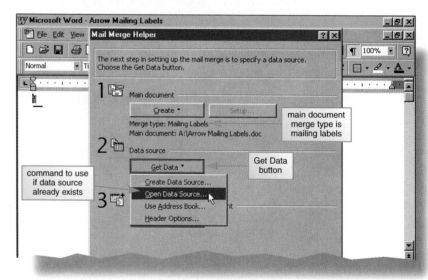

FIGURE 5-60

5 **Click Open Data Source. When Word displays the Open Data Source dialog box, click the Look in box arrow and then, if necessary, click 3½ Floppy (A:). Click the file name, Arrow Customer List, and then point to the Open button in the Open Data Source dialog box.**

Word displays the *Open Data Source dialog box* (Figure 5-61). You use the existing data source, Arrow Customer List, to generate the mailing labels.

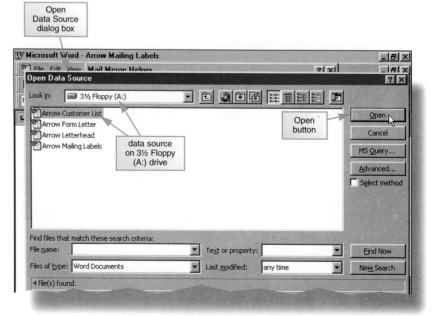

FIGURE 5-61

6 **Click the Open button.**

A Microsoft Word dialog box displays asking if you want to set up the main document, which is a mailing label layout in this case (Figure 5-62).

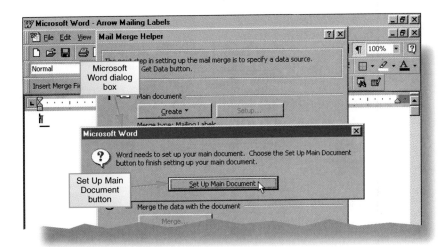

FIGURE 5-62

7 **Click the Set Up Main Document button. When the Label Options dialog box displays, click the desired Avery product number.**

Word displays the Label Options dialog box (Figure 5-63). If you have a dot matrix printer, your printer information will differ from this figure. The Product number list box displays the product numbers for all possible Avery mailing label sheets compatible with your printer. The Label information area displays details about the selected Avery product number.

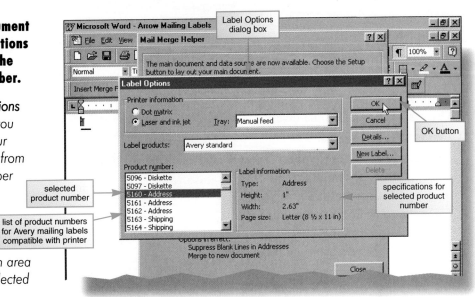

FIGURE 5-63

8 **Click the OK button.**

Word displays the Create Labels dialog box. You can insert merge fields into the Sample label area of this dialog box the same way you inserted merge fields into the main document for the form letter.

9 **Follow Steps 1 through 3 on pages WD 5.25 and WD 5.26 to address the mailing label. Point to the Insert Postal Bar Code button.**

The mailing label layout is complete (Figure 5-64).

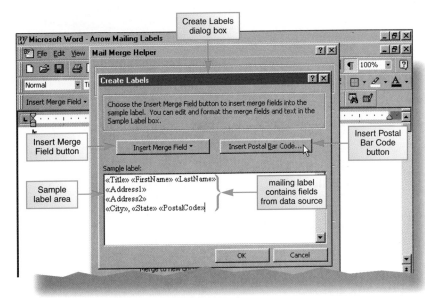

FIGURE 5-64

10 **Click the Insert Postal Bar Code button. When the Insert Postal Bar Code dialog box displays, click the Merge field with ZIP code box arrow and then click PostalCode in the list. Click the Merge field with street address box arrow and then click Address1 in the list.**

Word displays the Insert Postal Bar Code dialog box (Figure 5-65). A bar code contains the zip code and the first address line. Thus, PostalCode displays in the Merge field with ZIP code box and Address1 displays in the Merge field with street address box.

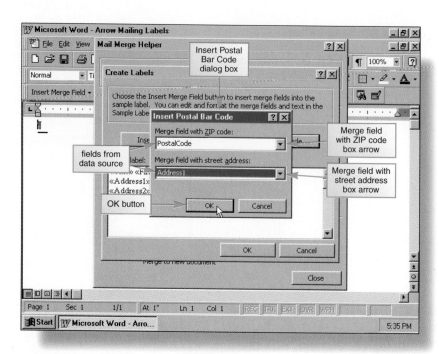

FIGURE 5-65

11 **Click the OK button in the Insert Postal Bar Code dialog box.**

Word returns to the Create Labels dialog box, which indicates where the bar code will print on each mailing label (Figure 5-66).

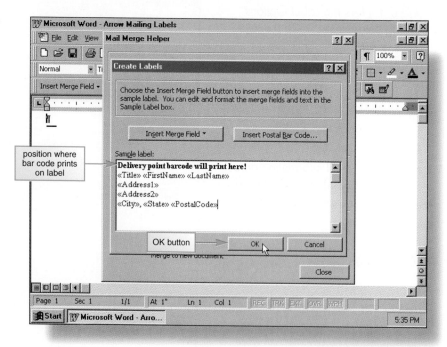

FIGURE 5-66

12 Click the OK button. Click the Close button in the Mail Merge Helper dialog box. When the main document displays in the document window, click the Merge to Printer button on the Mail Merge toolbar. When the Print dialog box displays, click the OK button.

Word returns to the document window with the mailing label layout as the main document (Figure 5-67). If your mailing labels display an error message indicating the zip code portion of the bar code is not valid, ignore the message because the bar codes will print correctly.

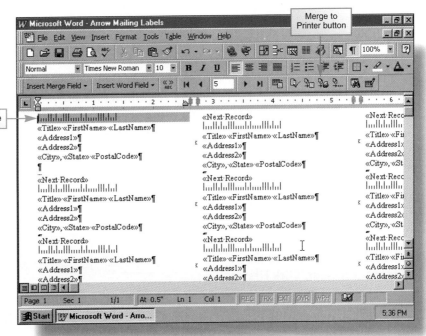

FIGURE 5-67

13 Retrieve the mailing labels from the printer.

The mailing labels print as shown in Figure 5-68. The mailing labels print in zip code order because earlier in this project you sorted the data source by zip code.

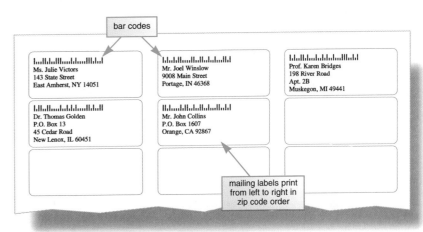

FIGURE 5-68

Saving the Mailing Labels

You should save the mailing labels again because you have made several changes since the initial save.

TO SAVE A DOCUMENT A SECOND TIME

① Click the Save button on the Standard toolbar.

Word saves the main document for the mailing labels on a floppy disk in drive A with the same file name, Arrow Mailing Labels.

Addressing and Printing Envelopes

Instead of generating mailing labels to affix to envelopes, your printer may have the capability of printing directly onto the envelopes. To print the label information directly on the envelopes, you will follow the same basic steps as you did to generate the mailing labels. Perform the following steps to address and print the envelopes.

Steps ## To Address and Print Envelopes from an Existing Data Source

1 **Click the New button on the Standard toolbar. Click File on the menu bar and then click Save As. Type** Arrow Envelopes **in the File name text box. If necessary, click the Save in box arrow and then click 3½ Floppy (A:). Click the Save button in the Save As dialog box. Click Tools on the menu bar and then click Mail Merge. When the Mail Merge Helper dialog box displays, click the Create button and then point to Envelopes.**

Word displays a new document window for the main document for the envelopes (Figure 5-69). The file name of the new document is Arrow Envelopes.

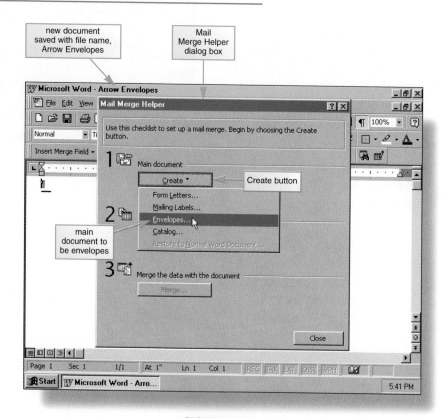

FIGURE 5-69

> ◆ **More** *About*
> **Envelopes**
>
> Instead of addressing envelopes from a data source, you can print an envelope(s) for a single address. Click Envelopes and Labels on the Tools menu, click the Envelopes tab, type the name, delivery address, and return address in the appropriate text boxes, then click the Print button in the Envelopes and Labels dialog box.

2 Click Envelopes. In the Microsoft Word dialog box, click the Active Window button. When the Mail Merge Helper dialog box displays, click the Get Data button and then click Open Data Source. When Word displays the Open Data Source dialog box, click the Look in box arrow and then, if necessary, click 3½ Floppy (A:). Click the file name, Arrow Customer List, and then click the Open button in the Open Data Source dialog box. In the Microsoft Word dialog box, click the Set Up Main Document button. If necessary, click the Envelope Options tab when the Envelope Options dialog box first opens.

Word displays the Envelope Options dialog box (Figure 5-70). The Envelope Options sheet is used to specify size of the envelopes. Depending on your printer, your Envelope Options sheet may differ from this figure.

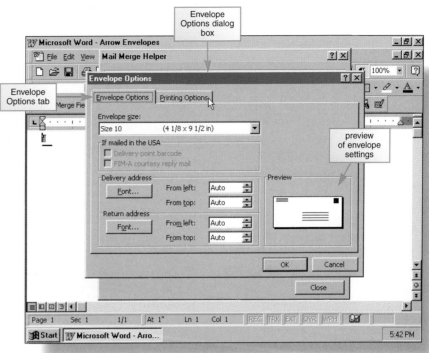

FIGURE 5-70

3 Click the Printing Options tab.

Word displays the Printing Options sheet in the Envelope Options dialog box (Figure 5-71). In the Feed method area, you can indicate how the envelopes are positioned in the printer. Depending on your printer, your Printing Options sheet may differ from this figure.

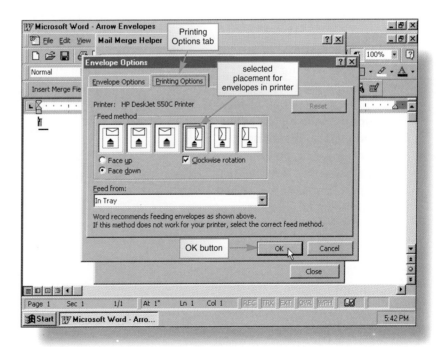

FIGURE 5-71

4 **Click the OK button.**

*Word displays the **Envelope address** dialog box. You insert merge fields into the Sample envelope address area of the this dialog box the same way you inserted merge fields into the main document for the mailing labels and the main document for the form letter.*

5 **Follow Steps 9 through 11 on pages WD 5.43 and WD 5.44 to address the envelopes with a bar code.**

Word displays the completed envelope layout (Figure 5-72).

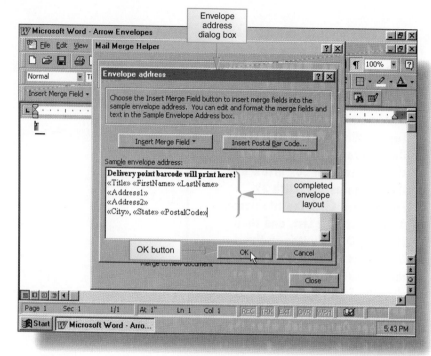

FIGURE 5-72

6 **Click the OK button in the Envelope address dialog box. When the Mail Merge Helper dialog box displays, click the Close button. When the main document displays in the document window, click the return address and type** Arrow Electronics **and then press the ENTER key. Type** 56 Madison Avenue **and then press the ENTER key. Type** Chicago, IL 60602 **and then click the Save button on the Standard toolbar. If necessary, insert envelopes in the printer. Click the Merge to Printer button on the Mail Merge toolbar. When the Print dialog box displays, click the OK button.**

Word returns to the document window with the envelope layout as the main document (Figure 5-73). If your envelope displays an error message indicating the zip code portion of the bar code is not valid, ignore the message because the bar code will print correctly.

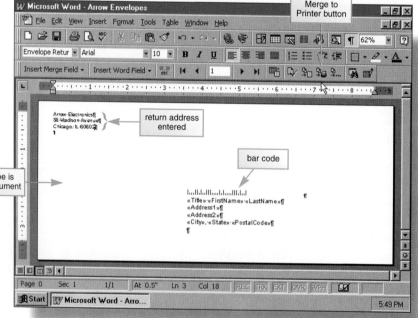

FIGURE 5-73

7 **Retrieve the envelopes from the printer.**

The envelopes print as shown in Figure 5-74. The envelopes print in zip code order because earlier in this project you sorted the data source by zip code.

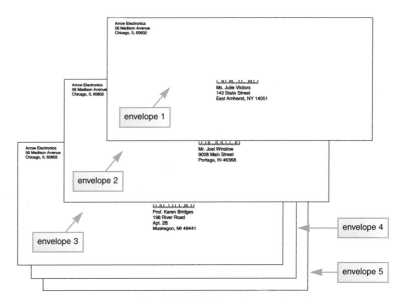

FIGURE 5-74

Closing All Open Files and Quitting Word

You currently have four files open: Arrow Customer List, Arrow Form Letter, Arrow Mailing Labels, and Arrow Envelopes. Rather than closing each one individually, you can close all open files at once as described in these steps.

TO CLOSE ALL OPEN DOCUMENTS

1 Press and hold the SHIFT key. While holding the SHIFT key, click File on the menu bar. Release the SHIFT key.

2 Click Close All.

3 If the Microsoft Word dialog box displays, click the Yes button to save any changes made to the individual documents. If you do not want the data records to be saved in sorted order (by zip code), you would click the No button when Word asks if you want to save changes to Arrow Customer List.

Word closes all open documents and displays a blank document window.

Project 5 is complete. Follow this step to quit Word.

TO QUIT WORD

1 Click the Close button in the Word window.

The Word window closes.

> **More** *About*
> **Closing Form Letters**
>
> Word always asks if you want to save changes when you close a main document, even if you just saved the document. If you are sure that no additional changes were made to the document, click the No button; otherwise, click the Yes button — just to be safe.

Project Summary

Project 5 introduced you to generating form letters and their corresponding mailing labels and envelopes. First, you created the Arrow Electronics letterhead, then identified the main document and created a data source. Next, you created the main document for the form letter. The form letter included merge fields and an IF field. In this project, you learned how to merge and print all the form letters, as well as only certain records in the data source. You also learned how to sort the data source records. Finally, you addressed and printed mailing labels and envelopes to accompany the form letters.

What You Should Know

Having completed this project, you now should be able to perform the following tasks:

▶ Address and Print Envelopes from an Existing Data Source *(WD 5.46)*

▶ Address and Print Mailing Labels from an Existing Data Source *(WD 5.41)*

▶ Bottom Border a Paragraph *(WD 5.8)*

▶ Close All Open Documents *(WD 5.49)*

▶ Create a Data Source in Word *(WD 5.13)*

▶ Create Company Letterhead *(WD 5.7)*

▶ Display Nonprinting Characters *(WD 5.7)*

▶ Enter the Salutation and the First Paragraph in the Form Letter *(WD 5.27)*

▶ Identify the Main Document *(WD 5.10)*

▶ Insert an IF Field into the Main Document *(WD 5.28)*

▶ Insert Merge Fields into the Main Document *(WD 5.25)*

▶ Insert the Current Date into a Document *(WD 5.24)*

▶ Merge the Documents and Print the Form Letters *(WD 5.34)*

▶ Print Field Codes in the Main Document *(WD 5.32)*

▶ Quit Word *(WD 5.49)*

▶ Redefine the Normal Style *(WD 5.21)*

▶ Save a Document a Second Time *(WD 5.45)*

▶ Save the Company Letterhead in a File *(WD 5.9)*

▶ Save the Main Document with a New File Name *(WD 5.21)*

▶ Selectively Merge and Print Records *(WD 5.36)*

▶ Sort the Data Records *(WD 5.39)*

▶ Start Word *(WD 5.6)*

▶ Switch from the Data Source to the Main Document *(WD 5.13)*

▶ Turn Field Codes On or Off for Display *(WD 5.31)*

▶ View Merged Data in the Main Document *(WD 5.40)*

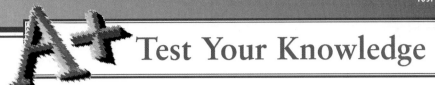

Test Your Knowledge

1 True/False

Instructions: Circle T if the statement is true or F if the statement is false.

T F   1. Sorting is the process of blending a data source into a main document.

T F   2. A data source contains the variable, or changing, text in a form letter.

T F   3. A data source is always a Word table.

T F   4. When a data source is the current document, the buttons on the Standard toolbar change.

T F   5. To redefine the Normal style, click the Normal Style button on the Standard toolbar to display the Redefine Style dialog box.

T F   6. To insert a merge field into the main document, type the beginning chevron, followed by the field name, followed by the ending chevron.

T F   7. A condition is composed of an expression, a comparison operator, and a final expression.

T F   8. Use one procedure to display field codes on the screen and another procedure to print them.

T F   9. When field codes are off, the word, MERGEFIELD, displays in front of every merge field in the main document.

T F   10. When merging a data source to a main document, Word by default suppresses empty fields from the data source.

2 Multiple Choice

Instructions: Circle the correct response.

1. To display the border palette, click the _____ button.
   a. Border Palette   b. Rule   c. Palette   d. none of the above

2. Each row in a data source is called a _____.
   a. character   b. field   c. record   d. file

3. The first row in a data source is called the _____.
   a. header row   b. data row   c. initial row   d. start row

4. To update a field, such as the current date, in the document window, press the _____ key.
   a. F6   b. F7   c. F8   d. F9

5. Which of the following is an invalid field name?
   a. FirstNameofCustomer   b. Title   c. Local_Resident   d. 1st_Name

6. In the main document, the Mail Merge toolbar is located between the _____ and the _____.
   a. title bar, menu bar   c. Formatting toolbar, ruler
   b. menu bar, Standard toolbar   d. Standard toolbar, Formatting toolbar

7. In an IF field, a null string is represented as _____.
   a. " " " "   b. "NULL"   c. "0"   d. " "

8. Which of the following mathematical operators stands for not equal to or does not match?
   a. !=!   b. <=   c. >=   d. none of the above

(continued)

Multiple Choice *(continued)*

9. Text expressions in an IF field must be surrounded by _____.
   a. equal signs (=)   b. apostrophes (')   c. quotation marks (")   d. hyphens (-)

10. When field codes are off, merge fields in the main document are surrounded by _____.
   a. quotation marks   b. chevrons   c. parenthesEs   d. none of the above

3 Understanding the Database Toolbar

Instructions: In Figure 5-75, arrows point to various buttons on the Database toolbar when a data source is the active document. In the spaces provided, identify each button.

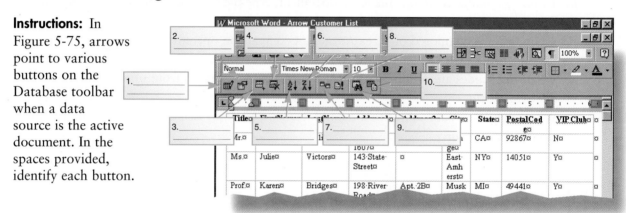

FIGURE 5-75

4 Understanding the Mail Merge Toolbar

Instructions: In Figure 5-76, arrows point to various buttons on the Mail Merge toolbar. In the spaces provided, identify each button.

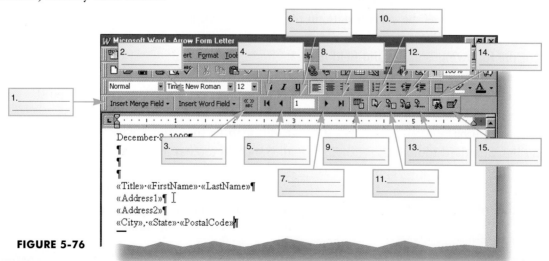

FIGURE 5-76

Use Help

1 Reviewing Project Activities

Instructions: Perform the following tasks using a computer.

1. Start Word. If the Office Assistant is on your screen, click it to display its balloon. If the Office Assistant is not on your screen, click the Office Assistant button on the Standard toolbar.
2. Type create a data source in the What would you like to do? text box. Click the Search button. Click the Create a new mail-merge data source in Word topic. Read and print the information.
3. Click the Help Topics button to display the Help Topics: Microsoft Word dialog box. Click the Contents tab. Double-click the Assembling Documents with Mail Merge book. Double-click the Customizing Mail Merge with Word Fields book. Double-click the Merge fields topic. Read and print the information.
4. Click the Help Topics button. Click the Index tab. Type styles in the top text box labeled 1 and then double-click the changing topic in the list box labeled 2. Read and print the information.
5. Click the Help Topics button. Click the Find tab. Type fields and then double-click the About fields topic. Read and print the information. Close any open Help window and the Office Assistant.

2 Expanding on the Basics

Instructions: Use Word Help to better understand the topics listed below. Answer the questions on your own paper or hand in the printed Help topic to your instructor.

1. In this project, you merged a main document to a data source. Sometimes when using mail merge, error messages display or you need to change existing settings. Use the Office Assistant to determine how to remedy these situations.
   a. You get a message saying your data file is a mail merge main document. How do you remove the main document designation from the data source?
   b. How do you change the mailing label or envelope size in an existing main document?
2. In this project, you created a data source as a Word table. Use the Contents tab in the Help Topics: Microsoft Word dialog box to answer the following questions about external data sources.
   a. What types of files, other than a Word table, can be used as a data source?
   b. What is a header source? When should you use one?
   c. What Office programs can you use to make a list of names and addresses for mail merge?
3. In this project, you addressed envelopes using the existing data source. Use the Index tab in the Help Topics: Microsoft Word dialog box to determine how to address a single envelope.
4. In this project, you created a condition in the mail merge main document. Use the Find tab in the Help Topics: Microsoft Word dialog box to give an example of a multiple selection rule (condition) using the And; also give an example using the Or. Then, explain each of the examples.

Apply Your Knowledge

1 Working with a Form Letter

Instructions: Start Word. Open the document, apply-5, from the Word folder on the Data Disk that accompanies this book. The document is a main document for Riverton College. You are to print field codes in the main document (Figure 5-77), edit and print a data source, and then merge the form letters to a file and the printer.

Perform the following tasks.

1. Click the Print button on the Standard toolbar.

2. Click File on the menu bar and then click Print. Click the Options button in the Print dialog box. Click Field codes to select the check box and then click the OK button. When the Print dialog box redisplays, click the OK button.

3. Click File on the menu bar and then click Print. Click the Options button in the Print dialog box. Click Field codes to turn off the check box and then click the OK button. When the Print dialog box redisplays, click the Close button.

4. Click the Edit Data Source button on the Mail Merge toolbar and then click the View Source button to display the data source, Riverton Graduate List, as a Word table.

5. Click the Add New Record button on the Database toolbar. Add a record containing your personal information; use SPS as the School.

6. Click Table on the menu bar and then click Table AutoFormat. When the Table AutoFormat dialog box displays, scroll through the list of formats, and then click Grid 8. Click the OK button.

7. Click in the LastName column of the data source. Click the Sort Ascending button on the Database toolbar.

8. Click File on the menu bar and then click Save As. Use the file name Revised Riverton Graduate List.

9. Click the Print button on the Standard toolbar.

10. Click the Mail Merge Main Document button on the Database toolbar.

11. Click the Merge to New Document button on the Mail Merge toolbar. Click the Print button on the Standard toolbar. Click File on the menu bar and then click the Close button. Click the No button in the Microsoft Word dialog box.

12. Click the Merge to Printer button on the Mail Merge toolbar. Click the OK button.

13. Press and hold the SHIFT key and then click File on the menu bar. Release the SHIFT key. Click Close All.

Riverton College
{ EMBED MS_ClipArt_Gallery }

(704) 392-1153
67 Marriot Street, Charlotte, NC 28208

{ TIME \@ "MMMM d, yyyy" }

{ MERGEFIELD Title } { MERGEFIELD FirstName } { MERGEFIELD LastName }
{ MERGEFIELD Address1 }
{ MERGEFIELD Address2 }
{ MERGEFIELD City }, { MERGEFIELD State } { MERGEFIELD PostalCode }

Dear { MERGEFIELD Title } { MERGEFIELD LastName }:

The Office of Registration at Riverton College would like to congratulate you on your upcoming completion of graduation requirements in the School of { IF { MERGEFIELD School } = "SPS" "Professional Studies" "Liberal Arts and Sciences" }. Providing you successfully complete all coursework toward your degree this semester, you will be eligible to attend the graduation ceremonies.

This year's ceremonies will be on the north lawn of the Reed Building on Sunday, May 9. The procession will start promptly at 12:30 p.m. from Room 100C of the Reed Building. Please arrive by 11:30 a.m. if you plan to be in the procession.

Regards,

Patricia Baker
Registrar

FIGURE 5-77

In the Lab

1 Creating a Data Source, Form Letter, and Mailing Labels

Problem: Janice Rivers, the owner of Rose Card and Gift Shop, has asked you to notify all customers of the shop's new holiday hours. You decide to send a form letter (Figure 5-78) to all customers.

Instructions:

1. Create the letterhead shown at the top of Figure 5-78 using a header. Save the letterhead with the file name Rose Letterhead.

2. Begin the mail merge process by clicking Tools on the menu bar and then clicking Mail Merge. Specify the current document window as the main document.

3. Create the data source shown in Figure 5-79.

4. In the Data Form dialog box, click the View Data Source button to view the data source in table form. Save the data source with the name Rose Customer List.

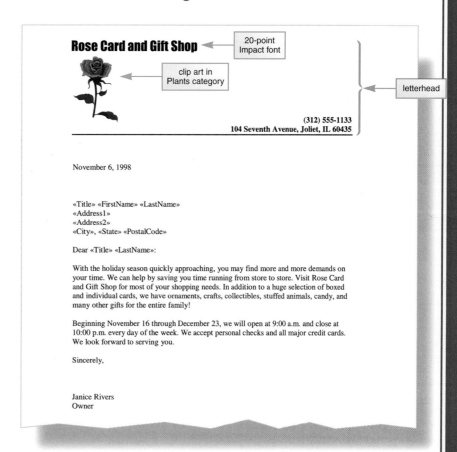

FIGURE 5-78

5. Print the data source.

6. Switch to the main document. Save the main document with a new file name, Rose Form Letter. Change the Normal style to a font size of 12 for the main document. Create the main document for the form letter shown in Figure 5-78. The current date should print at the top of the form letter.

7. Save the main document for the form letter again.

8. Print the main document.

Title	FirstName	LastName	Address1	Address2	City	State	PostalCode
Mr.	Ian	Peters	P.O. Box 19		Orland Park	IL	60462
Ms.	Charlotte	Winters	44 River Road		Joliet	IL	60435
Mrs.	Karen	Bissel	105 Lake Street	Apt. 3D	New Lenox	IL	60451
Dr.	John	Groves	P.O. Box 67		Mokena	IL	60448
Mr.	Samuel	Easton	123 Michigan Avenue	Apt. 5A	Joliet	IL	60435

FIGURE 5-79

(continued)

In the Lab

Creating a Data Source, Form Letter, and Mailing Labels *(continued)*

9. Merge and print the form letters.
10. Click the New button on the Standard toolbar and then address mailing labels using the same data source you used for the form letters. Put bar codes on the mailing labels.
11. Save the mailing labels with the name Rose Mailing Labels.
12. Print the mailing labels.
13. If your printer allows, address envelopes using the same data source you used for the form letters. Put bar codes on the envelopes. Save the envelopes with the name Rose Envelopes. Print the envelopes.

2 Creating a Data Source and a Form Letter with an IF Field

Problem: You are the owner of Magic Time! You have decided to use a form letter to offer a discount to all current customers (Figure 5-80). For those customers who recently ordered a full magic act, you offer a 20% discount; for those who ordered a mini performance, you offer a 10% discount. You decide to use an IF field for this task.

Instructions:

1. Create the letterhead shown at the top of Figure 5-80 using a header. Save the letterhead with the file name, Magic Time Letterhead.
2. Begin the mail merge process by clicking Tools on the menu bar and then clicking Mail Merge. Specify the current document window as the main document.
3. Create the data source shown in Figure 5-81.
4. In the Data Form dialog box, click the View Data Source button to view the data source in table form. Save the data source with the name Magic Time Customer List.
5. Print the data source.

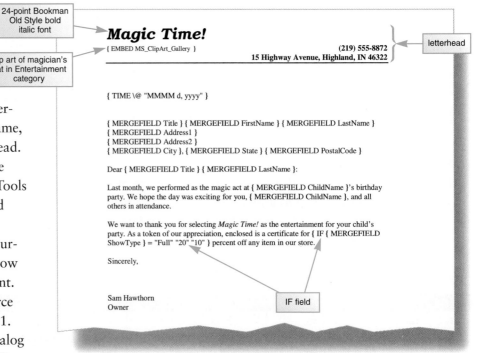

FIGURE 5-80

Title	FirstName	LastName	Address1	Address2	City	State	PostalCode	ChildName	ShowType
Mrs.	Juanita	Evans	175 Gordon Drive		Highland	IN	46322	Bobby	Full
Mr.	Frank	Zimmer	P.O. Box 15		Munster	IN	46321	Jackie	Mini
Ms.	Louise	Roseman	198 Hohman Avenue	Apt. 3A	Hammond	IN	46322	Julie	Mini
Mr.	Conrad	Jones	81 Duluth Street		Highland	IN	46322	Johnny	Full
Mrs.	Brenda	Duley	145 Calumet Avenue	Apt. 17	Hammond	IN	46323	Amanda	Mini

FIGURE 5-81

6. Switch to the main document. Save the main document with a new file name, Magic Time Form Letter. Change the Normal style to a font size of 12 for the main document. Create the main document for the form letter shown in Figure 5-80. The current date should print at the top of the form letter. The IF field tests if ShowType is equal to Full; if it is, then the discount is 20%; otherwise the discount is 10%.

7. Save the main document for the form letter again.

8. Print the main document with field codes on. Do not forget to turn the field codes off.

9. Merge and print the form letters.

3 Creating a Form Letter Using an Access Database as the Data Source

Problem: On Target Travel would like to thank its customers for their business (Figure 5-82). The customer list is stored in an Access database table. If you are using the *Complete Concepts and Techniques* book, the database file is on the Data Disk that accompanies this book; otherwise, see your instructor for the location of the database file. You are to use the Access database table as the data source in the form letters.

Instructions:

1. Create the letterhead shown at the top of Figure 5-82 using a header. Save the letterhead with the file name On Target Letterhead.

2. Begin the mail merge process by clicking Tools on the menu bar and then clicking Mail Merge. Specify the current document window as the main document.

FIGURE 5-82

(continued)

In the Lab

Creating a Form Letter Using an Access Database as the Data Source *(continued)*

3. In the Open Data Source dialog box, click the Files of type box arrow and then click MS Access Databases. Click On Target Client List and then click the Open button. Click Customers in the Microsoft Access dialog box and then click the OK button.

4. Click the Edit the Main Document button. Save the main document with a new file name, On Target Form Letters. Change the Normal style to a font size of 12 for the main document. Create the main document for the form letter shown in Figure 5-82 on the previous page. The current date should print at the top of the form letter. The IF field tests the Type field value: if Type is Personal, then print the word personal; otherwise print the word business.

5. Save the main document for the form letter again.

6. Print the main document with field codes. Do not forget to turn off the field codes after printing them.

7. Merge and print the form letters.

8. Click the New button on the Standard toolbar and address mailing labels using the same data source you used for the form letters. Put bar codes on the mailing labels.

9. Save the mailing labels with the name On Target Mailing Labels.

10. Print the mailing labels.

11. If your printer allows, address envelopes using the same data source you used for the form letters. Put bar codes on the envelopes. Save the envelopes with the name On Target Envelopes. Print the envelopes.

Cases and Places

The difficulty of these case studies varies: ❱ are the least difficult; ❱❱ are more difficult; and ❱❱❱ are the most difficult.

1 ❱ Your school is organizing a bazaar for the weekend of May 16 and May 17. The bazaar will have food booths, arts and crafts, door prizes, games, and contests. As event coordinator, you are responsible for recruiting your fellow classmates to assist during the bazaar. A variety of positions are required: food preparation, food sales, arts and crafts sales, booth setup, announcers, game directors, ticket collectors, cashiers, and more. Create a form letter persuading your classmates to assist during the bazaar. Be sure the form letter has an attractive letterhead containing the school name, address, and an appropriate clip art file. Obtain the names and addresses of five of your classmates and use them as records in the data source. Then, address and print accompanying labels or envelopes for the form letters.

2 ❱ You are coordinating the tenth-annual family reunion for your relatives. The reunion will be held at Grover Park in Wilmington on Saturday, August 8. You have reserved the pavilion at the park from 11:00 a.m. to 6:00 p.m. Each family is to bring a dish for eight to share. You will be providing burgers and brats for the grill, as well as all condiments and paper products. Family members should also bring mitts, bats, volleyballs, horseshoes, and other outdoor game equipment. Create a form letter announcing the family reunion to your relatives. Be sure the form letter has an attractive letterhead with your family name and an appropriate clip art file. Obtain the names and addresses of five of your family members and use them as records in the data source. Then, address and print accompanying labels or envelopes for the form letters.

3 ❱❱ You are currently seeking an employment position in your field of study. You already have prepared a resume and would like to send it to a group of potential employers. You decide to design a cover letter to send with the resume. Obtain a recent newspaper and cut out five classified advertisements pertaining to your field of study. Create the cover letter for your resume as a form letter. Be sure the cover letter has an attractive letterhead containing your name, address, and telephone number, as well as an appropriate clip art file. Use the information in the classified ads for the data source. The data source should contain potential employers' names, addresses, and position type. Use an IF field in your cover letter that prints the words, full-time or part-time, where appropriate, which will depend on whether or not it is a full-time position. Be sure to add a field to your data source for the comparison. Then, address and print accompanying labels or envelopes for the cover letters. Turn in the want ads with your printouts.

Cases and Places

4 ▶▶ Everyone has strong opinions about one or more of many subjects related to government issues (e.g., taxation, welfare, the justice system, etc.). Pick a subject of interest to you and then draft a letter persuading our congressmen to take some action regarding your position. Create your letter as a form letter. Be sure the letter has an attractive letterhead containing your name, address and telephone number, as well as an appropriate clip art file. Surf the Internet for five current senators or representatives. Use their names, addresses, party affiliation, and position as records in your data source. Use two IF fields in your form letter: one to print the party affiliation (Republican or Democrat), where appropriate, and the other to print their position (senator or representative), where appropriate. Be sure to add fields to your data source for these comparisons. Then, address and print accompanying labels or envelopes for the cover letters.

5 ▶▶ You are director of a local charity organization, which receives donations for many causes. This month's theme is health. Pick a health issue of concern to you (e.g., cancer, diabetes, AIDS, etc.) and then draft a letter persuading local businesses to donate to your charity so you can forward the contribution to the appropriate facility. Obtain the names of two facilities in your area, such as hospitals or hospices. Research your health issue either at the library or on the Internet to obtain impressive statistics and other information and then create a form letter containing your research findings. Be sure the letter has an attractive letterhead with an appropriate clip art file. Obtain the actual names and addresses of five major industries in your area. Use these businesses as records in your data source. Use an IF field in your form letter to print the name of the facility closest (e.g., hospital or hospice) to the business from which you seek a donation. Then, address and print accompanying labels or envelopes for the cover letters.

6 ▶▶▶ If Microsoft Access is installed on your system, you can use it to create a table and then use that table as the data source in a mail merge document. Start Access and then create the table in Project 5 on page WD 5.12 as an Access database table. You may need to use Help in Access to assist you in the procedure for creating and saving a database that contains a table. Quit Access. Start Word. Begin the mail merge process as discussed in Project 5. When specifying the data source, click Open Data Source. In the Open Data Source dialog box, change the file type to MS Access Databases and then click the database name of the file you created in Access. Create the form letter in Project 5 so it uses the fields in the Access database table. Then, address and print accompanying labels or envelopes for the cover letters.

7 ▶▶▶ If Microsoft Access is installed on your system, you can use it to create a table and then use that table as the data source in a mail merge document. Start Access and then create the table for the In the Lab 2 exercise as an Access table (Figure 5-81 on page WD 5.57). You may need to use Help in Access to assist you in the procedure for creating and saving a database that contains a table. Quit Access. Start Word. Begin the mail merge process as discussed in Project 5. When specifying the data source, click Open Data Source. In the Open Data Source dialog box, change the file type to MS Access Databases and then click the database name of the file you created in Access. Create the form letter in Figure 5-80 on page WD 5.56 so it uses the fields in the Access database table. Then, address and print accompanying labels or envelopes for the cover letters.

Microsoft Word 97

Creating a Professional Newsletter

Objectives:

You will have mastered the material in this project when you can:

- ❱ Define desktop publishing terminology
- ❱ Add ruling lines above and below paragraphs
- ❱ Insert special symbols in a document
- ❱ Format a document into multiple columns
- ❱ Format a dropped capital letter in a paragraph
- ❱ Position a graphic between columns
- ❱ Insert a column break
- ❱ Place a vertical rule between columns
- ❱ Create a pull-quote
- ❱ Use the Format Painter button
- ❱ Create a macro to automate a task
- ❱ Run a macro
- ❱ Delete a macro
- ❱ Change the color(s) in a graphic
- ❱ Add a text box to a graphic
- ❱ Place a border on a page

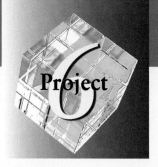

Project 6

From Academic to Zestful

A Newsletter for Every Interest

Women With Wheels. At-Home Dad. Penn State Sports Medicine Newsletter. From the church bulletin to the condominium association activity log, a newsletter exits to suit basically every interest. Each year an estimated 200,000 newsletters are published regularly in the United States, and more than 20,000 appear on the Internet. These numbers are growing as computer users discover desktop publishing software and the dynamic formatting features of word processing programs such as Microsoft Word 97.

Internet neophytes can surf to *NewbieNewz*,™ a free Net newsletter that offers helpful cyberspace advice and instruction. The two million American fathers who stay home with their preschoolers can cure their isolation and find helpful child-care and home business tips with *At-Home Dad*, which was started and is produced by a father who lost his job. The stress and special health problems affecting workers who work when the majority of people sleep are explored in *Shiftworker News*.

Other specialty newsletters have been created, such as *Catnip* for feline

---

Volume VII, No. 2

Women With Wheels ™

The Quarterly Newsletter on...

Automobile Rallying is Great Fun
by: Susan Frissell, Ph.D.

Now that Summer is here it is rally time! In the past couple of years, I've had the pleasure of being involved in several auto "rallies." Rallies with sport clubs, media associations, and specialty groups (convertibles, sport/GT cars). And, it's been far too much fun! In fact, the people, the enthusiasm, and the comradery are almost palpable.

There are rallies that are strictly for fun, and there are rallies for the serious driver. Time-and-Distance rallies are the type of rally you're more likely to find in connection with the avid sports-car club member. For instance, Corvette owners, Porsche owners, and the like, may participate in a Time-and-Distance rally where specific methods of timing, penalties and scoring are adhered to. Time-and-Distance rally scoring is based on the ability of contestants to maintain certain predetermined average speeds over a measured course. Time is an essential ingredient, although distance may also be used as a tie-breaker or as an additional...

the sole reason for participating in a rally. The first time out, participate for no other reason than to have a good time. Consider your first rally an opportunity to learn the ropes. You can learn to practice following route instructions, driving and/or navigating, you will have the chance to practice timing yourself and keeping track of the time. What I hope will be clear is that there are several basic ways of participating in (or running), a successful rally.

Just What is a Rally?

There are a wide variety of auto events that are classified as "rallies." A group of sports-car enthusiasts might get together and plan a picnic, following a specific route. Sponsored by the Club, this cruise may also be referred to as a "tour" or "caravan." As a member of The Midwest Automotive Media Association (M.A.M.A.), I participate in a test-drive of several new model-vehicles, provided by the manufacturers. We refer to our twice-a-year events as "rallies", and as members, we drive a specific route, switching cars and drivers at various checkpoints along the way.

Registration for most, if not all, rallies requires an entrance fee. This can range anywhere from $16 to a couple of thousand dollars (The Great North American Race). Generally, the fees are very reasonable, and will sometimes include snacks (cold drinks, cookies, etc.) at the checkpoints or rest stops, as well as mementos, such as T-shirts, key chains, etc., included in your packet for the early rally route instructions. They contain information to go to, and what average speeds to maintain. Along the route is your get-away.

Why rally... And it's easy to do, the family can stay... Winning or serious...

LANDSPEED LOUISE

SUMMER

AT-HOME DAD NETWORK ™

DAD-TO-DAD
With summer just around the corner, many DAD-to-DAD chapters will be taking their activities outside! A few events planned for the Atlanta chapter include: weekend camping and canoe trip, field trip to a horse ranch, and picnics in the park. So, put on the shorts and T-shirts and hit the outdoors! Speaking of T-shirts, DAD-to-DAD will have T-shirts available to purchase very soon for both children and adults. Look for further info in the next At-Home Dad newsletter. Also, please call me at (770) 643-5964, or dadtodad@aol.com if you need help either getting started or deciding on what activities are best.
Curtis Cooper - Founder, DAD-to-DAD

CHARLOTTESVILLE
March has been an active month for the Charlottesville-Albemarle Dad-to-Dad group. Three more fathers have expressed an interest in the group as a result of some television coverage, an ad in the C-Ville Weekly and a friendly invitation at Jungle Maxx. We've even had one very brave mother come to one of the play sessions. Also, Michael Duggan has worked hard to create a Home Page for our group on the Comet.Net Web Site. Use the address http://www.comet.net/clubs/dad-to-dad and check us out! Oprah presented the Parent of the Week Award to Curtis Cooper. The segment on Curtis was proud, and it proved to be an follow-up to the story about our...

Later that week, our group size... three! One father and his daughter... like to join us if we ever do a... playgroup. He's also interested... Dads' Night-Out Dinners. Another... and his child plan to join us on... We'll try to schedule two... playgroups for this month.
- Dan Dunsmore, Charlottesville

If you would like to send an update for publication about your... to-DAD chapter or any play... experiences, please send it out... will share it with the readers.

NETWORK BUZZ
Keith Dilley, the at-home dad of sextuplets (profiled in issue 3), has gone to "work" as an airline reservationist. (Ah, the easy life!) His kids are now 3 years old. To keep them in the playroom they use 3 metal baby gates on top of each other, slimed with vaseline.

Brian Basset, the cartoonist who draws Adam, the at-home dad comic strip, now has E-mail. Cyberdads can drop him a line at adamathome@aol.com. See page 7 for info on his new book.

...make the kids picky, they eat cold food, they take out the leftovers from the frig, open it up, we all grab a fork and go at it. This saves the plates so we don't have to do the dishes." Chris' wife Tasia was quick to point out, "What really annoys me is having dirty diapers in our bedroom." In a bizarre segment they ended the show with Chris and Casey modeling clothes. They brought in a fashion consultant who concluded that the clothes have to be of darker colors so when the baby throws up it won't show.

Casey told the consultant, "I've got to have everything with me at all times." He then came down the runway with a fisherman's vest which contained a pocket for everything, diaper, cell phone, baby monitor, bottles and even a remote control. Before the show Mommie told the consultant "...live in shorts, run around the house in... garage, so I... but comfortable th... out with a rep... flannel shirt, w... consultant ca... weekender So... which receive... with boots for...

If you get this early enough and have cable, check out CNBC's feature on this newsletter, Tues, May 28th at 7pm EST, on their show called *The Money Club*.

At-Home Dad readers Casey Spencer ...appeared on the "...25)..." for a...

PENN STATE

SPORTS MEDICINE NEWSLETTER
The Newsletter of Athletic Performance

Volume 5, Number 9, May '97

Table of Contents

lovers, published by Tufts University School of Veterinary Medicine, the *Frugal Bugle* for penny-pinchers, *Childfree Network* for individuals without children who desire equity in the corporate world, *Women with Wheels* for consumers wanting to learn about maintaining and purchasing cars, and *Naturally Well* for health-conscious individuals interested in homeopathic remedies. Other newsletter titles need no explanation: *Thrifty Traveler*, *Spirit of Route 66*, *FluteSounds*, *Growth Stock Outlook*, and *Dreaded Broccoli*.

Baby boomers' interests account for an upswing in specialized publications. For example, *Homeground*, a quarterly newsletter started by a former gardening columnist, and *Virtual Garden*, a newsletter on the Internet being read more than 35,000 times a week, are among the newsletters filling the gardening niche. Also, more than 30 health and nutrition newsletters have sprung up in the past decade with such titles as *Health After 50*, *Nutrition Advocate*, *What Doctors Don't Tell You*, *Health Wisdom for Women*, and *Yale Children's Health Letter*.

Internet users can find a plethora of electronic newsletters, some which also are available in printed versions. Investors might surf to the *Prime Time Investor Mutual Fund Family Newsletters*, which offers more than 100 newsletters discussing thousands of mutual funds and *The Right Investments*, giving daily performance results. Sports lovers can find *Sports Talk NFL News*, the *Trout Talk Fantasy Football Newsletter*, and the *Penn State Sports Medicine Newsletter*. Scientists can discover such diverse sites as the *NATO Science Forum*, the *Electronic Zoo*, and the *History of Australian Science Newsletter*.

A newsletter to evaluate other newsletters even exists. Each month the reviewers for *Newsletter Design* critique publications submitted by organizations. Calling itself a publication for "the desktop generation," *Newsletter Design* examines the overall layout, design, nameplate, shading, ruling lines, and graphics and then offers suggestions for improvement.

Americans are reading print and electronic newsletters in record numbers to satisfy their needs for education and entertainment. And with knowledge of basic design and the formatting features in word processing software, writers can satisfy this thirst for knowledge by using newsletters to express themselves.

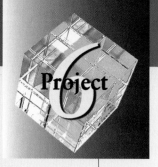

Project

6

Microsoft
Word 97

Creating a Professional Newsletter

Case Perspective

Tom Watson is president of Amateur Aviators, a club for the hobby pilot. Each month Tom prepares the club's newsletter. Because he has built two biplanes, he decides that this month's feature article will cover the basics of building a plane. He types the article in a Word document, covering items such as buying a kit, workspace, and hangar and concludes with a frequently asked questions and answers section. When finished, Tom realizes the article is quite long – about 650 words. Although the monthly newsletter usually is one page, he decides to make it two pages so the entire article will be in this newsletter. He also types the June announcements into a Word file containing about 150 words; the announcements remind members of the annual dues deadline, the July fly-in, and the Aviator's Catalog.

Now Tom's task is to design the newsletter so the How to Build a Plane article spans the first two columns of page 1 and then continues on page 2; the announcements always are located in the third column of the first page of the *Amateur Aviators* newsletter.

Introduction

Professional looking documents, such as newsletters and brochures, often are created using desktop publishing software. With **desktop publishing software**, you can divide a document into multiple columns, insert pictures and wrap text around them, change fonts and font sizes, add color and lines, and so on to make the document original and attractive. A traditionally held opinion of desktop publishing software, such as PageMaker or Ventura, is that it enables you to load an existing word processing document and enhance it through formatting not provided in your word processor. Word, however, provides you with many of the formatting features that you would find in a desktop publishing package. Thus, you can create professional newsletters and brochures directly within Word.

Project Six – Newsletter

Project 6 uses Word to produce the monthly newsletter shown in Figures 6-1 and 6-2 on the next two pages. The newsletter is a monthly publication for members of Amateur Aviators. Notice that it incorporates the desktop publishing features of Word. The newsletter is divided into three columns; includes a graphic of an airplane and a pull-quote, both with text wrapped around them; has both horizontal and vertical lines to separate distinct areas; has page borders; and uses different fonts, font sizes, and color for various characters and the graphic.

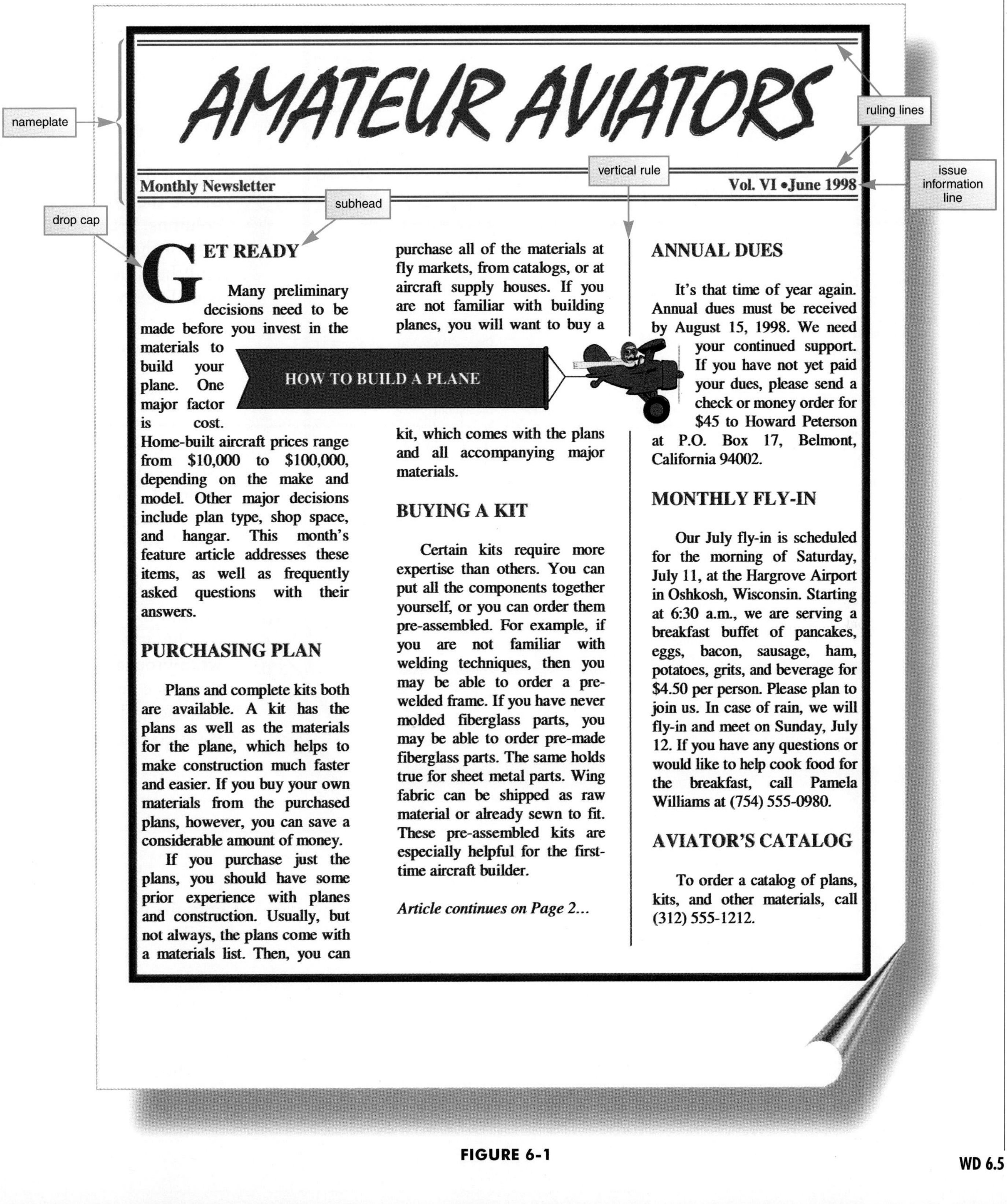

nameplate

AMATEUR AVIATORS

ruling lines

vertical rule

Monthly Newsletter

subhead

Vol. VI •June 1998

issue information line

drop cap

GET READY

Many preliminary decisions need to be made before you invest in the materials to build your plane. One major factor is cost. Home-built aircraft prices range from $10,000 to $100,000, depending on the make and model. Other major decisions include plan type, shop space, and hangar. This month's feature article addresses these items, as well as frequently asked questions with their answers.

PURCHASING PLAN

Plans and complete kits both are available. A kit has the plans as well as the materials for the plane, which helps to make construction much faster and easier. If you buy your own materials from the purchased plans, however, you can save a considerable amount of money.

If you purchase just the plans, you should have some prior experience with planes and construction. Usually, but not always, the plans come with a materials list. Then, you can

purchase all of the materials at fly markets, from catalogs, or at aircraft supply houses. If you are not familiar with building planes, you will want to buy a

HOW TO BUILD A PLANE

kit, which comes with the plans and all accompanying major materials.

BUYING A KIT

Certain kits require more expertise than others. You can put all the components together yourself, or you can order them pre-assembled. For example, if you are not familiar with welding techniques, then you may be able to order a pre-welded frame. If you have never molded fiberglass parts, you may be able to order pre-made fiberglass parts. The same holds true for sheet metal parts. Wing fabric can be shipped as raw material or already sewn to fit. These pre-assembled kits are especially helpful for the first-time aircraft builder.

Article continues on Page 2...

ANNUAL DUES

It's that time of year again. Annual dues must be received by August 15, 1998. We need your continued support. If you have not yet paid your dues, please send a check or money order for $45 to Howard Peterson at P.O. Box 17, Belmont, California 94002.

MONTHLY FLY-IN

Our July fly-in is scheduled for the morning of Saturday, July 11, at the Hargrove Airport in Oshkosh, Wisconsin. Starting at 6:30 a.m., we are serving a breakfast buffet of pancakes, eggs, bacon, sausage, ham, potatoes, grits, and beverage for $4.50 per person. Please plan to join us. In case of rain, we will fly-in and meet on Sunday, July 12. If you have any questions or would like to help cook food for the breakfast, call Pamela Williams at (754) 555-0980.

AVIATOR'S CATALOG

To order a catalog of plans, kits, and other materials, call (312) 555-1212.

FIGURE 6-1

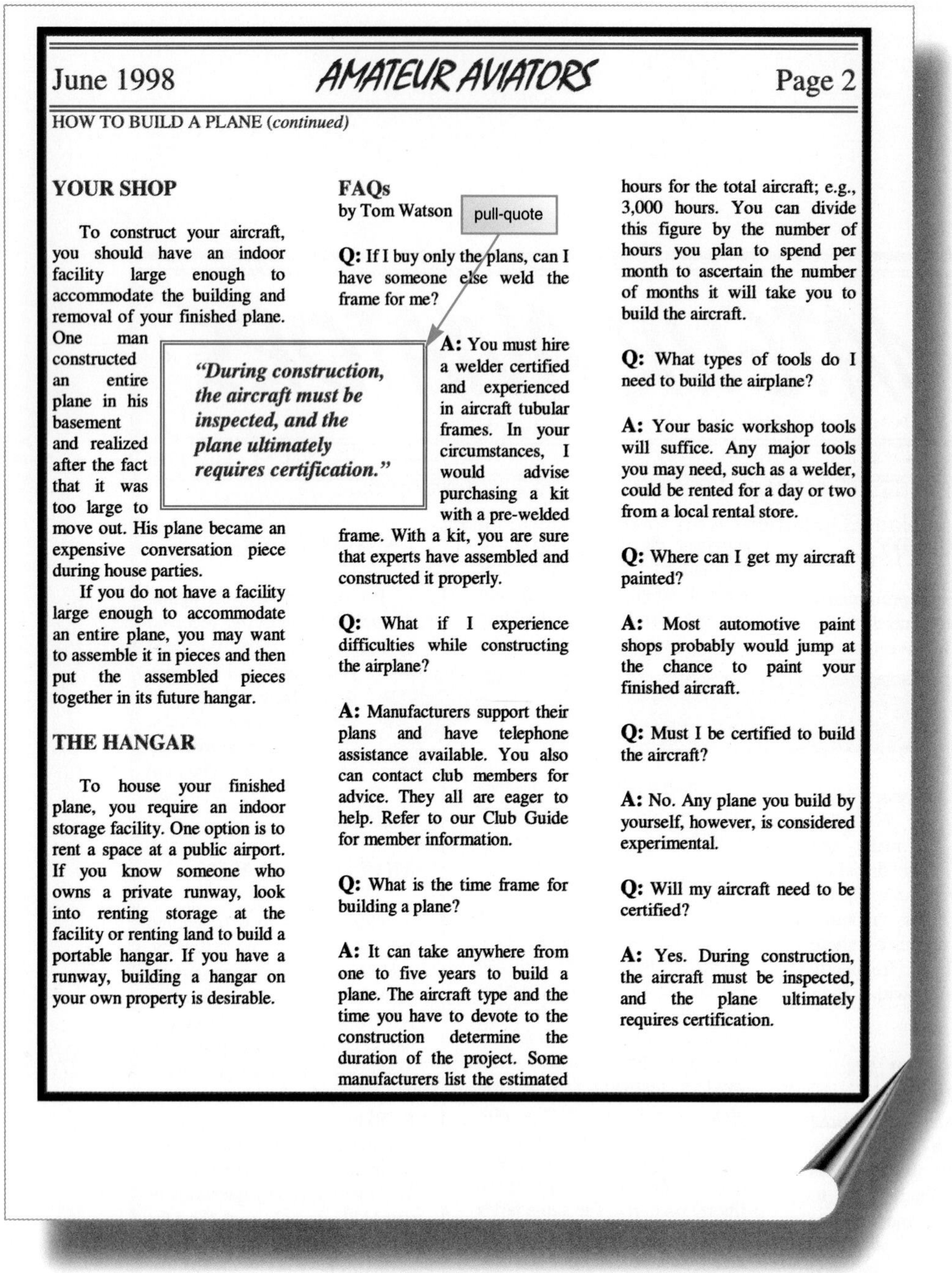

Desktop Publishing Terminology

As you create professional looking newsletters and brochures, you should be aware of several desktop publishing terms. In Project 6 (Figures 6-1 on the previous page and 6-2), the **nameplate,** or **banner,** is the top portion of the newsletter above the three columns. It contains the title of the newsletter and the **issue information line.** The horizontal lines in the nameplate are called **rules,** or **ruling lines.**

Within the body of the newsletter, a heading, such as GET READY, is called a **subhead.** The vertical line dividing the second and third columns on page 1 is a **vertical rule.** The text that wraps around the airplane graphic is referred to as **wrap-around text,** and the space between the graphic and the words is called the **run-around.**

June 1998 — *AMATEUR AVIATORS* — Page 2

HOW TO BUILD A PLANE *(continued)*

YOUR SHOP

To construct your aircraft, you should have an indoor facility large enough to accommodate the building and removal of your finished plane. One man constructed an entire plane in his basement and realized after the fact that it was too large to move out. His plane became an expensive conversation piece during house parties.

If you do not have a facility large enough to accommodate an entire plane, you may want to assemble it in pieces and then put the assembled pieces together in its future hangar.

THE HANGAR

To house your finished plane, you require an indoor storage facility. One option is to rent a space at a public airport. If you know someone who owns a private runway, look into renting storage at the facility or renting land to build a portable hangar. If you have a runway, building a hangar on your own property is desirable.

FAQs
by Tom Watson

pull-quote

Q: If I buy only the plans, can I have someone else weld the frame for me?

"During construction, the aircraft must be inspected, and the plane ultimately requires certification."

A: You must hire a welder certified and experienced in aircraft tubular frames. In your circumstances, I would advise purchasing a kit with a pre-welded frame. With a kit, you are sure that experts have assembled and constructed it properly.

Q: What if I experience difficulties while constructing the airplane?

A: Manufacturers support their plans and have telephone assistance available. You also can contact club members for advice. They all are eager to help. Refer to our Club Guide for member information.

Q: What is the time frame for building a plane?

A: It can take anywhere from one to five years to build a plane. The aircraft type and the time you have to devote to the construction determine the duration of the project. Some manufacturers list the estimated

hours for the total aircraft; e.g., 3,000 hours. You can divide this figure by the number of hours you plan to spend per month to ascertain the number of months it will take you to build the aircraft.

Q: What types of tools do I need to build the airplane?

A: Your basic workshop tools will suffice. Any major tools you may need, such as a welder, could be rented for a day or two from a local rental store.

Q: Where can I get my aircraft painted?

A: Most automotive paint shops probably would jump at the chance to paint your finished aircraft.

Q: Must I be certified to build the aircraft?

A: No. Any plane you build by yourself, however, is considered experimental.

Q: Will my aircraft need to be certified?

A: Yes. During construction, the aircraft must be inspected, and the plane ultimately requires certification.

FIGURE 6-2

Document Preparation Steps

Document preparation steps give you an overview of how the newsletter in Figures 6-1 and 6-2 will be developed. The following tasks will be completed in this project:

1. Create the nameplate.
2. Format the first page of the body of the newsletter.
3. Format the second page of the newsletter.
4. Enhance the newsletter with color using the Format Painter button and a macro.
5. Edit the graphic in the newsletter.

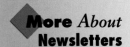

The following pages contain a detailed explanation of each of these tasks.

Because this project involves several steps requiring you to drag the mouse, you may want to cancel an action if you drag to the wrong location. Remember that you can always click the Undo button on the Standard toolbar to cancel your most recent action.

Starting Word

Follow these steps to start Word or ask your instructor how to start Word for your system.

TO START WORD

1. Click the Start button on the taskbar.
2. Click New Office Document on the Start menu. If necessary, click the General tab when the New Office Document dialog box first opens.
3. Double-click the Blank Document icon in the General sheet.
4. If the Word screen is not maximized, double-click its title bar to maximize it.

Office starts Word. After a few moments, an empty document titled Document1 displays on the Word screen.

Displaying Nonprinting Characters

It is helpful to display nonprinting characters that indicate where in the document you pressed the ENTER key, SPACEBAR, or TAB key. Thus, you should display the nonprinting characters as described below.

TO DISPLAY NONPRINTING CHARACTERS

1. If the Show/Hide ¶ button on the Standard toolbar is not already recessed, click it.

Word displays nonprinting characters in the document window, and the Show/Hide ¶ button on the Standard toolbar is recessed (Figure 6-3 on the next page).

Redefining the Normal Style

Recall from Project 5 that your desired document settings may differ from Word's default settings. In these cases, it is good practice to define your document settings and save these settings in the Normal style to ensure that the entire document follows the same style. Much of the text in the newsletter in Project 6 has a font size of 12. Use the steps on the next page to redefine the Normal style to a font size of 12, if your default is a font size other than 12. For a detailed example of the procedure summarized on the next page, refer to pages WD 5.21 through 5.23 in Project 5.

TO REDEFINE THE NORMAL STYLE

1 Click Format on the menu bar and then click Style.

2 When the Style dialog box displays, be sure Normal is selected in the Styles list box and then click the Modify button.

3 When the Modify Style dialog box displays, click the Format button and then click Font.

4 When the Font dialog box displays, click 12 in the Size list box and then click the OK button in the Font dialog box.

5 Click the OK button in the Modify Style dialog box, then click the Apply button in the Style dialog box.

Word redefines the Normal style to 12 point.

Changing All Margin Settings

As you may recall, Word is preset to use standard 8.5-by-11-inch paper, with 1.25-inch left and right margins and 1-inch top and bottom margins. For the newsletter in this project, you want the left, right, and top margins to be .5 inch and the bottom margin to be 1 inch. Thus, you want to change the left, right, and top margin settings as described in the following steps.

TO CHANGE ALL MARGIN SETTINGS

1 Click File on the menu bar and then click Page Setup.

2 When the Page Setup dialog box displays, type .5 in the Top text box and then press the TAB key twice; type .5 in the Left text box and then press the TAB key; type .5 in the Right text box and then point to the OK button (Figure 6-3).

3 Click the OK button to change the margin settings for this document.

Once you have completed Step 2, the Page Setup dialog box displays as shown in Figure 6-3. Depending on the printer you are using, you may need to set the margins differently for this project.

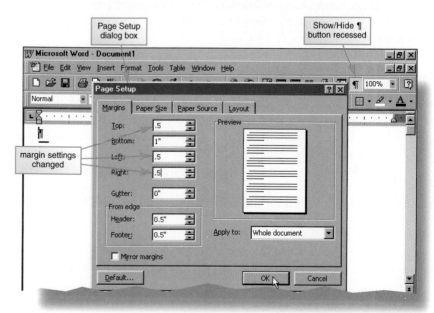

FIGURE 6-3

Creating the Nameplate

The nameplate in Project 6 consists of all the text above the multiple columns (see Figure 6-1 on page WD 6.5). The nameplate is composed of the newsletter title, AMATEUR AVIATORS, and the issue information line. The steps on the following pages illustrate how to create the nameplate for the first page of the newsletter in Project 6.

Entering the Newsletter Title

In Project 6, the newsletter title is formatted to 72-point Mistral teal, bold italic font. Follow these steps to format and enter the newsletter title.

TO FORMAT AND ENTER TEXT

1. Click the Font box arrow on the Formatting toolbar. Scroll to and then click Mistral (or a similar font) in the list.
2. Click the Font Size box arrow on the Formatting toolbar. Scroll to and then click 72 in the list.
3. Click the Bold button on the Formatting toolbar. Click the Italic button on the Formatting toolbar.
4. Click the Center button on the Formatting toolbar.
5. Click the Font Color button arrow on the Formatting toolbar and then click the color Teal.
6. Type AMATEUR AVIATORS and then press the ENTER key.
7. Click the Align Left button on the Formatting toolbar.

Word displays the newsletter title in 72-point Mistral teal, bold italic font (Figure 6-4).

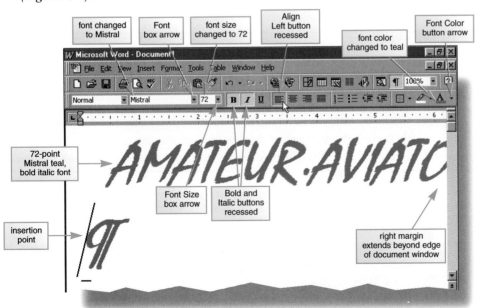

FIGURE 6-4

When you changed the margin settings earlier in this project, the right margin moved beyond the right edge of the document window. Thus, part of the newsletter title does not display in the document window.

Zooming page width brings both the left and right margins of a document into view in the document window. If the left and right margins do not both display in the document window, follow these steps to zoom page width.

TO ZOOM PAGE WIDTH

① Click the Zoom box arrow on the Standard toolbar.
② Click Page Width in the list.

Word brings both the left and right margins into view in the document window (Figure 6-5).

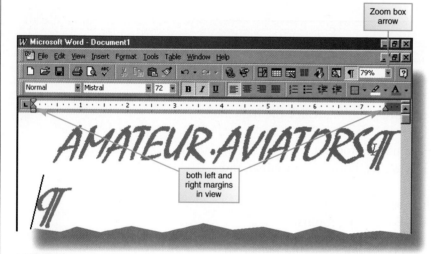

FIGURE 6-5

The next step is to add rules, or ruling lines, above and below the newsletter title.

Adding Ruling Lines to Divide Text

In Word, you use borders to create **ruling lines**. Borders can be placed on any edge of a paragraph(s), that is, the top, bottom, left, or right edges. Ruling lines generally display both above and below a paragraph. Perform the following steps to place ruling lines above and below the newsletter title.

TO ADD RULING LINES

① Click somewhere in the newsletter title.
② If necessary, click the Tables and Borders button on the Standard toolbar to display the Tables and Borders toolbar.
③ Click the Line Style box arrow on the Tables and Borders toolbar and then click the first set of double lines in the list.
④ Click the Line Weight box arrow on the Tables and Borders toolbar and then click 1 ½ pt.
⑤ Click the Border Color button on the Tables and Borders toolbar and then click the color Red.
⑥ Click the Outside Border button arrow on the Tables and Borders toolbar and then click Top Border. Click the Border button arrow again and then point to Bottom Border (Figure 6-6).
⑦ Click Bottom Border.
⑧ Click the Tables and Borders button on the Standard toolbar to remove the Tables and Borders toolbar. Click the Normal View button at the bottom of the Word screen.

Once you have completed Step 6, the newsletter title and Tables and Borders toolbar display as shown in Figure 6-6.

Recall that borders are part of paragraph formatting. If you press the ENTER key in a bordered paragraph, the border will carry forward to the next paragraph. To avoid this, move the insertion point outside of the bordered paragraph before pressing the ENTER key.

The next step is to enter the issue information line in the nameplate.

Inserting Symbols into a Document

The issue information line in this project contains the volume number and date of the newsletter. It also displays a large round dot between the volume number and the date of the newsletter. This special symbol, called a **bullet**, is not on the keyboard. You insert bullets and other special symbols, such as letters in the Greek alphabet and mathematical characters, using the Symbol dialog box. Perform the following steps to add a bullet symbol in the issue information line.

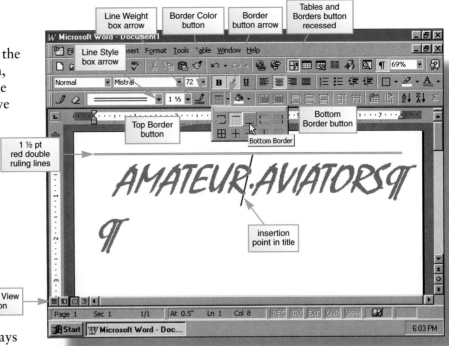

FIGURE 6-6

Steps **To Insert a Symbol into Text**

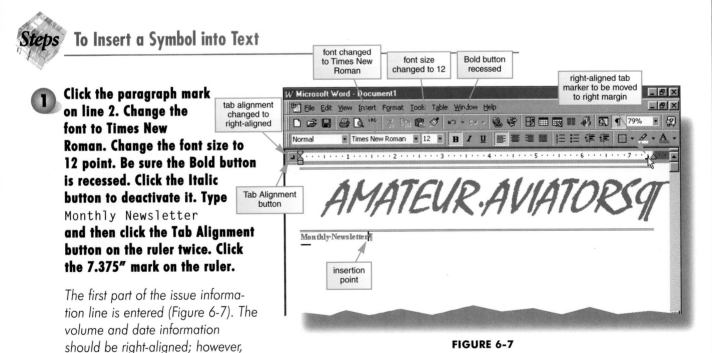

① Click the paragraph mark on line 2. Change the font to Times New Roman. Change the font size to 12 point. Be sure the Bold button is recessed. Click the Italic button to deactivate it. Type Monthly Newsletter **and then click the Tab Alignment button on the ruler twice. Click the 7.375″ mark on the ruler.**

The first part of the issue information line is entered (Figure 6-7). The volume and date information should be right-aligned; however, the words, Monthly Newsletter, should be at the left margin. Thus, you want one part of the paragraph

FIGURE 6-7

to be left-aligned and the other to be right-aligned. Because you can specify only one type of alignment for a single paragraph, you must use a right-aligned custom tab stop for the volume and date information. You cannot click a tab directly at the right margin, which explains why you click the 7.375″ mark and then drag the tab marker to the right margin.

2 Drag the right-aligned tab marker from the 7.375" mark on the ruler to the 7.5" mark on the ruler (where the gray meets the white). Press the TAB key. Type Vol. VI and then press the SPACEBAR. Click Insert on the menu bar and then point to Symbol.

The volume information displays at the right margin of the document (Figure 6-8). Notice the right-aligned tab marker is positioned directly on top of the right margin on the ruler.

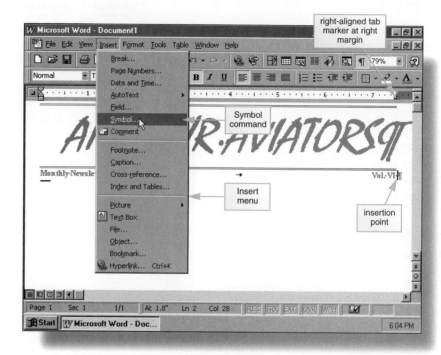

FIGURE 6-8

3 Click Symbol. If necessary, click the Symbols tab when the Symbol dialog box first opens. If necessary, click the Font box arrow in the Symbol dialog box and then click Symbol. If it is not already selected, click the bullet symbol. Click the Insert button.

*Word displays the **Symbol dialog box** (Figure 6-9). When you click a symbol in the list, it becomes enlarged so that you can see it more clearly. A selected symbol is highlighted. Because you clicked the Insert button, the bullet symbol appears in the document to the left of the insertion point. At this point, you can insert additional symbols or close the Symbol dialog box.*

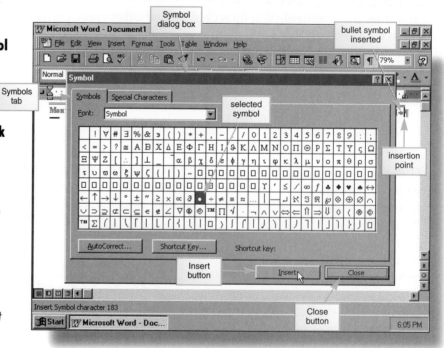

FIGURE 6-9

4 Click the Close button in the Symbol dialog box. Press the SPACEBAR. Type June 1998 and then press the ENTER key. Click in the issue information line. If necessary, click the Tables and Borders button on the Standard toolbar to display the Tables and Borders toolbar. Click the Border button arrow on the Tables and Borders toolbar and then click Bottom Border. Click the Tables and Borders button on the Standard toolbar. Click the Normal View button at the bottom of the Word screen. Click the paragraph mark on line 3. Click the Bold button on the Formatting toolbar to deactivate it. Click the Font Color button arrow on the Formatting toolbar and then click Automatic. Scroll up to display the entire nameplate.

The issue information line is complete (Figure 6-10).

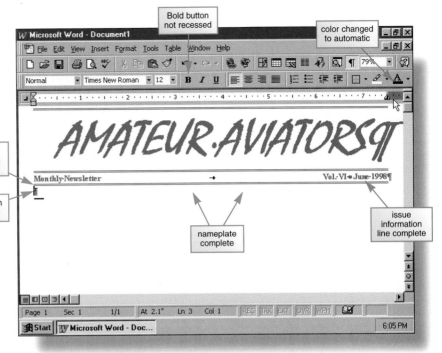

FIGURE 6-10

You also can insert ANSI characters into a document by entering the ANSI code directly into the document. The **ANSI characters** are a predefined set of characters, including both characters on the keyboard and special characters, such as the bullet symbol. To enter the ANSI code, make sure the NUM LOCK key is on. Press and hold the ALT key and then type the number zero followed by the ANSI code for the character. You *must* use the numeric keypad when entering the ANSI code. For a complete list of ANSI codes, see your Microsoft Windows documentation.

The nameplate is now complete. The next step is to enter and format the body of the newsletter.

Formatting the First Page of the Body of the Newsletter

The body of the newsletter in this project is divided into three columns (see Figure 6-1 on page WD 6.5). The airplane graphic displays across the first, second, and third columns on page 1. A vertical rule separates the second and third columns on page 1. The steps on the following pages illustrate how to format the first page of the body of the newsletter using these desktop publishing features.

More *About*
Newspaper Columns

Narrow columns are generally easier to read than wide ones; however, because columns can be too narrow, try to have between five and fifteen words per line. To do this, you may need to adjust the column width, the font size, or the leading. Leading is the line spacing, which can be adjusted through the Paragraph dialog box in Word.

Formatting a Document into Multiple Columns

With Word, you can create two types of columns: parallel columns and snaking columns. **Parallel columns**, or table columns, are created with the Insert Table button. You created parallel columns in Project 4. The text in **snaking columns**, or newspaper columns, flows from the bottom of one column to the top of the next. The body of the newsletter in Project 6 uses snaking columns.

When you begin a document in Word, it has one column. You can divide a portion of a document or the entire document into multiple columns. Within each column, you can type, modify, or format text.

To divide a portion of a document into multiple columns, you first must insert a section break. In this project, the nameplate is one column and the body of the newsletter is three columns. Thus, you must insert a continuous section break below the nameplate. *Continuous* means you want the new section on the same page as the previous section. Perform the following steps to divide the body of the newsletter into three columns.

Steps To Insert a Continuous Section Break

1 **With the insertion point on line 3, press the ENTER key twice. Click Insert on the menu bar and then click Break. Click Continuous in the Section breaks area of the Break dialog box. Point to the OK button.**

Word displays the Break dialog box (Figure 6-11). Continuous means you want the new section on the same page as the previous section.

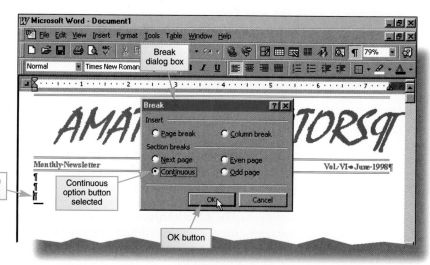

FIGURE 6-11

2 **Click the OK button.**

Word inserts a section break above the insertion point (Figure 6-12). The insertion point now is located in section 2.

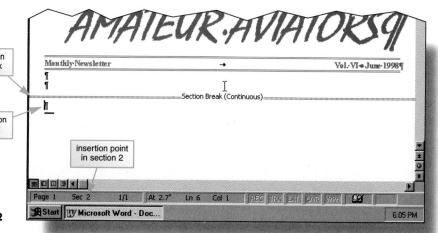

FIGURE 6-12

The next step is to format the second section to three columns.

 To Format Columns

1 **Be sure the insertion point is in section 2. Click the Columns button on the Standard toolbar.**

Word displays the columns list graphic below the Columns button (Figure 6-13).

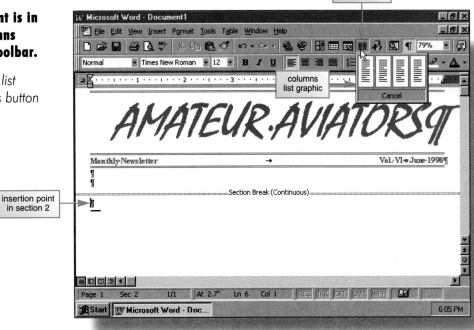

FIGURE 6-13

2 **Point to the third column in the columns list graphic (Figure 6-14).**

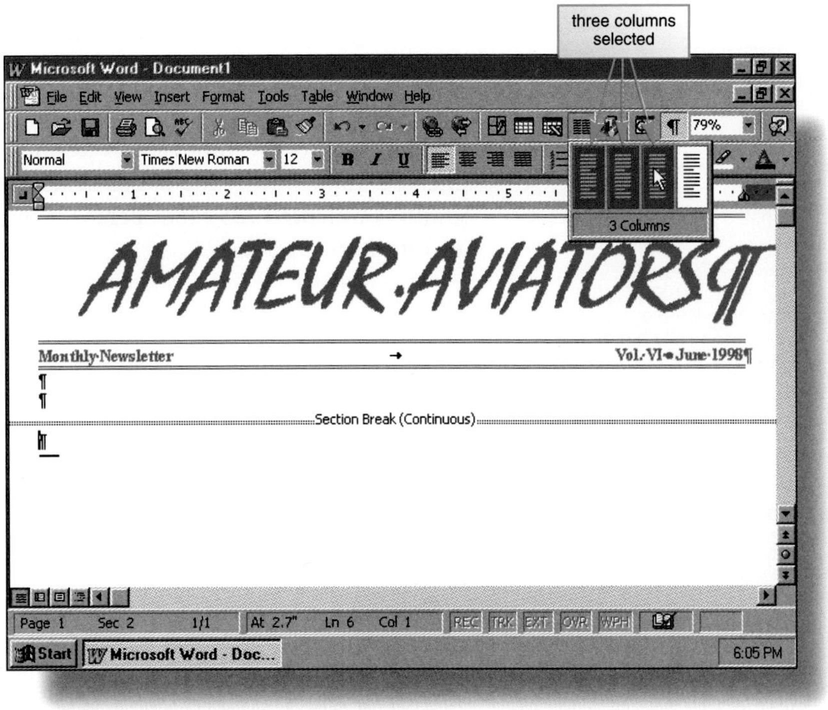

FIGURE 6-14

3 **Click the third column. If necessary, click the Zoom box arrow and then click Page Width.**

Word divides the section containing the insertion point into three evenly sized and spaced columns (Figure 6-15). Notice that the ruler indicates the size of the three columns. Word switches to page layout view because columns do not display properly in normal view.

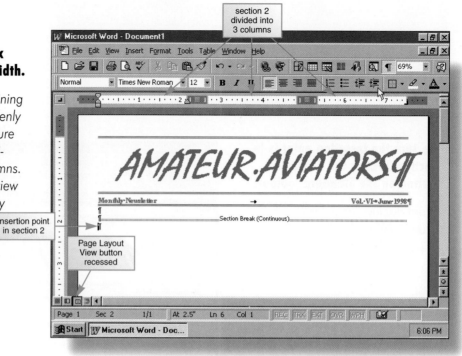

FIGURE 6-15

When you use the Columns button to create columns, Word creates columns of equal width. You can create columns of unequal width by clicking Columns on the Format menu.

Entering a Subhead and Associated Text

Subheads are headings placed throughout the body of the newsletter, such as GET READY. In this project, the subheads are bold and have a font size of 14. The text below the subheads is **justified**, which means that the left and right margins are aligned, like the edges of newspaper columns. The first line of each paragraph is indented .25 inch. Perform the following steps to enter the first subhead and its associated text.

Steps **To Enter Subheads and Associated Text**

1 **Change the font size to 14. Click the Bold button. Type** GET READY **and then click the Bold button. Change the font size back to 12 and then press the ENTER key twice. Drag the First Line Indent marker on the ruler to the .25″ mark.**

The first subhead is entered and the insertion point is indented .25 inch (Figure 6-16).

First Line Indent marker at .25″ mark on ruler

subhead entered

insertion point at .25″

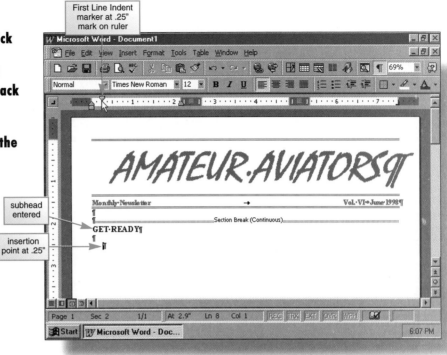

FIGURE 6-16

2 **Click the Justify button on the Formatting toolbar. Type the paragraph below the GET READY subhead. The paragraph is shown in Figure 6-18 on the next page.**

Word aligns both the left and right edges of the paragraph automatically (Figure 6-17). Notice that extra space is placed between some words when you justify text.

Justify button recessed

extra space inserted in justified paragraph

paragraph entered

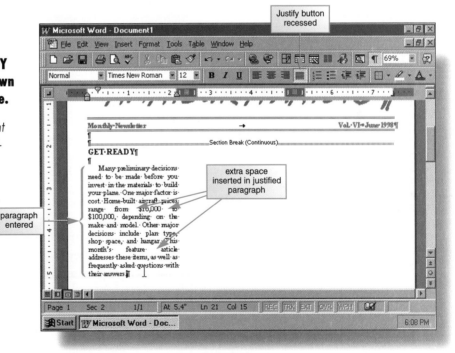

FIGURE 6-17

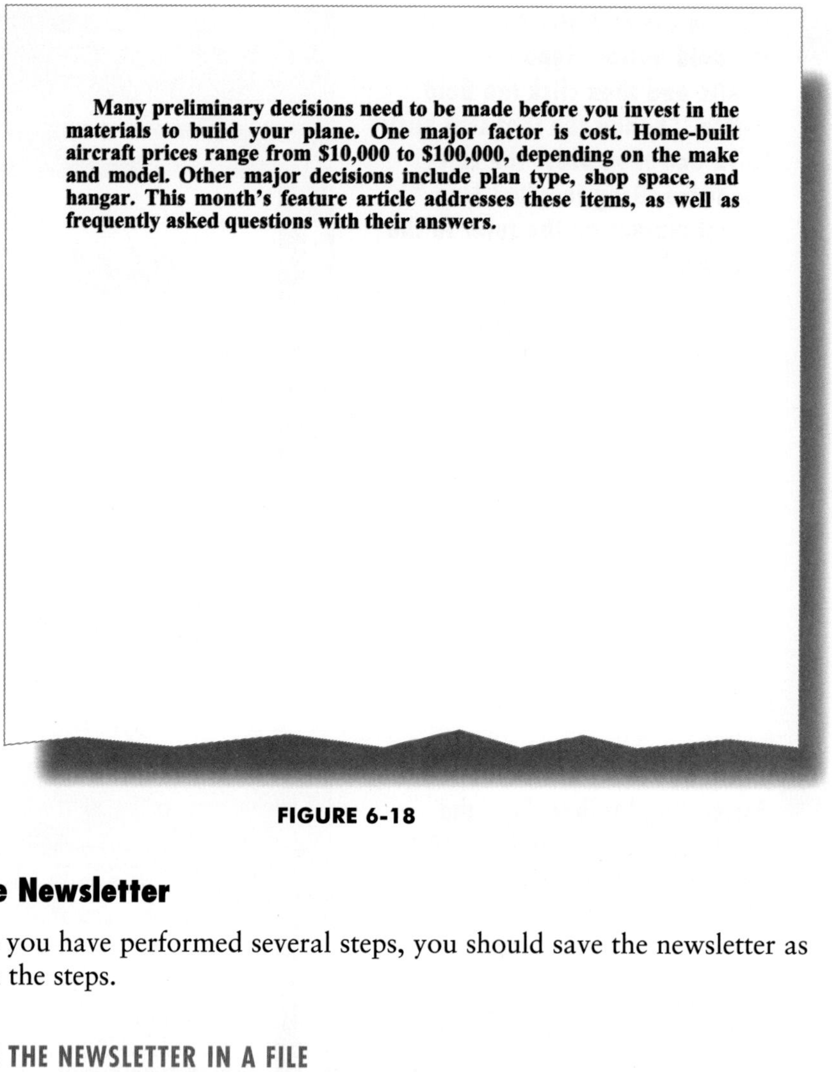

Many preliminary decisions need to be made before you invest in the materials to build your plane. One major factor is cost. Home-built aircraft prices range from $10,000 to $100,000, depending on the make and model. Other major decisions include plan type, shop space, and hangar. This month's feature article addresses these items, as well as frequently asked questions with their answers.

FIGURE 6-18

Saving the Newsletter

Because you have performed several steps, you should save the newsletter as described in the steps.

TO SAVE THE NEWSLETTER IN A FILE

1. Insert your floppy disk into drive A.
2. Click the Save button on the Standard toolbar.
3. Type Amateur Aviators Newsletter in the File name text box. Do not press the ENTER key.
4. Click the Save in box arrow and then click 3½ Floppy (A:).
5. Click the Save button in the Save As dialog box.

Word saves the document on a floppy disk in drive A with the file name, Amateur Aviators Newsletter (Figure 6-19).

Inserting the Remainder of the Newsletter Feature Article

Instead of entering the rest of this article into the newsletter for this project, you can insert the file named, How to Build a Plane Article, which is located on the Data Disk that accompanies this book, into the newsletter. This file contains the remainder of the newsletter article. Perform the following steps to insert the How to Build a Plane Article into the newsletter.

Steps To Insert a File into the Newsletter

1 **Press the ENTER key. Drag the first-line indent marker back to the 0" mark on the ruler. Press the ENTER key again. Insert the Data Disk that accompanies this book into drive A. Click Insert on the menu bar and then click File. If necessary, click the Look in box arrow and then click 3½ Floppy (A:). Double-click the Word folder. If it is not already recessed, click the Preview button. Click How to Build a Plane Article.**

Word displays the Insert File dialog box (Figure 6-19). The contents of the selected file (How to Build a Plane Article) display when the Preview button is recessed. The file will be inserted at the location of the insertion point in the document.

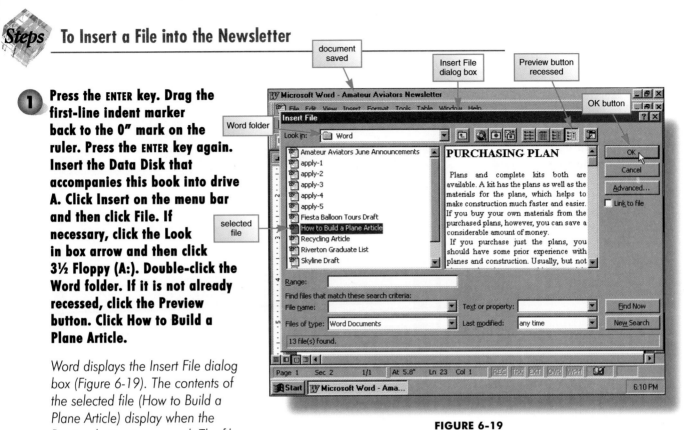

FIGURE 6-19

2 **Click the OK button. Replace the Data Disk with your floppy disk.**

Word inserts the file, How to Build a Plane Article, into the file Amateur Aviators Newsletter at the location of the insertion point (Figure 6-20).

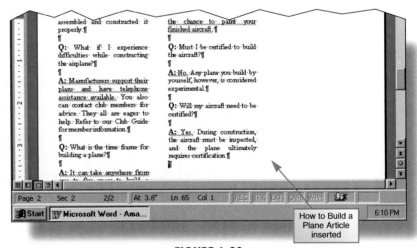

FIGURE 6-20

Creating a Dropped Capital Letter

You can format the first character or word in a paragraph to be dropped. A **dropped capital letter**, or **drop cap**, appears larger than the rest of the characters in the paragraph. The text in the paragraph wraps around the dropped capital letter. Perform the steps on the next page to create a dropped capital letter for the GET READY subhead in the newsletter.

Steps **To Create a Dropped Capital Letter**

1 Press the CTRL+HOME keys to scroll to the top of the document window. Click anywhere in the GET READY paragraph. Click Format on the menu bar and then point to Drop Cap.

The insertion point is in the GET READY paragraph (Figure 6-21).

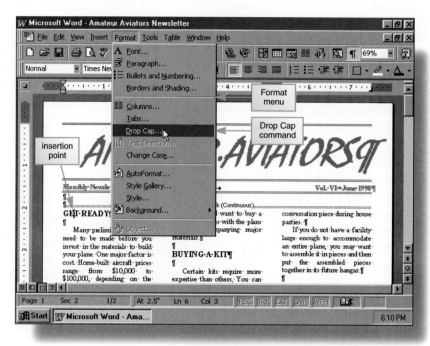

FIGURE 6-21

2 Click Drop Cap. Click Dropped in the Position area of the Drop Cap dialog box.

Word displays the Drop Cap dialog box (Figure 6-22).

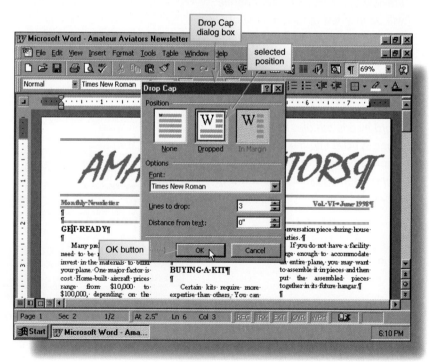

FIGURE 6-22

③ Click the OK button.

Word drops the letter G in the GET READY paragraph, and wraps subsequent text around the dropped capital G (Figure 6-23).

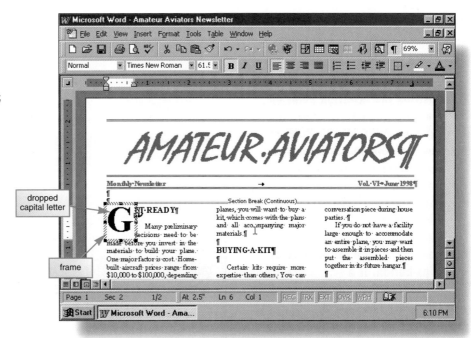

FIGURE 6-23

When you drop cap a letter, Word places a **frame** around it. A framed object is one that you can position anywhere on the page.

The next step is to insert the airplane graphic and position it across the first, second, and third columns.

Positioning Graphics on the Page

Recall that you insert a graphic into a document using the Picture command on the Insert menu. You can import graphics from the Microsoft Clip Gallery that accompanies Word, or you can import them from the Microsoft Clip Gallery Live page on the Web. In Project 4, after you imported the graphic, you turned off the Float over text check box in the Format Picture dialog box so the picture became part of a paragraph. In this project, you want to position the graphic across multiple columns; thus, you will not turn off the Float over text check box.

Perform the steps on the next page to download an airplane graphic from Microsoft's Clip Gallery Live Web page, import the clip art file into the document, and then position the graphic across the first, second, and third columns of page 1 in the newsletter.

NOTE: The steps on the next page assume you are using Microsoft Internet Explorer as your browser and that you have access to the Web. If you are not using Internet Explorer or you do not have access to the Web, you will need to perform a different set of steps. Your browser's handling of pictures on the Web will be discovered in Step 2. If necessary, you may be directed to follow the steps on page WD 6.23 to install the picture from the Data Disk that accompanies this book. If you do not have access to the Web, go directly to the steps on page WD 6.23.

More *About*
Graphics

The use of real photographs in a newsletter adds professionalism to the document. You can insert them yourself if you have a scanner; otherwise, you can work with a print shop. When using photos, you may need to crop, or trim out, the edges. If you have a scanner, you can crop the images on your own computer.

Steps To Download Clip Art from Microsoft's Clip Gallery Live Web Page

1 Scroll through the document and position the insertion point on the paragraph mark above the subhead PURCHASING PLAN in the first column. Click Insert on the menu bar, point to Picture, and then click Clip Art. If necessary, click the Clip Art tab when the Microsoft Clip Gallery dialog box first opens. Click the Connect to Web for additional clips button. If a Connect to Web for More Clip Art, Photos, Sounds dialog box displays, click its OK button. When the Clip Gallery Live window opens, click the Accept button in the left frame. Be sure the ClipArt button is recessed, click the Search button, type planes in the Enter keywords text box, then click the Find button.

Microsoft Clip Gallery Live displays in a new window (Figure 6-24). Recall that to download a file into the Microsoft Clip Gallery, you click the file name that displays below the clip art graphic.

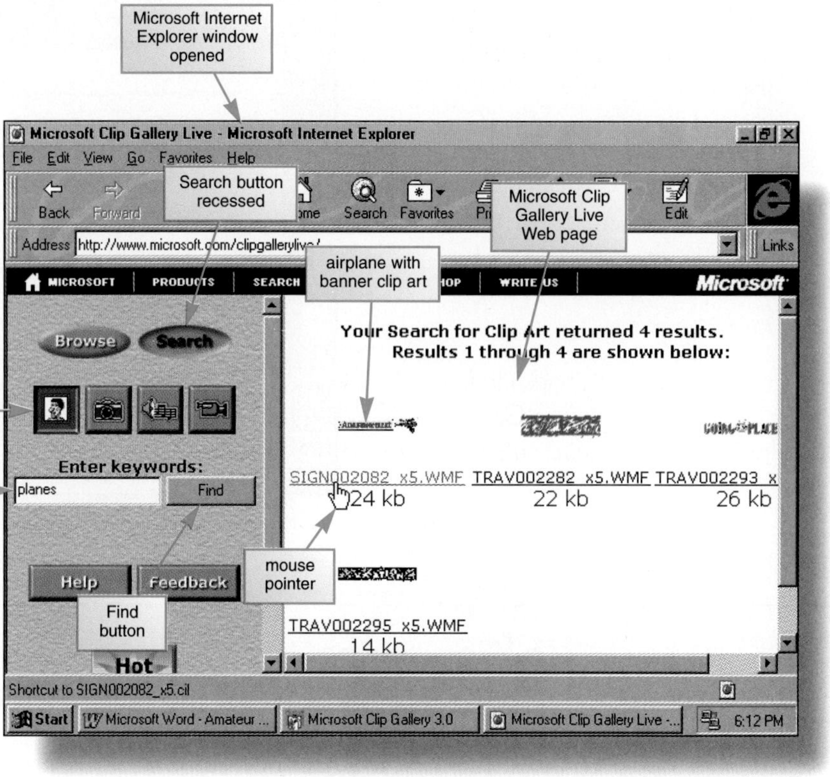

Microsoft Internet Explorer window opened

Microsoft Clip Gallery Live - Microsoft Internet Explorer

File   Edit   View   Go   Favorites   Help

Search button recessed

Back   Forward   ...me   Search   Favorites   Pr...   Edit

Microsoft Clip Gallery Live Web page

Address http://www.microsoft.com/clipgallerylive/   Links

MICROSOFT   PRODUCTS   SEARCH   ...OP   WRITE US   *Microsoft*

airplane with banner clip art

Browse   Search

ClipArt button recessed

Your Search for Clip Art returned 4 results.
Results 1 through 4 are shown below:

search text entered

Enter keywords:

planes   Find

SIGN002082_x5.WMF   TRAV002282_x5.WMF   TRAV002293_x
24 kb   22 kb   26 kb

Help   Feedback

mouse pointer

Find button

TRAV002295_x5.WMF
14 kb

Hot

Shortcut to SIGN002082_x5.cil

Start   Microsoft Word - Amateur...   Microsoft Clip Gallery 3.0   Microsoft Clip Gallery Live -...   6:12 PM

FIGURE 6-24

2 Click the file name SIGN002082_x5.WMF. (If your browser displays a dialog box asking whether you want to open the file or save the file, click Open and then click the OK button. If your browser displays a dialog box and Open is not an option, close your browser window, click the Close button in the Microsoft Clip Gallery dialog box, then go to the steps below).

Your browser downloads the file into your Microsoft Clip Gallery in the Downloaded Clips category (Figure 6-25).

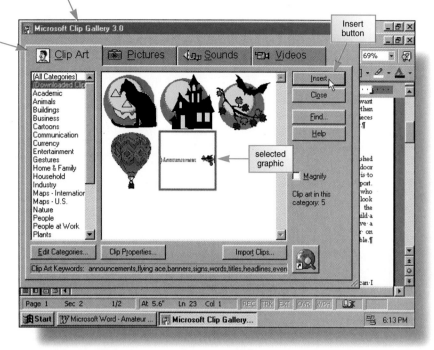

FIGURE 6-25

3 If it is not already selected, click the airplane graphic and then click the Insert button. Close your browser window.

Word inserts the airplane graphic into your document as a floating picture (Figure 6-26 on the next page).

If you do not have access to the Web, you have to install the clip art file into the Microsoft Clip Gallery from the Data Disk that accompanies this book as described in the following steps.

TO INSTALL THE CLIP ART FILE FROM THE DATA DISK

1 Position the insertion point on the paragraph mark above the subhead PURCHASING PLAN in first column.

2 Click Insert on the menu bar, point to Picture on the Insert menu, and then point to Clip Art on the Picture submenu.

3 Click Clip Art. If necessary, click the Clip Art tab when the Microsoft Clip Gallery dialog box first opens.

4 Insert the Data Disk that accompanies this book into drive A.

5 Click the Start button on the taskbar, point to Programs on the Start menu, and then click Windows Explorer. When the Exploring window displays, scroll to the top of the All Folders side of the window and then click 3½ Floppy (A:) to select drive A. Double-click the Word folder in the Contents side of the window to display the contents of the Data Disk.

6 Double-click the file name SIGN002082_x5.cil on the Data Disk. Close the Exploring window.

7 When the Microsoft Clip Gallery redisplays, click the airplane clip art and then click the Insert button. Replace the Data Disk with your floppy disk.

Word inserts the airplane clip art graphic into your document as a floating picture (Figure 6-26 below).

The next step is to specify how the text is to wrap around the graphic and then position the graphic across the first, second, and third columns of page 1 in the newsletter.

Steps **To Position a Graphic Anywhere on a Page**

1 **If necessary, click the airplane graphic to select it. If the Picture toolbar does not display, right-click the clip art graphic and then click Show Picture Toolbar on the shortcut menu. Point to the Format Picture button on the Picture toolbar.**

Word selects the airplane graphic (Figure 6-26). Recall that selected graphics display surrounded by sizing handles at each corner and middle location.

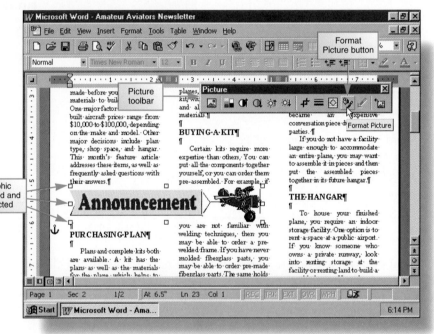

FIGURE 6-26

2 **Click the Format Picture button. When the Format Picture dialog box displays, click the Wrapping tab and then click Square in the Wrapping style area.**

*Word displays the Format Picture dialog box (Figure 6-27). The **wrapping styles** specify how the text in the document displays with the graphic.*

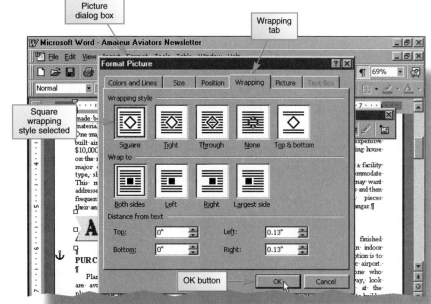

FIGURE 6-27

3 **Click the OK button. Point to the edge of the graphic so the mouse has a four-headed arrow attached to it.**

Word changes the wrapping style to square so the text boxes around the graphic (Figure 6-28). When the mouse has a four-headed arrow attached to it, you can drag the graphic to any location in the document.

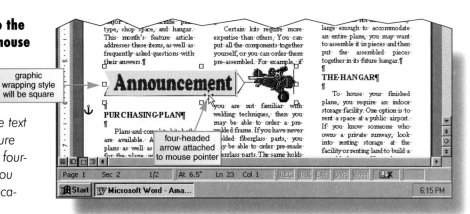

FIGURE 6-28

4 **Drag the graphic to the desired location. (Try to position the graphic as close as possible to Figure 6-29. You may have to drag the airplane graphic a couple of times to position it properly.) Click outside the graphic to remove the selection.**

As the graphic moves, a dotted border indicates its new location. When you release the mouse button, the graphic is positioned at the new location (Figure 6-29). Depending on the printer you are using, your wordwrap may occur in different locations.

FIGURE 6-29

Notice in Figure 6-29 on the previous page that the text in columns one and three wraps around the airplane graphic. Thus, it is called **wrap-around text**. The wrap around forms a square because of the wrapping style set in Step 2. The space between the airplane graphic and the wrap-around text is called the **run-around**.

The next step is to place the monthly announcements in column three of the newsletter.

Inserting a Column Break

Notice in Figure 6-1 on page WD 6.5 that the third column is not a continuation of the article. The third column contains several announcements. The How to Build a Plane article actually is continued on the second page of the newsletter. You want the monthly announcements to be separated into the third column. Thus, you must force a **column break** at the bottom of the second column. Word inserts a column break at the location of the insertion point.

The first step is to force the article to continue on the next page with a **next page section break** and then insert a column break at the bottom of the second column so the announcements always display in the third column.

Steps To Insert a Next Page Section Break

1 Scroll through the document to display the bottom of the second column of the first page in the document window. Click before the Y in the subhead YOUR SHOP. Click Insert on the menu bar and then click Break. Click Next page in the Section breaks area of the Break dialog box.

The insertion point is at the beginning of the subhead YOUR SHOP (Figure 6-30).

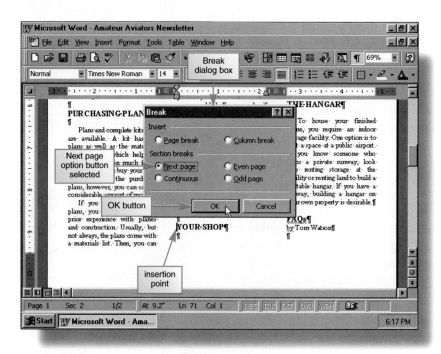

FIGURE 6-30

2 **Click the OK button.**

Word inserts a section break at the location of the insertion point (Figure 6-31). The rest of the article displays on page 2 of the document because the section break included a page break. On page 1, the bottom of the second column and the entire third column are empty.

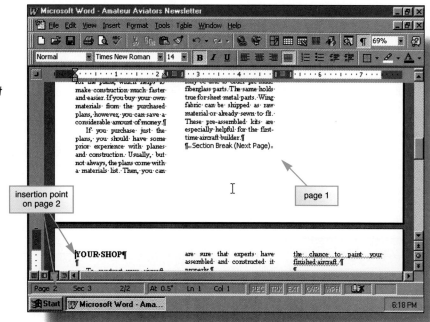

FIGURE 6-31

Because you want the monthly announcements to begin at the top of the third column, the next step is to enter a column break at the end of the text in the second column as shown in these steps.

 Steps **To Insert a Column Break**

1 **Position the insertion point at the end the second column on the first page of the newsletter. Press the ENTER key two times. Drag the First Line Indent marker to the 0″ mark on the ruler in column 2. Click the Italic button on the Formatting toolbar. Type** Article continues on Page 2... **and then click the Italic button again. Press the ENTER key. Click Insert on the menu bar and then click Break. Click Column break in the Break dialog box.**

The insertion point is immediately below the message, Article continues on Page 2 (Figure 6-32).

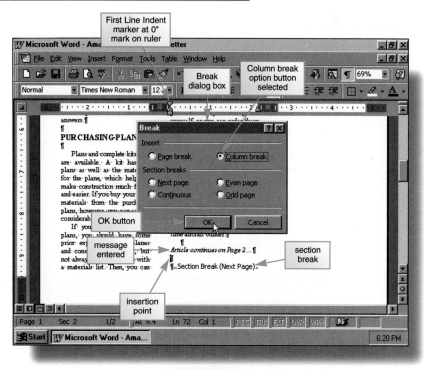

FIGURE 6-32

2 Click the OK button.

Word inserts a column break at the bottom of the second column and advances the insertion point to the top of the third column (Figure 6-33).

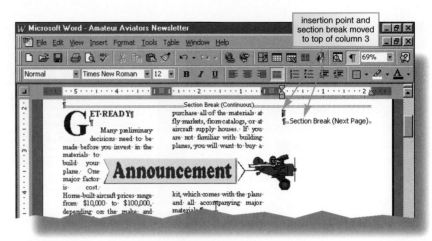

FIGURE 6-33

More *About* Jump Lines

An article that spans multiple pages should contain a jump or jump line, which informs the reader where to look for the rest of the article or story. The message on the first page is called a jump-to line, and a jump-from line marks the beginning of the continuation. The alignment of the jump-to and jump-from lines should be the same.

To eliminate having to enter the entire column of announcements into the newsletter, you can insert the file, Amateur Aviators June Announcements, which is located on the Data Disk that accompanies this book, into the third column of the newsletter. The file contains all of the announcements for this June issue.

TO INSERT A FILE INTO A COLUMN OF THE NEWSLETTER

1. Insert the Data Disk that accompanies this book into drive A.
2. With the insertion point at the top of the third column, click Insert on the menu bar and then click File.
3. When the Insert File dialog box displays, if necessary, click the Look in box arrow and then click 3½ Floppy (A:). If necessary, double-click the Word folder. If it is not already recessed, click the Preview button. If necessary, click Amateur Aviators June Announcements.
4. Click the OK button. Replace with the Data Disk with your floppy disk.

Word inserts the file, Amateur Aviators June Announcements, into the third column of the newsletter (Figure 6-34).

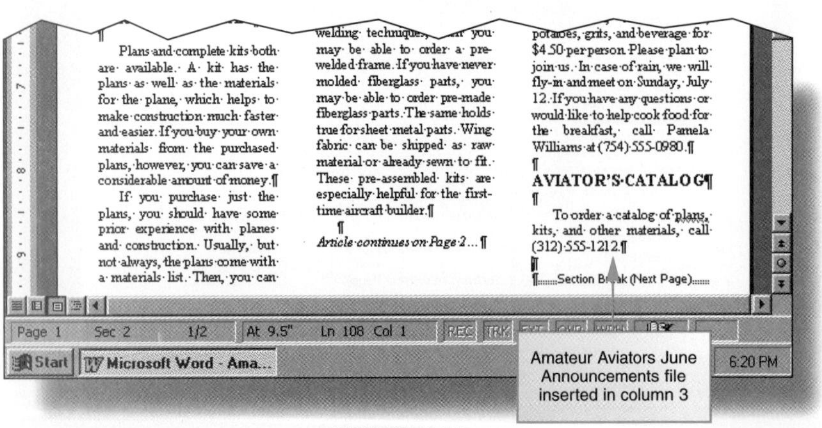

The next step is to place a vertical rule between the second and third columns in the newsletter.

Adding a Vertical Rule Between Columns

In newsletters, you often see a vertical rule separating columns. With Word, you can place a vertical rule between *all* columns by clicking the Columns command on the Format menu and then clicking the Line between check box.

FIGURE 6-34

In this project, you want a vertical rule between *only* the second and third columns. To do this, you add a left border placed several points from the text. Recall that a point is approximately 1/72 of an inch. Perform the following steps to add a vertical rule between the second and third column in the newsletter.

 Steps **To Add a Vertical Rule Between Columns**

1 **Drag the mouse from the top of the third column down to the bottom of the third column. Click Format on the menu bar and then point to Borders and Shading.**

Word highlights the entire third column of page 1 in the newsletter (Figure 6-35).

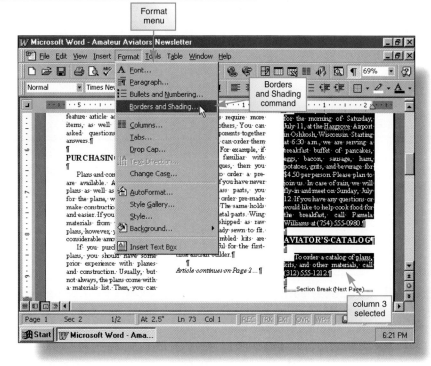

FIGURE 6-35

2 **Click Borders and Shading. If necessary, click the Borders tab when the Borders and Shading dialog box first opens. Point to the left side of the diagram in the Preview area.**

Word displays the Borders and Shading dialog box (Figure 6-36). By clicking sides of the diagram in the Preview area, you can apply borders to the selected paragraph(s).

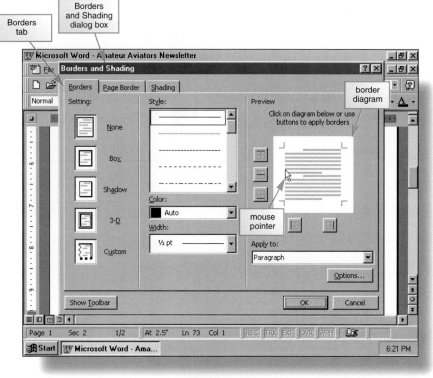

FIGURE 6-36

3 **Click the left side of the diagram in the Preview area. Point to the Options button.**

Word draws a border on the left edge of the diagram (Figure 6-37).

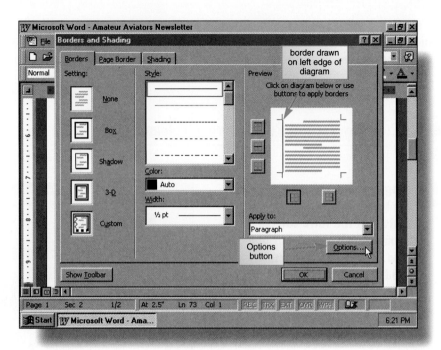

FIGURE 6-37

4 **Click the Options button. When the Border and Shading Options dialog box displays, change the Left text box to 15 pt.**

The Preview shows the border positioned 15 points from the left edge of the paragraph (Figure 6-38).

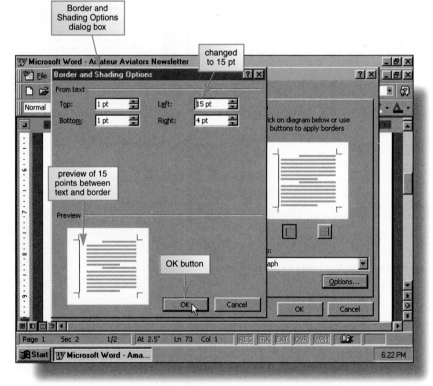

FIGURE 6-38

5 Click the OK button in the Borders and Shading Options dialog box. When the Borders and Shading dialog box redisplays, click its OK button. Click in the selection to remove the highlight.

Word draws a border positioned 15 points from the left edge of the text (Figure 6-39). A vertical rule displays between the second and third columns of the newsletter.

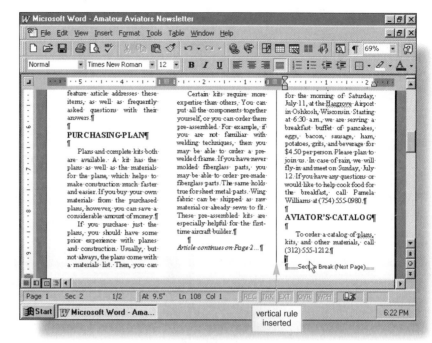

FIGURE 6-39

The first page of the newsletter is formatted completely.

Formatting the Second Page of the Newsletter

The second page of the newsletter continues the article that began in the first two columns of page 1 (see Figure 6-2 on page WD 6.6). The nameplate on the second page is more concise than the one on the first page of the newsletter. In addition to the text in the article, page two contains a pull-quote. The following pages illustrate how to format the second page of the newsletter in this project.

Creating the Nameplate on the Second Page

Because the document currently is formatted into three columns and the nameplate is a single column, the next step is to change the number of columns to one at the top of the second page. Recall that each time you change the number of columns in a document, you must insert a new section. You will then format the section to one column and enter the nameplate into the section as described in the steps on the next page.

More *About*
Vertical Rules

A vertical rule is used to guide the reader through the newsletter. If a multi-column newsletter contains a single article, then place a vertical rule between every column. If, however, different columns present different articles, then place a vertical rule between each article instead of each column.

Steps To Format the Second Page Nameplate

1 Scroll through the document and position the mouse pointer at the top left corner of the second page of the newsletter. Click Insert on the menu bar and then click Break. When the Break dialog box displays, click Continuous in the Section breaks area. Point to the OK button.

Word displays the Break dialog box (Figure 6-40). This section break will place the nameplate on the same physical page as the three columns of the continued article.

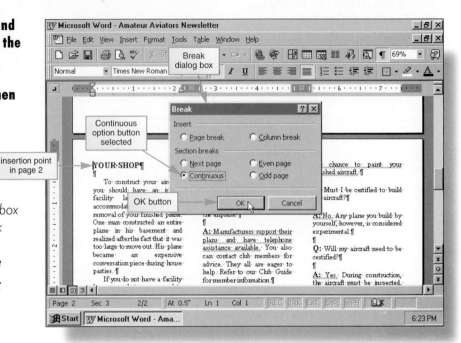

FIGURE 6-40

2 Click the OK button.

Word inserts a section break above the insertion point.

3 Press the UP ARROW key to position the insertion point in section 3 on the section break. Click the Columns button on the Standard toolbar. Point to the first column in the columns list graphic.

Word highlights the left column in the columns list graphic and displays 1 Column below the graphic (Figure 6-41). The current section, for the nameplate, will be formatted to one column.

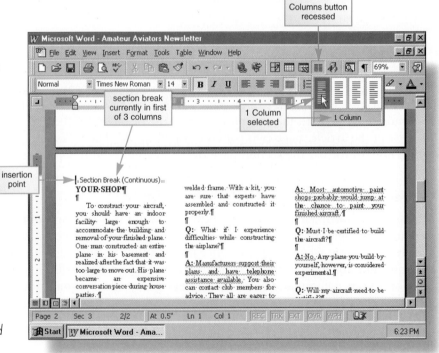

FIGURE 6-41

4 **Click the first column in the columns list graphic.**

Word formats the current section to one column (Figure 6-42).

section 3 is one column

section 4 is three columns

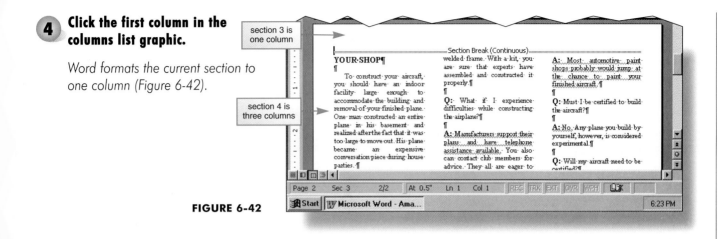

FIGURE 6-42

The next step is to enter the nameplate and a continued message at the top of the first column in the second page of the newsletter.

TO ENTER THE NAMEPLATE AND CONTINUED MESSAGE ON THE SECOND PAGE

1. Change the font size to 12. Click the Bold button on the Formatting toolbar. Press the ENTER key twice. Press the UP ARROW key. Change the font size to 20 point. Click the Font Color button arrow on the Formatting toolbar and then click the color Teal. Type June 1998 as the date.

2. Click the Tab Alignment button on the ruler as many times as necessary to change the alignment to centered. Click the 3.75" mark on the ruler to place a centered tab stop at that location. Change the font size to 28. Click the Bold and Italic buttons on the Formatting toolbar. Press the TAB key. Change the font to Mistral. Type AMATEUR AVIATORS and then click the Bold and Italic buttons. Change the font size back to 20. Change the font back to Times New Roman.

3. Click the Tab Alignment button on the ruler to change the alignment to right-aligned. Click the 7.375" mark on the ruler to place a right-aligned tab stop at that location. Drag the right-aligned tab marker to the 7.5" mark (the right margin). Press the TAB key. Type Page 2 and then press the ENTER key.

4. Click the line typed in Steps 1 through 3. Click the Tables and Borders button on the Standard toolbar. Click the Line Style box arrow and then click the first set of double lines in the list. Click the Border button arrow on the Tables and Borders toolbar and then click Top Border. Click the Border button arrow on the Tables and Borders toolbar and then click Bottom Border. Click the Tables and Borders button on the Standard toolbar.

5. Click the paragraph mark in line 2. Change the font size to 12. Type HOW TO BUILD A PLANE and then press the SPACEBAR. Click the Italic button on the Formatting toolbar. Type (continued) and then click the Italic button. Change the color back to Automatic. Press the ENTER key.

> ◆**M**ore *About*
> **Inner Page Nameplates**
>
> The top of the inner pages of the newsletter may or may not have a nameplate. If you choose to create one for your inner pages, it should not be the same as, or compete with, the one on the first page. Inner page nameplates usually contain only a portion of the nameplate from the first page of a newsletter.

The nameplate and article continued message for page two are complete (Figure 6-43 on the next page).

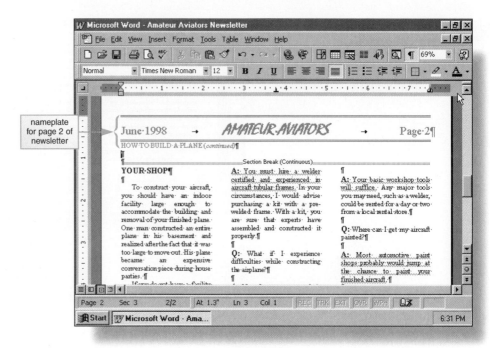

nameplate for page 2 of newsletter

FIGURE 6-43

Because you want to be sure the FAQs section of the newsletter begins at the top of the second column on page 2, you insert a column break at the bottom of the first column as described in these steps.

TO INSERT A COLUMN BREAK

1 Scroll to the bottom of the first column on page 2 and then position the insertion point to the left of the subhead, FAQs.

2 Click Insert on the menu bar and then click Break.

3 Click Column break in the Break dialog box and then click the OK button.

Word inserts a column break in the first column and positions the FAQs text at the top of the second column (Figure 6-44).

The next step is to insert a pull-quote between the first and second columns on page two of the newsletter.

Inserting a Pull-Quote

A **pull-quote** is a quotation pulled, or copied, from the text of the document and given graphic emphasis so it stands apart and grasps the attention of the reader. The newsletter in this project has a pull-quote on the second page between the first and second columns (see Figure 6-2 on page WD 6.6).

To create a pull-quote, you must copy the text in the existing document to the Clipboard and then paste it into a column of the newsletter. To position it between columns, you place a **text box** around it and then move it to the desired location. Perform the following steps to create the pull-quote.

More *About*
Pull-Quotes

Because of their bold emphasis, pull-quotes should be used sparingly in a newsletter. Pull-quotes are especially useful for breaking the monotony of long columns of text. Quotation marks are not required around a pull-quote; but if you use them, use curly (or smart) quotes instead of straight quotes.

Steps **To Create a Pull-Quote**

1 **Scroll to the bottom of the third column of the newsletter and highlight the entire last sentence of the article (do not select the paragraph mark).**

The text for the pull-quote is highlighted (Figure 6-44).

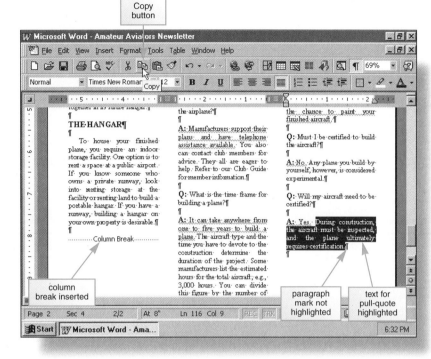

FIGURE 6-44

2 **Click the Copy button on the Standard toolbar. Scroll up the document and then click immediately below the THE HANGAR subhead in column 1 on page 2. Click the Paste button on the Standard toolbar. Type a quotation mark (") at the end of the pull-quote, and then type a quotation mark (") at the beginning of the pull-quote.**

The pull-quote displays below the THE HANGAR subhead (Figure 6-45).

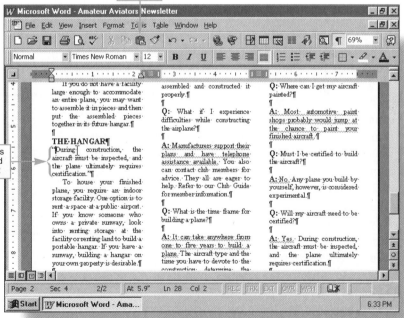

FIGURE 6-45

3 Select the entire pull-quote (do not select the paragraph mark). Click Insert on the menu bar and then point to Text Box (Figure 6-46).

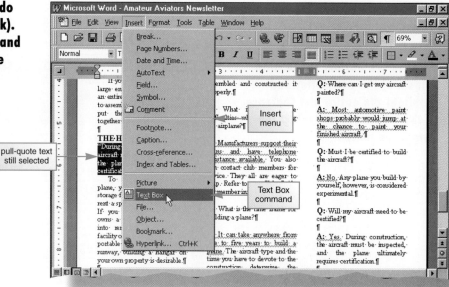

FIGURE 6-46

4 Click Text Box.

Word places a frame around the pull-quote, so that it may be positioned anywhere on the page and formatted.

5 Click the pull-quote. Click Format on the menu bar and then click Paragraph. If necessary, click the Indents and Spacing tab when the Paragraph dialog box first opens. In the Indentation area, change Left to 0.2″ and Right to 0.2″ to increase the amount of space between the left and right edges of the pull-quote and frame. In the Spacing area, change Before to 6 pt and After to 6 pt to increase the amount of space above and below the pull-quote.

Word displays the Paragraph dialog box (Figure 6-47). The pull-quote will have a 0.2-inch space on the left and right edges and 6 points - approximately one blank line - above and below it.

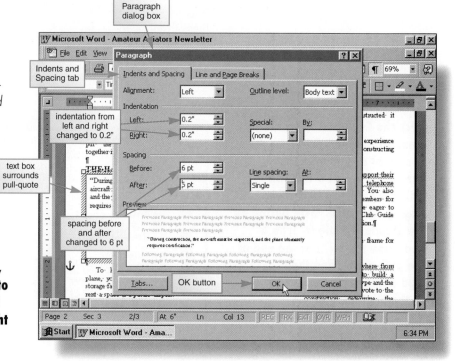

FIGURE 6-47

6 Click the OK button. Drag through the pull-quote text. Click the Font Size box arrow and then click 14. Click the Bold and Italic buttons on the Formatting toolbar. Click inside the pull-quote to remove the highlight.

Word displays the pull-quote left-aligned with a 0.2-inch space between the border and the frame on the left and right sides. Approximately one blank line displays between the border and frame on the top and bottom sides (Figure 6-48). Notice that Word places a border around the pull-quote. When you add a text box, Word automatically places a border around it and the Text Box toolbar displays. You want to change the border around the pull-quote.

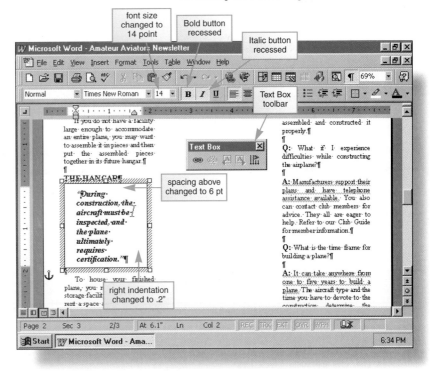

FIGURE 6-48

7 Click Format on the menu bar and then point to Text Box (Figure 6-49).

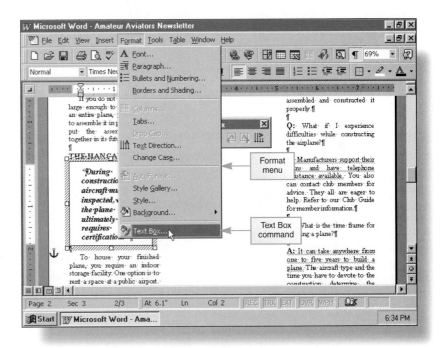

FIGURE 6-49

8 Click Text Box. If necessary, click the Colors and Lines tab when the Format Text Box dialog box first opens. Click the Line Color box arrow and then click the color Red. Click the Line Style box arrow and then click the 3 pt double lines graphic in the list.

Word displays the Format Text Box dialog box (Figure 6-50).

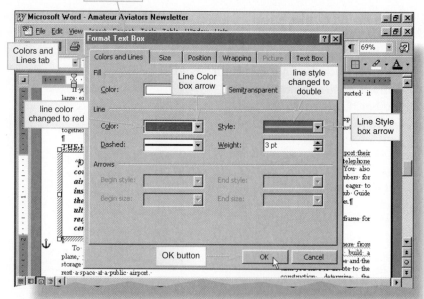

FIGURE 6-50

9 Click the OK button. Click the frame to select it and then point to the right-middle sizing handle on the frame.

Word changes the border around the text box (Figure 6-51).

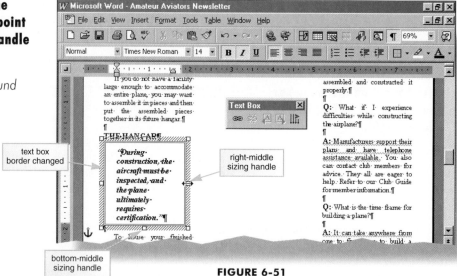

FIGURE 6-51

10 Drag the right-middle sizing handle to make the pull-quote a bit wider so the pull-quote text looks more balanced. Then, drag the bottom-middle sizing handle up to reduce the height of the pull-quote. Try to resize the pull-quote as close to Figure 6-52 as possible. Position the mouse pointer on the frame so it has a four-headed arrow attached to it.

The text in the pull-quote wraps more evenly (Figure 6-52).

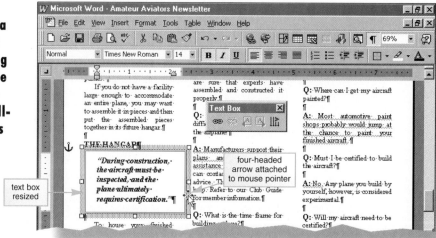

FIGURE 6-52

11 Drag the frame to its new position (Figure 6-53). You may need to drag it a couple of times to position it similarly to this figure. Try to position it as close to Figure 6-53 as possible. Depending on your printer, your wordwrap may occur in different locations. Click outside the frame to remove the selection.

The pull-quote is complete (Figure 6-53).

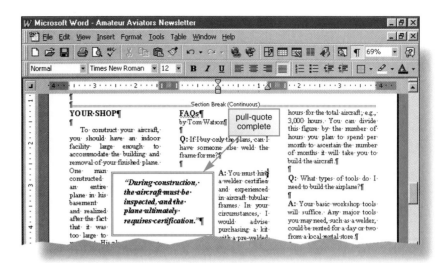

FIGURE 6-53

The second page of the newsletter is complete. Save this project again by clicking the Save button on the Standard toolbar.

The next step is to enhance the newsletter with colors and borders.

Enhancing the Newsletter with Color and a Page Border

You already have added color to many of the characters and lines in the newsletter in Project 6. You also want to color all of the subheads, edit the airplane graphic, and add a border around each page of the newsletter. The following pages illustrate these tasks.

The first step is to color the dropped capital letter.

TO COLOR THE DROP CAP

1 Scroll to the top of the newsletter and then select the dropped capital letter by clicking to its left.

2 Click the Font Color button arrow on the Formatting toolbar and then click the color Violet.

Word changes the color of the dropped capital letter to violet (Figure 6-54 on the next page).

Using the Format Painter Button

All of the subheads are to be colored violet. Instead of selecting each subhead one at a time and then changing its color with the Font Color button, you can change the color of the first subhead and then copy its formatting (which includes the color) to another location. To do this, use the **Format Painter button** on the Standard toolbar as shown on the next page.

More *About*
Printing Color

Some printers do not have enough memory to print a wide variety of images and color. In these cases, the printer prints up to a certain point on a page and then chokes – resulting in only the top portion of the document printing. Check with your instructor whether your printer has enough memory to work with colors.

More *About*
Highlighting

To add color to an e-mail communication or online document, you highlight the text instead of changing the font's color. Highlighting this text alerts the reader to the text's importance, much like a highlight marker does in a textbook. To highlight text, select it, click the Highlight button arrow, and then click the desired color.

Steps **To Use the Format Painter Button**

1 **Drag through the remaining characters in the subhead, ET READY. (It may be easier to drag from right to left because of the frame around the dropped capital letter.) Click the Font Color button on the Formatting toolbar. Click somewhere in the subhead GET READY, other than the drop cap. Click the Format Painter button on the Standard toolbar. Move the mouse pointer into the document window.**

*The mouse pointer changes to an I-beam with a small paint brush to its left when the **Format Painter button** is recessed (Figure 6-54). The insertion point is in the 14-point Times New Roman violet, bold font of the subhead GET READY. The format painter has copied this font.*

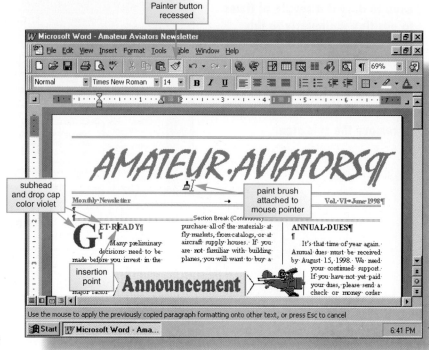

FIGURE 6-54

2 **Scroll through the newsletter to the next subhead, PURCHASING PLAN. Select the subhead by clicking to its left. Click outside the selection to remove the highlight.**

Word copies the 14-point Times New Roman violet, bold font to the PURCHASING PLAN subhead (Figure 6-55). The Format Painter button on the Standard toolbar is no longer recessed.

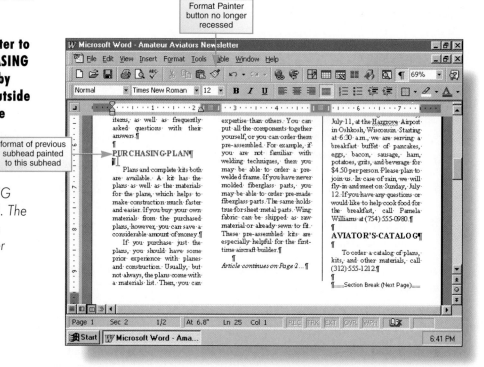

FIGURE 6-55

If you want to copy character formatting to multiple locations in a document, double-click the Format Painter button, which will remain recessed until you click it again. Highlight each location to which you want the format copied. When you are finished copying the character formatting, click the Format Painter button again to restore the normal I-beam pointer.

In this newsletter, you want each subhead to be the color violet. You could use the Format Painter button to color each subhead. Because several subheads remain, an easier technique is to create a macro for the character formatting as discussed in the next section.

Using a Macro to Automate a Task

A **macro** is composed of a series of Word commands or instructions that are grouped together as a single command. This single command is a convenient way to automate a difficult or lengthy task. Macros often are used by Word users for formatting or editing activities, to combine multiple commands into a single command, or to display a dialog box with a single keystroke.

To create a macro, you begin the **Word macro recorder** and then record a series of actions. The recorder is similar to a movie camera, in that it records all actions you perform on a document over a period of time. Once the macro is recorded, you can run it any time you want to perform that same set of actions.

When Word records a macro, it stores a series of instructions using Visual Basic, its **macro language**. **Visual Basic** is a powerful programming language available with Word. If you are familiar with programming techniques, you can write your own macros or edit one recorded earlier.

The macro for this project will format characters to the 14-point Times New Roman violet, bold font when you press the ALT+V keys. Perform the following steps to record this macro.

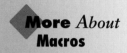

More *About* **Macros**

If you are familiar with computer programming techniques, you can edit an existing macro. To do this, click Macro on the Tools menu, click Macros on the Macro submenu, click the name of the macro in the Macros dialog box, and then click the Edit button to display the macro contents in the Visual Basic Editor window. When finished, save the macro and then click Close on the File menu.

 Steps To Record a Macro

1 **Position the insertion point in the BUYING A KIT subhead. Point to the REC indicator on the status bar.**

Because the BUYING A KIT subhead already is formatted to 14-point Times New Roman bold, the formatting required for the macro will require only the addition of the color violet (Figure 6-56). Thus, the positioning of the insertion point in this step is for convenience only; it is not required.

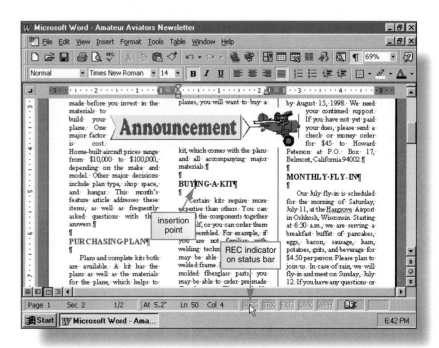

FIGURE 6-56

2 Double-click the REC indicator on the status bar. When the Record Macro dialog box displays, type FormatSubheads in the Macro name text box. Point to the Keyboard button.

*Word displays the **Record Macro** dialog box (Figure 6-57). Macro names must begin with a letter, can contain only letters and numbers with no spaces, and can be a maximum length of 80 characters. You can assign a macro to a button on a toolbar, a command in a menu, or a shortcut key. For this macro, you want to press the ALT+V keys to make selected characters the 14-point Times New Roman violet, bold font.*

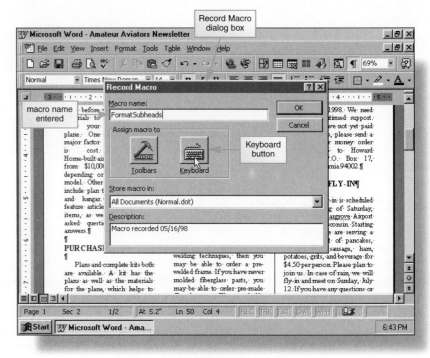

FIGURE 6-57

3 Click the Keyboard button. When the Customize Keyboard dialog box displays, press the ALT+V keys and then point to the Assign button.

*Word displays the **Customize Keyboard** dialog box (Figure 6-58). The shortcut keys you pressed display in the Press new shortcut key text box. If the shortcut key already has a function in Word, it displays in the Currently assigned to area. In this case, ALT+V is unassigned.*

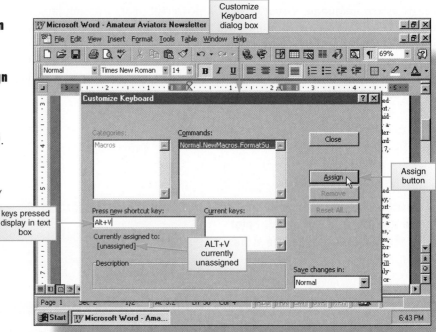

FIGURE 6-58

4 **Click the Assign button and then point to the Close button in the Customize Keyboard dialog box.**

Word assigns the shortcut key to the macro named FormatSubheads (Figure 6-59).

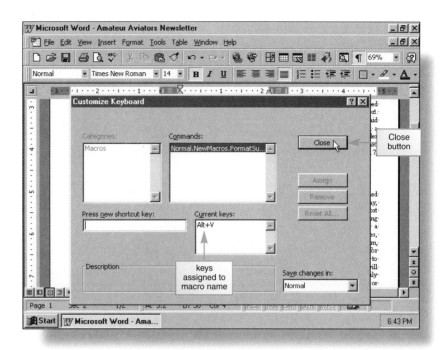

FIGURE 6-59

5 **Click the Close button.**

*Word displays a **Stop Recording toolbar** in the document window (Figure 6-60).*

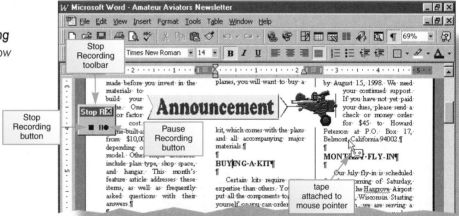

FIGURE 6-60

6 **Click Format on the menu bar and then point to Font (Figure 6-61).**

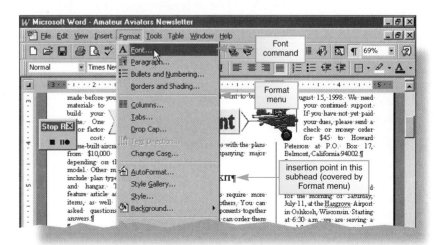

FIGURE 6-61

7 **Click Font. If necessary, click the Font tab when the Font dialog box first opens. Click the Color box arrow; scroll to and then click Violet in the list. Be sure the font is Times New Roman, the font style is Bold, and the font size is 14. Point to the OK button.**

Word displays the Font dialog box (Figure 6-62). The formatting for the subheads, 14-point Times New Roman violet, bold font, is selected.

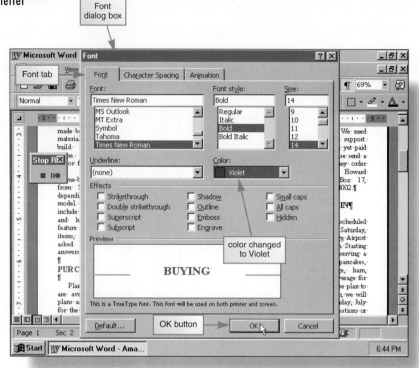

FIGURE 6-62

8 **Click the OK button. Point to the Stop Recording button on the Stop Recording toolbar.**

Word stores the settings in the Font dialog box in the FormatSubheads macro (Figure 6-63). A portion of the subhead is formatted with the color violet.

9 **Click the Stop Recording button.**

Word closes the Stop Recording toolbar and dims the REC indicator on the status bar (see Figure 6-64).

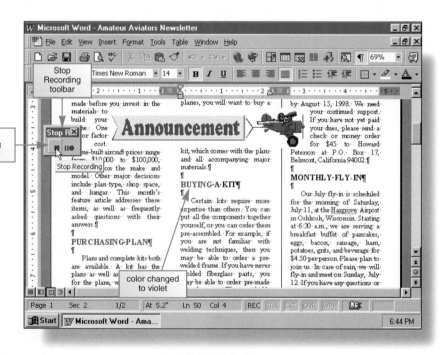

FIGURE 6-63

Other Ways

1. On Tools menu point to Macro, click Record New Macro, enter macro name, click Keyboard in Record Macro dialog box, press shortcut keys, click Assign button, click Close button, record macro, click Stop Recording button in Macro Record dialog box

If, while recording a macro, you want to perform some actions that should not be part of the macro, click the **Pause Recording button** on the Stop Recording toolbar to suspend the recording (Figure 6-60 on the previous page). When you want to continue recording, click the Pause Recording button again.

The next step is to run the macro using the shortcut keys ALT+V as shown in the following steps.

Steps To Run a Macro

1 **Select the BUYING A KIT subhead (Figure 6-64).**

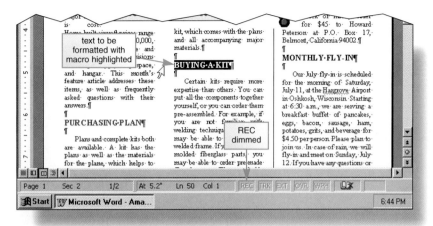

FIGURE 6-64

2 **Press the ALT+V keys. Click outside the highlight to remove the selection.**

Word locates the instructions stored for the macro ALT+V and then performs its instructions (Figure 6-65). The characters in the subhead are the 14-point Times New Roman violet, bold font.

FIGURE 6-65

The remaining subheads and the pull-quote in the newsletter must be colored as described in the steps below.

TO COLOR THE REMAINING TEXT IN THE NEWSLETTER

1 Select the ANNUAL DUES subhead and then press the ALT+V keys.
2 Repeat the procedure in Step 1 for each of these subheads: MONTHLY FLY-IN, AVIATOR'S CATALOG, YOUR SHOP, THE HANGAR, and FAQs.
3 Select the pull-quote by dragging from the left quotation mark through the right quotation mark. Click the Font Color button arrow on the Formatting toolbar and then click the color Teal. Click outside the selection to remove the highlight.

The characters in the newsletter are colored (Figure 6-66 on the next page).

Word stores macros in the Normal template; thus, they are available to every Word document on your system. For this reason, you should delete the macro just created by following the steps on the next page.

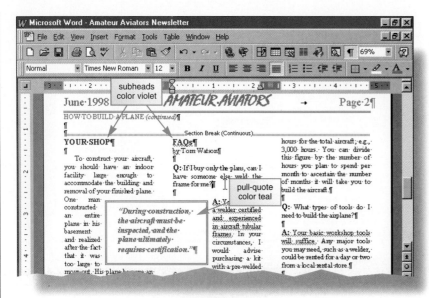

FIGURE 6-66

TO DELETE A MACRO

1. Click Tools on the menu bar, point to Macro, and then click Macros.
2. Click the macro name FormatSubheads in the Macro name list.
3. Click the Delete button.
4. Click the Yes button in the Microsoft Word dialog box. Click the Close button in the Macros dialog box.

Word deletes the FormatSubheads macro; thus, ALT+V is no longer assigned to any Word instructions.

The next step is to change the color of the airplane graphic and change the slogan in the banner object of the graphic.

Editing a Graphic

The banner object of the airplane graphic in the newsletter is yellow. To change its color and add text to it, you use the **Drawing toolbar**. Through the drawing toolbar, you can create **drawing objects** such as rectangles, squares, polygons, ellipses, and lines. Perform the following steps to edit the airplane graphic.

 To Edit a Graphic

1. **Scroll through the document and then click the airplane graphic to select it. Click the Drawing button on the Standard toolbar.**

   The airplane graphic is selected (Figure 6-67). The **Drawing button** *on the Standard toolbar is recessed, and the Drawing toolbar displays at the bottom of the Word screen.*

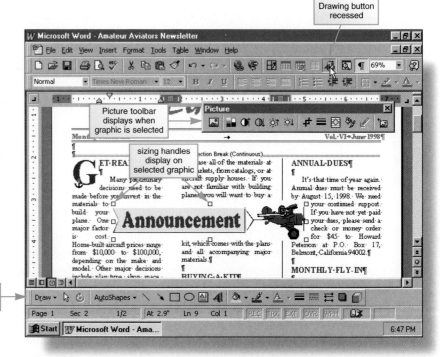

FIGURE 6-67

2 Click the Draw button on the Drawing toolbar and then point to Ungroup on the Draw menu (Figure 6-68).

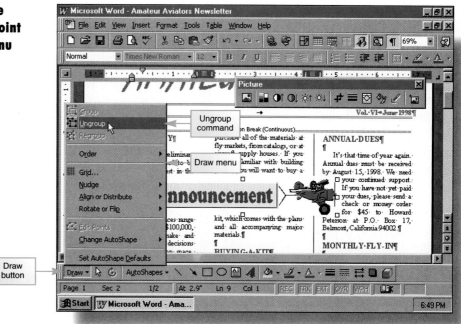

FIGURE 6-68

3 Click Ungroup.

The airplane graphic is separated into its individual objects (Figure 6-69). You can edit each individual object.

FIGURE 6-69

4 Click outside the graphic to deselect the objects. Click the letter A in the word, Announcement. While holding down the SHIFT key, click each remaining letter in the word, Announcement. If you accidentally click any other object, click outside the graphic and begin this step again.

Word selects each letter in the word, Announcement (Figure 6-70). Be careful not to select any other object in the graphic.

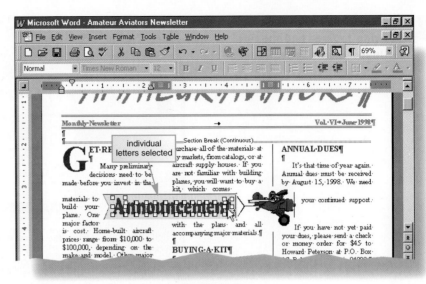

FIGURE 6-70

5 Click the Cut button on the Standard toolbar. Click the banner object to select it. Click the Fill Color button arrow on the Drawing toolbar and then point to the color Teal.

Word removes the word, Announcement, from the banner (Figure 6-71). The banner object has sizing handles, indicating it is selected.

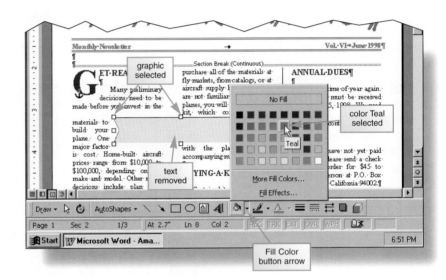

FIGURE 6-71

6 Click the color Teal. Click the Text Box button on the Drawing toolbar. Point in the banner object about .25 inch from its top and left edges.

Word colors the inside of the banner teal (Figure 6-72). The mouse pointer changes to a plus sign when the Text Box button is recessed. You drag the mouse pointer to outline a **text box***, in which you then can type.*

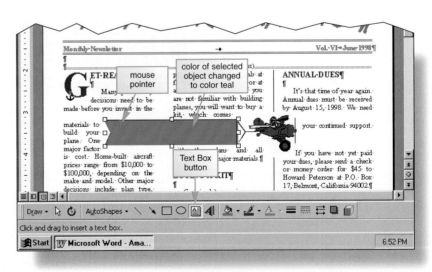

FIGURE 6-72

7 Drag so a text box approximately 2 inches wide and .25 inch high displays in the banner object. Point to the Fill Color button on the Drawing toolbar.

Word creates a text box inside the banner object (Figure 6-73). The Fill Color button displays the color teal because it is the most recently selected color.

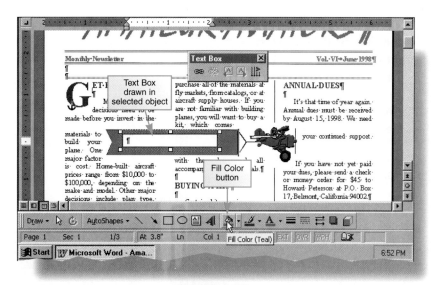

FIGURE 6-73

8 Click the Fill Color button on the the Drawing toolbar. Click the Font Color button arrow and then point to the color White.

Word displays the list of available font colors (Figure 6-74).

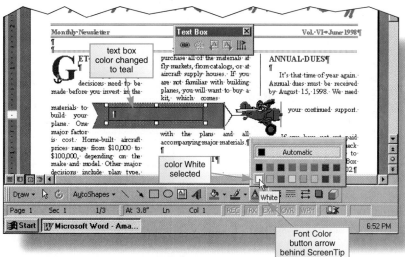

FIGURE 6-74

9 Click the color White and then click the Bold button on the Formatting toolbar. Type HOW TO BUILD A PLANE in the text box.

Word displays the slogan in a text box in the banner object (Figure 6-75). Notice the text box has a border around it.

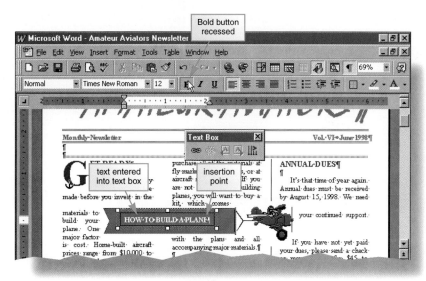

FIGURE 6-75

10 Click Format on the menu bar and then click Text Box. If necessary, click the Colors and Lines tab when the Format Text Box dialog box first opens. Click the Line Color box arrow and then click No Line.

Word displays the Format Text Box dialog box (Figure 6-76).

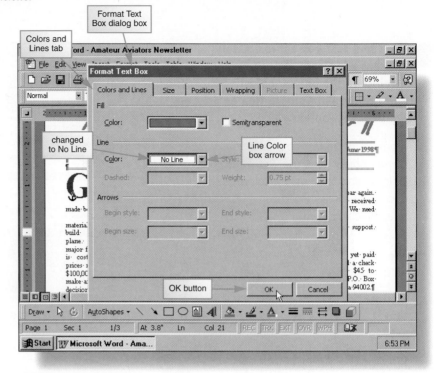

FIGURE 6-76

11 Click the OK button. Click the Draw button on the Drawing toolbar and then point to Regroup.

Word removes the border from around the text box (Figure 6-77). Because you are finished editing the airplane, you want to regroup the individual objects into one large object.

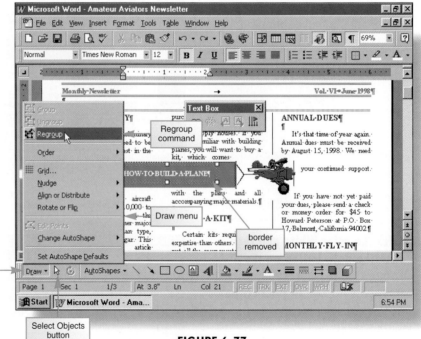

FIGURE 6-77

12 Click Regroup. (If the Regroup command is dimmed, click the Select Objects button on the Drawing toolbar, drag the dotted rectangle around the entire graphic, click the Draw button on the Drawing toolbar, and then click Group to regroup the objects into a single object.) Click the Drawing button on the Standard toolbar to remove the Drawing toolbar. Click outside the graphic to remove the selection.

Word regroups the individual objects into a single object (Figure 6-78). The Drawing toolbar no longer displays at the bottom of the screen.

FIGURE 6-78

The final step in enhancing the newsletter is to add a border around each page.

Adding a Page Border

You have added borders to the edges of a paragraph(s). In Word, you can also add a border around the perimeter of an entire page. These page borders add professionalism to your documents. Perform the following steps to add a teal page border to the pages of the newsletter.

More *About* **Graphics**

Some images in the Microsoft Clip Gallery are Windows metafiles, and you may edit any of the metafiles. Other graphics supplied with Office, also in the Clip Gallery, are called bitmap images. You cannot edit bitmap images. To determine the file type, click the Clip Properties button in the Clip Gallery dialog box.

 Steps To Add a Page Border

1 Click Format on the menu bar and then click Borders and Shading. If necessary, click the Page Border tab when the Borders and Shading dialog box first opens. Click the Box option in the Setting area; scroll to the bottom of the Style list box and then click the last style in the list; click the Color box arrow and then click Teal; point to the Options button.

Word displays the Borders and Shading dialog box (Figure 6-79). The page border is set to a 3-point Teal box.

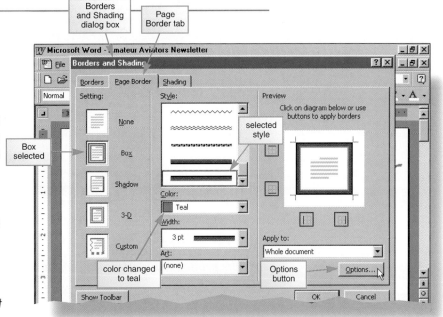

FIGURE 6-79

2 Click the Options button. When the Border and Shading Options dialog box displays, click the Measure from box arrow and then click Text. Change the Top setting to 4 pt and the bottom setting to 0 pt.

Word displays the Border and Shading Options dialog box (Figure 6-80).

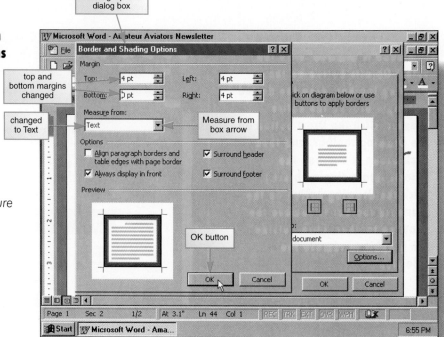

FIGURE 6-80

3 Click the OK button in the Border and Shading Options dialog box. When the Borders and Shading dialog box redisplays, click its OK button.

Word places a page border on each page of the newsletter (Figure 6-81).

FIGURE 6-81

The newsletter is complete. You should save the document again, print it, and then quit Word.

TO SAVE AND PRINT THE DOCUMENT

1 Click the Save button on the Standard toolbar.

2 Click the Print button on the Standard toolbar.

The printed newsletter is shown in Figures 6-1 and 6-2 on pages WD 6.5 and WD 6.6.

TO QUIT WORD

❶ Click the Close button in the Word window.

The Word window closes.

Project Summary

Project 6 introduced you to creating a professional looking newsletter using desktop publishing features. You created a nameplate with ruling lines. You formatted the body of the newsletter into three columns and added a vertical rule between the second and third columns. You learned how to move graphics and a pull-quote between columns. You used the Format Painter button and learned how to create a macro. Finally, you edited a graphic and added a page border to the newsletter.

What You Should Know

Having completed this project, you should now be able to perform the following tasks:

▶ Add a Page Border *(WD 6.51)*
▶ Add a Vertical Rule Between Columns *(WD 6.29)*
▶ Add Ruling Lines *(WD 6.10)*
▶ Change All Margin Settings *(WD 6.8)*
▶ Color the Drop Cap *(WD 6.39)*
▶ Color the Remaining Text in the Newsletter *(WD 6.45)*
▶ Create a Dropped Capital Letter *(WD 6.20)*
▶ Create a Pull-Quote *(WD 6.35)*
▶ Delete a Macro *(WD 6.46)*
▶ Display Nonprinting Characters *(WD 6.7)*
▶ Download Clip Art from Microsoft's Clip Gallery Live Web Page *(WD 6.22)*
▶ Edit a Graphic *(WD 6.46)*
▶ Enter Subheads and Associated Text *(WD 6.17)*
▶ Enter the Nameplate and Continued Message on the Second Page *(WD 6.33)*
▶ Format and Enter Text *(WD 6.9)*
▶ Format Columns *(WD 6.15)*
▶ Format the Second Page Nameplate *(WD 6.32)*

▶ Insert a Column Break (WD 6.27 and WD 6.34)
▶ Insert a Continuous Section Break *(WD 6.14)*
▶ Insert a File into a Column of the Newsletter *(WD 6.28)*
▶ Insert a File into the Newsletter *(WD 6.19)*
▶ Insert a Next Page Section Break *(WD 6.26)*
▶ Insert a Symbol into Text *(WD 6.11)*
▶ Install the Clip Art File from the Data Disk *(WD 6.23)*
▶ Position a Graphic Anywhere on a Page *(WD 6.24)*
▶ Quit Word *(WD 6.53)*
▶ Record a Macro *(WD 6.41)*
▶ Redefine the Normal Style *(WD 6.8)*
▶ Run a Macro *(WD 6.45)*
▶ Save and Print the Document *(WD 6.52)*
▶ Save the Newsletter in a File *(WD 6.18)*
▶ Start Word *(WD 6.7)*
▶ Use the Format Painter Button *(WD 6.40)*
▶ Zoom Page Width *(WD 6.10)*

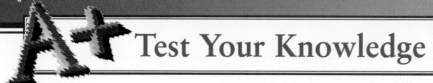 Test Your Knowledge

1 True/False

Instructions: Circle T if the statement is true or F if the statement is false.

T F   1. Word 97 provides many of the desktop publishing features you would find in a specialized package.

T F   2. The space between an object and the text that wraps around the object is called run-around.

T F   3. To format the first character of a paragraph as a dropped capital letter, click the Drop Cap button on the Formatting toolbar.

T F   4. Snaking columns are created with the Columns button on the Standard toolbar.

T F   5. The default number of columns in a document is one.

T F   6. To move a graphic between or across columns, the Float over text check box must be deselected.

T F   7. When you insert a text box, Word places a border around it.

T F   8. A pull-quote is a quotation mark displayed in a font size larger than 40 points.

T F   9. The Drawing toolbar displays below the Formatting toolbar.

T F   10. A paragraph border displays around the perimeter of a page.

2 Multiple Choice

Instructions: Circle the correct response.

1. In the desktop publishing field, the _____ is located at the top of a newsletter.
   a. box border
   b. nameplate
   c. wrap-around text
   d. pull-quote
2. To insert special characters and symbols into a document, _____.
   a. click Symbol on the Insert menu
   b. press and hold the ALT key and then type a zero followed by the ANSI character code
   c. either a or b
   d. neither a nor b
3. Each section in a document can have its own _____.
   a. number of columns
   b. margins settings
   c. headers
   d. all of the above

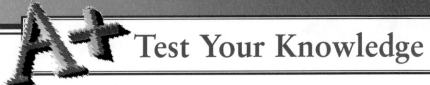

4. To add a vertical rule between columns, select the column and then _____.
   a. on the Tools menu, click Vertical Rule
   b. on the Format menu, click Borders and Shading
   c. click the Rule button on the Standard toolbar
   d. click the Rule button on the Drawing toolbar

5. Which of the following is a valid macro name?
   a. Print Hard Copy
   b. Print2HardCopies
   c. Print&SaveDocument
   d. both b and c are valid macro names

6. When Word records a macro, it stores a series of instructions using _____.
   a. Visual Basic
   b. Excel
   c. Access
   d. PowerPoint

7. To copy the formatting of text, click the text, click the _____ on the Standard toolbar, then select the text where you want to copy the formatting.
   a. Copy button
   b. Paste button
   c. Format Painter button
   d. Copy button and then the Paste button

8. When the first letter in a paragraph is larger than the rest of the characters in the paragraph, the letter is called a _____.
   a. large cap
   b. big cap
   c. drop cap
   d. enlarged cap

9. The REC indicator is located on the _____.
   a. vertical scroll bar
   b. horizontal scroll bar
   c. status bar
   d. taskbar

10. To add a page border, _____.
    a. on the Format menu, click Borders and Shading
    b. on the Format menu, click Page Border
    c. right-click the page and then click Border on the shortcut menu
    d. click the Page Border button on the Standard toolbar

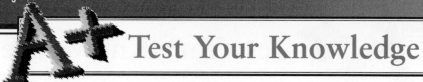

Test Your Knowledge

3 Understanding the Drawing Toolbar

Instructions: In Figure 6-82, arrows point to several of the buttons on the Drawing toolbar. In the spaces provided, briefly explain the purpose of each button.

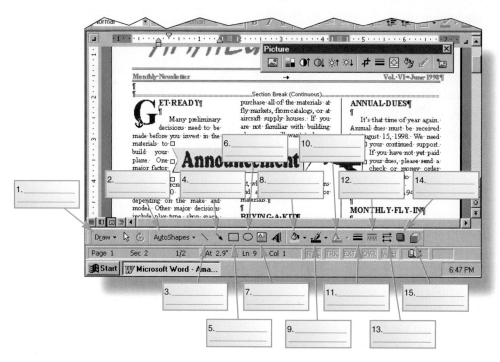

FIGURE 6-82

4 Understanding Desktop Publishing Terminology

Instructions: In the spaces provided, briefly define each of the desktop publishing terms listed.

TERM	DEFINITION
1. nameplate	
2. ruling line	
3. vertical rule	
4. issue information line	
5. subhead	
6. wrap-around text	
7. run-around	
8. pull-quote	
9. banner	
10. drop cap	

Use Help

1 Reviewing Project Activities

Instructions: Perform the following tasks using a computer.

1. Start Word.
2. If the Office Assistant is on your screen, click it to display its balloon. If the Office Assistant is not on your screen, click the Office Assistant button on the Standard toolbar.
3. Type macros in the What would you like to do? text box. Click the Search button. Click the Using macros to automate tasks link. Read the information. Use the shortcut menu or the Options button to print the information.
4. Click the Help Topics button to display the Help Topics: Microsoft Word dialog box. Click the Contents tab. Double-click the Changing the Appearance of Your Page book. Double-click the Positioning Text Using Newspaper Columns book. Double-click the Newspaper columns topic. Click each of the links and read their Help information. Right-click each link's help information and then click Print Topic on the shortcut menu.
5. Click the Help Topics button. Click the Index tab. Type page borders and then double-click the page borders, adding topic. Click the Add a border to a page in a document link. Read and print the information.
6. Click the Help Topics button. Click the Find tab. Type format painter and then double-click the Copy character and paragraph formats topic. Read and print the information.
7. Close any open Help window(s) by clicking its Close button. Close the Office Assistant.

2 Expanding on the Basics

Instructions: Use Word Help to better understand the topics listed below. Answer the questions on your own paper or hand in the printed Help topic to your instructor.

1. In this project, you created a page border to enhance the newsletter. Use the Office Assistant to determine the definition of a watermark and then determine how to add one to a Word document.
2. In this project, you created newspaper, or snaking, columns in the newsletters. Use the Contents tab in the Help Topics: Microsoft Word dialog box to answer the following questions about newspaper columns.
   a. How do you change the number of newspaper columns in a section?
   b. How can you change the width of a newspaper column in a section?
   c. How do you remove newspaper columns from a section?
3. In this project, you used a macro. Use the Index tab in the Help Topics: Microsoft Word dialog box to answer the following questions about macros.
   a. What if, when you record a macro, you accidentally perform an action you do not want to record?
   b. Can a macro be renamed? If so, how?
4. In this project, you inserted the bullet symbol into the newsletter. Use the Find tab in the Help Topics: Microsoft Word dialog box to answer these questions about symbols.
   a. How do you enter the following international symbols into a document? ò, ó, Ö, ø, ¿, ß
   b. How do you assign a symbol to a shortcut key?

Apply Your Knowledge

1 Editing an Embedded Object

Instructions: Start Word. Performing the steps below, you are to edit a Windows metafile. The edited graphic is shown in Figure 6-83.

Perform the following tasks.

1. Click Insert on the menu bar, point to Picture, and then click Clip Art. If necessary, click the Clip Art tab when the Microsoft Clip Gallery dialog box first opens. Click the Signs category and then click the scales graphic. Click the Insert button to insert the scales graphic into the document window.

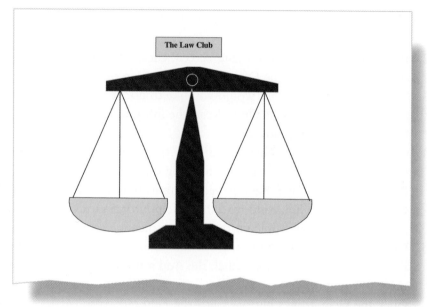

FIGURE 6-83

2. Click the Drawing button on the Standard toolbar to display the Drawing toolbar.
3. Click the Draw button on the Drawing toolbar and then click Ungroup.
4. Click the left scale in the graphic to select it. Click the Fill Color button arrow on the Drawing toolbar and then click the color Gold to change the scale's color to gold. Click the Line Color button arrow on the Drawing toolbar and then click the color Dark Red to change the line color to dark red.
5. Repeat Step 4 for the right scale.
6. Click the stand in the graphic to select it. Click the Fill Color button arrow on the Drawing toolbar and then click the color Violet. Click the Line Color button arrow on the Drawing toolbar and then click the color Gold.
7. Click the Text Box button on the Drawing toolbar and then drag a text box above the graphic about .25 inch high by 1.50 inches long to create a text box.
8. Change the font size to 12. Click the Bold button and the Center button on the Formatting toolbar. Click the text box and then type `The Law Club` as the club name. Resize the text box, if necessary. With the text box still selected, click the Font Color button arrow on the Drawing toolbar and then click the color Violet.
9. Click the Fill Color button arrow on the Drawing toolbar and then click the color Gold. Click the Line Color button arrow on the Drawing toolbar and then click the color Violet.
10. Save the edited graphic with The Law Club Graphic as the file name.
11. Print the edited graphic.

In the Lab

1 Creating a Newsletter from an Article and Announcements on File

Problem: You are an associate editor of the *Village News* newsletter for the Village of New Treppor. The 32nd edition is due out next Monday. The Village's new recycling program is to be the feature article (Figure 6-84). The recycling article and the announcements have been prepared and are on the Data Disk that accompanies this book.

Instructions:

1. Change the top, left, and right margins to .5 inch; change the bottom margin to .75 inch. Depending on your printer, you may need different margin settings.
2. Redefine the Normal style to a font size of 12.
3. Create the nameplate using the formats identified in Figure 6-84. Create a continuous section break below the nameplate. Format section 2 to three columns.
4. Insert the recycling article into section 2 below the nameplate. The article is in a file called Recycling Article in the Word folder on the Data Disk that accompanies this book. If necessary, switch to Page Layout View.
5. Insert a column break at the end of the recycling article. Insert the announcements into column 3 of section 2. The article is in a file called Village News Announcements in the Word folder on the Data Disk that accompanies this book.

(continued)

3-point dark red page border

72-point Algerian dark red, bold font

14-point Times New Roman dark red font

Times New Roman dark red, bold italic font for pull-quote

14-point Times New Roman teal, bold font for subheads

3-point green ruling lines

VILLAGE NEWS

Weekly Newsletter   No. 32 • July 20, 1998

RECYCLING

Beginning this Monday, the Village will initiate a curbside recycling program. To participate, simply pick up a green recycling bin at the Village Hall. The hours are Monday to Friday from 8:00 a.m. to 4:30 p.m. and Saturday from 8:00 a.m. to 1:00 p.m. The first recycling bin is free to each Village resident. Additional bins may be obtained for a fee of $3.50. The following sections of this newsletter outline the types of material that may be recycled.

"The first recycling bin is free to each Village resident."

BOTTLES & CANS

Both clear and colored food and drink glass bottles and aluminum cans may be recycled. Labels do not need to be removed; nor do the containers need to be washed. Broken bottles are not accepted.

PAPER

Most paper can be recycled. We require that you separate paper into the three individual groups: newspapers, magazines and catalogs, and mixed paper.

Inserts and advertisements may be left in the newspapers. Mixed paper includes white and colored paper, cardboard, cereal boxes, junk mail, and brown paper bags. Plastic window envelopes are recyclable.

Contaminated paper products may not be recycled and include paper coated with food, covered with wax, soaked in oil, or laminated.

PLASTIC

Types 1 and 2 plastic jugs and bottles are accepted. Milk jugs and soda bottles generally are recyclable in our program; motor oil and anti-freeze containers are not. Check the bottom of the jug or bottle for the code number. Because caps are not recyclable, remove all bottle caps from jugs and bottles.

OTHER NOTES

Johnny's Grocery in the Village Square will accept plastic grocery and produce sacks for recycling. The store is open 24-hours a day for your convenience.

HELP WANTED

Our fifth annual Summerfest is scheduled for the weekend of August 8 and 9. Activities include arts and crafts booths, volleyball games, antique car show, food and drink stands, live entertainment, children's contests, and bingo. We need volunteers to collect tickets, staff booths, and coordinate events. If you are interested, please call Jean at 555-2312.

WAFFLE BREAKFAST

The Village is sponsoring a Waffle Breakfast at the VFW on Center Street on Saturday, August 16, from 6:30 to 10:00 in the morning. Meal includes a waffle, 2 eggs, bacon or sausage, and juice. Cost is $3.99 per adult and $1.99 per child. The food is being donated by The Country Kitchen. All proceeds from this event will be donated to the Charity House. Please plan to attend.

DID YOU KNOW?

You can pay your water bills at the Village Bank or at Johnny's Grocery. If you have any questions, please come in and ask.

FIGURE 6-84

In the Lab

Creating a Newsletter from an Article and Announcements on File *(continued)*

6. Format the newsletter according to Figure 6-84 on the previous page. Place a vertical rule between the second and third columns. Use the Format Painter button and a macro to automate some of your formatting tasks.
7. Save the document with Village News Newsletter as the file name.
8. Print the newsletter.

2 Creating a Newsletter from an Article on File

Problem: You are secretary for the National Campers Society and responsible for the monthly preparation of *Campers Society*, a newsletter for the club. The September edition, due out in two weeks, is to rate Trail Blaze Park in the feature article (Figure 6-85). The Trail Blaze Park review article has been prepared and is on the Data Disk that accompanies this book. You need to type the announcements.

Instructions:

1. Change the top, left, and right margins to .5 inch; change the bottom margin to .75 inch. Depending on your printer, you may need different margin settings.
2. Redefine the Normal style to a font size of 12.
3. Create the nameplate using the formats identified in Figure 6-85. Create a continuous section break below the nameplate. Format section 2 to three columns.
4. Insert the Trail Blaze Article file into section 2 below the nameplate. The article is in a file called Trail Blaze Article in the Word folder on the Data Disk that accompanies this book. If necessary, switch to Page Layout View.
5. Insert a column break at the end of Trail Blaze Article. Enter the announcements into column 3 of section 2. The first line of each paragraph is indented .25 inch.
6. Format the newsletter according to Figure 6-85. The clip art is in the Screen Beans category of the Microsoft Clip Gallery; resize the clip art to 45%. Place a vertical rule between the second and third columns. Use the Format Painter button and a macro to automate some of your formatting tasks.
7. Save the document with Campers Society Newsletter as the file name.
8. Print the newsletter.

3 Creating a Newsletter from Scratch

Problem: You are the editor of *Surfing Today*, a new monthly newsletter for the subscribers to the Internet. The first edition is due out in November. An introduction to the Internet is to be the feature article (Figure 6-86 on page WD 6.62). You need to enter the feature article, as well as announcements.

In the Lab

3-point green
page border

48-point Arial
Black blue,
bold font

CAMPERS SOCIETY

½-point red
triple ruling lines

14-point Times
New Roman
blue font

Monthly Newsletter   Issue 66 • September 1998

FOUR STARS!

Trail Blaze Park in Round Lake, Illinois, receives a four-star rating from the National Campers Society. Located on more than 7,500 acres of beautiful rolling hills with thousands of oak trees and roomy campsites, the park has two lakes stocked with game fish and another lake for swimming and boating. The park provides comfortable, clean camping facilities with both outdoor and indoor activities for all ages. This article highlights the features of Trail Blaze Park.

clip art fill color
light blue, line
color blue-gray

14-point Times New
Roman green, bold
font for subheads

RECREATION

One major attraction of this park is that all activities are free to all overnight guests. For the camper that enjoys the outdoors, Trail Blaze Park provides swimming in a clear water lake or an Olympic-sized heated pool, tennis, basketball, horseshoes, hiking, nature walks, canoeing, ping-pong, golf, shuffleboard, rowboating, fishing, and horseback riding. For children, the fun includes hayrides, video games, four playgrounds, and wagon rides.

Evening activities include bingo, movies, concerts, and square dances. An enclosed recreation room has frequent nighttime children's programs, such as games, sing-a-longs, scavenger hunts, and cartoons.

FACILITIES

The park has 550 hook-up sites. Of these, 200 are full hook-ups that include water, sewer, and 30-amp electric for $18 per day. The remaining 350 are water and 20-amp electric for $15 per day. A total of 75 primitive, or tent, sites are available for $10 per day.

The park provides modern restrooms, hot showers, laundry facilities, and public telephones. A camp store is located at the park's entrance that supplies snacks, groceries, firewood, camping supplies, and fishing supplies. No fishing license is required!

For reservations, directions, or more information, call Karen at (847) 555-8867.

MEMBER DISCOUNTS

As a National Campers Society member, you are entitled to many benefits. Discounts include a 10 percent reduction on campsites at over 3,000 parks nationwide; members-only RV and auto insurance protection at low rates; 15 percent discount on parts and supplies at participating facilities; and an annual coupon book. To receive your free National Campers Society card and a complete benefits guide, call Mike at (312) 555-0088.

FREE CATALOG

Campers Discount Supply has air conditioners, awnings, jacks, heaters, refrigerators, fans and vents, kitchen accessories, generators, trailer parts, covers, and many more hard-to-find camping supplies. For a free color catalog, call toll-free at (800) 555-4400.

REMINDER

Annual dues of $40 must be paid by September 30. Please send check to National Campers Society, P.O. Box 776, Chicago, IL 60601.

FIGURE 6-85

Instructions:

1. Change the top, left, and right margins to .5 inch; change the bottom margin to .75 inch. Depending on your printer, you may need different margin settings.
2. Redefine the Normal style to a font size of 12.
3. Create the nameplate using the formats identified in Figure 6-86 on the next page. Create a continuous section break below the nameplate. Format section 2 to three columns.

(continued)

In the Lab

Creating a Newsletter from Scratch *(continued)*

4. If necessary, switch to Page Layout View. Enter the Internet article into section 2 below the nameplate.

5. Insert a continuous section break at the end of the Internet article. Format section 3 to two columns. Type the announcements into section 3 at the bottom of the page.

6. Format the newsletter according to Figure 6-86. Place a vertical rule between all columns in section 2; place a vertical rule between the columns in section 3. Use the Line between check box in the Columns dialog box (Format menu) to do this. Use the Format Painter button and a macro to automate some of your formatting tasks.

7. Save the document with Surfing Today Newsletter as the file name.

8. Print the newsletter.

3-point dark blue page border

72-point Arial Narrow green, bold font

½-point pink double ruling lines

SURFING TODAY

14-point Times New Roman green font

Monthly Newsletter

Vol. I • No. 1 • November 1998

WELCOME

For this first monthly issue of Surfing Today, we plan to introduce you to the basics of the Internet. With each subsequent issue, you will be exposed to another exciting feature of the Internet. For example, how to do research; view stock prices; shop for services and merchandise; display weather maps; obtain pictures, movies, audio clips, and information stored on computers around the world; and converse with people worldwide.

clip art in Maps – International category of Microsoft Clip Gallery

14-point Times New Roman dark blue, bold font for subheads

THE INTERNET

The Internet is a collection of networks, each of which is composed of a collection of smaller networks; for example,

on a college campus, the network in the student lab can be connected to the faculty computer network, which is connected to the administration network, and they all can connect to the Internet.

Networks are connected with high-, medium-, and low-speed data lines that allow data to move from one computer to another. The separate networks connect to the Internet through computers.

WORLD WIDE WEB

Modern computer systems have the capability to deliver information in a variety of ways, such as graphics, sound, video clips, animation, and, of course, regular text. On the Internet, this multimedia capability is available in the form of hypermedia, which is any variety of computer media.

Hypermedia is accessed through the use of a hypertext link, or simply link, which is a special software pointer that points to the location of the computer on which the hypermedia is stored and to the hypermedia itself. A link can point to hypermedia on any computer hooked into the Internet that is running the proper software. Thus, a hypertext link on a computer in New York can point to a picture on a computer in Los Angeles.

The collection of hypertext links throughout the Internet creates an interconnected network of links called the World Wide Web, which also is referred to as the Web, or WWW. Each computer within the Web containing hypermedia that can be referenced by hypertext links is called a Web site. Thousands of Web sites around the world can be accessed through the Internet.

2¼-point bright green ruling line

FAQs

Frequently Asked Questions, or FAQs, are a common type of informal publishing on the Internet. A FAQ file answers questions of interest to a particular group of people. For example, one FAQ file addresses questions on Internet documentation styles for research papers.

NEXT MONTH

Next month's issue will discuss how to use Netscape Navigator, an Internet browser. Netscape Navigator provides graphical display of plain and formatted text, hypertext, online access to graphs, images, audio and video clips, and multimedia and hypermedia documents.

FIGURE 6-86

Cases and Places

The difficulty of these case studies varies: ❶ are the least difficult; ❷❷ are more difficult; and ❸❸❸ are the most difficult.

1 ❶ Your school has decided to publish a one-page monthly newsletter to be sent to the community. You have been assigned the task of designing the newsletter and writing the first issue. The newsletter should contain an informative article about the school. Select a topic about your school that would interest the community; e.g., a curricula, the fitness center, the day care center, the bookstore, the Student Government Organization, registration, the student body, a club, a sports team, and so on. Obtain information for your article by interviewing a campus employee or a student, visiting the school library, or reading brochures published by your school. The article should span the first two columns of the newsletter, and the third column should contain announcements for the school. Enhance the newsletter with color, ruling lines, and a page border. Use an appropriate clip art graphic or a pull-quote in the newsletter.

2 ❶ You are a member of the Pen Pal Club, which unites people across the world. The club publishes a monthly newsletter for its members. Each newsletter features one member and lists announcements. You are the feature member this month; thus, you have been assigned the task of designing and writing the newsletter. The newsletter should contain an interesting article about you; e.g., interests, hobbies, employment, major, family, friends, and so on. The article should span the first two columns of the newsletter, and the third column should contain announcements for the club. Enhance the newsletter with color, ruling lines, and a page border. Use an appropriate clip art graphic or a pull-quote in the newsletter.

3 ❷❷ You are an associate editor of *Village News*, a one-page newsletter for the Village of New Treppor. Last week's edition is shown in Figure 6-84 on page WD 6.59. The 33rd edition is due out in three weeks. Your assignment is to decide on a feature article for the *Village News* newsletter and develop some announcements. Use your home community as the basis for your feature article and announcements. Your article could address an item such as one of these: an issue facing the community, a major upcoming event, a celebration, a new program, an election or campaign, and so on. Visit the Chamber of Commerce or other government agency in your community to obtain background information for your article. The newsletter should contain both the feature article and community announcements. Enhance the newsletter with color, ruling lines, and a page border using colors different from those used in Figure 6-84. Use an appropriate clip art graphic or a pull-quote in the newsletter.

Cases and Places

4 ▶▶ You are secretary for the National Campers Society and responsible for the monthly preparation of *Campers Society*, a one-page newsletter for the club. Last month's edition is shown in Figure 6-85 on page WD 6.61. The October edition is due out in two weeks. Your assignment is to decide on a feature article for *Campers Society* and develop some announcements. The feature article cannot rate a campground; instead, develop a feature article of interest to campers. For example, your feature article could discuss types of recreational vehicles, items to pack for a camping trip, how to care for your camper, or any other item of interest to you. Visit a campground, the library, or a local dealership for information for your article. The newsletter should contain both the feature article and announcements, which you need to develop. Enhance the newsletter with color, ruling lines, and a page border using colors different from those used in Figure 6-85. Use an appropriate clip art graphic or a pull-quote in the newsletter.

5 ▶▶ You are the editor of *Surfing Today*, a one-page monthly newsletter for the subscribers to the Internet. Last month's edition is shown in Figure 6-86 on page WD 6.62. The next edition is due out in two weeks. Your assignment is to decide on a feature article for *Surfing Today* and develop some announcements. The feature article should provide information about some aspect of the Internet. Your article could address an item such as one of these: a Web browser, how to develop a home page, an interesting Internet site, HTML, an Internet provider, and so on. Surf the Internet for information in your article. The newsletter should contain both the feature article and announcements, which you need to develop. Enhance the newsletter with color, ruling lines, and a page border using colors different from those in Figure 6-86. Use an appropriate clip art graphic or a pull-quote in the newsletter.

6 ▶▶▶ You are a member of the local chapter of a computer user group. The group has decided to publish a two-page monthly newsletter. You must decide on a title for the newsletter. Your assignment is to design the newsletter and develop the first issue. The newsletter should have a feature article and some announcements for the user group. Your feature article should address a computer-related item such as a new hardware platform, an interesting software application, an exciting Internet site, price comparisons, a local computer center, and so on. Use the Internet, textbooks, teachers, user manuals, user guides, and magazines for information in your article. The newsletter should contain both the feature article that spans both pages of the newsletter and user group announcements on the first page of the newsletter. Enhance the newsletter with color, ruling lines, and a page border. Use an appropriate clip art graphic and a pull-quote in the newsletter.

7 ▶▶▶ You are a member of a package vacation club. Because you have a background in desktop publishing, you prepare the monthly two-page newsletter for club members. Your assignment is to design the newsletter and develop the next issue. The newsletter should have a feature article and some announcements for club members. Your feature article should discuss some exciting vacation site, which can be anywhere in the world. Use the Internet, a local travel agency, literature or brochures, or a public library for information on your travel spot. The newsletter should contain the feature article that spans both pages of the newsletter and user group announcements on the first page of the newsletter. Enhance the newsletter with color, ruling lines, and a page border. Use an appropriate clip art graphic and a pull-quote in the newsletter.

Using WordArt to Add Special Text Effects to a Word Document

Case Perspective

Recall that in Project 6, you were asked to design the June newsletter for the Amateur Aviators. Thus, you created the newsletter shown in Figures 6-1 and 6-2 on pages WD 6.5 and WD 6.6 and submitted it to the club president, Tom Watson, for his approval. He was very impressed with the design you created. Now, he has asked you to enhance the title somehow. He wants it to have a bit more pizzazz. You decide to look into the capabilities of WordArt, a supplementary Office application that allows you to create interesting text effects.

You will need the newsletter created in Project 6 so you can modify the title. (If you did not create the newsletter, see your instructor for a copy of it.) You will use WordArt to add special text effects to the title. WordArt is an application included with Microsoft Office. Depending on how Office was installed on your system, you may not have WordArt. If Office was installed using the Typical setup option, then you will need to run the Setup program again to install WordArt.

Introduction

Microsoft Office includes supplemental applications (WordArt, Equation, Organization Chart, and Graph) that allow you to create a visual object and then insert the object into an Office document. With WordArt, you create text with special effects; Equation allows you to create mathematical equations; you create company organization charts with Organization Chart; and Graph enables you to create charts. Thus, a **visual object** can be a graphic, equation, or chart. The application used initially to create the object is referred to as the **source application**.

When you insert, or **embed**, an object into an Office document, the object becomes part of the Office document. Because the Office document contains the embedded object, the Office document is referred to as the **container file**. In some cases, when you double-click an object embedded into an Office document, the object's source application opens inside the Office application, allowing you to edit the object directly from within Office. Any changes you make to the object are reflected immediately in the Office document.

This Integration Feature illustrates the procedure to use WordArt to add special text effects to the title of the *Amateur Aviators* newsletter. The revised newsletter is shown in Figure 1 on the next page. Notice the title waves and has a gradient color scheme.

title created in WordArt and embedded into Word document

Amateur Aviators

Monthly Newsletter   **Vol. VI • June 1998**

GET READY

Many preliminary decisions need to be made before you invest in the materials to build your plane. One major factor is cost. Home-built aircraft prices range from $10,000 to $100,000, depending on the make and model. Other major decisions include plan type, shop space, and hangar. This month's feature article addresses these items, as well as frequently asked questions with their answers.

PURCHASING PLAN

Plans and complete kits both are available. A kit has the plans as well as the materials for the plane, which helps to make construction much faster and easier. If you buy your own materials from the purchased plans, however, you can save a considerable amount of money.

If you purchase just the plans, you should have some prior experience with planes and construction. Usually, but not always, the plans come with a materials list. Then, you can purchase all of the materials at fly markets, from catalogs, or at aircraft supply houses. If you are not familiar with building planes, you will want to buy a

HOW TO BUILD A PLANE

kit, which comes with the plans and all accompanying major materials.

BUYING A KIT

Certain kits require more expertise than others. You can put all the components together yourself, or you can order them pre-assembled. For example, if you are not familiar with welding techniques, then you may be able to order a pre-welded frame. If you have never molded fiberglass parts, you may be able to order pre-made fiberglass parts. The same holds true for sheet metal parts. Wing fabric can be shipped as raw material or already sewn to fit. These pre-assembled kits are especially helpful for the first-time aircraft builder.

Article continues on Page 2…

ANNUAL DUES

It's that time of year again. Annual dues must be received by August 15, 1998. We need your continued support. If you have not yet paid your dues, please send a check or money order for $45 to Howard Peterson at P.O. Box 17, Belmont, California 94002.

MONTHLY FLY-IN

Our July fly-in is scheduled for the morning of Saturday, July 11, at the Hargrove Airport in Oshkosh, Wisconsin. Starting at 6:30 a.m., we are serving a breakfast buffet of pancakes, eggs, bacon, sausage, ham, potatoes, grits, and beverage for $4.50 per person. Please plan to join us. In case of rain, we will fly-in and meet on Sunday, July 12. If you have any questions or would like to help cook food for the breakfast, call Pamela Williams at (754) 555-0980.

AVIATOR'S CATALOG

To order a catalog of plans, kits, and other materials, call (312) 555-1212.

FIGURE 1

Removing the Current Title

To create the WordArt object, the first step is to open the Amateur Aviators Newsletter file and then remove the current title as described in the following steps.

TO REMOVE THE CURRENT TITLE

1. Start Word and then open the Amateur Aviators Newsletter file created in Project 6. (If you did not create the newsletter in Project 6, see your instructor for a copy of it.)
2. If it is not already recessed, click the Show/Hide ¶ button on the Standard toolbar.
3. Drag through the title to select it. Be careful NOT to select the paragraph mark following the title. Right-click the selection (Figure 2).
4. Click Cut on the shortcut menu.

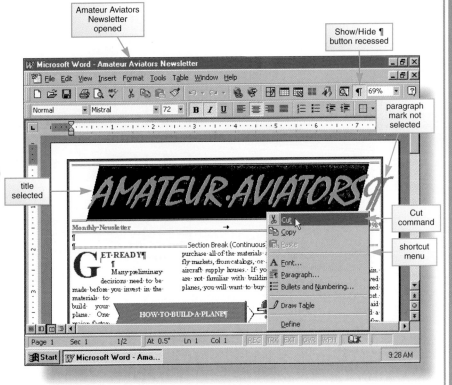

FIGURE 2

Word removes the title from the newsletter (Figure 3 on the next page). The insertion point is positioned where the title originally was located. It is important to leave the original paragraph mark to ensure enough room (72-point, in this case) is available for the WordArt object.

Creating a WordArt Object

As discussed earlier, **WordArt** is an application that enables you to add special text effects to a document. In this Integration Feature, you will use WordArt to create a new title for the *Amateur Aviators* newsletter. WordArt is the source application because that is where the title will be created. The Word document is the container file because it will contain the **WordArt object**, the title. The following pages explain how to insert a WordArt object into a Word document and then use WordArt to add special effects to the text itself.

The first step in creating a WordArt object is to **insert,** or **embed**, the object into a Word document. WordArt inserts at the location of the insertion point. Follow the steps on the next page to insert a WordArt object into a Word document.

Steps **To Insert a WordArt Object into a Word Document**

1 **Click Insert on the menu bar, point to Picture, and then point to WordArt.**

Notice the insertion point is positioned on the paragraph mark on line 1 of the newsletter (Figure 3).

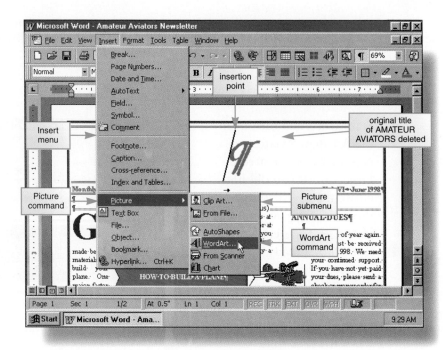

FIGURE 3

2 **Click WordArt. When the WordArt Gallery dialog box displays, if necessary, click the style in the upper-left corner.**

The WordArt Gallery dialog box displays (Figure 4). Because you will add your own special text effects, the style in the upper-left corner is selected.

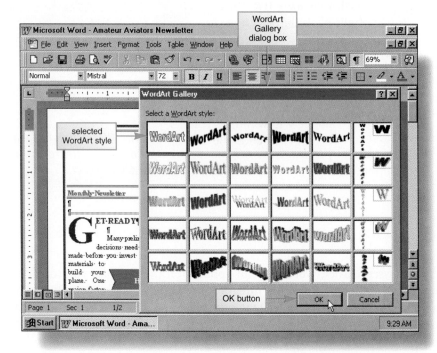

FIGURE 4

③ **Click the OK button. When the Edit WordArt Text dialog box displays, type** Amateur Aviators **and then click the Font box arrow. Scroll to and then click Impact. Click the Size box arrow, scroll to and then click 60.**

The Edit WordArt Text dialog box displays (Figure 5). In this dialog box, you can enter the WordArt text, and change its font and font size.

④ **Click the OK button.**

The WordArt text (object) displays in the document window (Figure 6 on the next page).

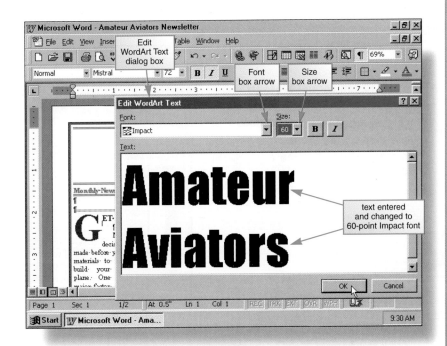

FIGURE 5

Notice in Figure 6 on the next page that when the WordArt object is selected, the **WordArt toolbar** displays.
Recall that selected objects display with **sizing handles** at their middle and corner locations. If, for some reason, you wanted to change the WordArt text, its font, or its font size, you would click the **Edit Text button** on the WordArt toolbar to display the Edit WordArt text dialog box.

To change the size (width and height) of WordArt text, you drag the sizing handles on the selected WordArt object to the appropriate locations – just as you resize any other graphic.

If, for some reason, you wanted to delete WordArt text, you would right-click the WordArt object and then click the Cut button on the shortcut menu.

Adding Special Effects to WordArt Text

The next step is to enhance the WordArt text. Enhancing includes changing its color, shape, and location. The steps on the following pages outline these enhancements.

Formatting the WordArt Text

In Figure 6, the WordArt text (the title) is formatted so the text in the newsletter wraps around it; you do not want the newsletter text to wrap around the WordArt text. In addition, you want to add color to the WordArt text. Perform the steps on the next page to format the WordArt text.

▶OtherWays

1. Click Insert WordArt button on Drawing toolbar, select WordArt style, enter WordArt text, click OK button

◆ More *About* **Special Effects**

If you want WordArt to format your text, click the desired WordArt style in the WordArt Gallery dialog box (Figure 4). If you want to rotate your text, click the Free Rotate button on the WordArt toolbar, drag a corner of the WordArt object in the direction you want it rotated, and then click the Free Rotate button again to deselect it.

Steps **To Format the WordArt Text**

1 Point to the Format WordArt button on the WordArt toolbar (Figure 6). If your screen does not display the WordArt toolbar, right-click the WordArt object and then click Show WordArt Toolbar.

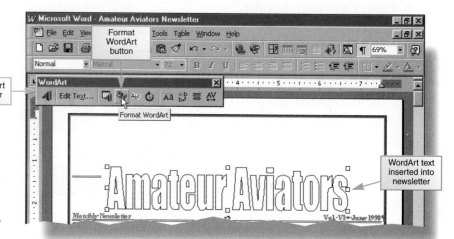

FIGURE 6

2 Click the Format WordArt button. If necessary, click the Wrapping tab when the Format WordArt dialog box first opens. Click None in the Wrapping style area.

The Format WordArt dialog box displays (Figure 7). In the Wrapping sheet, you can specify how the words in the document will wrap around the WordArt object.

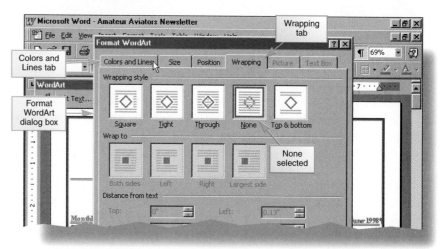

FIGURE 7

3 Click the Colors and Lines tab. Click the Fill Color box arrow and then point to Fill Effects.

The options in the Colors and Lines sheet display (Figure 8). In this sheet, you can change the color of the WordArt text.

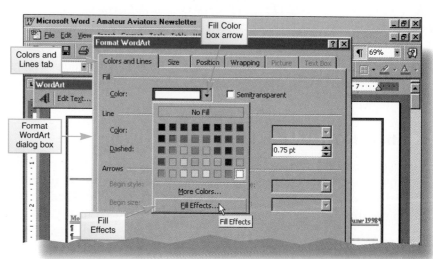

FIGURE 8

4 **Click Fill Effects. When the Fill Effects dialog box displays, if necessary, click the Gradient tab, and then click Two colors. Click the Color 1 box arrow and then click Teal. Click the Color 2 box arrow and then click White.**

The Fill Effects dialog box displays (Figure 9). In this dialog box, you can change the color scheme for the WordArt text.

5 **Click the OK button in the Fill Effects dialog box and then click the OK button in the Format WordArt dialog box.**

The WordArt text displays formatted with a teal-to-white gradient color scheme (Figure 10 below).

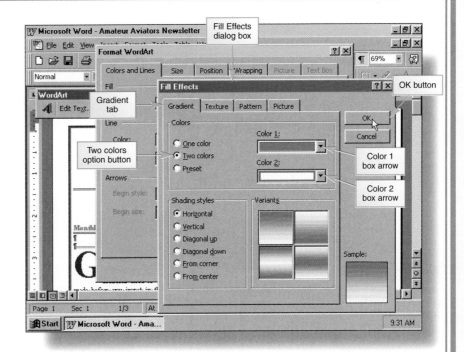

FIGURE 9

Moving WordArt Text

Notice in Figure 10 that the WordArt text is positioned on top of the newsletter text; this is because you changed wrapping to none in the previous steps. Now, you can move the WordArt text as you would any other drawing object. That is, drag the WordArt object to the desired location as shown in the steps below.

 Steps To Move a WordArt Object

1 **If the WordArt object is not selected, click it to select it. Point in the WordArt object so the mouse pointer displays a four-headed arrow.**

*The mouse pointer changes to include a **four-headed arrow** when positioned in a WordArt object (Figure 10).*

FIGURE 10

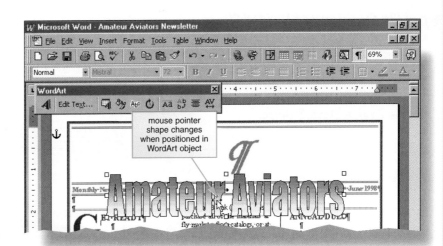

2 **Drag the WordArt object to the desired location.**

As you drag, a dotted outline moves to show where the dropped WordArt object will display if the mouse button is released at that location (Figure 11).

FIGURE 11

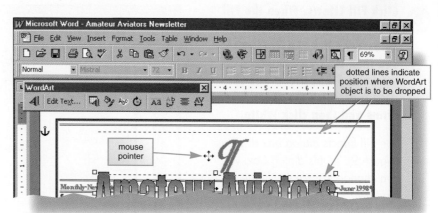

3 **Release the mouse button.**

The WordArt object is moved to the desired location (Figure 12).

FIGURE 12

Changing the WordArt Shape

WordArt provides a variety of shapes to make your WordArt text more interesting. Perform the following steps to change the WordArt text to a wavy shape.

Steps **To Change the WordArt Shape**

1 **Click the WordArt Shape button on the WordArt toolbar. Point to the Double Wave 2 shape.**

WordArt displays a graphic list of available shapes (Figure 13). The WordArt text forms itself into the selected shape when you click a shape.

FIGURE 13

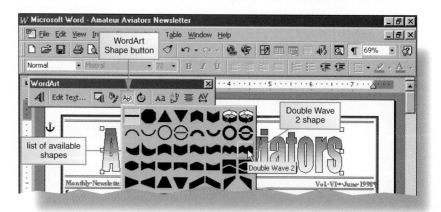

2 **Click Double Wave 2. Click below the WordArt text as shown in the figure to remove the selection and remove the WordArt toolbar. Click the Show/Hide ¶ button on the Standard toolbar to remove nonprinting characters from the screen.**

The title displays in the double wave 2 shape (Figure 14). The WordArt text is complete.

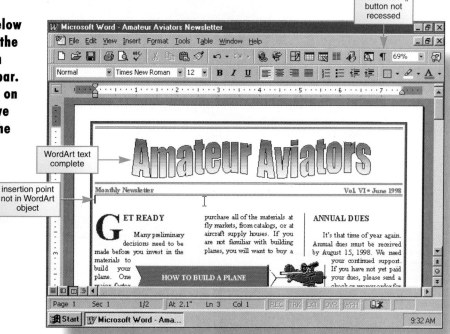

FIGURE 14

Saving and Printing the Newsletter and Quitting Word

The revision of the newsletter is now complete. You should save it with a new file name, print it, and then quit Word.

Summary

This Integration Feature introduced you to the concept of embedding an object created in WordArt into a Word document. You learned how to insert a WordArt object, add WordArt special features to the WordArt text, and move the WordArt object.

What You Should Know

Having completed this Integration Feature, you now should be able to perform the following tasks:

- Change the WordArt Shape *(WDI 2.8)*
- Format the WordArt Text *(WDI 2.6)*
- Insert a WordArt Object into a Word Document *(WDI 2.4)*
- Move a WordArt Object *(WDI 2.7)*
- Remove the Current Title *(WDI 2.3)*

In the Lab

1 Using Help

Instructions: Start Word. If the Office Assistant is on your screen, click it to display its balloon. If the Office Assistant is not on your screen, click the Office Assistant button on the Standard toolbar. Type share information in the What would you like to do? text box. Click the Search button. Click the Use linked and embedded objects to share information between Office programs topic. Read and print the information. Click the Help Topics button to display the Help Topics: Microsoft Word dialog box. Click the Find tab. Type WordArt and then double-click the Arrange text and graphics on a page topic. Read and print the information. Close any open Help window or dialog box by clicking its Close button. Close the Office Assistant.

2 Embedding a WordArt Object into a Newsletter

Problem: You created the *Village News* newsletter shown in Figure 6-84 on page WD 6.59 in Project 6. You decide to redo the title, VILLAGE NEWS, using WordArt.

Instructions: Open the file Village News Newsletter from your floppy disk. (If you did not create the newsletter, see your instructor for a copy of it.) Delete the current title from the document. Be sure not to delete the paragraph mark following the title. Insert a WordArt object at the location of the title using the Insert command on the Picture menu. Enter the title VILLAGE NEWS, use the font Courier New, the font size 66, and bold it. Format the WordArt object to no wrapping and gradient colors of Dark Red to White. Change the shape of the WordArt text to Deflate Bottom. Quit WordArt. Save the file using the Save As command on the File menu with Village News Newsletter Revised as the file name. Print the revised file.

3 Embedding a WordArt Object into a Newsletter

Problem: You created the *Surfing Today* newsletter shown in Figure 6-86 on page WD 6.62 in Project 6. You decide to redo the title, SURFING TODAY, using WordArt.

Instructions: Open the file Surfing Today Newsletter from your floppy disk. (If you did not create the newsletter, see your instructor for a copy of it.) Delete the current title from the document. Be sure not to delete the paragraph mark following the title. Insert a WordArt object at the location of the title using the Insert command on the Picture menu. Enter the title SURFING TODAY, use the font Comic Sans MS, and the font size 60. Format the WordArt object to no wrapping and gradient colors of Sky Blue to Sea Green. Change the shape of the WordArt text to Wave 1. Quit WordArt. Save the file using the Save As command on the File menu with Surfing Today Newsletter Revised as the file name. Print the revised file.

Index